Lecture Notes in Computer Science 8507

Commenced Publication in 1973
Founding and Former Series Editors:
Gerhard Goos, Juris Hartmanis, and Jan van Leeuwen

Shigeru Yamashita   Shin-ichi Minato (Eds.)

Reversible Computation

6th International Conference, RC 2014
Kyoto, Japan, July 10-11, 2014
Proceedings

Volume Editors

Shigeru Yamashita
Ritsumeikan University
College of Information Science and Engineering
1-1-1 Noji Higashi, Kusatsu, Shiga 525-8577, Japan
E-mail: ger@cs.ritsumei.ac.jp

Shin-ichi Minato
Hokkaido University
Graduate School of Information Science and Technology
North 14 West 9, Sapporo 060-0814, Japan
E-mail: minato@ist.hokudai.ac.jp

ISSN 0302-9743   e-ISSN 1611-3349
ISBN 978-3-319-08493-0   e-ISBN 978-3-319-08494-7
DOI 10.1007/978-3-319-08494-7
Springer Cham Heidelberg New York Dordrecht London

Library of Congress Control Number: 2014941620

LNCS Sublibrary: SL 2 – Programming and Software Engineering

Typesetting: Camera-ready by author, data conversion by Scientific Publishing Services, Chennai, India

Printed on acid-free paper

Springer is part of Springer Science+Business Media (www.springer.com)

Preface

Reversible computing is a model of computing where the computational process is in some measure reversible; either in a logical or physical sense, and in certain areas, both. Reversible computation is of importance to a broad range of areas of computer science, engineering, mathematics, and physics including low-power circuit design, coding/decoding, program debugging, testing, databases, discrete event simulation, reversible algorithms, reversible specification formalisms, reversible programming languages, process algebras, and the modeling of biochemical systems. Furthermore, reversible logic provides a basis for describing and working with quantum computation and its applications as well as other emerging computational technologies.

RC 2014 was the 6th in a series of annual meetings designed to gather researchers for the dissemination and discussion of novel results and concepts in all aspects of reversible computation. The first five events were held in York, UK (2009), Bremen, Germany (2010), Ghent, Belgium (2011), Copenhagen, Denmark (2012) and Victoria, Canada (2013). RC 2014 was thus the first of the meetings to be held in Asia. This volume comprises the proceedings for RC 2014.

The RC 2014 program included three invited talks by Irek Ulidowski, Naoki Takeuchi and Simon Devitt. For each talk, the full paper appears in these proceedings. The first paper "Concurrency and Reversibility" is by Irek Ulidowski, Iain Phillips and Shoji Yuen. The second paper "Reversible Computing Using Adiabatic Superconductor Logic" is by Naoki Takeuchi, Yuki Yamanashi and Nobuyuki Yoshikawa. The third paper "Classical Control of Large-Scale Quantum Computers" is by Simon Devitt. We thank the invited speakers for their contributions to RC2014.

The call for papers attracted 27 submissions. All contributed papers were reviewed by at least three members of the RC 2014 Program Committee or their designated sub-reviewers. Based on those reviews and extensive discussion by the Program Committee, 14 papers were selected for presentation at RC 2014 to make up sessions on automata, notation and languages for reversible computation, synthesis and optimization of reversible and quantum circuits, as well as validation and representation of quantum logic.

The list of Program Committee members is provided elsewhere in this volume. We take this opportunity to thank these 15 experts from across the international reversible computation community for their hard work and dedication to the quality of RC 2014. We also thank additional reviewers for their important contributions. It has been our great pleasure to have served as Program Co-chairs for RC 2014 and as editors for these proceedings.

Financial support for RC 2014 was provided by JST ERATO MINATO Discrete Structure Manipulation System Project and by the Department of

Computer Science, College of Information Science and Engineering, Ritsumeikan University. The invited talk by Irek Ulidowski was supported by the Department of Computer Science, University of Leicester.

We also acknowledge organizational support provided by Lisa Jungmann and Robert Wille, University of Bremen, and by Nurul Ain Binti Adnan and Yousef Mohammed Alhamdan, Ritsumeikan University.

We also should thank D. Michael Miller, University of Victoria, and Irek Ulidowski, University of Leicester for their valuable suggestions and guidance.

To conclude, we offer our sincere appreciation to Frank Holzwarth and Anna Kramer, Springer, Heidelberg, Germany, for their assistance and guidance on the use of the OCS online manuscript submission and review system, and in the preparation of these proceedings.

July 2014   Shin-ichi Minato
                                                                  Shigeru Yamashita

Organization

Program Committee Co-chairs

Shin-ichi Minato	Hokkaido University, Japan
Shigeru Yamashita	Ritsumeikan University, Japan

Program Committee

Holger Bock Axelsen	University of Copenhagen, Denmark
Alexis De Vos	University of Ghent, Belgium
Simon Gay	University of Glasgow, UK
Markus Grassl	Centre Quantum Tech, Singapore
Jarkko J. Kari	University of Turku, Finland
Martin Kutrib	University of Giessen, Germany
Kazutaka Matsuda	University of Tokyo, Japan
D. Michael Miller	University of Victoria, Canada
Jackie Rice	University of Lethbridge, Canada
Yasuhiro Takahashi	NTT, Japan
Irek Ulidowski	University of Leicester, UK
Janis Voigtländer	University of Bonn, Germany
Robert Wille	University of Bremen, Germany
Tetsuo Yokoyama	Nanzan University, Japan
Paolo Zuliani	Newcastle University, UK

Organizing Committee

Nurul Ain Binti	Adnan Ritsumeikan University, Japan
Yousef Mohammed	Alhamdan Ritsumeikan University, Japan
Lisa Jungmann	University of Bremen, Germany
Shin-ichi Minato	Hokkaido University, Japan
Robert Wille	University of Bremen, Germany
Shigeru Yamashita	Ritsumeikan University, Japan

Additional Reviewers

Krysia Broda
Markus Holzer
Sebastian Jakobi
Andreas Malcher
Andreas Maletti
Daniel Morrison

Ville Salo
Shigeyuki Sato
Michal Szabados
Rick Thomas
Michael Kirkedal Thomsen
Ilkka Törmä

Sponsors

RC 2014 was sponsored by JST ERATO MINATO Discrete Structure Manipulation System Project and by the Department of Computer Science, College of Information Science and Engineering, Ritsumeikan University. The invited talk by Irek Ulidowski was supported by the Department of Computer Science, University of Leicester.

Table of Contents

Concurrency and Reversibility

Irek Ulidowski[1], Iain Phillips[2], and Shoji Yuen[3]

[1] Department of Computer Science, University of Leicester, England
[2] Department of Computing, Imperial College London, England
[3] Graduate School of Information Science, Nagoya University, Japan

Abstract. Reversible computation has attracted increasing interest in recent years, with applications in hardware, software and biochemistry. In this paper we show how to model reversibility in concurrent computation as realised abstractly in terms of event structures. Two different forms of event structures are presented and it is shown how to extend them with reversibility.

1 Introduction

Reversing computation in concurrent and distributed systems has many promising applications as well as technical and conceptual challenges. Several different forms of undoing of computation have been identified recently. *Backtracking* and reversing of computation that preserves *causal order* were considered in, for example, [8, 16, 13, 4, 14, 5, 9] with applications including recovery-oriented systems and reversible debugging. Reversing *out of causal order*, however, which is a very common mode of operation in, for example, biochemical systems has not been studied widely. The first attempt was made by Phillips, Ulidowski and Yuen [21] where an extension of the reversible process calculus CCSK with the execution control operator was proposed. This was followed by a study of a form of reversible event structure [22] based on a generalisation of Winskel's enabling relation [26]. Phillips and Ulidowski proposed then in [19] reversible event structures that focused on analysing conflict and causation as first-class notions in the setting of reversible computation.

The last decade has produced a good understanding of how causal reversibility can be described in the settings of operational semantics and process calculi, and how to model reversibility logically and in terms of behavioural equivalences. Research on reversing process calculi can be traced back perhaps to Berry and Boudol's Chemical Abstract Machine [3]. Danos and Krivine reversed CCS in [6, 7], and Phillips and Ulidowski proposed a general method for reversing process calculi in [16, 17]. Reversible structures that compute forwards and backwards asynchronously were developed by Cardelli and Laneve [4]. Mechanisms for controlling reversibility based on a rollback construct were devised by Lanese, Mezzina, Schmitt and Stefani [12] for a reversible higher-order π calculus [13], and an alternative mechanism based on the execution control operator was proposed in [21]. Event Identifier Logic (EIL), which extends Hennessy-Milner logic [11] with reverse modalities, was introduced in [20]. EIL corresponds to hereditary history-preserving bisimulation equivalence [2] within a particular true-concurrency model

S. Yamashita and S. Minato (Eds.): RC 2014, LNCS 8507, pp. 1–14, 2014.

of stable configuration structures [10]. Moreover, natural sublogics of EIL correspond to coarser equivalences, several of them defined in terms of reversible events, sets of concurrent reversible events or pomsets of reversible events. These equivalences and other behavioural equivalences based in the reversible setting were studied for the first time in [18].

In this paper we show how to understand and model reversibility in concurrent computation as realised abstractly in terms of event structures. In Section 2 we introduce the notions of events, configurations, computation and configuration systems. Then in Sections 3 and 4, we recall two different forms of event structures and show how to extend them with reversibility. Numerous examples are used to illustrate our approach. The last section contains conclusions and lists some future challenges.

2   Events and Configurations

We represent the behaviour of systems and processes in the setting of event structures where units of behaviour are modelled by *events*. Since we aim to cover a wide range of systems and processes, events will represent activities such as incrementing the value of a variable, sending a message, as well as entering a room, putting a coin into a vending machine, or creating a bond between two molecules. Events have names and we assume that no two different events have the same name. We shall use a, b, c, d, e, f to denote events. A system or a process is then represented as an *event structure* which is a set of events and a number of relations on events. Event structures were defined by Winskel [26] following earlier work by Nielsen, Plotkin and Winskel [15]. They were further developed in, for example, [24, 23, 27] and [25]. There are many ways in which events can be related, and this determines how events are performed or undone. For example, a number of events can *cause* each other thus occurring in a sequence. Also, events can be *independent* from each other, or some events may be in *conflict* with other events. Alternatively, an *enabling* relation on events is used.

Event structures compute (or execute) by either performing events or undoing events, thus moving from one state to another state. A state is simply a set of events that have occurred and have not been undone yet, and is called a *configuration*. The act of moving from a configuration to another configuration is a computation step and is represented by a transition relation: $C \rightarrow C'$ means that configuration C evolves to configuration C' by performing and/or undoing some events. A sequence of computation steps is called an execution (or computation). For example, the execution $\varnothing \rightarrow \{a\} \rightarrow \{a, b\}$ says that, initially, no event has occurred, then event a takes place, and finally event b occurs. We note that any initial subsequence of an execution is also an execution. Events can also be undone. We take the view that undoing an event e means that e is removed from the current configuration, and it is as if e had never occurred, apart possibly from indirect effects, such as e having caused another event f before e was reversed. When we undo e in configuration $\{e, f\}$ we regress to $\{f\}$: this is often written as $\{e, f\} \dashrightarrow \{f\}$ instead of $\{e, f\} \rightarrow \{f\}$ to indicate that an event is undone and to match the notation used in figures. The computation of event structures is thus represented by a *configuration system*. Configuration systems are closely related to *configuration structures*, which have a notion of *configuration* and a notion of concurrent or *step* transition. These were introduced by van Glabbeek and Goltz in [10] and later generalised by van Glabbeek and Plotkin in [23]. Let $\mathfrak{P}(E)$ denote the powerset of a set E. A configuration structure is a pair $\mathcal{C} = (E, \mathsf{C})$ where E is a set of events and $\mathsf{C} \subseteq \mathfrak{P}(E)$ is a set of configurations. For configurations X, Y, we let $X \to Y$ if $X \subseteq Y$ and for every Z, if $X \subseteq Z \subseteq Y$ then Z is a configuration. Since all the events in $Y \smallsetminus X$ are independent, they can happen concurrently as a single step.

We sometime write $X \xrightarrow{A} Y$ where $A = Y \smallsetminus X$ instead of $X \to Y$. Note that if $Y = X \cup \{a\}$ and $X, Y \in \mathsf{C}$ then $X \to Y$. This may no longer hold in the reversible setting. Consider $E = \{a, b\}$. Suppose that a causes b, so that b cannot occur unless a has already occurred. Then $\{b\}$ is not a possible configuration using forwards computation. However, if a is reversible, we can do a (namely, $\varnothing \to \{a\}$) followed by b ($\{a\} \to \{a, b\}$), followed by reversing a ($\{a, b\} \dashrightarrow \{b\}$) to reach $\{b\}$. Thus both $\varnothing$ and $\{b\}$ are configurations, but we do not have $\varnothing \xrightarrow{b} \{b\}$.

A definition of configuration systems appropriate for the reversible setting was first given in [19]. We first establish our notation before we recall the definition. We let $A, B, X, Y, Z, \ldots$ range over sets of events. If an event e is reversible, we have a corresponding reverse event $\underline{e}$. We write $\underline{B}$ for $\{\underline{e} : e \in B\}$.

Definition 2.1. *A configuration system is a quadruple* $\mathcal{C} = (E, F, \mathsf{C}, \to)$ *where E is a set of events, $F \subseteq E$ are the reversible events, $\mathsf{C} \subseteq \mathfrak{P}(E)$ is the set of configurations and* $\to \subseteq \mathsf{C} \times \mathfrak{P}(E \cup \underline{F}) \times \mathsf{C}$ *is a labelled transition relation such that if* $X \xrightarrow{A \cup \underline{B}} Y$ *then:*

- $A \cap X = \varnothing$ *and* $B \subseteq X \cap F$ *and* $Y = (X \smallsetminus B) \cup A$;
- $X \xrightarrow{A' \cup \underline{B'}} Z \xrightarrow{(A \smallsetminus A') \cup (\underline{B \smallsetminus B'})} Y$ *(where* $Z = (X \smallsetminus B') \cup A' \in \mathsf{C}$*) for every* $A' \subseteq A$ *and* $B' \subseteq B$.

We say that $A \cup \underline{B}$ *is enabled at X if there is Y such that* $X \xrightarrow{A \cup \underline{B}} Y$. *A transition* $X \xrightarrow{A \cup \underline{B}} Y$ *is mixed if both A and B are non-empty. If $B = \varnothing$ we say the transition is* forwards, *and if $A = \varnothing$ the transition is* reverse.

For simplicity, we do not discuss in depth mixed transitions in this paper. Most examples concern transitions where A and $\underline{B}$ are singleton sets. As a result, the transitions denote either performing an event or undoing an event.

Finally, we define reachable configurations. Let $\mathcal{C} = (E, F, \mathsf{C}, \to)$ be a configuration system. We say that configuration X is a *reachable* configuration if $\varnothing \xrightarrow{A_1 \cup \underline{B_1}} \cdots \xrightarrow{A_n \cup \underline{B_n}} X$ where $A_i \subseteq E$ and $B_i \subseteq F$ for each $i = 1, \ldots, n$.

3 Reversible Event Structures with Causality and Precedence

In this section we consider event structures where the causation, concurrency and precedence relations on events dictate how they compute.

In order to explore different forms of relations between events and how this impacts on performing and undoing of events, we shall consider mostly very small event structures, namely those that have three events a, b and c. Even in such a simple setting we will be able to describe most of the important forms of executing events forwards and in reverse. The events a, b, c are depicted by the three dimensions of the cube in Figure 1. Note that any of the four edges of any dimension (representing an event) denotes an *occurrence* of the event. The bottom-left vertex represents the empty configuration $\varnothing$ (the origin of computation) and the top-right vertex represents the configuration $\{a, b, c\}$. If there are no constraints the events can happen in any order, denoted by following the edges from the origin, or simultaneously, denoted by taking some diagonals in the cube. For simplicity we do not display transitions of simultaneous events in our figures.

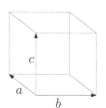

Fig. 1.

Causality is a binary irreflexive relation on events. It tells us which events cause which other events. We write $a \prec b$ to mean a causes b, so b cannot take place before a has occurred.

If $a \prec b$ and $b \prec c$ and $a \prec c$, namely $\prec$ is transitive, then we know that an execution contains b if it contains a, and c is in an execution if b is. The execution is $\varnothing \rightarrow \{a\} \rightarrow \{a, b\} \rightarrow \{a, b, c\}$. This is depicted in the left cube in Figure 2 by the sequence of thick arrows. An alternative way to represent an execution is with a sequence of events, for example, abc is the execution of the system with $a \prec b$, $b \prec c$ and $a \prec c$. And we can also write $\varnothing \xrightarrow{a} \{a\} \xrightarrow{b} \{a, b\} \xrightarrow{c} \{a, b, c\}$.

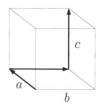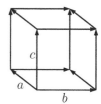

Fig. 2.

The cube on the right in Figure 2 shows all possible executions when a, b and c are *independent*, except those executions that involve steps (sets of simultaneous events) which we do not display for clarity. If events are not related by causality or other relations, then they are independent. This means that the events can take place in any order; hence six complete executions abc, acb, bac, bca, cab and cba are depicted. Each square of thick arrows represents graphically the independence of the events; we see that the events can happen in any order so we call them *concurrent* events. We have step transitions here, for example $\varnothing \rightarrow \{a, b, c\}$ and $\{a\} \rightarrow \{a, b, c\}$, but we do not display them in Figure 2. Also, there are several mixed transitions, for example, performing b and undoing a from $\{a\}$ is represented by $\{a\} \rightarrow \{b\}$, or $\{a\} \xrightarrow{b, \underline{a}} \{b\}$.

If $a \prec b$ and $a \prec c$, meaning that a causes both b and c, and b, c are independent, then there are only two complete executions: abc and acb. Correspondingly, $a \prec c$ and $b \prec c$ (namely, both a and b cause c) results in abc and bac.

So far we have illustrated how causality or independence (concurrency) affects the execution. Another very useful relation on events is *precedence*: $a \lhd b$,

read as event a *precedes* event b, means that if both a and b occur then a occurs first. The precedence relation has a dual interpretation: $b \rhd a$ says that b *prevents* a, meaning that if b is present in a configuration, then a cannot occur. Precedence is a form of *asymmetric*
conflict [1]. Consider a system where
$a \lhd b$ and $b \lhd a$, meaning that once either a or b occurs the other event cannot occur afterwards. In other words,
a and b are in *conflict*, often denoted
as $a \sharp b$. If, additionally, $a \prec c$, then we
have two complete executions ac and
b depicted by the left cube in Figure 3.
We can use the precedence relation to

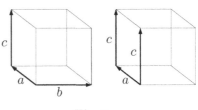

Fig. 3.

disable events. For example, if $b \lhd b$, then b can never occur, and if we also have $a \lhd c$ then ac and c are the only complete executions (see the cube on the right in Figure 3).

There are other forms of execution of the three events a, b, c which cannot be achieved by any combination of the causation, concurrency and precedence relations: we discuss this in the next section.

Next, we recall three forms of undoing events. *Backtracking* is when events are undone in the inverse order they occurred. The system $a \prec b \prec c$ in configuration $\{a, b, c\}$ backtracks by undoing c first, then undoing b and, lastly, undoing a. The left cube in Figure 4 shows the system backtracking c and then b (dashed arrows pointing in the opposite direction) from $\{a, b, c\}$, which is written as $\{a, b, c\} \dashrightarrow \{a, b\} \dashrightarrow \{a\}$.

Consider $a \prec b$ and $a \prec c$: a occurs first and then b, c can occur independently. Once in the configuration
$\{a, b, c\}$ we have no way of working
out which of b and c occurred last.
Since the events are independent, the
order of performing or undoing them
does not matter. So *causal reversing*,
or simply reversing, is undoing where

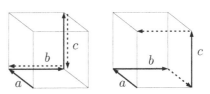

Fig. 4.

(a) independent events can be undone in any order irrespective of the order they have actually occurred, and (b) events that cause other events can only be undone after the caused events are undone first.

Both backtracking and reversing are *cause-respecting*, meaning that events caused by other events are undone first before the other events can be undone. There are, however, many important examples of undoing things *out-of-causal order*. In fact, this form of undoing plays the vital rôle the mechanisms driving long-running transactions and biochemical reactions. As an example, consider the following pattern of behaviour shown in the right cube of Figure 4. Event a causes event b. Once we have b, a is not needed so it is undone. Finally, c occurs and cannot be undone, and then b is undone. Informally speaking, a can be thought as the *catalyst* of b, and b as the catalyst of c. The execution is $\varnothing \to \{a\} \to \{a,b\} \dashrightarrow \{b\} \to \{b,c\} \dashrightarrow \{c\}$. Note that we undo a, the cause of b, before we undo b. Overall, we can reach $\{c\}$ from $\varnothing$ via a combination of forwards and reverse moves but we cannot reach $\{c\}$ by executing forwards only.

Since there are different forms of undoing events, the question is how to model undoing of events formally. In [19] we extend the causation and precedence relations to define additionally undoing of events. Recall that $\underline{a}, \underline{b}, \underline{c}$ denote undoing of a, b, c. We can extend the causation relation $<$ with pairs $x < \underline{y}$, meaning that event y can be undone if y has occurred and x has occurred and has not been undone yet. For example, $a < \underline{a}$ means that a can be undone if it has occurred. Correspondingly, we also extend our precedence relation $\vartriangleleft$ with pairs $\underline{x} \vartriangleleft y$, meaning that x cannot be undone if y is present. What we have described informally so far are *reversible asymmetric event structures* ([19]):

Definition 3.1. A reversible asymmetric event structure (RAES) is a quadruple $\mathcal{E} = (E, F, <, \vartriangleleft)$ where E is a set of events and $F \subseteq E$ are those events of E which are reversible, and for any $a, b, c, e \in E$ and $\alpha \in E \cup \underline{F}$:

1. $\vartriangleleft \subseteq (E \cup \underline{F}) \times E$ is the *precedence* relation (with $a \vartriangleleft b$ if and only if $b \vartriangleright a$), which is irreflexive;
2. $< \subseteq E \times (E \cup \underline{F})$ is the *direct causation* relation, which is irreflexive and well-founded, and such that $\{e \in E : e < \alpha\}$ is finite and $\vartriangleleft$ is acyclic on $\{e \in E : e < \alpha\}$;
3. $a < \underline{a}$ for all $a \in F$;
4. if $a < \alpha$ then not $a \vartriangleright \alpha$;
5. $a \lll b$ implies $a \vartriangleleft b$, where *sustained direct causation* $a \lll b$ means that $a < b$ and if $a \in F$ then $b \vartriangleright \underline{a}$;
6. $\lll$ is transitive;
7. if $a \,\|\, c$ and $a \lll b$ then $b \,\|\, c$, where $\|$ is defined to be $\vartriangleleft \cap \vartriangleright$.

Causation can be explained in two different ways. Event a causes event b ($a < b$) means either (1) in any execution (computation), if b occurs then a occurs earlier or (2) if b is enabled at configuration X then we must have $a \in X$. The two views are equivalent if there is no reversing. Consider three events with $a < b < c$. Taking view (1) we deduce that $a < c$. View (2) also allows us to deduce that $a < c$, provided that X is left-closed (downwards closed under $<$), which will be the case for forward-only computation. Thus causation is transitive.

In the setting of reversible computation the second view of causation is simpler, and is adopted in this paper. If all reversing is causal, then all configurations are left-closed, and so it is still natural to require $<$ to be transitive. If, however, there is non-causal reversing, which leads to non-left-closed configurations (such as $\{b,c\}$ and $\{c\}$ in our example), it is no longer reasonable to insist on $<$ being transitive. If $a < b < c$ then a may have been reversed after b occurs, and before c occurs. Therefore, direct causation in RAESs is non-transitive. We introduce additionally the concept of sustained causation, where $a \lll b$ means that a causes b and a cannot reverse until b reverses. This is the analogue of standard causation for forwards computation, and we therefore take sustained causation to be transitive (condition 6 in Definition 3.1).

Next we consider the issue of *conflict inheritance*, namely if $a < b$ and $a \,\sharp\, c$ then $b \,\sharp\, c$, in the reversible setting. If $a < b$ and $a \,\sharp\, c$ and a is reversible, then we can undo a in $\{a, b\}$ to reach $\{b\}$. And there is nothing in $\{b\}$ to prevent c from taking place, so we expect that $\{b, c\}$ is a configuration, and b and c are not in conflict. Hence, there is no conflict inheritance with respect to $<$. However, we still have conflict inheritance with respect to sustained causation $a \lll b$ (condition 7 in Definition 3.1).

Definition 3.2. Let $\mathcal{E} = (E, F, <, \lhd)$ be an RAES. We define the associated configuration system $C(\mathcal{E}) = (E, F, \mathsf{C}, \to)$ as follows. Let C consist of those $X \subseteq E$ such that $\lhd$ is well-founded on X. For $X \in \mathsf{C}$ and $A \subseteq E$, $B \subseteq F$, we define $X \xrightarrow{A \cup B} Y$ if and only if $X, Y \in \mathsf{C}$ and $Y = (X \smallsetminus B) \cup A$ and $A \cup \underline{B}$ is *enabled* at X, which is

- $A \cap X = \varnothing$, $B \subseteq X$;
- for every $a \in A$, if $c < a$ then $c \in X \smallsetminus B$;
- for every $a \in A$, if $c \rhd a$ then $c \notin X \cup A$;
- for every $b \in B$, if $d < \underline{b}$ then $d \in X \smallsetminus (B \smallsetminus \{b\})$;
- for every $b \in B$, if $d \rhd \underline{b}$ then $d \notin X \cup A$.

We are now able to model undoing of events. If we add $x < \underline{x}$, for all $x \in \{a, b, c\}$, and $\underline{a} \lhd b$, $\underline{b} \lhd c$ to $a < b < c$ and $a < c$, then we achieve backtracking in Figure 4. Note that only c can be undone in $\{a, b, c\}$ because $\underline{a} \lhd b$, $\underline{b} \lhd c$ and the presence of b, c prevents undoing of a, b, respectively.

In order to achieve causal reversing we impose the following global conditions: all events are reversible ($x < \underline{y}$ if and only if $x = y$ for all x), and causes are undone if and only if their effects are not present ($x < y$ if and only if $\underline{x} \lhd y$ for all x, y). In the case of the system $a < b, a < c$ we add the following to achieve causal reversibility: $a < \underline{a}$, $b < \underline{b}$, $c < \underline{c}$ and $\underline{a} \lhd b$, $\underline{a} \lhd c$. Here, once $\{a, b, c\}$ is reached, b, c can be undone in any order, and a can only be undone when b, c are not present (due to $\underline{a} \lhd b$, $\underline{a} \lhd c$). Overall, we have $\{a, b, c\} \to \{a, b\} \to \{a\}$ and $\{a, b, c\} \to \{a, c\} \to \{a\}$, and clearly $\{a\} \to \varnothing$.

Finally, we model the out-of-causal-order RAES in Figure 4. We have $a < b < c$ but no $a < c$ (so $<$ is not transitive) and $a < \underline{a}$, $b < \underline{b}$ (there is no $c < \underline{c}$ since c is irreversible). That a, b are undone only when b, c are present is ensured by $b < \underline{a}$, $c < \underline{b}$, respectively. In order to stop reversing b immediately after it occurs we add $\underline{b} \lhd a$. And, $\underline{a} \lhd b$, $\underline{a} \lhd c$ prevent a from re-occurring when b or c are present. As a result, there is a single execution $\varnothing \to \{a\} \to \{a, b\} \to \{b\} \to \{b, c\} \to \{c\}$.

The work on reversing asymmetric event structures in [19] led to several interesting results concerning reachable configurations. For example, we have given conditions under which finite and reachable configurations are guaranteed to be reachable without intermediate infinite configurations. Our models are general enough to allow several forms of reversibility to be defined and analysed, including the causal and *inverse causal* disciplines.

4   Reversible Event Structures with Enablings

There are forms of execution of three events a, b, c which cannot be achieved by any combination of the causation, concurrency and precedence relations. For example, consider an event that is caused by a disjunction of events: namely a or b causes c. This is called *disjunctive causation*. If no other relation holds of a, b, c, then there is an execution where only a occurs before c, there is another execution where only b occurs prior to c, and there are two executions where both a and b precede c. These complete executions acb, bca, abc and bac are depicted in the left cube in Figure 5. This event structure can be defined using the *enabling* relation as in [15, 26] as we shall see below. Another example of a relation on events that cannot be expressed in terms of causality, concurrency and precedence is *resolvable conflict*. Consider a temporary conflict between a and b which becomes resolved once a third event c occurs. This is represented by the executions acb, bca, cab and cba in the cube on the right in Figure 5. This event structure cannot be expressed with the traditional enabling relation; instead a more general enabling rela-

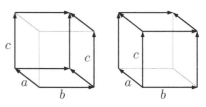

Fig. 5.

tion from [23] or our *enabling with prevention* relation, that we recall below, are necessary.

Firstly, we recall some definitions from [26]. Event structures are triples $\mathcal{E} = (E, \mathsf{Con}, \vdash)$ where E is a set of events with typical elements e, e', $\mathsf{Con} \subseteq \mathcal{P}_{\mathrm{fin}}(E)$ is the *consistency* relation which is non-empty and satisfies the property $Y \subseteq X \in \mathsf{Con}$ implies $Y \in \mathsf{Con}$ (downwards closure), and $\vdash \subseteq \mathsf{Con} \times E$ is the *enabling* relation which satisfies the *weakening* condition $X \vdash e$ and $X \subseteq Y \in \mathsf{Con}$ implies $Y \vdash e$ for all $e \in E$. We omit brackets for singleton sets in expressions $X \vdash e$ where convenient. Informally, configurations are the sets of events that have occurred (in accordance with Con and $\vdash$). More formally, we let $\mathcal{E} = (E, \mathsf{Con}, \vdash)$ be an event structure. The set $S(\mathcal{E})$ of *configurations* of $\mathcal{E}$ consists of $X \subseteq E$ which are

- *consistent*: every finite subset of X is in Con;
- *secured*: for all $e \in X$ there is a sequence of events $e_0, \ldots, e_n \in X$ such that $e_n = e$ and for all $i < n$, $\{e_0, \ldots, e_{i-1}\} \vdash e_i$.

We shall now present several examples of event structures with enablings and their corresponding configurations.

Consider the events a, b with all subsets of $\{a, b\}$ in Con, and the enabling relation $\varnothing \vdash a$, $a \vdash b$. We notice that $\{a\}$ is a configuration because $\{a\} \in \mathsf{Con}$ and a is enabled without any preconditions: $\varnothing \vdash a$. Once a takes place, b can happen because $\{a, b\} \in \mathsf{Con}$ and b is enabled by the already performed a: $a \vdash b$. We can say here that a *causes* b and b cannot take place before a happens first.

Some events are in *conflict*: they cannot happen in the same computation. Consider the events a, b as above and the event c which is conflict with a. This is represented by $\{a,c\} \notin \mathsf{Con}$ and, by the downwards closure property, $\{a,b,c\} \notin \mathsf{Con}$. The enabling relation is $\varnothing \vdash a$, $a \vdash b$ and $\varnothing \vdash c$. The configurations are $\varnothing$, $\{a\}, \{a,b\}$ and $\{c\}$ representing that either a or c can happen initially, but once one has taken place the other cannot happen; see left cube in Figure 6. Some events are independent of each other, or concurrent. Consider the events a, b and c, with no events in conflict. The enabling relation is $\varnothing \vdash a$, $a \vdash b$ and $\varnothing \vdash c$. Since a and c are not in conflict, $\varnothing \vdash a$, $\varnothing \vdash c$ imply that a, c can happen independently of one another, in any order. Moreover, b and c are independent and can happen in any order provided that b always fol-

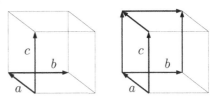

Fig. 6.

lows a. The configurations are $\varnothing$, $\{a\}, \{a,b\}, \{c\}, \{a,c\}, \{a,b,c\}$, and can be seen in the cube on the right in Figure 6.

We now show how to define the disjunctive causation event structure from Figure 5. If we let the enabling relation as $\varnothing \vdash a$, $\varnothing \vdash b$, and $a \vdash c$ with $b \vdash c$, then we can deduce that $\{c\}$ is not a configuration since we have no $\varnothing \vdash c$. All other subsets of $\{a,b,c\}$ are configurations.

As we aim to generalise event structures with enablings to the reversible setting, we shall use this equivalent definition of a configuration. Let $\mathcal{E} = (E, \mathsf{Con}, \vdash)$ be an event structure. A set $X \subseteq E$ is a *configuration* of $\mathcal{E}$ if there is an infinite sequence $X_0, \dots$ with $X = \bigcup_{n=0}^{\infty} X_n$, $X_0 = \varnothing$, $X_n \subseteq X_{n+1}$ and X_n consistent (all $n \in \mathbb{N}$), where for every $n \in \mathbb{N}$, and every $e \in X_{n+1} \setminus X_n$, there is a rule $X' \vdash e$ with $X' \subseteq_{\mathrm{fin}} X_n$.

As in Section 3, there is a natural notion of computation for configurations in this setting. A transition relation can now be defined to represent how a new event can happen in a configuration giving rise to a bigger configuration. Given configurations X, Y we have $X \to Y$ if $Y = X \cup \{e\}$ (with $e \notin X$) and $X' \vdash e$, for some e and $X' \subseteq_{\mathrm{fin}} X$. A computation of the event structure $\mathcal{E}$ is a computation (sequence of transitions) starting from $\varnothing_{\mathcal{E}}$, the empty configuration of $\mathcal{E}$. Subsequently we omit $\mathcal{E}$ in $\varnothing_{\mathcal{E}}$. As an illustration, $\varnothing \to \{c\} \to \{a,c\} \to \{a,b,c\}$ is a computation of the event structure in the right cube in Figure 6. We also have $\varnothing \to \{a\} \to \{a,c\} \to \{a,b,c\}$ and $\varnothing \to \{a\} \to \{a,b\} \to \{a,b,c\}$.

Finally, we consider undoing of events. Let E be a set of events. We define the corresponding set of *undone* events (strictly speaking, events that are to be undone) to be $\underline{E} = \{\underline{e} : e \in E\}$, where $\underline{E}$ is disjoint from E. For $e \in E$, let e^* be either e or $\underline{e}$; we sometimes use the notation $X + e^*$ to mean either $X \cup \{e\}$ or $X \setminus \{e\}$ respectively. *Reversible event structures* were first introduced in [22]:

Definition 4.1. A reversible event structure (RES for short) is a triple $\mathcal{E} = (E, \mathsf{Con}, \vdash)$ where E and Con are as before and $\vdash \subseteq \mathsf{Con} \times \mathfrak{P}(E) \times (E \cup \underline{E})$ is the *enabling* relation satisfying:

1. if $X \otimes Y \vdash e^*$ then $(X \cup \{e\}) \cap Y = \varnothing$;
2. if $X \otimes Y \vdash \underline{e}$ then $e \in X$;

3. *weakening*: if $X \oslash Y \vdash e^*$ and $X \subseteq X' \in \mathsf{Con}$ then $X' \oslash Y \vdash e^*$, provided $X' \cap Y = \varnothing$.

When $Y = \varnothing$ we shall write $X \oslash Y \vdash e^*$ as $X \vdash e^*$. Also we omit brackets for singleton sets in expressions $X \oslash Y \vdash e^*$ where convenient.

Our enabling relation $\vdash$ extends the enabling relation of Winskel in two directions. Firstly, it permits reversing of events as e^* in $X \oslash Y \vdash e^*$ can be an undone event. Secondly, it allows us to specify some of the events that prevent e^* (here those in Y) in addition to the events that enable e^* (those in X). For example, $\{a, b\} \oslash \{c, d\} \vdash \underline{a}$ says that a can be undone in a configuration which contains a and b and does not contain c and d.

We are ready to define an RES for resolvable conflict in Figure 5.

Example 4.2. We let Con be $\mathfrak{P}(\{a, b, c\})$. The enabling relation is as follows: $\varnothing \vdash c$, $\varnothing \oslash b \vdash a$ and $\varnothing \oslash a \vdash b$, meaning that initially, either a or b can take place if the other event is not present. We also have $c \vdash a$ and $c \vdash b$, which imply that both a and b can happen after c.

Example 4.3. Consider an RES with a single event e and the enabling rule $\varnothing \vdash e$. The sets $\varnothing$ and $\{e\}$ are configurations. If we add another rule $e \vdash \underline{e}$ then this allows us to regress from $\{e\}$ to $\varnothing$. The sets $\varnothing$ and $\{e\}$ are reachable from $\varnothing$ in any number of steps; they are configurations according to Definition 4.5 below. And, there is an infinite computation sequence $\varnothing, \{e\}, \varnothing, \{e\}, \ldots$.

This example shows that sets of events can grow and and shrink as reversible computation progresses. Also, sets of events may grow non-monotonically as, for example, in $a_0, b, a_1, \underline{b}, a_2, b, a_3, \underline{b}, a_4, \ldots$. So we shall use limits of infinite sequences of subsets of E in order to define configurations as in [22] (recall that $S \subseteq \mathbb{N}$ is *cofinite* if $\mathbb{N} \setminus S$ is finite):

Definition 4.4. Let $X_0, \ldots$ be an infinite sequence of subsets of E. We say that $X = \lim_{n \to \infty} X_n$ if for every $e \in E$:

1. $\{n \in \mathbb{N} : e \in X_n\}$ is either finite or cofinite;
2. $e \in X$ if and only if $\{n : e \in X_n\}$ is cofinite.

We note that a sequence of sets does not necessarily have a limit. The sequence $\varnothing, \{e\}, \varnothing, \{e\}, \ldots$ in Example 4.3 has no limit, since e belongs to infinitely many sets and does not belong to infinitely many sets. However if $X_n \subseteq X_{n+1}$ (all $n \in \mathbb{N}$) then $\lim_{n \to \infty} X_n$ exists and is $\bigcup_{n=0}^{\infty} X_n$. A finite sequence $X_0, \ldots, X_n$ can be extended to an infinite sequence by letting $X_m = X_n$ for all $m > n$; the extended sequence has the limit X_n. In Example 4.3 the sequence $\varnothing, \{e\}$ can be extended to an infinite sequence $\varnothing, \{e\}, \{e\}, \ldots$ and has the limit $\{e\}$.

Next we state the definition of a configuration for an RES ([22]). As the notational convention we write $\underline{e} \in A \setminus B$ to mean $e \in B \setminus A$.

Definition 4.5. Let $\mathcal{E} = (E, \mathsf{Con}, \vdash)$ be an RES. A set $X \subseteq E$ is a *configuration* of $\mathcal{E}$ if there is an infinite sequence $X_0, \ldots$ with $X = \lim_{n \to \infty} X_n$, $X_0 = \varnothing$ and $X_n \cup X_{n+1}$ consistent (all $n \in \mathbb{N}$), where for every $n \in \mathbb{N}$, and every $e^* \in X_{n+1} \setminus X_n$, there is a rule $X' \oslash Y' \vdash e^*$ such that:

1. $X' \subseteq_{\text{fin}} X_n$ and $X' + e^* \subseteq X_{n+1}$;
2. $Y' \cap (X_n \cup X_{n+1}) = \varnothing$.

We require $X_n \cup X_{n+1}$ to be consistent, as configurations can only be extended in a consistent fashion. However, there is no requirement that $X_i \cup X_j$ is consistent if $j > i + 1$ because events in X_i which are inconsistent with X_j can be reversed in constructing $X_{i+1}, \ldots, X_{j-1}$. Also, we note that the X_is in the above definition can grow smaller as well as bigger as computation progresses. Moreover, a finite sequence $X_0, \ldots, X_n = X$ that satisfies the conditions of Definition 4.5 is sufficient for X to be a configuration. The sequence $\varnothing, \{e\}$ in Example 4.3 can be extended to an infinite sequence and, since the conditions of Definition 4.5 are satisfied, its limit $\{e\}$ is a configuration.

We return to Example 4.2. We note that although $\{a, b\} \in \mathsf{Con}$, $\{a, b\}$ is not a configuration according to Definition 4.5. Consider $\varnothing$, $\{a\}$, $\{a, b\}$ and b: there is no enabling $X' \otimes Y' \vdash b$ such that $X' \subseteq_{\text{fin}} \{a\}$ and $Y' \cap \{a, b\} = \varnothing$. Correspondingly for the sequence $\varnothing$, $\{b\}$, $\{a, b\}$ and a. Hence, $\{a, b\}$ is not a configuration.

It can be easily shown that RESs are a generalisation of event structures: RESs with enablings $X \otimes \varnothing \vdash e$ are just event structures of Winskel [26]. Moreover, our configurations in such setting are just the traditional configurations. We can also show that our generalised enabling rules are powerful enough that we no longer need the consistency relation.

We are now ready to define a transition relation between configurations of an RES. Again, as in Section 2, we shall use the dashed arrow notation for the part of the transition relation that represents undoing of events. Given configurations X, Y of an RES $\mathcal{E}$ we let

– $X \to Y$ if $Y = X \cup \{e\}$ and $X' \otimes Z \vdash e$ for some e, X', Z with $e \notin X$, $X' \subseteq_{\text{fin}} X$ and $Z \cap (X \cup \{e\}) = \varnothing$;
– $X \dashrightarrow Y$ if $Y = X \smallsetminus \{e\}$ and $X' \otimes Z \vdash \underline{e}$ for some e, X', Z with $X' \subseteq_{\text{fin}} X$ and $Z \cap X = \varnothing$.

In contrast to Section 2, this transition relation represents only either performing a single event or undoing a single event. Having given the transition relation, we can now define a configuration system for an RES. Given an RES $\mathcal{E} = (E, \mathsf{Con}, \vdash)$, the associated configuration system $C(\mathcal{E})$ is $(E, E, \mathsf{C}, \to)$ where C is the set of configurations for $\mathcal{E}$ as in Definition 4.5.

We now show how to represent different forms of undoing of events in RESs. Consider events a and b with $\varnothing \vdash a$ and $a \vdash b$. We have that a causes b so if we wish to achieve causal reversing we need to add the following to the definition of $\vdash$: $b \vdash \underline{b}$ and $a \otimes b \vdash \underline{a}$. The configuration $\{a, b\}$ can regress to $\{a\}$ by undoing b as allowed by $b \vdash \underline{b}$. But it cannot regress to $\{b\}$ because $a \otimes b \vdash \underline{a}$ can only be applied in a configuration that contains a and does not contain b. See Figure 7(i).

If undoing events in the same order as they occurred is required, we instead add to the definition of $\vdash$ the following: $a \vdash \underline{a}$ and $b \otimes a \vdash \underline{b}$. This means that a can be reversed in any configuration that contains a (with or without b), and b can be reversed only when a is not present. Since a causes b, this means that b can be reversed only when a is reversed. See Figure 7(ii) where reverse transitions are

(i)   (ii)   (iii)

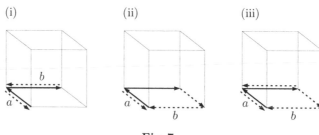

Fig. 7.

indicated by dashed lines. Finally, if we would like instead that a and b are reversed in any order, then we would extend the enabling relation simply with $b \vdash \underline{b}$ and $a \vdash \underline{a}$. See Figure 7(iii).

Finally, we give an example where we get an infinite configuration as a limit of a non-monotonically increasing sequence ([22]).

Example 4.6. Let $\mathcal{E} = (E, \mathsf{Con}, \vdash)$ where $E = \{a_i : i \in \mathbb{N}\} \cup \{b_j : j \in \mathbb{N}\}$ and Con consists of $\{a_i, b_0, \ldots, b_j\}$ (any $i, j \in \mathbb{N}$) plus deducible subsets, with

$$\varnothing \vdash a_0 \quad a_i \vdash b_i \quad \{a_i, b_i\} \vdash \underline{a_i} \quad b_i \vdash a_{i+1} \quad (\text{all } i \in \mathbb{N})$$

Informally, a_i is the catalyst of b_i, for all i, so once b_i occurs a_i can be undone.

The only possible computation of $\mathcal{E}$ is $a_0, b_0, \underline{a_0}, a_1, b_1, \underline{a_1}, \ldots$. It produces the following sequence of sets of events, which grow non-monotonically:

$$\varnothing,$$
$$\{a_0\}, \ \{a_0, b_0\}, \ \{b_0\},$$
$$\{b_0, a_1\}, \ \{b_0, a_1, b_1\}, \ \{b_0, b_1\},$$
$$\{b_0, b_1, a_2\}, \ \{b_0, b_1, a_2, b_2\}, \ \{b_0, b_1, b_2\}, \ \ldots$$

Each of the sets is a configuration and this sequence has limit the infinite set $\{b_j : j \in \mathbb{N}\}$, so $\{b_j : j \in \mathbb{N}\}$ is also a configuration. Note that each a_i appears finitely often in the sequence, while each b_j appears cofinitely often.

5   Discussion and Conclusions

We indicate briefly several areas of ongoing research in reversing event structures.

We aim to investigate the expressiveness of event structures defined with our enabling relation with prevention (for forwards-only events), and compare them with other forms of event structures. In particular, it remains to be seen whether or not we can encode event structures of van Glabbeek and Plotkin [23], which are defined by a very general form of enabling relation ($X \vdash Y$ where X, Y are sets of events), as our event structures from Section 4, or vice versa.

The examples in the previous section indicate that it ought to be possible to represent an arbitrary RAES as a special form of RES. Given an RAES if $X_a = \{e \mid e < a\}$ and $Y_a = \{f \mid a \vartriangleleft f\}$, then the enabling rule $X_a \oslash Y_a \vdash a$ captures the idea that a can occur if all events in X_a have occurred (and are present) and if no events from Y_a are present. It should be then routine to define conditions 3 to 7 of RAESs in terms of our enabling relation. For example, condition 3 is expressed as if $X \oslash Y \vdash \alpha$ and $a \in X$, then $a \notin Y$: this is already guaranteed by condition 1 in Definition 4.1. Since disjunctive causation cannot be expressed in RAESs, RESs are strictly more expressive that RAESs.

Another challenge is to define step and mixed transitions between configurations in the RES setting. In order to define the notion of a set of enabled events and past events (as in Definition 3.2), we need to devise a way of dealing with enabling rules that are obtained via weakening (Definition 4.1). Assume that we wish to check if $A \cup B$ is enabled at X. Clearly, we require $A \cap X = \varnothing$ and $B \subseteq X$. If $a \in A$ and $X_a \oslash Y_a \vdash a$, then we also require that $X_a \subseteq X \setminus B$ and $(X \cup A) \cap Y_a = \varnothing$. However, the last condition will not necessarily hold for rules gotten from $X_a \oslash Y_a \vdash a$ by weakening. Assume that $X_a \cup \{d\}$ is consistent and $d \notin X_a, Y_a, X$. Then $(X_a \cup \{d\}) \oslash Y_a \vdash a$ is an enabling obtained from $X_a \oslash Y_a \vdash a$ by weakening, but $X_a \cup \{d\}$ is not a subset of $X \setminus B$.

Concluding, we have shown how to model reversibility in concurrent computation as realised by two different forms of events structures, namely event structures defined in terms of the causation and precedence relations and event structures defined by the enabling relation. We have presented causal reversibility as well as out-of-causal-order reversibility.

Acknowledgements. The first author thanks the University of Leicester for granting Academic Study Leave and acknowledges partial support from the JSPS Invitation Fellowship grant S13054.

References

[1] Baldan, P., Corradini, A., Montanari, U.: Contextual Petri nets, asymmetric event structures, and processes. Information and Computation 171(1), 1–49 (2001)
[2] Bednarczyk, M.A.: Hereditary history preserving bisimulations or what is the power of the future perfect in program logics. Technical Report ICS PAS, Polish Academy of Sciences (1991)
[3] Berry, G., Boudol, G.: The chemical abstract machine. Theoretical Computer Science 96(1), 217–248 (1992)
[4] Cardelli, L., Laneve, C.: Reversible structures. In: 9th International Conference on Computational Methods in Systems Biology, pp. 131–140. ACM (2011)
[5] Cristescu, I., Krivine, J., Varacca, D.: A compositional semantics for the reversible p-calculus. In: Proceedings of LICS 2013, pp. 388–397. IEEE Computer Society (2013)
[6] Danos, V., Krivine, J.: Reversible communicating systems. In: Gardner, P., Yoshida, N. (eds.) CONCUR 2004. LNCS, vol. 3170, pp. 292–307. Springer, Heidelberg (2004)
[7] Danos, V., Krivine, J.: Transactions in RCCS. In: Abadi, M., de Alfaro, L. (eds.) CONCUR 2005. LNCS, vol. 3653, pp. 398–412. Springer, Heidelberg (2005)
[8] Danos, V., Krivine, J.: Formal molecular biology done in CCS-R. In: Proceedings of BioConcur 2003. ENTCS, vol. 180, pp. 31–49 (2007)

[9] Giachino, E., Lanese, I., Mezzina, C.A.: Causal-consistent reversible debugging. In: Gnesi, S., Rensink, A. (eds.) FASE 2014 (ETAPS). LNCS, vol. 8411, pp. 370–384. Springer, Heidelberg (2014)

[10] van Glabbeek, R.J., Goltz, U.: Refinement of actions and equivalence notions for concurrent systems. Acta Informatica 37, 229–327 (2001)

[11] Hennessy, M., Milner, R.: Algebraic laws for non-determinism and concurrency. Journal of the ACM 32, 137–161 (1985)

[12] Lanese, I., Mezzina, C.A., Schmitt, A., Stefani, J.-B.: Controlling reversibility in higher-order pi. In: Katoen, J.-P., König, B. (eds.) CONCUR 2011. LNCS, vol. 6901, pp. 297–311. Springer, Heidelberg (2011)

[13] Lanese, I., Mezzina, C.A., Stefani, J.-B.: Reversing higher-order pi. In: Gastin, P., Laroussinie, F. (eds.) CONCUR 2010. LNCS, vol. 6269, pp. 478–493. Springer, Heidelberg (2010)

[14] Lanese, I., Mezzina, C.A., Stefani, J.-B.: Controlled reversibility and compensations. In: Glück, R., Yokoyama, T. (eds.) RC 2012. LNCS, vol. 7581, pp. 233–240. Springer, Heidelberg (2013)

[15] Nielsen, M., Plotkin, G.D., Winskel, G.: Petri nets, event structures and domains, part I. Theoretical Computer Science 13, 85–108 (1981)

[16] Phillips, I.C.C., Ulidowski, I.: Reversing algebraic process calculi. In: Aceto, L., Ingólfsdóttir, A. (eds.) FOSSACS 2006. LNCS, vol. 3921, pp. 246–260. Springer, Heidelberg (2006)

[17] Phillips, I.C.C., Ulidowski, I.: Reversing algebraic process calculi. Journal of Logic and Algebraic Programming 73, 70–96 (2007)

[18] Phillips, I.C.C., Ulidowski, I.: A hierarchy of reverse bisimulations on stable configuration structures. Mathematical Structures in Computer Science 22, 333–372 (2012)

[19] Phillips, I., Ulidowski, I.: Reversibility and asymmetric conflict in even structures. In: D'Argenio, P.R., Melgratti, H. (eds.) CONCUR 2013. LNCS, vol. 8052, pp. 303–318. Springer, Heidelberg (2013)

[20] Phillips, I.C.C., Ulidowski, I.: Event Identifier Logic. Mathematical Structures in Computer Science 24, 1–51 (2014)

[21] Phillips, I.C.C., Ulidowski, I., Yuen, S.: A reversible process calculus and the modelling of the ERK signalling pathway. In: Glück, R., Yokoyama, T. (eds.) RC 2012. LNCS, vol. 7581, pp. 218–232. Springer, Heidelberg (2013)

[22] Phillips, I.C.C., Ulidowski, I., Yuen, S.: Modelling of bonding with processes and events. In: Dueck, G.W., Miller, D.M. (eds.) RC 2013. LNCS, vol. 7948, pp. 141–154. Springer, Heidelberg (2013)

[23] van Glabbeek, R.J., Plotkin, G.D.: Configuration structures, event structures and Petri nets. Theoretical Computer Science 410(41), 4111–4159 (2009)

[24] van Glabbeek, R.J., Plotkin, G.D.: Event structures for resolvable conflict. In: Fiala, J., Koubek, V., Kratochvíl, J. (eds.) MFCS 2004. LNCS, vol. 3153, pp. 550–561. Springer, Heidelberg (2004)

[25] Varacca, D., Yoshida, N.: Typed event structures and the linear π-calculus. Theoretical Computer Science 411(19), 1949–1973 (2010)

[26] Winskel, G.: Event structures. In: Brauer, W., Reisig, W., Rozenberg, G. (eds.) APN 1986. LNCS, vol. 255, pp. 325–392. Springer, Heidelberg (1987)

[27] Winskel, G.: Events, causality and symmetry. Computer Journal 54(1), 42–57 (2011)

Reversible Computing
Using Adiabatic Superconductor Logic

Naoki Takeuchi, Yuki Yamanashi, and Nobuyuki Yoshikawa

Department of Elecrical and Computer Engineering, Yokohama National University,
Hodogaya, Yokohama 240-8501, Japan
takeuchi-naoki-kx@ynu.jp, {yamanasi,nyoshi}@ynu.ac.jp

Abstract. The adiabatic quantum-flux-parametron (AQFP), which is adiabatic superconductor logic, is well suitable to realize reversible computing, because of the extremely high energy efficiency. In AQFP logic, dynamic energy dissipation can be significantly reduced by varying potential energy adiabatically during a switching event, which prevents non-adiabatic energy dissipation. In this paper, we report recent research results toward reversible computing using AQFP logic. First, we show experimental demonstrations of adiabatic switching operations of an AQFP gate. Then we discuss the minimum energy dissipation for an adiabatic switching operation using numerical analyses. Finally, we report reversible computing using AQFP gates and discuss the minimum energy dissipation required for logic operations using logically and physically reversible gates.

Keywords: reversible computing, physical reversibility, superconductor logic, adiabatic device, QFP.

1   Introduction

The connection between information and energy has recently been attracting significant attention as part of efforts related to increasing energy-efficiency, which is now considered to be the most important metric in modern computer design [1,2]. One of the most important theories in this field is the Landauer's principle [3], whereby Rolf Landauer predicted that the erasure of 1-bit information generates heat of more than $k_B T \ln 2$ in order to compensate for a reduction in entropy, where k_B is the Boltzmann constant and T is temperature. This principle imposed the Landauer bound of $k_B T \ln 2$ as the minimum energy dissipation on irreversible logic operations, such as AND and OR, which erase 1-bit information at every logic operation. The minimum power consumption in modern semiconductor-based computers can be defined using this principle because they primarily conduct irreversible logic operations [4-7]. After long discussions and numerical analyses of this energy bound [8-10], some very recent experimental demonstrations that confirmed its validity have been reported [11,12].

S. Yamashita and S. Minato (Eds.): RC 2014, LNCS 8507, pp. 15–25, 2014.

In order to go beyond this bound, Edward Fredkin established a theory of reversible computing [13], where the entropy of information is conserved during computation to prevent the heat generation resulting from the entropy reduction. He introduced the Fredkin gate [13] as a 3-in/3-out reversible logic gate, which is logically reversible [14] because its inputs are uniquely determined from its outputs, thereby conserving the entropy during computation. As part of the effort to achieve practical reversible logic gates, several physical models and devices have been proposed [15-18]. However, no reversible logic operations have been demonstrated to date, and the minimum energy bound for logic operations using practical devices is not clear yet. Thus, discussions on reversible computing remain theoretical, and the question as to whether reversible computing is achievable using practical logic devices has yet to be resolved.

One of the obstacles to the achievement of reversible computing is that reversible logic gates must be built by using very low-power devices, whose bit energy should be $\sim k_B T$ or even smaller. Adiabatic quantum-flux-parametron [19,20], which is adiabatic superconductor logic, is a good candidate for such use because the bit energy can go below $k_B T$ due to adiabatic switching operations [21]. Another obstacle is that a reversible logic gate must be physically, as well as logically, reversible [22].

In the present study, we report recent research results toward reversible computing using AQFP gates. In Chap. 3, we show experimental demonstrations of adiabatic switching operations of AQFP gates. In Chap. 4, we discuss the minimum energy dissipation for the adiabatic operations. In Chap. 5, we show the first practical reversible logic gate using AQFP logic and discuss the minimum energy dissipation for reversible computing.

2   Adiabatic Quantum-Flux-Parametron Logic

Figure 1 shows the circuit schematic of an AQFP gate, which is composed of two superconducting loops including Josephson junctions, J_1 and J_2. The operation principle of an AQFP gate is based on that of a quantum-flux-parametron (QFP) gate invented by Eiichi Goto [23]. In AQFP logic, we focus on operating QFP gates in an adiabatic operation mode with optimized circuit parameters [20]. Excitation fluxes are applied to the superconducting loops through transformers composed of L_1, L_2, L_{x1}, and L_{x2} using ac excitation currents, I_x. Then one single-flux-quantum (SFQ) is stored either in the left loop or in the right loop, depending on the input current, I_{in}. As a result, the logic state can be represented by the direction of the output current, I_{out}. Because AQFP gates are driven by ac excitation currents, static power consumption is zero. Moreover, dynamic energy dissipation can be significantly reduced by adiabatic switching operations, as will be described later.

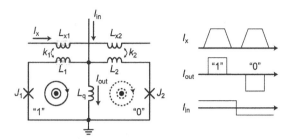

Fig. 1. AQFP gate. Excitation fluxes are applied using I_x, and one SFQ is stored either in the left loop or in the right loop, which correspond to logic "1" and "0", respectively.

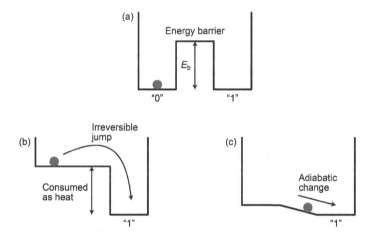

Fig. 2. (a) Potential energy of a binary switch. The particle corresponds to the circuit state. (b) Non-adiabatic switching operation. (c) Adiabatic switching operation. The circuits state changes without irreversible state transition.

The potential energy of a binary switch can be represented by double-well potential as shown in Fig. 2(a). In most logic devices, including complementary metal-oxide-semiconductor (CMOS) logic and rapid single-flux-quantum (RSFQ) logic [24], the circuit state non-adiabatically changes during a switching event as shown in Fig. 2(b), and the applied energy equal to or larger than the energy barrier, E_b, is dissipated as heat. Also, E_b should be much larger than the thermal energy, k_BT. Therefore, in non-adiabatic logic, energy much larger than k_BT is dissipated at every switching operation; the bit energy of state-of-the-art CMOS circuits is approximately $10^5 k_BT$ [25,26], those of energy-efficient superconductor logics are at least $10^3 k_BT$ [27-29]. On the other hand, in adiabatic logic such as AQFP, the circuit state changes adiabatically by tilting the single-well potential after removing the energy barrier as shown in Fig. 2(c), which enables switching operations with energy dissipation much smaller than E_b. Moreover, because energy dissipation is proportional to operation frequencies in adiabatic logic [21, 22], sub-k_BT bit energy is achievable by lowering operation frequencies.

3   Experimental Demonstration of Adiabatic Switching Operations

In order to experimentally demonstrate adiabatic switching operations of AQFP logic, we measured extremely small energy dissipation of an AQFP gate using the superconducting resonator-based method [30]. Figure 3 shows the circuit schematic for the method, where an AQFP gate is magnetically coupled with the superconducting resonator composed of L and C. When the Q between the resonator and each port, Q_{es}, is sufficiently high, most of the energy applied by a power supply is dissipated by the AQFP gate. In such a coupling condition, the power consumption of an AQFP gate, P_{qfp}, is given by the insertion loss, S_{21}, as follows:

$$P_{qfp} = \frac{P_{in}}{2} S_{21}(1 - S_{21}),$$ (1)

where P_{in} is the input microwave power. Figure 4(a) shows the micrograph of a 5 GHz superconducting resonator and an AQFP gate for the power measurement, that we designed and fabricated using the Nb Josephson process, the AIST standard process (STP2) [31]. We measured S_{21} of the resonator using a network analyzer and calculated P_{qfp} using Eq. (1). Figure 4(b) shows the measurement results of S_{21} implemented in the liquid He at 4.2 K, where the sudden drop of S_{21} for $P_{in} \sim$ -57 dBm indicates that the AQFP gate starts to switch by applied enough energy through the resonator. Assuming the loss of the measurement system to be 4.0 dB, P_{qfp} was ~50 pW for P_{in} = -57 dBm, which corresponds to the bit energy of only 10 zJ = 170 k_BT at 5 GHz operation. Furthermore, the bit energy corresponds to 10% of the energy barrier given by $E_b = I_c\Phi_0$, where I_c is a critical current of Josephson junctions and Φ_0 is an SFQ. From the above results, we have successfully demonstrated the adiabatic switching operation of AQFP gates, where the bit energy is much smaller than the energy barrier as described in Chap. 2.

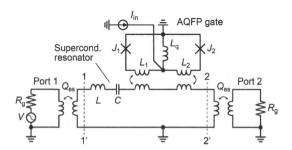

Fig. 3. Superconducting resonator-based method to measure power consumption of an AQFP gate. The AQFP gate is supplied with energy for switching by the resonator through magnetic coupling. Most of the energy applied by the power supply is dissipated by the AQFP gate for sufficiently high Q_{es}.

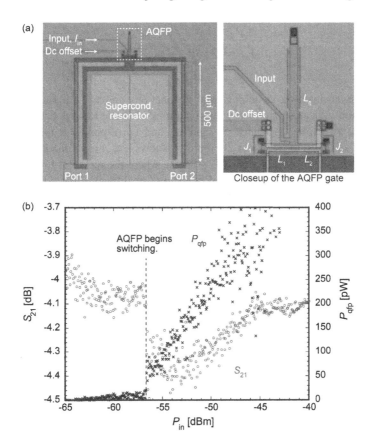

Fig. 4. Measurement of power consumption of an AQFP gate at 5 GHz operation for $I_c = 50$ μA. (a) Micrograph. (b) Measurement results. P_{qfp} increases as P_{in} increases, because excitation fluxes applied by the resonator changes potential energy of the AQFP gate more quickly.

4   Minimum Energy Dissipation for Adiabatic Switching Operations

In this chapter, we discuss the minimum energy dissipation required for adiabatic switching operations using analytical estimation of bit energy and numerical analyses on a bit error rate (BER) [21]. In Chap. 3, the AQFP gate was designed using critically damped Josephson junctions for high-speed operations, where the McCumber parameter [32], β_c $(= Q^2)$, was adjusted to be ~1. For adiabatic switching operations, energy dissipation can be further reduced by using underdamped junctions with higher β_c, because the intrinsic switching time of junctions reduces and the circuit state changes more adiabatically. This gives analytical estimation of the bit energy, E_{bit}, as follows:

$$E_{bit} = 2I_c\Phi_0 \frac{\tau_{sw}}{\tau_{rf}}, \tag{2}$$

where τ_{sw} is an intrinsic switching time of junctions and τ_{rf} is a rise/fall time of I_x. This equation indicates that energy dissipation in adiabatic logic is determined by the ratio of the two time constants, τ_{sw} and τ_{rf}, and corresponds to the non-adiabatic dissipation of $I_c\Phi_0$ for $\tau_{sw} = \tau_{rf}$. Figure 5 shows E_{bit} as a function of τ_{rf} using underdamped Josephson junctions ($\beta_c \sim 2600$), where the red solid line shows circuit simulation results and the blue dashed line shows analytical estimation using Eq. (2). The figure shows energy dissipation reduces linearly with an increase in τ_{rf}, and finally E_{bit} reaches below the Landauer bound of $k_BT \ln2$ [3] for $\tau_{rf} \sim 1000$ ps at 4.2 K.

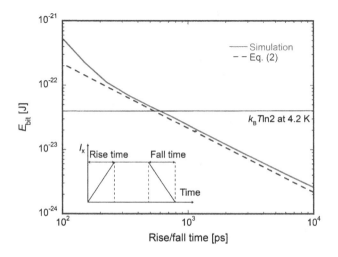

Fig. 5. Bit energy as a function of a rise/fall time of ac excitation currents for underdamped Josephson junctions ($\beta_c \sim 2600$) for $I_c = 50$ µA. Simulation results agree well with the analytical estimation. Energy dissipation reduces almost linearly with an increase in the rise/fall time.

In order to confirm if such an extremely small E_{bit} is attainable at a finite temperature, we calculated BERs at 4.2 K for different τ_{rf} with the same circuit parameters. Figure 6 shows the simulation results of the BERs for τ_{rf} of 200 ps, 1000 ps, and 2000 ps, as a function of I_x, where the bias of 0% corresponds to an excitation flux of Φ_0. The plotted markers show simulation results and the lines show fitting curves using a complementary error function. We confirmed that the BER for each τ_{rf} was much smaller than 10^{-23} for the bias of 0%, and all the fitting curves were almost the same. This is because the BERs of AQFP gates are determined by the energy barrier of $I_c\Phi_0$ and do not depend on operation frequencies. These results show that the bit energy of an AQFP gate can be arbitrarily reduced by increasing the rise/fall time while keeping low BERs, and that there is no minimum bit energy in AQFP logic, unless the entropy decreases.

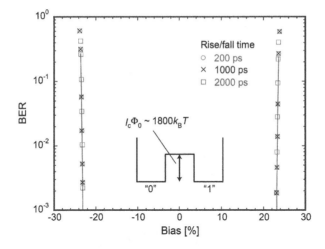

Fig. 6. Bit error rates at 4.2 K for different rise/fall times. Junctions are underdamped ($\beta_c \sim$ 2600) and $I_c = 50$ μA. The bias of 0% corresponds to the excitation flux of Φ_0. BERs are determined by the energy barrier of $I_c\Phi_0$, therefore energy dissipation can be arbitrarily reduced by increasing the rise/fall time.

5   Reversible Computing Using AQFP Gates

We have demonstrated that AQFP gates can operate in an adiabatic mode, and that energy dissipation during a switching event can be arbitrarily reduced by increasing junctions' Q or lowering operation frequencies. In this chapter, we show the first practical reversible logic gate, which we designated as the reversible quantum-flux-parametron (RQFP) gate [33], and discuss the minimum energy dissipation required for reversible computing using AQFP gates.

Fig. 7(a) shows the block diagram of the RQFP gate, where a, b, and c are input ports, and x, y, and z are output ports. An RQFP gate is composed of three AQFP majority (MAJ) gates and three AQFP splitter (SPL) gates. In AQFP logic, MAJ gates and SPL gates have the same circuit topologies and the direction of data flow decides the function, MAJ or SPL. Therefore, the circuit topology of the RQFP gate is totally symmetrical and data can propagate bi-directionally, which indicates that the RQFP gate is physically, as well as logically, reversible. Also, the RQFP gate is considered to be a primitive gate in reversible computing, because MAJ gates, NOT gates, and constant inputs constitute a logical primitive. Fig. 7(b) shows the simulation results of energy dissipation per clock cycle for logic operations using an RQFP gate. For all input data combinations, energy dissipation reduces almost linearly with an increase in a rise/fall time of excitation currents, which shows that all the gates in the RQFP gate operate adiabatically. Therefore, it can be concluded that there is no minimum energy dissipation for logic operations using RQFP gates, or logically and physically reversible gates. On the other hand, there exists minimum energy dissipation for logic operation using irreversible gates because of the physical irreversibility. To the best of our knowledge, this is the first numerical demonstrations that show no minimum energy bound for reversible computing using practical logic devices.

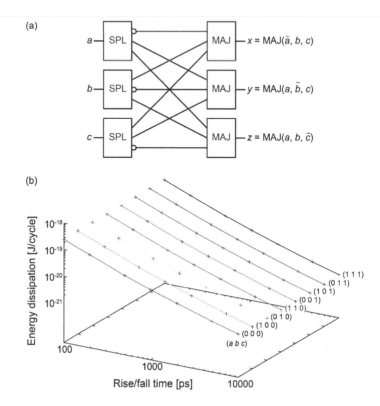

Fig. 7. RQFP gate. (a) Block diagram, where MAJ(a, b, c) = $ab+bc+ca$. (b) Simulation results of energy dissipation of an RQFP gate with several input and output buffers. All the junctions are underdamped ($\beta_c \sim 2600$) and $I_c = 50$ µA. Energy dissipation reduces almost linearly with an increase in the rise/fall time due to the physical reversibility.

Figure 8(a) shows the micrograph of an RQFP gate with input and output buffer gates that we designed and fabricated using the STP2. The circuits are driven by three phase excitation currents, I_{x1}, I_{x2}, and I_{x3}, and dc superconducting quantum interference devices (dc-SQUIDs) were used for readout of output data. Figure 8(b) shows low-speed experimental test results at 100 kHz, implemented in the liquid He at 4.2 K. The figure shows correct logic operations of the RQFP gate. We also experimentally confirmed the logical and physical reversibility of the RQFP gate [33]. Although energy dissipation was too small to measure in this low-speed demonstration, we expect that it will be possible to measure that of RQFP gates by using superconducting resonator-based method [30] at a higher operation frequency ($\sim$ 1 GHz) [34].

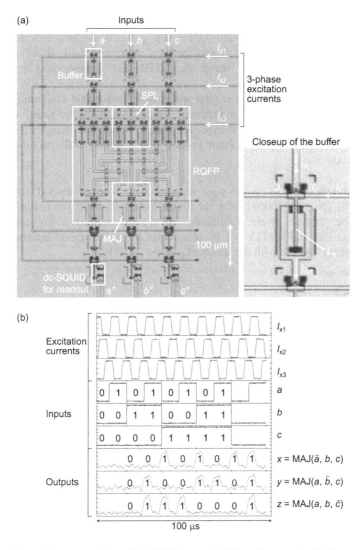

Fig. 8. Experimental demonstration of the RQFP gate. (a) Microphotograph. (b) Low-speed test results. The results show the correct logic operations of the RQFP gate.

6   Conclusion

We reported recent research results toward reversible computing using adiabatic superconductor logic, or AQFP gates. First we experimentally demonstrated adiabatic switching operations of AQFP gates using a superconducting resonator. Then we numerically demonstrated that bit energy of an AQFP gate can be arbitrarily reduced by increasing Q or lowering operation frequencies, which shows that there is no minimum energy dissipation for adiabatic switching operations. Finally, we reported the first practical reversible logic gate, which we designated as the RQFP gate. RQFP gates are logically and physically reversible because of the symmetric circuit topology composed of AQFP MAJ gates and AQFP SPL gates. We numerically demonstrated that there is no minimum energy bound for logic operations using RQFP gates. Also, we fabricated an RQFP gate using the STP2 and demonstrated correct logic operations.

We believe that our research results will enable "reversible computing" to move from the theoretical stage into practical usage. Additionally, these results will facilitate detailed discussions and investigations related to the energy efficiency, and the hardware complexity associated reversible computing will become realizable using actual devices.

Acknowledgement. This work was supported by a Grant-in-Aid for Scientific Research (S) (No. 22226009) from the Japan Society for the Promotion of Science (JSPS). The circuits were fabricated in the clean room for analog-digital superconductivity (CRAVITY) of National Institute of Advanced Industrial Science and Technology (AIST) with the standard process 2 (STP2).

References

1. Ball, P.: Computer engineering: Feeling the heat. Nature 492, 174–176 (2012)
2. Service, R.F.: Computer science. What it'll take to go exascale. Science 335, 394–396 (2012)
3. Landauer, R.: Irreversibility and Heat Generation in the Computing Process. IBM J. Res. Dev. 5, 183–191 (1961)
4. Keyes, R.W.: Fundamental limits in digital information processing. Proc. IEEE. 69, 267–278 (1981)
5. Lloyd, S.: Ultimate physical limits to computation. Nature 406, 1047–1054 (2000)
6. Meindl, J.D., Davis, J.A.: The fundamental limit on binary switching energy for terascale integration (TSI). IEEE J. Solid-State Circuits 35, 1515–1516 (2000)
7. Zhirnov, V.V., Cavin, R.K., Hutchby, J.A., Bourianoff, G.I.: Limits to binary logic switch scaling-a gedanken model. Proc. IEEE. 9, 1934–1939 (2003)
8. Shizume, K.: Heat generation required by information erasure. Phys. Rev. E 52, 3495–3499 (1995)
9. Dillenschneider, R., Lutz, E.: Memory Erasure in Small Systems. Phys. Rev. Lett. 102, 1–4 (2009)
10. Sagawa, T., Ueda, M.: Minimal Energy Cost for Thermodynamic Information Processing: Measurement and Information Erasure. Phys. Rev. Lett. 102, 250602 (2009)
11. Bérut, A., Arakelyan, A., Petrosyan, A., Ciliberto, S., Dillenschneider, R., Lutz, E.: Experimental verification of Landauer's principle linking information and thermodynamics. Nature 483, 187–189 (2012)
12. Orlov, A.O., Lent, C.S., Thorpe, C.C., Boechler, G.P., Snider, G.L.: Experimental Test of Landauer's Principle at the Sub-k_BT Level. Jpn. J. Appl. Phys. 51, 06FE10 (2012)
13. Fredkin, E., Toffoli, T.: Conservative logic. Int. J. Theor. Phys. 21, 219–253 (1982)
14. Bennett, C.H.: Logical Reversibility of Computation. IBM J. Res. Dev. 17, 525–532 (1973)
15. Keyes, R.W., Landauer, R.: Minimal Energy Dissipation in Logic. IBM J. Res. Dev. 14, 152–157 (1970)

16. Likharev, K.: Dynamics of some single flux quantum devices: I. Parametric quantron. IEEE Trans. Magn. 13, 242–244 (1977)
17. Semenov, V.K., Danilov, G.V., Averin, D.V.: Negative-inductance SQUID as the basic element of reversible Josephson-junction circuits. IEEE Trans. Appiled Supercond. 13, 938–943 (2003)
18. Wenzler, J., Dunn, T., Toffoli, T., Mohanty, P.: A nanomechanical Fredkin gate. Nano Lett. 14, 89–93 (2014)
19. Takeuchi, N., Ozawa, D., Yamanashi, Y., Yoshikawa, N.: An adiabatic quantum flux parametron as an ultra-low-power logic device. Supercond. Sci. Technol. 26, 035010 (2013)
20. Takeuchi, N., Ehara, K., Inoue, K., Yamanashi, Y., Yoshikawa, N.: Margin and Energy Dissipation of Adiabatic Quantum-Flux-Parametron Logic at Finite Temperature. IEEE Trans. Appl. Supercond. 23, 1700304 (2013)
21. Takeuchi, N., Yamanashi, Y., Yoshikawa, N.: Simulation of sub-$k_\mathrm{B}T$ bit-energy operation of adiabatic quantum-flux-parametron logic with low bit-error-rate. Appl. Phys. Lett. 103, 62602 (2013)
22. Likharev, K.K.: Classical and quantum limitations on energy consumption in computation. Int. J. Theor. Phys. 21, 311–326 (1982)
23. Hosoya, M., Hioe, W., Casas, J., Kamikawai, R., Harada, Y., Wada, Y., Nakane, H., Suda, R., Goto, E.: Quantum flux parametron: a single quantum flux device for Josephson supercomputer. IEEE Trans. Appiled Supercond. 1, 77–89 (1991)
24. Likharev, K.K., Semenov, V.K.: RSFQ logic/memory family: a new Josephson-junction technology for sub-terahertz-clock-frequency digital systems. IEEE Trans. Appl. Supercond. 1, 3–28 (1991)
25. Mukhopadhyay, S.: Switching energy in CMOS logic: How far are we from physical limit (2006), http://nanohub.org/resources/1250
26. Zhirnov, V., Cavin, R., Gammaitoni, L.: Minimum Energy of Computing, Fundamental Considerations (2014), http://dx.doi.org/10.5772/57346
27. Mukhanov, O.A.: Energy-Efficient Single Flux Quantum Technology. IEEE Trans. Appl. Supercond. 21, 760–769 (2011)
28. Herr, Q.P., Herr, A.Y., Oberg, O.T., Ioannidis, A.G.: Ultra-low-power superconductor logic. J. Appl. Phys. 109, 103903 (2011)
29. Tanaka, M., Ito, M., Kitayama, A., Kouketsu, T., Fujimaki, A.: 18-GHz, 4.0-aJ/bit Operation of Ultra-Low-Energy Rapid Single-Flux-Quantum Shift Registers. Jpn. J. Appl. Phys. 51, 053102 (2012)
30. Takeuchi, N., Yamanashi, Y., Yoshikawa, N.: Measurement of 10 zJ energy dissipation of adiabatic quantum-flux-parametron logic using a superconducting resonator. Appl. Phys. Lett. 102, 052602 (2013)
31. Nagasawa, S., Hashimoto, Y., Numata, H., Tahara, S.: A 380 ps, 9.5 mW Josephson 4-Kbit RAM operated at a high bit yield. IEEE Trans. Appl. Supercond. 5, 2447–2452 (1995)
32. McCumber, D.E.: Effect of ac Impedance on dc Voltage-Current Characteristics of Superconductor Weak-Link Junctions. J. Appl. Phys. 39, 3113 (1968)
33. Takeuchi, N., Yamanashi, Y., Yoshikawa, N.: Reversible logic gate using adiabatic superconducting devices. submitted to Appl. Phys. Lett.
34. Takeuchi, N., Ortlepp, T., Yamanashi, Y., Yoshikawa, N.: High-Speed Experimental Demonstration of Adiabatic Quantum-Flux-Parametron Gates Using Quantum-Flux-Latches. IEEE Trans. Appl. Supercond. 24, 1300204 (2014)

Classical Control of Large-Scale Quantum Computers

Simon J. Devitt

Ochanomizu University, 2-1-1 Otsuka, Bunkyo-ku, Tokyo 112-8610, Japan
National Institute of Informatics, 2-1-2 Hitotsubashi, Chiyoda-ku, Tokyo, Japan

Abstract. The accelerated development of quantum technology has reached a pivotal point. Early in 2014, several results were published demonstrating that several experimental technologies are now accurate enough to satisfy the requirements of fault-tolerant, error corrected quantum computation. While there are many technological and experimental issues that still need to be solved, the ability of experimental systems to now have error rates low enough to satisfy the fault-tolerant threshold for several error correction models is a tremendous milestone. Consequently, it is now a good time for the computer science and classical engineering community to examine the *classical* problems associated with compiling quantum algorithms and implementing them on future quantum hardware. In this paper, we will review the basic operational rules of a topological quantum computing architecture and outline one of the most important classical problems that need to be solved; the decoding of error correction data for a large-scale quantum computer. We will endeavour to present these problems independently from the underlying physics as much of this work can be effectively solved by non-experts in quantum information or quantum mechanics.

Keywords: quantum computing, topological quantum computing, classical processing.

1 Introduction

Quantum technology, specifically large-scale quantum computation, has been a significant research topic in physics since the early 1990's. Since the publication of the first quantum algorithms [1], illustrating the computational power of quantum computers, millions of dollars has been invested worldwide and numerous technological advances have been made [2–7]. It is now routine for multiple experimental laboratories to fabricate and control small arrays of quantum bits (qubits) and perform proof of principal experiments demonstrating small quantum algorithms and protocols [8]. Quantum technology has also moved into the industrial sector via protocols such as Quantum Key Distribution (QKD) and Quantum random number generators and many non-physicists are aware of the D-Wave quantum computer, which while scientifically controversial is an attempt to build a analogue quantum computer capable of solving certain types of optimisation problems [9–11].

S. Yamashita and S. Minato (Eds.): RC 2014, LNCS 8507, pp. 26–39, 2014.

Recent experimental results in 2014 have demonstrated that two experimental systems can be built with high enough accuracy to satisfy the constraints of fault-tolerant, error corrected quantum computation [12, 13]. As error rates on qubit arrays is high compared to classical nano-electronics, extensive error correction is required to successfully perform computation [1, 14–17]. One of the most seminal results in quantum information theory is the fault-tolerant threshold theorem [18]. This theorem states that provided the fundamental error rate associated with qubits and quantum gates falls below a threshold, then arbitrarily long quantum computation is possible with a polylogarithmic overhead in physical resources. This threshold is a function of the type of quantum error correction code used for the computer [14–17] and extensive research has been performed to derive new codes, with high thresholds, that are amenable to experimental architectures. Arguably the most successful class of codes that have been developed are known as topological quantum codes [19–23]. Topological quantum codes are defined over a lattice (of arbitrary dimension depending on the code, but the most common are 2- and 3-dimensional) of physical qubits. The code itself can be defined over small, physically local groups of qubits while the properties of the encoded information is a global property of the entire lattice. This is what defines the code as topological. These codes are arguably preferred in quantum computer development as they exhibit comparably high fault-tolerant thresholds and they are adaptable to the physical constraints of experimental quantum systems.

Irrespective of the actual quantum code chosen to protect a quantum computer, it is well known that operating such as system requires extensive *classical* control infrastructure. This is not simply related to the control of the physical device hardware needed to operate a qubit (lasers, signal generators etc...), but it is also required to decode error correction information produced by the computer. This classical control software development is in its infancy and has received little attention within the fields of quantum information and classical computer science [24, 25]. While there has been much work at the more abstract level of quantum algorithm design and circuit optimisation [26–32], we now have to go one step deeper and connect the high level work to the physical constraints of the quantum hardware.

This paper will introduce one of the main classical computer science and engineering problems associated with controlling a large scale quantum computer. We will focus on a specific form of quantum computer; namely a system that is built using an error correction code known as Topological Quantum Clusters (TQC) [33, 34]. This code has received significant attention in recent years due to multiple hardware architectures utilising it in designing large scale systems [23, 35–40]. We won't discuss the details of how information to be encoded or manipulated. Instead we will focus on the basic error correction properties of the code and what this implies for classical processing of this data. In section 2 we will provide some background information on the basic definitions of qubits and quantum logic. In section 3 we will provide a brief introduction to the TQC model. This will not be an in depth introduction, but should provide enough material to grasp the classical problems that need to be solved. Finally, in section 5 we will examine the processing that needs to be developed to perform dynamic error correction on the system and discuss the potential problems associated with the massive amount of classical data produced by the computer.

2   Quantum Computers

A qubit is the quantum analogue of a bit. Its state is defined as a vector of dimension 2, where $|0\rangle = (1, 0)^T$ is the vector notation for the value corresponding to binary 0, and $|1\rangle = (0, 1)^T$ correspond to 1. The state of one qubit q can be written as the linear combination $|q\rangle = a_0|0\rangle + a_1|1\rangle$, where $a_i \in \mathbb{C}$ and $\sum_i |a_i|^2 = 1$; this is a *superposition* of the two basis states, a concept with no analogy in classical computing. Given the principal of superposition, an array of n qubits can be in an equal superposition of all binary states from $|0\rangle$ unto $|2^{n-1}\rangle$, i.e. $\sum_{i=0}^{2^n-1} a_i|\mathrm{BIN}(i)\rangle$, where a_i are complex numbers and $\mathrm{BIN}(i)$ is the binary expansion of i.

Measurement: In quantum computing, *measuring* a state is the only way to observe results of calculation. Measuring an arbitrary quantum state $|q\rangle = a_0|0\rangle + a_1|1\rangle$ can result in two outcomes: $|0\rangle$ (with probability $|a_0|^2$), or $|1\rangle$ (with probability $|a_1|^2$). Moreover, the measurement will *collapse* the state leaving it in the state corresponding to the measurement result.

The goal of a quantum algorithm is to manipulate the amplitudes of each binary state, a_i, such that the *incorrect* answers have very low amplitudes, $a_j \approx 0$, $j = $ incorrect while the *correct* answers have amplitudes close to one, $a_j \approx 1$, $j = $ correct. This will ensure that after an algorithm is completed, we have a very high probability, when we measure every qubit, to measure the correct answer. The simplest initial state is to initialise each qubit in the computer in the $|+\rangle = (|0\rangle + |1\rangle)/\sqrt{2}$ such that each $a_i = 1/2^{(n/2)}$, $\forall i$. Therefore, initially, every possible binary state will have an equal probability of being measured. The quantum algorithm will then manipulate these amplitudes to suppress the amplitudes of incorrect answers and increase the amplitude of correct ones. At any given time the state of the quantum computer is represented by a n-dimensional complex vector $|\psi\rangle = (a_0, a_1, a_2, ..., a_{2(n-1)})^T$.

Quantum Gates: Quantum *gates* act on qubits and modify their states and hence modify the amplitudes of each binary state, a_i. They are represented as unitary (guaranteeing a gate is reversible, a necessity in quantum theory) matrices. An n-qubit gate, G, is described by a $2^n \times 2^n$ matrix and its action on the state of the quantum computer is described by simply computing $|\psi'\rangle = G|\psi\rangle$, where $|\psi'\rangle$ is the output and $|\psi\rangle$ is the input. It has been shown that any valid operation, G, can be decomposed into a discrete alphabet of single qubit and 2-qubit gates and consequently we only need to realise a small set of primitive qubit operations to realise any arbitrary computation. Shown below is an example of such an alphabet, consisting of four single qubit gates and one two-qubit gate.

$$X = \begin{pmatrix} 0 & 1 \\ 1 & 0 \end{pmatrix} Z = \begin{pmatrix} 1 & 0 \\ 0 & -1 \end{pmatrix} H = \frac{1}{\sqrt{2}} \begin{pmatrix} 1 & 1 \\ 1 & -1 \end{pmatrix} \text{CNOT} = \begin{pmatrix} 1 & 0 & 0 & 0 \\ 0 & 1 & 0 & 0 \\ 0 & 0 & 0 & 1 \\ 0 & 0 & 1 & 0 \end{pmatrix} T = \begin{pmatrix} 1 & 0 \\ 0 & e^{-i\pi/8} \end{pmatrix}$$

(1)

These gates form a *universal gate set* (technically, $\mathbb{S} = \{H, T, \text{CNOT}\}$ are sufficient for universality, we include X and Z because of their relevance for QEC), i.e., arbitrary quantum gates can be decomposed into products of these gates [1]. (This is similar to the classical case where all gates can be represented by equivalent circuits consisting of NAND gates only.).

The properties of quantum information allow us to create certain states that have no classical analogue. These states are called *entangled* states. For example, if we prepare two qubits in the initial state $|+\rangle|0\rangle$ and apply the two qubit CNOT gate (where the control qubit is the one in the $|+\rangle$ state), we get the output $|b\rangle = \frac{1}{\sqrt{2}}(|00\rangle + |11\rangle)$. This state is known as a Bell state and it has properties that no classical computational state has. Specifically if we measure one of the qubits in the $|0\rangle$ state, the second qubits is also found to be in the $|0\rangle$ state. Similarly for the $|1\rangle$ state. This behaviour is unique to quantum-bits and creation and manipulation of these types of states is an identifying feature when proving, experimentally, you have a true quantum system. Entanglement is a fundamental property of quantum information and forms the basis of the TQC model we will discuss in the next section.

3 Topological Cluster State Computation

The original formalism for quantum computation is the circuit based model [1]. This is where we have an array of qubits that is operated on by a pre-defined sequence of quantum gates to realise an algorithm. There is another method of performing quantum computation, known as the measurement based model (MBM) [41]. In this model, we pre-define what is known as a Universal Resource State (URS). A URS is a lattice of qubits where entanglement connections have been formed before any computation begins. This URS can be thought of as a graph, where each vertex represents a qubit and each edge is a two-qubit quantum gate that establishes entanglement between two vertices. Once this resource state has been prepared, quantum gates are realised by measuring individual qubits in well defined ways. As computation proceeds, qubits are *consumed* as they are measured. The first MBM was defined over a regular, 2-dimensional grid of qubits with nearest neighbour connections [Figure 1]. In this model, qubits are measured, column-by-column, to realise quantum gates. Essentially each *row* of qubits represented the world line of a given qubit of information and each *column* represented individual time steps of computation. As each column is measured, information is teleported to the next column and a quantum gate is applied during this teleportation.

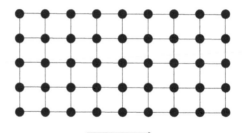

Qubits measured column-by-column to perform computation

Fig. 1. A standard 2D lattice of qubits used for measurement based quantum computation. Qubits are measured from left to right and information is teleported from column to column. Processing occurs during this teleportation, applying quantum gates.

This 2-dimensional MBM showed that arbitrary computation could be achieved using a pre-defined URS, but it did not incorporate any error correction protocols to protect against noise.

The Topological Cluster State model is a MBM of quantum computation that incorporates a sophisticated topological error correction model by construction. It was derived from the seminal work of Kitaev [19] and extended to a 3-dimensional entangled lattice of qubits that forms the initial URS [33]. The fundamental unit cell of this lattice is illustrated in Figure 2. Again, each vertex in the image represents a physical qubit while each edge represents a two-qubit gate applied to form an entanglement bond. Preparing this state requires initialising each qubit in the $|+\rangle$ state, and applying a CZ gate between any two qubits connected by an edge. A CZ gate can be achieved by applying the CNOT gate, interleaved by two H gates on the target qubit [1]. The total size of the 3-dimensional Topological cluster is dictated by the total resources needed for an algorithm. i.e. how many encoded qubits and gates does the algorithm need and how strong the error correction needs to be to successfully complete computation. For large quantum algorithms, the size of this lattice could be billions if not trillions of physical qubits [42].

3.1   Error Correction

The primary job of the TQC model is to perform error correction. The structure of the 3-dimensional lattice establishes certain symmetries that can be used to detect and correct errors that occur during the preparation and/or consumption of the state.

Arbitrary noise on a qubit can be decomposed into a series of bit-flips (X gates) and phase flips (Z gates). A phase flip is a gate which can convert the state $|+\rangle = (|0\rangle + |1\rangle)/\sqrt{2}$ into $|-\rangle = (|0\rangle - |1\rangle)/\sqrt{2}$ and has no classical analogue. A general error operator, E, acting on a single qubit can be written in the form,

$$E|\psi\rangle = k_I|\psi\rangle + k_x X|\psi\rangle + k_z Z|\psi\rangle + k_{xz} XZ|\psi\rangle \tag{2}$$

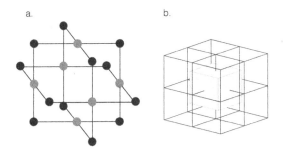

Fig. 2. Figure a) represents the unit cell of the lattice. Each of the Face qubits (red) are used to calculate the parity of the cell. The non-face qubits of Figure a) are face qubits on identical unit cells that are offset by half a lattice spacing along the three axes of the lattice.

where $\{|k_I|^2, |k_x|^2, |k_y|^2, |k_{xz}|^2\}$ are the probabilities that the qubit experiences an X error, a Z error or both [1]. Therefore, to protect qubits against noise, we just need the ability to detect and correct for bit- and phase-flips.

The unit cell of the topological cluster has certain symmetries. Namely, if you measure the six face qubits of the unit cell (illustrated in red in Figure 2a)) in the basis $\{|+\rangle, |-\rangle\}$ (known as an X-basis measurement) and you calculate the classical parity of the results (identifying the bit-value zero if we measure the qubit in $|+\rangle$ and one if we measure it in $|-\rangle$), you will always get an even parity result under modulo 2 addition. i.e. while the individual measurements themselves are random, the symmetries of the quantum state of the unit cell will conspire (through the property of entanglement) to always generate an even parity result when you combine the measured values of these six qubits. Now, let us consider two of these unit cells side by side and the consequence of a Z-error on the qubit shared on a face [Figure 3a)]. In quantum information the *order* in which you apply quantum gates is important. For example, the output of the operation $XZ|\psi\rangle$ is not necessarily the same as the output of the operation $ZX|\psi\rangle$, this is because the gates X and Z do not *commute*, i.e. $XZ - ZX \neq 0$. Instead, for these two operations the following holds, $XZ = -ZX$. What does this mean when we measure our six face qubits of the unit cell when a qubit experiences an error? If no error occurs, then the six measurement, when combined modulo 2, gives us an even parity result. If one of those qubits experiences a Z-error prior to being measured in the X-basis the fact that $XZ = -ZX$ means that the measurement of the erred qubit will flip from $|\pm\rangle$ to $|\mp\rangle$. Consequently, if the initial parity of the six measurements was even, it will flip to odd. Hence for the two unit cells shown in Figure 3a) when we measure the 11 face qubits and we observe a negative parity of the two sets of measurements,

---

[1] This is not a completely general description of a noise channel, but introducing the formalism for a general channel would require us to delve more into the mathematics of qubits.

we can identify that a Z-error must have occurred on the qubit sharing a face between the two cells. Similarly errors on the other five face qubits are detected by parity flips with the other unit cells bordering the five other faces [Figure 3b)].

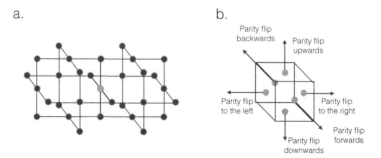

Fig. 3. A single error on a face qubit of a unit cell will cause two parity flips on the cells which share the qubit [Figure a)]. The six neighbouring cells bordering a given cell allows us to uniquely determine which qubit experienced an error [Figure b)].

An obvious question arises. We have so far only considered the six qubits on each of the faces of the unit cell. What about the other remaining qubits lying on edges? If we stack together eight unit cells into a cube, at it's centre is an identical unit cell. The face qubits associated with this unit cell correspond to the qubits on the edges of the eight cells in the cube. The topological lattice embeds two self similar lattices, one which we call the primal lattice and the other which we call the dual[2]. Face qubits on primal unit cells correspond to edge qubits on dual cells and visa versa. These two self similar lattices also explains how X-errors are corrected. In the previous paragraph we only considered Z errors because the Z-gate didn't commute with the X-basis measurement of each face qubit and consequently the parity of the six face measurements flipped when an error occurred. Again, without going into the mathematical detail, the symmetries of the topological lattice allows us to convert X-errors on a qubit into Z-errors on other qubits. If an X-error occurs on a given qubit, the entanglement bonds connecting qubits can convert this X-error into Z-errors on all the qubits it is connected to [34, 43]. If you examine the structure of the unit cell [Figure 2a)] you will note that a given face qubit is only connected to qubits on the edge of a unit cell. Therefore an X-error occurring on a face qubit will be converted to Z-errors on edge qubits (which correspond to face qubits on dual cells). Therefore, all errors can be converted to Z-errors in either the primal or dual lattices and detecting these parity flips in both spaces is sufficient for correcting arbitrary errors on each individual qubit.

We discussed how single errors can be corrected by examining the parity of neighbouring cells, the next issue is what happens when multiple errors occur.

---

[2] Which is primal and which is dual is arbitrary.

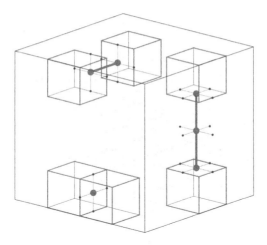

Fig. 4. From Ref. [34]. Errors create parity flips on various unit cells. Multiple errors can form chains. Parity flips are only observed at the endpoints of chains.

This is shown in Figure 4. As the parity condition for a unit cell is calculated modulo two we only see an odd parity if an odd number of errors have occurred. If an even number occur then the parity will remain even. Therefore, if there is a chain of errors we will only see a parity flip for the two unit cells at the endpoint of the error chain. In the case of isolated errors, endpoints are of neighbouring cells. Hence decoding the error correction information requires us to match up the endpoints (which we detect via the calculation of a cells parity) with the actual physical sets of errors that occurred (which are not directly detected.

In quantum information we assign a probability, p, that a given qubit will experience a bit (X) and/or phase (Z) error over some time interval, t. This probability encapsulates the physical sources of noise such as environmental decoherence and control that could effect the operation of the qubit. Provided that $p < 1$, increasing numbers of errors occurring in a given time interval become exponentially less probable. Consequently, the most probable event that gives rise to the observed set of parity flips in the topological cluster is the one with the fewest number of errors. Given a set of parity flips measured in the topological cluster we connect them in a pairwise fashion such that the total length of all connections is minimised. This is a well known classical problem and was solved by Edmonds in 1967 [44] who developed a classical algorithm for minimum weight perfect matching who's runtime scales polynomially with the number of nodes (which in our case corresponds to the number of parity flips we observe).

4   Physical Data Flow in an Operational Computer

What occurs in a physical quantum computer built using this model? For the TQC model, the physical quantum hardware is responsible for preparing the lattice.

If we assume that the physical qubits in the quantum computer are single particles of light (photons), then each photon is prepared from a source and sent through the quantum computer to be entangled with its neighbours [36]. Each 2-dimensional cross-section of the lattice is prepared sequentially as photons "flow" through the quantum hardware.

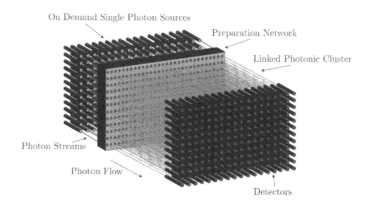

Fig. 5. From Ref. [24]. Architecture for an optical quantum computer. Single photons are prepared, sent through a preparation network which is responsible for creating the topological lattice. After the lattice is prepared it flows into detector arrays which performs measurement to perform computation.

Photons are continuously injected into the rear of the preparation network. Each passes through a network of quantum devices, which act to link them together into the topological lattice. Each quantum device operates on a fundamental clock cycle, T, and each device operates in a well-defined manner. Once a given photon has been connected to its relevant neighbours, it does not have to wait until the rest of the lattice is constructed, it can be measured immediately. This is exactly how the actual computer will operate. The lattice is consumed at the same rate at which it is created, hence in the third dimension there only exists a small number of 2D cross-sections at any given time.

As one dimension of the topological lattice is identified as simulated time, the total 2D cross section defines the actual size of the quantum computer. The lattice is built such that when each 2D cross-section is measured, all encoded information is teleported to the next successive layer along the direction of simulated time allowing an algorithm to be implemented (in a similar manner to standard cluster state computation [41]).

In Figure 6 we illustrate the structure of the detection system. A given unit cell flows through a set of nine optical fibres which carry the individual photons that have been linked together in the lattice. As they flow into the detectors the parity of the cell is calculated as,

$$P(i,j,T) = (s_{(i,j)}^{T-1} + s_{(i-1,j)}^{T} + s_{(i,j-1)}^{T} + s_{(i,j+1)}^{T} + s_{(i+1,j)}^{T} + s_{(i,j)}^{T+1}) \bmod 2 \quad (3)$$

where $s_{i,j}^{T}$ is the detection result $(1,0)$ of detector (i,j) at time T.

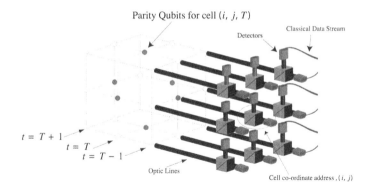

Fig. 6. Detection array for a topological quantum computer where each qubit is a single photon

Error decoding and correction must occur in real-time as the computer is operating in order to ensure the system will operate correctly. Hence the classical data processing much be done efficiently, fast and in a highly parallel way.

5 The Decoding Problem

The error correction decoding problem is a classical software and hardware optimisation problem to effectively perform the minimum weight perfect matching algorithm to an arbitrarily large topological lattice running at high speeds. Resource estimates for topological quantum computing has shown that to successfully implement fully error corrected, large-scale algorithms would require an enormous topological lattice [42]. The results of Ref. [42] indicate that a lattice of the order of a billion cells in cross-section, running for a year at 10 nanoseconds per cross-sectional sheet is necessary to factor a 1024-bit number using Shor's algorithm. At 6-bits of raw data per cell, we would need to classically process on the order of $(6 \times 10^9)/(30 \times 10^{-9}) = 2 \times 10^{17}$ bits/second of data to perform error correction decoding for the entire computation.

This clearly is a phenomenal amount of data that needs to be processed while the computer is running. Clearly we require a large amount of parallel processing and a modular classical processing framework to decode error correction data for a full-scale machine. There has been work attempting to address this problem which falls into two categories. The first is further optimisation of the minimum weight perfect matching algorithm. The Blossom V algorithm is currently used when performing simulations of the topological cluster state model [45] and we can examine its performance for large lattices [Figure 7]. From this figure (which was produced by running the algorithm on a standard laptop) shows that Blossom V runs far too slowly to handle the processing of error correction data for a large-scale computer. This necessitates further optimisation of the algorithm. Work by Fowler and others [46, 47] attempts to rectify this problem, but at

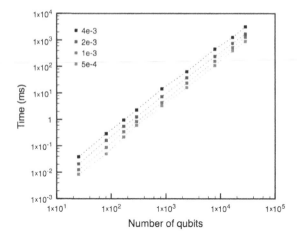

Fig. 7. Processing speed of Blossom V [45] as a function of the total number of qubits in a 2D cross-section of the topological lattice. Each curve represents a different physical error rate of each qubit, p. This plot was produced with a standard laptop with no further optimisation.

this stage no benchmarking has been performed using this package. The second category is dedicated hardware implementations of the decoding operations [24]. There are several steps which is illustrated in Figure. 8.

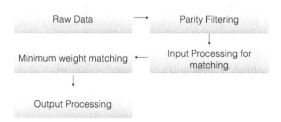

Fig. 8. Processing stages for error decoding in the topological model

The raw data is the bit streams coming directly from the quantum hardware. Parity filtering is the first step, where the co-ordinates of unit cells that have experienced a parity flip are retained and all other data is disregarded. This can reduce the amount of information as the probability that a unit cell of the lattice will experience a parity flip is of the order of the error rate of each qubit, p, which will be approximately 0.1% [48]. The next step is to convert the collection of co-ordinates into a graph which is used as input for the minimum weight matching algorithm. This data will produce a lookup table associating a vertex number for the graph with the co-ordinate of the relevant cell. The matching algorithm comes next and will produce a list of bi-partite connections telling us which nodes in the graph are connected. Output processing then converts these nodes back into the cell co-ordinates allowing us to correct the actual errors.

Each of these stages will have to be handled by dedicated circuits, built primarily for speed. This has not currently been done and we do not have evidence if current technology is sufficient to achieve fast enough speeds for quantum computing systems. For various physics related reasons, we do not wish to slow down the operational speed of the quantum hardware to accommodate slow classical processing. The speed of the classical system mush be commensurate with the quantum system (which can vary between 10ns and 10ms depending on the underlying technology). The first generation of quantum computers will be slow, so the demands on the classical hardware should not be too significant in the short term. But more futuristic technology is being developed [49] and will run at much higher clock rates. Designing the classical system with these faster systems in mind should ensure that quantum computer development is not bottlenecked by the necessary classical systems being underdeveloped.

Acknowledgements. We wish to thank Ashley Stephens for producing the image in Figure 7.

References

1. Nielsen, M., Chuang, I.: Quantum Computation and Information, 2nd edn. Cambridge University Press (2000)
2. Gaebel, T., Domhan, M., Popa, I., Wittmann, C., Neumann, P., Jelezko, F., Rabeau, J., Stavrias, N., Greentree, A., Prawer, S., Meijer, J., Twamley, J., Hemmer, P., Wrachtrup, J.: Room Temperature coherent control of coupled single spins in solid. Nature Physics (London) 2, 408–413 (2006)
3. Hanson, R., Awschalom, D.: Coherent manipulation of single spins in semiconductors. Nature (London) 453, 1043–1049 (2008)
4. Press, D., Ladd, T.D., Zhang, B., Yamamoto, Y.: Complete quantum control of a single quantum dot spin using ultrafast optical pulses. Nature (London) 456, 218–221 (2008)
5. Politi, A., Matthews, J., O'Brien, J.: Shor's quantum factoring algorithm on a photonic chip. Science 325, 1221 (2009)
6. Pla, J., Tan, K.Y., Dehollain, J.P., Lim, W.H., Morton, J.J.L., Jamieson, D.N., Dzurak, A.S., Morello, A.: A single-atom electron spin qubit in Silicon. Nature (London) 489, 541–545 (2012)
7. Lucero, E., Barends, R., Chen, Y., Kelly, J., Mariantoni, M., Megrant, A., O'Malley, P., Sank, D., Vainsencher, A., Wenner, J., White, T., Yin, Y., Cleland, A.N., Martinis, J.: Computing prime factors with a Josephson phase qubit quantum processor. Nature Physics 8, 719–723 (2012)
8. Ladd, T., Jelezko, F., Laflamme, R., Nakamura, Y., Monroe, C., O'Brien, J.: Quantum Computing. Nature (London) 464, 45–53 (2010)
9. Vinci, W., Albash, T., Mishra, A., Warburton, P.A., Lidar, D.A.: Distinguishing Classical and Quantum Models for the D-Wave Device. arxiv:1403.4228 (2014)

10. Boixo, S., Ronnow, T.F., Wecker, S.I.Z.W.D., Lidar, D., Martinis, J., Troyer, M.: Quantum annealing with more than one hundred qubits. Nature Physics 10, 218 (2014)
11. Shin, S., Smith, G., Smolin, J., Vazirani, U.: How "Quantum" is the D-Wave Machine? arxiv:1401.0787 (2014)
12. Barends, R., Kelly, J., Megrant, A., Veitia, A., Sank, D., Jeffrey, E., White, T., Mutus, J., Fowler, A., Campbell, B., Chen, Y., Chen, Z., Chiaro, B., Dunsworth, A., Neill, C., O'Malley, P., Roushan, P., Vainsencher, A., Wenner, J., Korotkov, A., Cleland, A., Martinis, J.: Logic gates at the surface code threshold: Superconducting qubits poised for fault-tolerant quantum computing. arXiv:1402.4848 (2014)
13. Choi, T., Debnath, S., Manning, T., Figgatt, C., Gong, Z.X., Duan, L.M., Monroe, C.: Optimal quantum control of multi-mode couplings between trapped ion qubits for scalable entanglement. arxiv:1401.1575 (2014)
14. Devitt, S., Munro, W., Nemoto, K.: Quantum error correction for beginners. Rep. Prog. Phys. 76, 76001 (2013)
15. Steane, A.: Quantum Computing and Error Correction. Decoherence and its implications in quantum computation and information transfer. In: Gonis, Turchi (eds.), pp. 284–298. IOS Press, Amsterdam (2001), quant-ph/0304016 (2001)
16. Calderbank, A., Rains, E., Shor, P., Sloane, N.: Quantum Error Correction via Codes Over GF(4). IEEE Trans. Inform. Theory 44, 1369 (1998)
17. Knill, E., Laflamme, R., Viola, L.: Theory of Quantum Error Correction for General Noise. Phys. Rev. Lett. 84, 2525 (2000)
18. Aharonov, D., Ben-Or, M.: Fault-tolerant Quantum Computation with constant error. In: Proceedings of 29th Annual ACM Symposium on Theory of Computing, p. 46 (1997)
19. Kitaev, A.: Quantum Computations: algorithms and error correction. Russ. Math. Serv. 52, 1191 (1997)
20. Dennis, E., Kitaev, A., Landahl, A., Preskill, J.: Topological Quantum Memory. J. Math. Phys. 43, 4452 (2002)
21. Raussendorf, R., Harrington, J., Goyal, K.: A Fault-tolerant one way quantum computer. Ann. Phys. 321, 2242 (2006)
22. Raussendorf, R., Harrington, J.: Fault-tolerant quantum computation with high threshold in two dimensions. Phys. Rev. Lett. 98, 190504 (2007)
23. Fowler, A., Mariantoni, M., Martinis, J., Cleland, A.: Surface codes: Towards practical large-scale quantum computation. Phys. Rev. A 86, 32324 (2012)
24. Devitt, S., Fowler, A., Tilma, T., Munro, W., Nemoto, K.: Classical Processing Requirements for a Topological Quantum Computing Systems. Int. J. Quant. Inf. 8, 1 (2010)
25. Duclos-Cianci, G., Poulin, D.: Fault-Tolerant Renormalization Group Decoded for Abelian Topological Codes. Quant. Inf. Comp. 14, 721 (2014)
26. Kliuchnikov, V., Maslov, D., Mosca, M.: Asymptotically optimal approximation of single qubit unitaries by Clifford and T circuits using a constant number of ancillary qubits. Phys. Rev. Lett. 110, 190502 (2013)
27. Meter, R.V., Itoh, K.: Fast Quatum Modular Exponentiation. Phys. Rev. A. 71, 052320 (2005)
28. Zalka, C.: Fast Versions of Shor's quantum factoring algorithm. quant-ph/9806084 (1998)
29. Vedral, V., Barenco, A., Ekert, A.: Quantum Networks for elementary arithmetic operations. Phys. Rev. A. 54, 147 (1996)

30. Choi, B., Meter, R.V.: A $\Theta(\sqrt{n})$-depth Quantum Adder on a 2D NTC Quantum Computer Architecture. ACM Journal on Emerging Technologies in Computer Systems (JETC) 7, 11 (2011)
31. Cleve, R., Watrous, J.: Fast Parallel circuits for the quantum fourier transform. In: Proc. 41st Annual IEEE Symposium on Foundations of Computer Science (FOCS 2000), pp. 526–536 (2000)
32. Meter, R.V., Itoh, K.: Fast Quantum Modular Exponentiation. Phys. Rev. A. 71, 52320 (2005)
33. Raussendorf, R., Harrington, J., Goyal, K.: Topological fault-tolerance in cluster state quantum computation. New J. Phys. 9, 199 (2007)
34. Fowler, A., Goyal, K.: Topological cluster state quantum computing. Quant. Inf. Comp. 9, 721 (2009)
35. Stock, R., James, D.: A Scalable, high-speed measurement based quantum computer using trapped ions. Phys. Rev. Lett. 102, 170501 (2009)
36. Devitt, S., Fowler, A., Stephens, A., Greentree, A., Hollenberg, L., Munro, W., Nemoto, K.: Architectural design for a topological cluster state quantum computer. New. J. Phys. 11, 083032 (2009)
37. Nemoto, K., Trupke, M., Devitt, S., Stephens, A., Buczak, K., Nobauer, T., Everitt, M., Schmiedmayer, J., Munro, W.: Photonic architecture for scalable quantum information processing in NV-diamond. arXiv:1309.4277 (2013)
38. Jones, N.C., Meter, R.V., Fowler, A., McMahon, P., Kim, J., Ladd, T., Yamamoto, Y.: A Layered Architecture for Quantum Computing Using Quantum Dots. Phys. Rev. X 2, 31007 (2012)
39. Meter, R.V., Ladd, T., Fowler, A., Yamamoto, Y.: Distributed Quantum Computation Architecture Using Semiconductor Nanophotonics. Int. J. Quant. Inf. 8, 295 (2010)
40. Monroe, C., Raussendorf, R., Ruthven, A., Brown, K., Maunz, P., Duan, L.M., Kim, J.: Large Scale Modular Quantum Computer Architecture with Atomic Memory and Photonic Interconnects. Phys. Rev. A 89, 22317 (2014)
41. Raussendorf, R., Briegel, H.J.: A One way Quantum Computer. Phys. Rev. Lett. 86, 5188 (2001)
42. Devitt, S., Stephens, A., Munro, W., Nemoto, K.: Requirements for fault-tolerant factoring on an atom-optics quantum computer. Nature Communications 4, 2524 (2013)
43. Gottesman, D.: PhD Thesis (Caltech). quant-ph/9705052 (1997)
44. Edmonds, J.: Paths, trees, and flowers. Canadian J. Math. 17, 449 (1965)
45. Kolmogorov, V.: Blossom V: A new implementation of a minimum cost perfect matching algorithm. Math. Prog. Comp. 1, 43 (2009)
46. Fowler, A., Whiteside, A., Hollenberg, L.: Towwards practical classical processing for the surface code: Timing analysis. Phys. Rev. A. 86, 042313 (2012)
47. Fowler, A.: Minimum weight perfect matching in $O(1)$ parallel time. arxiv:1307.1740 (2013)
48. Stephens, A.: Fault-tolerant thresholds for quantum error correction with the surface code. Phys. Rev. A. 89, 022321 (2014)
49. Kane, B.: A Silicon-Based nuclear spin Quantum Computer. Nature (London) 393, 133 (1998)

Degrees of Reversibility for DFA and DPDA

Martin Kutrib[1] and Thomas Worsch[2]

[1] Institut für Informatik, Universität Giessen
Arndtstr. 2, 35392 Giessen, Germany
`kutrib@informatik.uni-giessen.de`
[2] Karlsruhe Institute of Technology
`worsch@kit.edu`

Abstract. The notion of k-reversibility is generalized to pushdown automata. A pushdown automaton is said to be (k, l)-reversible if its predecessor configurations can uniquely be computed by a pushdown automaton with input lookahead of size k and stack lookahead of size l. It turns out that there are problems which can be solved by $(k + 1, 1)$-reversible pushdown automata, but not by (k, l)-reversible pushdown automata. So, infinite hierarchies dependent on the degree of reversibility are shown. On the other hand, any reversible pushdown automaton of degree $(k, l+1)$ can be simulated by a reversible pushdown automaton of degree $(k, 1)$. So, there are no hierarchies induced by the size of the stack lookahead. These results complement the situation for finite automata which is also discussed and presented in our setting.

Keywords: Reversible finite state machines, gradual reversibility, pushdown automata, lookahead, hierarchies of languages.

1 Introduction

Reversibility is a fundamental principle in physics. Since abstract computational models may serve as prototypes of computing devices which can be physically constructed, it is interesting to know whether these abstract models are able to obey physical laws. The observation that loss of information results in heat dissipation [9] strongly suggests to study computations without loss of information. Many different formal models have been studied in connection with reversibility. For example, reversible Turing machines have been introduced in [4] (see [3,10] for improved constructions). Reversibility in finite state machines has been studied in [2,11] and reversibility in pushdown machines is investigated in [8].

Reversibility in the context of computing devices with discrete internal states that evolve in discrete time refers to the possibility to letting the computation step back and forth deterministically. This implies that any configuration has at most one predecessor that, in addition, has to be computable by a device of the same type as the given one. For example, given a reversible finite-state machine it is required that the backward steps in time are performed by another finite-state machine derived from the given one. An observation in [2,11] is that there are regular languages which are not reversible, so there are finite-state machines

S. Yamashita and S. Minato (Eds.): RC 2014, LNCS 8507, pp. 40–53, 2014.

that cannot be simulated by any reversible finite-state machine. However, it turned out [2] that this inherent irreversibility may depend on the size of the input window of the devices. If this size is increased *for backward computations*, more languages become reversible. This result led to the definition of so-called *k*-reversible languages. However, in [2] the machines are also considered from the learning theory point of view. So, they are restricted to have one accepting state only. Here we stick with standard definitions and generalize the notion of *k*-reversibility to finite-state devices with an additional resource. In particular, the resource pushdown store or stack is considered.

The rest of this paper is organized as follows. In the next section we recall some basic definitions including deterministic finite-state machines with input lookahead, and define devices that are reversible of a certain degree. Then we present an example of a regular language that is reversible of degree two but not reversible of degree one. This example is generalized to an infinite degree hierarchy of regular languages, thus, obtaining the results of [2] in our setting.

Section 4 is devoted to the study of degrees of reversibility for pushdown machines. The handling of the additional resource makes the definitions of the degrees more involved. A pushdown machine is said to be reversible of degree (k, l) if its predecessor configurations can uniquely be computed by a pushdown machine with input lookahead of size k and stack lookahead of size l. The situation for finite automata is complemented and contrasted by proving that there are problems which can be solved by reversible pushdown machines of degree $(k + 1, 1)$, but not by any reversible pushdown machine of degree (k, l). On the other hand, any reversible pushdown machine of degree $(k, l + 1)$ can be simulated by a reversible pushdown machine of degree $(k, 1)$. So, there are no hierarchies induced by the size of the stack lookahead. However, the stack lookahead is suitable to decrease the descriptional complexity of pushdown automata. The lookahead can be used to obtain machines with significantly fewer states and/or stack symbols.

Finally, in Section 5 we are interested in the question whether for any regular respectively realtime deterministic context-free language there is some degree k of reversibility so that the language is accepted by a device of the corresponding type with degree k. Or else, whether there are regular (or deterministic context-free) languages that cannot be accepted by any reversible finite automaton (or reversible pushdown automaton) of any degree. We consider the important subclasses of *finite* and *unary* languages as well as the general question.

2   Preliminaries and Definitions

Let Σ^* denote the *set of all words* over the finite alphabet Σ. The *empty word* is denoted by λ, and $\Sigma^+ = \Sigma^* \setminus \{\lambda\}$. For convenience, we use $\Sigma^{\leq k}$ for the *set of all words* over Σ whose length is at most $k \geq 0$. Furthermore, we write $a^{\leq k}$ for $\{a\}^{\leq k}$. Hence $\Sigma \Sigma^{\leq k-1}$ is the set of all non-empty words of length at most k. For the *length of w* we write $|w|$. We denote by $\mathrm{prf}_k(w)$ the longest prefix of w which has length at most k and analogously by $\mathrm{suf}_k(w)$ the longest suffix of w which has length at most k.

In the following we consider computing machines with a finite number of discrete internal states. The machines have a read-only input tape, may be equipped with further resources, and evolve in discrete time, where each computation step is driven by a *deterministic transition function* δ. Given a *configuration* representing the complete "global state" of a device, the transition function is used to compute the successor configuration resulting after one step. The transition function depends on the current internal state and on the status of further resources the machine is equipped with. It gives the successor state and maybe changes the status of the resources.

A first study of reversibility of such devices has been done in [4] for Turing machines. Deterministic Turing machines are called *reversible* if any configuration occurring in any computation has at most one predecessor which, in addition, is computable by a deterministic Turing machine, say, with transition function $\delta^{\leftarrow}$. Generalizing this convention, we assume that for any reversible computing machine with discrete internal states and transition function δ the reverse transition function is denoted by $\delta^{\leftarrow}$.

In the following, two devices are said to be *equivalent* if they accept the same language.

3   Degree of Reversibility for Finite Automata

We first look at the simplest type of device in question, deterministic finite automata which can accept the regular languages. *Forward* automata read their input from left to right as usual, and *backward* automata from right to left.

A *deterministic finite automaton with lookahead* k, (k)-DFA for short, is a system $\langle S, \Sigma, \delta, s_0, k, F \rangle$, where S is the finite set of *internal states*, Σ is the finite set of *input symbols*, $s_0 \in S$ is the *initial state*, $k \geq 1$ is the *size of the input window* (lookahead), $F \subseteq S$ is the set of *accepting states*, and $\delta \colon S \times \Sigma \Sigma^{\leq k-1} \to S$ is the (possibly partial) *transition function*.

A classical deterministic finite automaton (DFA) is a (1)-DFA. A *configuration* of a (k)-DFA is a triple $(u, s, v) \in \Sigma^* \times S \times \Sigma^*$, where s is the current state and uv is the complete input. The part $u \in \Sigma^*$ is to the left and the part $v \in \Sigma^*$ to the right of the input head. The *input window* of a forward DFA is $W = \mathrm{prf}_k(v)$, for a backward DFA it is $W = \mathrm{suf}_k(u)$. The initial configuration for forward computations on input w is defined to be (λ, s_0, w).

For a configuration (u, s, v) its *successor configuration* is (u', s', v') where $s' = \delta(s, W)$ and $(u', v') = (u\,\mathrm{prf}_1(v), \mathrm{suf}_{|v|-1}(v))$ for forward computations and $(u', v') = (\mathrm{prf}_{|u|-1}(u), \mathrm{suf}_1(u)v)$ in the backward case. The head always moves 1 symbol further, even if $k \geq 2$. There is no successor configuration if $W = \lambda$. The relation from one configuration to the next one is denoted $\vdash$, and its reflexive transitive closure by $\vdash^*$. The *language accepted* by a forward (k)-DFA M is $L(M) = \{\, w \in \Sigma^* \mid (\lambda, s_0, w) \vdash^* (w, s_f, \lambda),\ \text{for some } s_f \in F \,\}$.

Now we turn to *reversibility* of DFA. In general, it is required that any configuration must have at most one predecessor. However, this definition raises a couple of questions. For example, how difficult it is to compute the unique predecessor configuration. On the other hand, the notion of reversibility can be relaxed slightly. For example, when for a fixed constant $k \geq 1$ the k symbols most recently read in a forward computation are known, and the immediate predecessor configuration is unique for all computations that lead to the current configuration along these k symbols seen in the input window. From this point of view, it turns out to be interesting to allow some lookahead $k \geq 1$ for the backward computation (see [2]), although the lookahead for the forward DFA is still 1.

We emphasize that the task of the reverse DFA is to compute predecessor configurations and *not* to accept a specific language. Therefore the indication of initial state and accepting states for the reverse DFA is meaningless.

A forward DFA is said to be *reversible of degree k* (REV(k)-DFA) if and only if there exists a backward (k)-DFA with transition function $\delta^{\leftarrow}$ inducing a relation $\vdash^{\leftarrow}$ from one configuration to the next, so that

$$(u, s, v) \vdash^{\leftarrow} (u', s', v') \text{ if and only if}$$

(i) $(u', s', v') \vdash (u, s, v)$,
(ii) if $|u| \geq k$, then $(\mathrm{prf}_{|u|-k}(u), \hat{s}, \mathrm{suf}_k(u)v) \vdash^* (u', s', v') \vdash (u, s, v)$ for all $\hat{s} \in S$ so that $(\mathrm{prf}_{|u|-k}(u), \hat{s}, \mathrm{suf}_k(u)v) \vdash^* (u, s, v)$, and
(iii) if $1 \leq |u| < k$, then $(\lambda, s_0, u) \vdash^* (u', s', v') \vdash (u, s, v)$.

So, the lookahead of the backward DFA is used to determine the unique predecessor configuration from all computations that lead to the current configuration along the symbols seen in the input window.

Example 1. The regular language $\{ a^m b^n \mid m \geq 0, n \geq 1 \}$ is accepted by the REV(2)-DFA $M = \langle \{s_0, s_1\}, \{a, b\}, \delta, s_0, 2, \{s_1\} \rangle$, where the transition functions δ and $\delta^{\leftarrow}$ are shown in Figure 1. The crucial part of the computation appears at the borderline between the a's and b's in the input. Figure 2 demonstrates that it can be done reversibly by the (2)-DFA M.

In addition, consider exemplarily the configuration $(baab, s_1, bb)$ that is unreachable in any computation starting from an initial configuration, and the configuration $(aaab, s_1, bb)$ that is reachable. Both have two predecessor configurations, namely $(baa, s_0, bbb), (baa, s_1, bbb)$ and $(aaa, s_0, bbb), (aaa, s_1, bbb)$. However, in both cases the predecessor configuration is unique, when the computation comes along the last two input symbols. For the first case we have $(ba, s_0, abbb) \vdash (baa, s_0, bbb) \vdash (baab, s_1, bb)$ and $(ba, s_1, abbb) \not\vdash^* (baab, s_1, bb)$. □

Essentially, in [11] it has been shown that the regular language of Example 1 cannot be accepted by any REV(1)-DFA. So, one gets the following corollary already known from [2].

Corollary 2. *There are languages accepted by REV(2)-DFA that cannot be accepted by any REV(1)-DFA.*

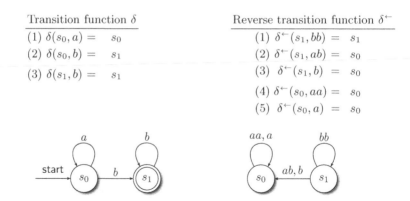

Transition function δ	Reverse transition function $\delta^{\leftarrow}$
(1) $\delta(s_0, a) = s_0$	(1) $\delta^{\leftarrow}(s_1, bb) = s_1$
(2) $\delta(s_0, b) = s_1$	(2) $\delta^{\leftarrow}(s_1, ab) = s_0$
(3) $\delta(s_1, b) = s_1$	(3) $\delta^{\leftarrow}(s_1, b) = s_0$
	(4) $\delta^{\leftarrow}(s_0, aa) = s_0$
	(5) $\delta^{\leftarrow}(s_0, a) = s_0$

Fig. 1. Example of a REV(2)-DFA accepting the language a^*b^+ (double circled states are accepting). The DFA is depicted at the left and the reverse (2)-DFA is depicted at the right. The labels on the edges indicate the *complete* content of the input window (but only 1 symbol is "consumed"). There is no REV(1)-DFA accepting this language.

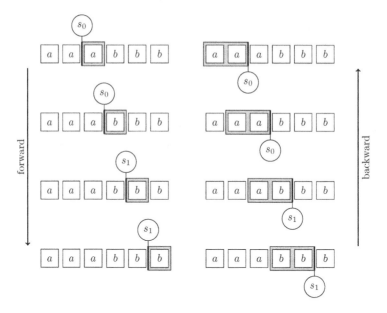

Fig. 2. A forward and its corresponding backward computation

Reversible deterministic finite automata have also been studied in the context of algorithmic learning theory [2,7]. In the former reference the notion of k-reversible languages has been introduced in a slightly different setting. However, there an infinite and strict hierarchy of regular language families is derived depending on the lookahead size in backward computations. We generalize Example 1 and Corollary 2 obtaining the result of [2]. So one can speak about the *degree of reversibility of regular languages*.

Example 3. Let $k \geq 1$ be an integer. Then the language $\{ a^m b^n \mid m \geq 0, n \geq k \}$ is accepted by the REV$(k + 1)$-DFA

$$M = \langle \{s_0, s_1, \ldots, s_k\}, \{a, b\}, \delta, s_0, k + 1, \{s_k\} \rangle$$

as depicted in Figure 3. However, the language *cannot* be accepted by any REV(k)-DFA.   □

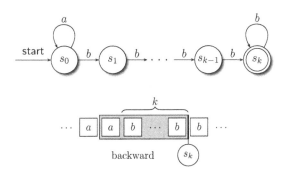

Fig. 3. Example of a REV$(k+1)$-DFA accepting the language $a^* b^k b^*$. This DFA is not a REV(k)-DFA and there is no other REV(k)-DFA accepting this language.

Theorem 4. *For any integer $k \geq 1$, there are regular languages accepted by REV$(k + 1)$-DFA that cannot be accepted by any REV(k)-DFA.*

Proof. For $k \geq 1$ let M be any DFA accepting $\{ a^m b^n \mid m \geq 0, n \geq k \}$. Consider the input words $w_r = b^{k-1} b^r$ for $r \geq 0$ and denote by s_r the state of M after reading w_r. For increasing r M must ultimately enter a loop of accepting states; denote by $y \geq 1$ the length of the loop. Let w_x be the shortest word leading to a state belonging to the loop; then $s_x = s_{x+y}$ and $x \geq 1$. This means that $\mathrm{suf}_k(w_x) = \mathrm{suf}_k(w_{x+y}) = b^k$ and therefore any reverse automaton with lookahead at most k will enter the *same* state when doing one step backwards.

On the other hand, because of the minimality of x state s_{x-1} is not part of the loop while s_{x+y-1} is. Therefore undoing the last step after inputs w_x and w_{x+y} respectively should lead to *different* states which therefore requires a lookahead whose size is at least $k + 1$.   □

4   Degree of Reversibility for Pushdown Machines

Now we turn to generalize the results of the previous section to more powerful finite state devices having an additional resource. Here we consider the resource *pushdown store* or *stack* and obtain the so-called pushdown automata, whose deterministic variants have important applications in parser theory. They capture the deterministic context-free languages that can still be parsed in linear time (see, for example, [1]). The additional resource allows a more involved definition of lookaheads and, thus, degrees of reversibility. On the one hand, there is the possible lookahead on the input as for (k)-DFA. On the other hand, we consider a lookahead on the stack, that is, the machine can see the topmost l stack symbols. It turns out that the latter is interesting from a descriptional complexity point if view only.

General deterministic pushdown automata that are not allowed to perform λ-steps are weaker than DPDA that may move on λ input [6]. However, in [8] it has been shown that every reversible pushdown automaton can be simulated by a *realtime* reversible pushdown automaton, that is, without λ-steps. This realtime reversible machine can effectively be constructed from the given one. Therefore, in order to simplify matters we do not allow λ-steps from the outset.

A *deterministic pushdown automaton with lookaheads k and l* $((k,l)$-DPDA) is a system $M = \langle S, \Sigma, \Gamma, \delta, s_0, k, l, \perp, F \rangle$, where S is the finite set of *internal states*, Σ is the finite set of *input symbols*, Γ is the finite set of *stack symbols*, $s_0 \in S$ is the *initial state*, $k \geq 1$ is the *size of the input window*, $l \geq 1$ is the *size of the stack window*, $\perp \in \Gamma$ is the so-called *bottom-of-stack symbol*, which initially appears on the stack, $F \subseteq S$ is the set of *accepting states*, and $\delta : S \times \Sigma \Sigma^{\leq k-1} \times \Gamma \Gamma^{\leq l-1} \to S \times \Gamma^*$ is the (possibly partial) *transition function*.

A classical deterministic pushdown automaton (DPDA) is a deterministic pushdown automaton with lookaheads $k = 1$ and $l = 1$. A *configuration* of a (k,l)-DPDA is a quadruple (u, s, v, γ), where s is the current state, $u \in \Sigma^*$ is the part of the input to the left of the input head, and $v \in \Sigma^*$ the part of the input to the right of the input head, and $\gamma \in \Gamma^*$ is the current content of the stack, the leftmost symbol of γ being the top symbol. On input w the initial configuration is defined to be $(\lambda, s_0, w, \perp)$.

For a configuration $(u, s, v, Z\gamma)$ its *successor configuration* is $(u', s', v', \beta\gamma)$ where $(s', \beta) = \delta(s, W, \mathrm{prf}_l(Z\gamma))$. As for DFA the input window is denoted W and the change from (u, v) to (u', v') depends on whether it is a forward or a backward computation. There are no successor configurations for (u, s, λ, γ) and for (u, s, v, λ). The size of the stack can only decrease (by exactly 1) if $\beta = \lambda$; this is usually called a pop operation. If $|\beta| = 1$ the top of stack symbol is exchanged, leaving the size of the stack unchanged. If $|\beta| > 1$ the size of the stack increases (by $|\beta| - 1$); we call this a push operation.

As before, we denote the relation from one configuration to the next one by $\vdash$. The *language accepted* by a (k,l)-DPDA M is

$$L(M) = \{ w \in \Sigma^* \mid (\lambda, s_0, w, \perp) \vdash^* (w, s_f, \lambda, \gamma), \text{ for some } s_f \in F \text{ and } \gamma \in \Gamma^* \}.$$

Now we turn to reversible DPDA. Classical reversible pushdown automata have been introduced in [8], where reversibility is considered only for configurations that are reachable from some valid initial configuration.

As for DFA here we also consider configurations unreachable from initial configurations and, moreover, relax the notion of reversibility slightly. A configuration must have a unique predecessor for all computations that lead to the current configuration along the symbols seen in the input window and are consistent with the symbols at the top of the stack. As before, for reverse computations the head moves from right to left.

A DPDA is said to be *reversible of degree* (k, l) (REV(k, l)-DPDA) if and only if there exists a reverse (k, l)-DPDA with transition function $\delta^\leftarrow$ inducing a relation $\vdash^\leftarrow$ from one configuration to the next, so that

$$(u, s, v, \gamma) \vdash^\leftarrow (u', s', v', \gamma') \text{ if and only if}$$

(i) $(u', s', v', \gamma') \vdash (u, s, v, \gamma)$,

(ii) if $|u| \geq k$, then $(\mathrm{prf}_{|u|-k}(u), \hat{s}, \mathrm{suf}_k(u)v, \hat{\gamma}) \vdash^* (u', s', v', \gamma') \vdash (u, s, v, \gamma)$ for all $\hat{s} \in S$, $\hat{\gamma} \in \Gamma^*$ so that $(\mathrm{prf}_{|u|-k}(u), \hat{s}, \mathrm{suf}_k(u)v, \hat{\gamma}) \vdash^* (u, s, v, \gamma)$, and

(iii) if $1 \leq |u| < k$, then $(\lambda, s_0, u, \bot) \vdash^* (u', s', v', \gamma') \vdash (u, s, v, \gamma)$.

Example 5. For any integer $k \geq 1$, the deterministic linear context-free language $\{a^n b a^m b a^n \mid n \geq 1, m \geq k\}$ is accepted by the REV$(k + 1, 1)$-DPDA $M = \langle\{s_0, s_1, \ldots, s_{k+4}\}, \{a, b\}, \{a, \bot\}, \delta, s_0, k + 1, 1, \bot, \{s_{k+4}\}\rangle$, where the transition functions δ and $\delta^\leftarrow$ are as follows, for $x \in \{a^{k+1}\} \cup \{a^p baa^q \mid p + q = k - 1\}$, $2 \leq i \leq k + 1$, and $Z \in \Gamma$:

Transition function δ			Reverse transition function $\delta^\leftarrow$		
(F1) $\delta(s_0, a, \bot)$	$=$	$(s_1, \bot)$	(B1) $\delta^\leftarrow(s_{k+4}, x, \bot)$	$=$	$(s_{k+3}, \bot)$
(F2) $\delta(s_1, a, Z)$	$=$	(s_1, aZ)	(B2) $\delta^\leftarrow(s_{k+3}, x, Z)$	$=$	(s_{k+3}, aZ)
(F3) $\delta(s_1, b, Z)$	$=$	(s_2, Z)	(B3) $\delta^\leftarrow(s_{k+3}, a^k b, Z)$	$=$	(s_{k+2}, Z)
(F4) $\delta(s_i, a, Z)$	$=$	(s_{i+1}, Z)	(B4) $\delta^\leftarrow(s_{k+2}, a^{k+1}, Z)$	$=$	(s_{k+2}, Z)
(F5) $\delta(s_{k+2}, a, Z)$	$=$	(s_{k+2}, Z)	(B5) $\delta^\leftarrow(s_{k+2}, ba^k, Z)$	$=$	(s_{k+1}, Z)
(F6) $\delta(s_{k+2}, b, Z)$	$=$	(s_{k+3}, Z)	(B6) $\delta^\leftarrow(s_i, a^{\leq k-i+1} aba^{i-2}, Z)$	$=$	(s_{i-1}, Z)
(F7) $\delta(s_{k+3}, a, a)$	$=$	(s_{k+3}, λ)	(B7) $\delta^\leftarrow(s_1, a^{\leq k-1} aa, a)$	$=$	(s_1, λ)
(F8) $\delta(s_{k+3}, a, \bot)$	$=$	$(s_{k+4}, \bot)$	(B8) $\delta^\leftarrow(s_1, a, \bot)$	$=$	$(s_0, \bot)$

Rule (F1) is used to read the first a of the input and to change to state s_1 in order to record that at least one a appeared. While in s_1 the remaining input prefix of the form a^* is read and stored. When a b appears in the input, (F3) and (F4) are used to count the number of a's in the infix up to k. If there are sufficiently many a's, the computation continues in s_{k+2} until the second b appears in the input (using (F5) and (F6)). By (F7), now the number of stored a's from the prefix is compared with the number of a's from the suffix. Since the very first a has not been stored, there should be one more a in the suffix than in the stack. Finally, if the bottom-of-stack symbol is seen in state s_{k+3}, automaton M reads the last a from the suffix and changes into the sole accepting state s_{k+4} by (F8), and the computation necessarily stops.

For the backward computation the transitions of $\delta^\leftarrow$ are used. Note, that in forward computations any state s_{i+1} can only be reached from state s_i and possibly from state s_{i+1} itself. Since there is only one transition of δ that changes to state s_{k+4}, (B1) reverses this step for all lookahead contents that allows a computation to reach s_{k+4}. For further input symbols a from the suffix, the only transition of δ that changes to state s_{k+3} is (F7) which pops the symbol from the top of the stack. So, (B2) are constructed to reverse the popping by pushing the current input symbol, again for all lookahead contents that allow a computation to reach s_{k+3}. In forward computations M changes from state s_{k+2} to s_{k+3} if and only if the current input symbol is a b, whereby the stack remains unchanged. This step can uniquely be reversed by (B3). While in state s_{k+2}, the power of the lookahead is used. As long as there are only a's in the input window, all possible computations along these a's lead M to state s_{k+2} (B4). When the window content becomes ba^k, all possible computations along these sequence of symbols lead M to start to reverse the forward counting. Similarly for further contents of the input window given in rule (B6). So, by (B5) and (B6) the state s_1 is reached. The only possibility in forward computations to reach s_1 is by a's. Therefore, (B7) reverses the pushing of the prefix by popping whenever the stack is not empty. Finally, by (B8) the leftmost a is read when the stack is empty, which leads to state s_0. $\Box$

4.1 Degrees by Input Lookahead

We use the languages of Example 5 as witnesses for an infinite and tight hierarchy of languages acceptable by reversible pushdown automata of a degree that depends on the size of the input window only. Large stack windows do not help.

Theorem 6. *For any integer $k \geq 1$, there are deterministic linear context-free languages accepted by $REV(k+1,1)$-DPDA that cannot be accepted by any $REV(k,l)$-DPDA, for an arbitrary $l \geq 1$.*

Proof. By Example 5, the language $L_k = \{\, a^n b a^m b a^n \mid n \geq 1, m \geq k \,\}$ is accepted by some $REV(k+1,1)$-DPDA. So, it remains to be shown, that L_k cannot be accepted by any $REV(k,l)$-DPDA, $l \geq 1$. To this end, assume in contrast to the assertion that L_k is accepted by some $REV(k,l)$-DPDA $M = \langle S, \Sigma, \Gamma, \delta, s_0, k, l, \bot, F \rangle$. During the computation of M on input prefixes a^+ no combination of state and content of the pushdown store may appear twice: If

$$(\lambda, s_0, a^n b a^m b a^n, \bot) \vdash^* (a^{p_1}, s_1, a^{n-p_1} b a^m b a^n, \gamma_1)$$
$$\vdash^+ (a^{p_1+p_2}, s_1, a^{n-p_1-p_2} b a^m b a^n, \gamma_1)$$

is the beginning of an accepting computation, then so is

$$(\lambda, s_0, a^{n-p_2} b a^m b a^n, \bot) \vdash^* (a^{p_1}, s_1, a^{n-p_1-p_2} b a^m b a^n, \gamma_1),$$

but $a^{n-p_2} b a^m b a^n$ does not belong to L_k. This implies that each height of the pushdown store may appear only finitely often and, thus, that the height increases arbitrarily. So, M runs into a loop while processing a's, that is, the combination of a state and, for any fixed number h, some h topmost pushdown symbols α appear again and again. To render the loop more precisely, let $(a^{n-x}, s, a^x b a^m b a^n, \alpha\gamma)$ be a configuration of the loop. Then there is a successor configuration with the same combination of state and topmost pushdown symbols $(a^{n-x+y}, s, a^{x-y} b a^m b a^n, \alpha\beta)$. We may choose α so that during the computation starting in $(a^{n-x}, s, a^x b a^m b a^n, \alpha\gamma)$ no symbol of γ is touched, that is, $\alpha\beta = \alpha\gamma'\gamma$. Therefore, the computation continues as

$$(a^{n-x+y}, s, a^{x-y} b a^m b a^n, \alpha\gamma'\gamma) \vdash^+ (a^{n-x+2y}, s, a^{x-2y} b a^m b a^n, \alpha\gamma'\gamma'\gamma).$$

Now we turn to the input suffixes. While M processes the input suffixes a^+, no combination of state and content of the pushdown store may appear twice. If

$$(a^n b a^m b, s_2, a^n, \gamma_2) \vdash^* (a^n b a^m b a^{q_1}, s_3, a^{n-q_1}, \gamma_3)$$
$$\vdash^+ (a^n b a^m b a^{q_1+q_2}, s_3, a^{n-q_1-q_2}, \gamma_3)$$

results in an accepting computation, then so does

$$(a^n b a^m b, s_2, a^{n-q_2}, \gamma_2) \vdash^* (a^n b a^m b a^{q_1}, s_3, a^{n-q_1-q_2}, \gamma_3),$$

but $a^n b a^m b a^{n-q_2}$ does not belong to L_k. This implies that each height of the pushdown store appears only finitely often. Moreover, in any accepting computation the pushdown store has to be decreased until some symbol of γ appears. Otherwise, we could increase the number of a's in the prefix by y to drive M through an additional loop. The resulting computation would also be accepting but the input does not belong to L_k. Together we conclude that M runs into a loop that decreases the height of the pushdown store while processing the a's of the suffix, and that there are only finitely many combinations of state and content of the pushdown store which are accepting.

Now we consider the computations on the input infixes of the form a^+ in between the two symbols b. While processing these infixes the height of the pushdown store cannot be decreased by more than a constant. Otherwise we obtain the same contradiction as for the computation on the prefixes. Moreover, M cannot increase the height of the pushdown store by more than a constant while processing the infixes. Otherwise, the computation on the suffixes cannot decrease the height sufficiently, and there would be infinitely many accepting combinations of state and content of the pushdown store, which contradicts the previous observation. Therefore, on these infixes M processes a loop that, in total, neither increases nor decreases the height of the pushdown store by more than a constant.

We will now derive a contradiction to the assumption that L_k is accepted by M. Consider two different numbers $k < m_1 < m_2$ and some $n \geq 1$ so that M accepts $a^n b a^{m_1} b a^n$ and $a^n b a^{m_2} b a^n$ in the same combinations of state and content of the pushdown store, say in state s_p with γ_p in the pushdown store, at the end of the infix computation and in the same combinations of state and content of the pushdown store, say s_f and γ_f, at the overall end of the computation. By the considerations above, such numbers exist. So, we have the forward computations

$$(\lambda, s_0, a^n b a^{m_1} b a^n, \bot) \vdash^{n+1} (a^n b, s_1, a^{m_1} b a^n, \gamma_1)$$
$$\vdash^{k-1} (a^n b a^{k-1}, s_2, a^{m_1-k+1} b a^n, \gamma_2) \vdash (a^n b a^k, s_3, a^{m_1-k} b a^n, \gamma_3)$$
$$\vdash^{m_1-k} (a^n b a^{m_1}, s_p, b a^n, \gamma_p) \vdash^* (a^n b a^{m_1} b a^n, s_f, \lambda, \gamma_f)$$

and

$$(\lambda, s_0, a^n b a^{m_2} b a^n, \bot) \vdash^{n+1} (a^n b, s_1, a^{m_2} b a^n, \gamma_1)$$
$$\vdash^k (a^n b a^k, s_3, a^{m_2-k} b a^n, \gamma_3) \vdash^{m_2-m_1-1} (a^n b a^{k+m_2-m_1-1}, s_4, a^{m_1-k+1} b a^n, \gamma_4)$$
$$\vdash (a^n b a^{k+m_2-m_1}, s_5, a^{m_1-k} b a^n, \gamma_5) \vdash^{m_1-k} (a^n b a^{m_2}, s_p, b a^n, \gamma_p)$$
$$\vdash^* (a^n b a^{m_2} b a^n, s_f, \lambda, \gamma_f).$$

Since M is (k, l)-reversible, we obtain

$$(a^n b a^{m_1} b a^n, s_f, \lambda, \gamma_f) \vdash^{\leftarrow *} (a^n b a^{m_1}, s_p, b a^n, \gamma_p)$$
$$\vdash^{\leftarrow m_1-k} (a^n b a^k, s_3, a^{m_1-k} b a^n, \gamma_3)$$

and

$$(a^n b a^{m_2} b a^n, s_f, \lambda, \gamma_f) \vdash^{\leftarrow *} (a^n b a^{m_2}, s_p, b a^n, \gamma_p)$$
$$\vdash^{\leftarrow m_1-k} (a^n b a^{k+m_2-m_1}, s_5, a^{m_1-k} b a^n, \gamma_5).$$

Since during the $m_1 - k$ steps of both backward computations the input look-ahead is always a^k and the stacks are even identical, $(s_3, \gamma_3) = (s_5, \gamma_5)$ and, in particular, $(s_2, \gamma_2) = (s_4, \gamma_4)$ follow. Since M is deterministic, the beginning of the accepting computation on input $a^n b a^{k+m_2-m_1-1} b a^n$ is

$$(\lambda, s_0, a^n b a^{k+m_2-m_1-1} b a^n, \bot) \vdash^{n+1} (a^n b, s_1, a^{k+m_2-m_1-1} b a^n, \gamma_1)$$
$$\vdash^k (a^n b a^k, s_3, a^{m_2-m_1-1} b a^n, \gamma_3) \vdash^{m_2-m_1-1} (a^n b a^{k+m_2-m_1-1}, s_4, b a^n, \gamma_4)$$
$$= (a^n b a^{k+m_2-m_1-1}, s_2, b a^n, \gamma_2).$$

By the forward computations above, the beginning of the computation on input $a^n b a^{k-1} b a^n$ is as follows:

$$(\lambda, s_0, a^n b a^{k-1} b a^n, \bot) \vdash^{n+1} (a^n b, s_1, a^{k-1} b a^n, \gamma_1) \vdash^{k-1} (a^n b a^{k-1}, s_2, b a^n, \gamma_2).$$

So, the computation on input $a^n b a^{k-1} b a^n$ is accepting, too, a contradiction. □

4.2   No Degrees by Stack Lookahead

Now we turn to the question whether there are hierarchies with respect to the size of the stack lookahead, and answer it negatively. In fact, any reversible pushdown machine of degree $(k, l+1)$ can be simulated by a reversible pushdown machines of degree $(k, 1)$. So, in general, a lookahead on the stack does not help to obtain reversibility. We present two different simulation principles based on where the information of the topmost stack symbols is maintained. This could be in additional registers of the states or in the stack symbols. Both methods are constructive. From a practical point of view, states are somehow more active resources while stack symbols are more passive. So, it depends on the application which principle is more suitable.

Theorem 7. *Let $k, l \geq 1$ be integers and M be an $REV(k, l)$-DPDA with m states and n stack symbols. Then an equivalent $REV(k, 1)$-DPDA with n stack symbols and at most $m \cdot \frac{n^{l+1}}{n-1}$ states can effectively be constructed.*

The second construction groups up to l stack symbols into one. However, the construction has to overcome the problem, that, when the original automaton pops a symbol, the simulating one has to access the symbol below the topmost.

Theorem 8. *Let $k, l \geq 1$ be integers and M be an $REV(k, l)$-DPDA with m states and n stack symbols. Then an equivalent $REV(k, 1)$-DPDA with m states and at most $\frac{n^{l+1}}{n-1} \cdot (n^l + 1)$ stack symbols can effectively be constructed.*

5   Beyond the Degrees

So far, it turned out that lookaheads on the input gradually increase the capability to perform reverse computations. On the other hand, lookaheads on the stack do not. However, the latter are suitable to decrease the descriptional complexity of pushdown automata. The lookahead can be used to obtain machines with significantly fewer states and/or stack symbols.

Now we are interested in the question whether all regular respectively realtime deterministic context-free languages are captured by REV-DFA respectively by REV-DPDA. Or else, whether there are regular (or deterministic context-free) languages that cannot be accepted by any REV-DFA (or REV-DPDA) of any degree. For the important subclass of *finite* languages, the answer to the latter question is *no*.

Proposition 9. *Any finite language is accepted by some $REV(1)$-DFA.*

Proof. For any finite language one can obtain a DFA M whose state graph is a finite tree and, thus, M is reversible of degree 1.   □

For a second important subclass, the unary languages, reversibility is always obtained as well, but the degree for REV-DFA cannot be bounded by any number.

Proposition 10. *For any unary regular language L there is an integer $k \geq 1$ so that L is accepted by some $REV(k)$-DFA.*

Proof. Basically, the state graph of any DFA accepting a unary language consists of an initial tail that leads into a cycle. If both parts are non-empty, the DFA cannot be reversible of degree 1, since the first state of the cycle has two predecessors. However, with an input lookahead whose size is one more than the length of the initial tail the DFA can compute its predecessor state uniquely. □

The necessity to provide arbitrary degrees to accept unary regular languages is not applicable for pushdown automata.

Proposition 11. *Any unary (deterministic) context-free language is accepted by some $REV(1,1)$-DPDA.*

Proof. In [5] it is shown that any unary context-free language is regular. The assertion now follows from a result in [8] that provides a $REV(1,1)$-DPDA for any regular language. Basically, the idea is to store the history of a DFA computation on the pushdown store. Since in this way the predecessor configuration is always unique, the construction applies here as well. □

Finally, we consider the general cases and show that there are languages for which even an arbitrarily large degree cannot help.

Theorem 12. *There are regular languages which cannot be accepted by any $REV(k)$-DFA for any degree $k \geq 1$. There are realtime deterministic context-free languages which cannot be accepted by any $REV(k,l)$-DPDA for any degree (k,l), $k,l \geq 1$.*

Proof. Theorem 4 and Theorem 6 revealed that there are regular languages accepted by $REV(2)$-DFA that cannot be accepted by any $REV(1)$-DFA and that there are context-free languages accepted by $REV(2,1)$-DPDA that cannot be accepted by any $REV(1,l)$-DPDA, $l \geq 1$.

Let $L \subseteq \Sigma^*$ be such a language, respectively, and $\# \notin \Sigma$ be a symbol. Define a regular substitution by $s(a) = a\#^*$, for $a \in \Sigma$. Language $s(L)$ consists of all words from L with an arbitrary number of $\#$ between each two symbols from Σ.

Clearly, $s(L)$ is still accepted by some DFA respectively DPDA. On the other hand, for any $k \geq 1$, language $s(L)$ contains all words from $s(L) \cap (\Sigma \#^k)^*$. So, when accepting such words there is always at most one symbol of Σ in the lookahead. Therefore, if $s(L)$ would be reversible for input lookahead size k, a direct construction would show that it is reversible for input lookahead size 1 as well, a contradiction. □

References

1. Aho, A.V., Ullman, J.D.: The theory of parsing, translation, and compiling. Parsing, vol. I. Prentice-Hall Inc., Englewood Cliffs (1972)
2. Angluin, D.: Inference of reversible languages. J. ACM 29(3), 741–765 (1982)
3. Axelsen, H.B., Glück, R.: A simple and efficient universal reversible Turing machine. In: Dediu, A.-H., Inenaga, S., Martín-Vide, C. (eds.) LATA 2011. LNCS, vol. 6638, pp. 117–128. Springer, Heidelberg (2011)

4. Bennett, C.H.: Logical reversibility of computation. IBM J. Res. Dev. 17, 525–532 (1973)
5. Ginsburg, S., Rice, H.G.: Two families of languages related to ALGOL. J. ACM 9(3), 350–371 (1962)
6. Harrison, M.A.: Introduction to Formal Language Theory. Addison-Wesley, Reading (1978)
7. Kobayashi, S., Yokomori, T.: Learning approximately regular languages with reversible languages. Theoret. Comput. Sci. 174, 251–257 (1997)
8. Kutrib, M., Malcher, A.: Reversible pushdown automata. J. Comput. System Sci. 78, 1814–1827 (2012)
9. Landauer, R.: Irreversibility and heat generation in the computing process. IBM J. Res. Dev. 5, 183–191 (1961)
10. Morita, K., Shirasaki, A., Gono, Y.: A 1-tape 2-symbol reversible Turing machine. Trans. IEICE E72, 223–228 (1989)
11. Pin, J.E.: On reversible automata. In: Simon, I. (ed.) LATIN 1992. LNCS, vol. 583, pp. 401–416. Springer, Heidelberg (1992)

Trace Complexity of Chaotic Reversible Cellular Automata*

Jarkko Kari, Ville Salo, and Ilkka Törmä

TUCS – Turku Centre for Computer Science, Finland
University of Turku, Finland
{jkari,vosalo,iatorm}@utu.fi

Abstract. Delvenne, Kůrka and Blondel have defined new notions of computational complexity for arbitrary symbolic systems, and shown examples of effective systems that are computationally universal in this sense. The notion is defined in terms of the trace function of the system, and aims to capture its dynamics. We present a Devaney-chaotic reversible cellular automaton that is universal in their sense, answering a question that they explicitly left open. We also discuss some implications and limitations of the construction.

Keywords: cellular automaton, reversible, chaos, computational complexity, trace, symbolic system.

1 Introduction

A significant branch of dynamical systems research is the study of computability and computational complexity of finitely presented systems. In the literature, there are usually multiple incomparable notions of computability and computational universality for a sufficiently popular model, like cellular automata [16,18,4]. Traditionally, for a model to be considered computationally universal, it is sufficient for it to be able to simulate the computation process of any Turing machine in a suitably transparent way. However, seemingly minor variations to the formal definition (if one is presented) may reduce a universal system into a trivial one. A related notion is that of *intrinsic* universality, which refers to the ability of simulating any other instance of the same model in some formally defined way. In cellular automata, intrinsic universality is usually defined with respect to block simulations, although in earlier research this notion had usually also been left undefined. See [8] for a discussion on the implications of not defining these notions rigorously. In the context of reversible computation, intrinsic universality of reversible Turing machines has been discussed in [1].

In [5], a new definition of computational universality was proposed that can be applied to a wide range of discrete dynamical systems, including cellular automata, shift spaces, tag systems, and Turing machines, which can be viewed as dynamical systems in more than one way [9]. It is an update of the definition

---

* Research supported by the Academy of Finland Grant 131558.

S. Yamashita and S. Minato (Eds.): RC 2014, LNCS 8507, pp. 54–66, 2014.

given in [6], and aims to capture the dynamical complexity of the system, so that systems that are dynamically too simple (like the identity map on a set) or allow too much freedom (like the shift map) would not be universal.

The computational universality presented in [5] intuitively means the hardness of deciding prediction problems like 'for subsets U, V, W of the state space, is there a point in U that is mapped by the dynamics to V, and stays there until it enters W.' For example, one would show that Turing machines are computationally universal by defining U as the singleton set containing the initial configuration, V as the set of all configurations, and W as the set of final configurations. Of course, for the definition to be sensible, the subsets need to be restricted in some way. In symbolic systems, whose elements are infinite sequences of symbols, we require that the sets are clopen, that is, they are defined by the contents of finitely many coordinates.

One of the main observations in [5] is that universal systems tend to be 'at the edge of chaos': the dynamics appears chaotic, but has underlying structure that gives rise to the universality. They give examples of effective systems that are both universal and chaotic in the sense of Devaney [7], but the existence of a universal chaotic cellular automaton is explicitly left open. In this article, we contruct a reversible universal chaotic cellular automaton, answering this question in the positive. Note that although reversible cellular automata were shown to be able to simulate arbitrary computation already in [11], and their construction seems to be universal in the sense of [5], it is not chaotic.

2   Definitions

Let $\mathbb{M}$ be either $\mathbb{N}$ or $\mathbb{Z}$, and let S be a finite alphabet. The set $S^{\mathbb{M}}$, equipped with the product topology, is called the *full $\mathbb{M}$-shift on S*, and its elements are called *configurations*. The monoid $(\mathbb{M}, +)$ acts on $S^{\mathbb{M}}$ by the *shift maps* $\sigma^m : S^{\mathbb{M}} \to S^{\mathbb{M}}$ for $m \in \mathbb{M}$, defined by $\sigma^m(x)_n = x_{n+m}$. We denote $\sigma^1 = \sigma$. For a word $w \in S^n$ and $x \in S^{\mathbb{M}}$, we say that w *occurs in* x, denoted $w \sqsubset x$, if there exists $m \in \mathbb{M}$ such that $w = x_{[m,m+n-1]}$. This notation is extended to sets of configurations in the obvious way. An $\mathbb{M}$-*shift space* is a topologically closed set $X \subset S^{\mathbb{M}}$ satisfying $\sigma(X) \subset X$. Equivalently, a shift space is defined by a set $F \subset S^*$ of *forbidden words* as $\mathcal{X}_F = \{x \in S^{\mathbb{M}} \mid \forall w \in F : w \not\sqsubset x\}$. If F is finite, $\mathcal{X}_F$ is a *shift of finite type* (SFT for short). We denote $\mathcal{B}_n(X) = \{w \in S^n \mid w \sqsubset X\}$ and $\mathcal{B}(X) = \bigcup_{n \in \mathbb{N}} \mathcal{B}_n(X)$.

A *block map* is a continuous function $f : X \to Y$ between shift spaces $X, Y \subset S^{\mathbb{M}}$ that satisfies $f \circ \sigma|_X = \sigma|_Y \circ f$. Alternatively, a block map is defined by a *local rule* $\hat{f} : \mathcal{B}_{a+m+1}(X) \to \mathcal{B}_1(Y)$, where $a, m \in \mathbb{N}$ are the *anticipation* and *memory* of $\hat{f}$, by $f(x)_n = \hat{f}(x_{[n-m,n+a]})$. The interval $\{-m, \dots, a\} \subset \mathbb{M}$ is called the *neighborhood* of $\hat{f}$. In the case $\mathbb{M} = \mathbb{N}$, we must have $m = 0$. If $X = Y = S^{\mathbb{M}}$, then f is called a *cellular automaton* (CA for short), and a bijective CA is called *reversible*, since its inverse function is also a CA. We sometimes identify a CA and its local rule, but this should always be clear from the context.

A *symbolic system* is a tuple (X, f), where X is a compact metric space with countable clopen basis (equivalently, homeomorphic to a closed subset of a full shift), and $f : X \to X$ is continuous. The system is *effective* if the clopen basis of X can be enumerated so that complementation, intersection and f-preimage are computable operations. It is *chaotic* (in the sense of Devaney [7]) if

- it is sensitive (there exists $\epsilon > 0$ such that for all $x \in X$ and $\delta > 0$ there exist $y \in X$ and $n \in \mathbb{N}$ with $d(x, y) < \delta$ and $d(f^n(x), f^n(y)) \geq \epsilon$),
- it is transitive (for all nonempty open sets $U, V \subset X$, there exists $n \in \mathbb{N}$ with $U \cap f^n(V) \neq \emptyset$), and
- the f-periodic points (those $x \in X$ for which $f^n(x) = x$ for some $n \in \mathbb{N}$) are dense in X.

In particular, every $\mathbb{Z}$-shift space (X, σ) with the left shift is a symbolic system, as is (X, f) for every block map $f : X \to X$. These are the only kinds of symbolic systems we use in this article; the full definition is given only for completeness, and to state the definitions of universality given in [5].

Example 1. For a cellular automaton $f : S^{\mathbb{Z}} \to S^{\mathbb{Z}}$, most dynamical notions have combinatorial characterizations. For example, f is transitive if and only if for all words $u, v \in S^{2\ell+1}$ of the same odd length, there exists a configuration $x \in S^{\mathbb{Z}}$ and $n \in \mathbb{N}$ such that $x_{[-\ell,\ell]} = u$ and $f^n(x)_{[-\ell,\ell]} = v$.

A *Muller automaton* is a quintuple $A = (Q, q_0, \Sigma, \delta, F)$, where Q is a finite *state set*, $q_0 \in Q$ an *initial state*, Σ a finite *input alphabet*, $\delta : Q \times \Sigma \to Q$ a *transition function* and $F \subset 2^Q$ a set of *accepting subsets of states*. A Muller automaton runs deterministically on infinite words $w \in \Sigma^{\mathbb{N}}$ analogously to a standard finite automaton, and accepts if the set of states that are visited infinitely often during the computation is in the set F. The language accepted by A is denoted L_A. For a language $L \subset A^*$, we denote by $L^\omega \subset A^{\mathbb{N}}$ the set of infinite concatenations of the words of L. In particular, if L is regular, then L^ω is accepted by a Muller automaton. See [17] for a reference on Muller automata, and other types of finite automata on infinite words.

In this article, a *Turing machine* is a sextuple $M = (Q, \Sigma, q_0, q_f, B, \delta)$, where Q is a finite *state set*, Σ a finite *input alphabet*, $q_0, q_f \in Q$ are the *initial and final states*, $B \in \Sigma$ is the *blank letter* and $\delta \subset Q \times (\Sigma \times \Sigma \cup \{/\} \times \{+, 0, -\}) \times Q$ a *transition relation*. Turing machines are run on two-way infinite tapes, and the initial input is placed immediately to the right of the head. The interpretation of a quadruple $[q_1, a, b, q_2] \in \delta$ in the case $a, b \in \Sigma$ is that if M is in state q_1 and reading the letter a, it may rewrite it to b and go to state q_2. In the case $a = /$ and $b \in \{+, 0, -\}$, if M is in state q_1, it may go to state q_2 and move one step in the direction indicated by b. Two quadruples $[q_1, a, b, q_2]$ and $[q'_1, a', b', q'_2]$ *overlap in domain* if $q_1 = q'_1$ and $a, a' \in \Sigma \implies a = a'$. They *overlap in range* if $q_2 = q'_2$ and $a, a' \in \Sigma \implies b = b'$. If no distinct quadruples overlap in domain (range), then M is *deterministic (reversible, respectively)*. As usual, the language of a Turing machine is the set of input words on which is eventually halts.

We use the following terminology for certain classes in the arithmetical and analytical hierarchies. A set $N \subset \mathbb{N}$ is called Σ_1^0 if it is recursively enumerable, and Π_1^0 if its complement is. The set is called Σ_1^1, if there exists an oracle Turing machine M such that

$$N = \{n \in \mathbb{N} \mid \exists f : \mathbb{N} \to \mathbb{N} : M \text{ never halts on input } n \text{ with oracle } f\}.$$

These are not the standard definitions of the classes, but characterizations whose proofs can be found, for example, in [15, Theorem 1.3]. Hardness and completeness of a set with respect to these classes is defined using Turing reductions. When classifying subsets of other countable sets than $\mathbb{N}$, for example $\{0,1\}^*$, we assume that they are in some natural and computable bijection with $\mathbb{N}$.

In [12], it was proved that deterministic reversible Turing machines are capable of simulating any deterministic Turing machine (first proved in [2] for *multi-tape* Turing machines). We will not go into the details of the notion of simulation, but it is easy to see that it implies the following lemmas.

Lemma 1. *There exists a deterministic reversible Turing Machine M whose language is Σ_1^0-complete.*

Lemma 2. *There exists a deterministic reversible Turing Machine M, whose tape alphabet contains 0, 1 and $\#$, such that the set*

$$L = \{w \in \{0,1\}^* \mid \exists u \in (0^*1)^\omega : M \text{ never halts on } w\#u\}$$

is Σ_1^1-complete, and the head never steps left of the origin on right-infinite inputs.

3   Traces and Computational Universality

In this section, we recall the definition of computational universality for an effective symbolic system (X, f), as given in [5]. First, a *clopen partition* of X is a finite collection $\mathcal{C} = (C_s)_{s \in \Sigma}$ of mutually disjoint clopen subsets of X such that $X = \bigcup_{s \in \Sigma} C_s$, labeled by a finite set Σ. The partition can be seen as an observation or experiment, with input $x \in X$ resulting in the unique label $\pi_{\mathcal{C}}(x) = s_0 \in \Sigma$ such that $x \in C_{s_0}$. More information can be extracted from x if we apply the dynamics function f to it and repeat the experiment, obtaining the result $\pi_{\mathcal{C}}(f(x)) \in \Sigma$. Iterating the idea leads to the following definition.

Definition 1. *Let (X, f) be a symbolic system, and let $\mathcal{C} = (C_s)_{s \in \Sigma}$ be a clopen partition of X. For $x \in X$, the f-itinerary of x via $\mathcal{C}$ is the infinite sequence $\pi_{\mathcal{C}}^f(x) \in \Sigma^{\mathbb{N}}$ defined by $\pi_{\mathcal{C}}^f(x)_n = \pi_{\mathcal{C}}(f^n(x))$ for all $n \in \mathbb{N}$. The $\mathcal{C}$-trace shift of f is the $\mathbb{N}$-shift space $\tau_{f,\mathcal{C}} = \{\pi_{\mathcal{C}}^f(x) \mid x \in X\}$. In the case $X \subset S^{\mathbb{Z}}$, we denote by $\tau_{f,n}$ the trace with respect to the partition $\mathcal{C}_n = (C_w)_{w \in S^{2n+1}}$, where $C_w = \{x \in X \mid x_{[-n,n]} = w\}$ for all $w \in S^{2n+1}$.*

Example 2. Let $f : S^{\mathbb{Z}} \to S^{\mathbb{Z}}$ be a cellular automaton, and let $n \in \mathbb{N}$. Then the trace shift $\tau_{f,n}$ is obtained by taking, for each $x \in S^{\mathbb{Z}}$, the sequence

$$x_{[-n,n]}, f(x)_{[-n,n]}, f^2(x)_{[-n,n]}, f^3(x)_{[-n,n]}, \cdots$$

of the central words occurring in the evolution of the initial state x under f.

The article [5] defines the following two decision problems.

Definition 2. *Let* (X, f) *be an effective symbolic system. The* infinite time prediction problem *asks whether we have* $\tau_{f,\mathcal{C}} \cap L_A \neq \emptyset$ *for a given partition* $\mathcal{C} = (C_s)_{s \in \Sigma}$ *and Muller automaton* A *on the alphabet* Σ. *The* finite time prediction problem *asks whether we have* $\mathcal{B}(\tau_{f,\mathcal{C}}) \cap L \neq \emptyset$ *for a given partition* $\mathcal{C} = (C_s)_{s \in \Sigma}$ *and regular language* $L \subset \Sigma^*$. *We say that* (X, f) *is* computationally universal *if its finite time prediction problem is* Σ_1^0-*complete.*

As hinted in Section 1, the most obvious way of showing that an effective symbolic system (X, f) is computationally universal in the above sense is to construct a simulation of a Turing machine M (or some other universal computational device) by f, and identify three disjoint clopen sets $C_0, C_1, C_2 \subset X$ that correspond to the classes of initial, intermediate, and halting configurations of M. Then the instance 01^*2 of the finite time prediction problem is positive if and only if M halts on one of the the the initial configurations in C_0.

Example 3. We continue Example 2. In the finite time prediction problem for $(S^{\mathbb{Z}}, f)$, we are given a clopen partition of $S^{\mathbb{Z}}$, which we (for now) assume to be $\mathcal{C}_n$ for some $n \in \mathbb{N}$, and a regular language L over the alphabet S^{2n+1}. For example, if $S = \{0, 1\}$ and $n = 1$, then L may be given as the regular expression $([000][010])^*[111] + [100]^*[111]$ (note that the 'letters' of this regular expression are binary words of length 3). If there exists $x \in \{0, 1\}^{\mathbb{Z}}$ such that, for example, $x_{[-1,1]} = 000$, $f(x)_{[-1,1]} = 010$ and $f^2(x)_{[-1,1]} = 111$, then the answer to the finite time prediction problem with these inputs is 'yes', since the language of the $\mathcal{C}_1$-trace shift of f contains the word $[000][010][111] \in L$.

Examples of chaotic universal effective symbolic systems and universal cellular automata were provided in [5], but it was explicitly left open whether a universal cellular automaton can be chaotic.

The notion of universality given in the earlier work [6] is also equivalent to the Σ_1^0-completeness of a prediction problem, but instead of Muller automata, the definition uses a temporal logic that specifies subsets of the state space. We will not digress into this subject, as it is not necessary for stating and proving the main results of this article.

4   Main Results

In this section, we prove that a chaotic reversible cellular automaton can be computationally universal and even have a maximally hard infinite time prediction problem. In the proof, we use the following well-known lemma, found explicitly in [10].

Lemma 3. *A reversible cellular automaton is chaotic (in the sense of Devaney) if and only if it is transitive.*

We are now ready to state and prove our main theorem.

Theorem 1. *There exists a chaotic reversible cellular automaton whose finite-time prediction problem is Σ_1^0-complete, even when restricted to the radius-one partition $\mathcal{C}_1$. In particular, the automaton is computationally universal in the sense of Definition 2.*

Proof. We first describe the general idea of the construction. The configurations of the reversible CA we construct are divided into 'compartments', each of which may contain one read-write head of a reversible Turing machine. The automaton simulates the Turing machines separately in each compartment, changing the direction of the simulation if they halt, and no information can be passed between the compartments. The compartments and the machines are also constantly shifted to the left. When one of the machines halts, it sends a signal to the right.

Now, in the trace shift we wish to see the following pattern: the left wall of a compartment, then some empty space, then the Turing machine head in its initial state followed by an input word, then another empty stretch, and finally the right-moving signal emitted by the halting machine. If we see such a pattern, the machine must have halted, since the signal cannot have come from the other side of the wall, and it cannot be the result of a left-moving signal bouncing off the wall, for no such signal was seen earlier. Finally, the transitivity of the CA follows from the constant shifting of the compartments and the fact that they never communicate, so that every central pattern of a configuration can eventually be replaced by arbitrary data.

Let $M = (\Sigma, Q, \delta, B, q_0, q_f)$ be the reversible Turing Machine of Lemma 1. We may assume that the head of M makes a move only on every third step, that it does not make a move in state q_0 for two steps when run backwards or forwards, that it always takes at least $2|w| + 2$ steps for M to halt on an input word w, and that it always halts after an even number of steps or runs forever. Denote $S = \Sigma \times (Q \cup \tilde{Q} \cup \{\leftarrow, \rightarrow\})$, where $\tilde{Q} = \{\tilde{q} \mid q \in Q\}$ is a disjoint copy of Q, and define a reversible cellular automaton f_M on $S^{\mathbb{Z}}$ as follows.

We partition each configuration $x \in S^{\mathbb{Z}}$ into segments whose second track is of the form $\leftarrow^m q \rightarrow^n$, where $q \in Q \cup \tilde{Q}$, or $\leftarrow^{m+1} \rightarrow^{n+1}$, for some (possibly infinite) $m, n \geq 0$. Namely, each cell of x is contained in at least one pattern of this form, and when we take the maximal ones, the partition is uniquely determined. On these segments, f_M simulates a computation of M (backwards in time if $q \in \tilde{Q}$) in a standard way. Namely, consider a cell in state $(a, q) \in \Sigma \times Q$. If $[q, a, b, r] \in \delta$ for some $b \in \Sigma$ and $r \in Q$, the cell will update to (b, r). Each two-cell pattern $(a, q)(b, \rightarrow)$ such that $[q, /, +, r] \in \delta$ for some $b \in \Sigma$ will update to $(a, \leftarrow)(b, r)$, and analogously for a 0- or $-$-move. In all other cases (no applicable quadruple exists, or the segment ends), the cell becomes $(a, \tilde{q})$. To such cells, the quadruples and the time-reversal rule are applied in the reverse direction: $[r, b, a, q] \in \delta$ results in $(b, \tilde{r})$ and so on. All cells not mentioned here retain their state. Thus the first track acts as the tape, the endpoints of the segments never move, and if the simulation cannot be carried on then it changes direction. For $x \in S^{\mathbb{Z}}$, denote by $r(x) \in S^{\mathbb{Z}}$ the configuration obtained from x by changing every $q \in Q$ to $\tilde{q}$, and vice versa; it is easy to see that $r \circ f_M \circ r = f_M^{-1}$, which implies that f_M is reversible. See Figure 1 for a visualization of the dynamics of f_M.

Now, let $D = \{\square, \boxtimes, \boxslash, \boxtimes\}$, and denote $R = S \times D$. The cells in D represent particles traveling to the left or to the right, with the fourth one containing one of each. We define a CA g on $R^{\mathbb{Z}}$ that functions as follows:

1. Apply f_M to the first track.
2. Shift each particle to its direction, unless it would cross the barrier between two segments, in which case change its direction.
3. If a cell contains the final state of M in its first track, apply the bijection $\square \leftrightarrow \boxslash, \boxtimes \leftrightarrow \boxtimes$ to the second track.

See Figure 2 for a visualization. Since each of the three steps is clearly reversible, so is g. Finally, define $h = \sigma \circ g^2$, which is likewise reversible, and denote by $\pi_S : R \to S$ and $\pi_D : R \to D$ the obvious projections from R.

Now, let $w \in \Sigma^*$ be arbitrary, and denote by $L(w) \subset R^*$ the regular language

$$(B, \to, \square)(B, \leftarrow, \square)^*(B, q_0, \square)(w \times (\to, \square)^{|w|})(B, \to, \square)^*(B, \to, \boxslash) \quad (1)$$

The words of the language $L(w)$ consist of the left border of a segment, then some 'empty' cells, followed by the initial state of M and its input word, then more empty cells, and finally a right-moving particle. Let $U(w) \subset (R^3)^{\mathbb{N}}$ be the open set of all configurations that have a prefix $v \in (R^3)^*$ such that the middle components of the triples in v form a word in $L(w)$, and none of the letters of v contain a left-moving particle. We claim that $\tau_{h,1} \cap U(w)$ is nonempty if and only if M halts on w, which is Σ_1^0-complete.

First, assume that M halts on w after exactly $2n + 2$ steps, where $n \geq |w|$, and define $x \in R^{\mathbb{Z}}$ by

$$x_i = \begin{cases} (B, \to, \square), & \text{if } i \leq -n, \\ (B, \leftarrow, \square), & \text{if } -n < i < 0, \\ (B, q_0, \square), & \text{if } i = 0, \\ (w_{i-1}, \to, \square), & \text{if } 1 \leq i \leq |w|, \\ (B, \to, \square), & \text{if } i > |w|. \end{cases}$$

Denote $y = h^{-n}(x)$. We claim that $(h^i(y)_{[-1,1]})_{i \in \mathbb{N}} \in U(w)$. To prove that, we first remark that for all $k, \ell \in \mathbb{Z}$ such that $3|\ell| \geq |k|$ we have $\pi_S(g^k(x)_\ell) = \pi_S(x_\ell)$, since only the single Turing Machine head can introduce changes to the S-component of the configuration, and it only moves every third step by assumption. This means that for all $i \in \mathbb{Z}$ we have $\pi_S(h^i(y)_0) = \pi_S(x_{i-n})$.

Since M does not halt in $2n$ steps, the second track of every configuration in $\{h^i(y) \mid i \in \{0, \ldots, 2n\}\}$ contains no particles. But since M halts at step $2n + 2$, there exists $k \in \mathbb{Z}$ with $|k| \leq \frac{n}{3}$ such that $\pi_D(h^{2n+1}(y)_{k-n-1}) = \pi_D(g^{2n+2}(x)_k) = \boxslash$. Since the single Turing Machine head will not enter the final state for another $4n + 4$ steps, we have $\pi_D(h^i(y)_0) = \square$ for every $i \in \{2n + 1, \ldots, 3n - k + 1\}$, and $\pi_D(h^{3n-k+2}(y)_0) = \boxslash$. Furthermore, no letter in $(h^i(y)_{[-1,1]})_{i \in \mathbb{N}}$ contains a left-moving particle, and together with the previous paragraph, this shows that $(h^i(y)_{[-1,1]})_{i \in \mathbb{N}} \in U(w)$, and thus $\tau_{h,1} \cap U(w) \neq \emptyset$. See Figure 3 for a visualization that will also be helpful in the converse direction.

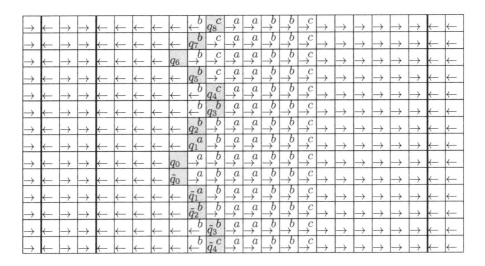

Fig. 1. A spacetime diagram of the reversible cellular automaton f_M simulating the reversible Turing machine M. Each row is (the central pattern of) a configuration of $S^{\mathbb{Z}}$, and time increases upwards. The shaded cells contain a Turing machine head, and the thick vertical lines mark the borders of segments. The initial state of M is q_0, which is preceded in the simulation by the 'backward' state $\tilde{q}_0$, and a, b, c are elements of the tape alphabet. To save space, M does not move only every third step in this figure.

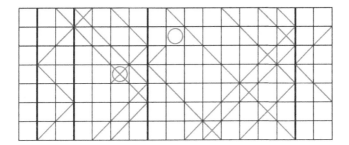

Fig. 2. A spacetime diagram of g, showing the dynamics of the particles. The thick lines mark the borders of segments, and the circles denote the final state of M. Other information from the first track is not shown. The particles are drawn in gray for clarity.

Second, assume that $y \in R^{\mathbb{Z}}$ is such that $(h^i(y))_{i \in \mathbb{N}} \in U(w)$, with the $*$-symbols in the definition of $L(w)$ being replaced by numbers $n-1, m-|w|-1 \in \mathbb{N}$, so that we have $h^n(y)_0 = (B, q_0, \square)$ and $h^{n+m}(y)_0 = (B, \rightarrow, \boxtimes)$. Let $x = h^n(y)$. Since the segments used in the simulation of M never move under the action of g, the interval $I = [-n, m]$ is contained in a single segment of y, and contains its left endpoint. The segment contains a Turing Machine head, and as above,

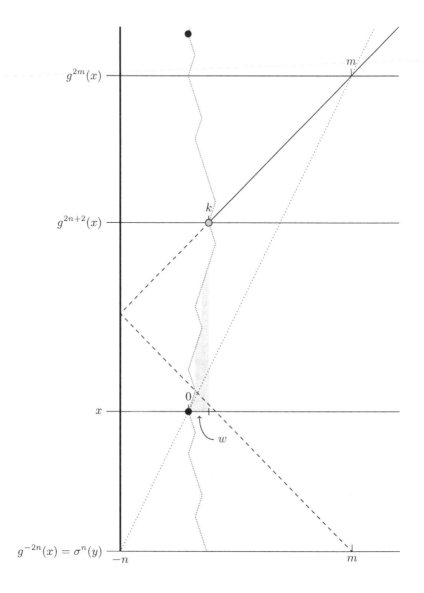

Fig. 3. A schematic spacetime diagram of g. The black (gray) circles represent the initial (final) states of M (at coordinates 0 and k, respectively), and the densely dotted line traces the read-write head of M as it carries out its computation. The sparsely dotted line corresponds to the central coordinates of the configurations $h^{i-n}(x)$ for $i \in \mathbb{N}$. The thick vertical line is a border of segments, the diagonal line is a particle, and the dashed continuation is its hypothetical path assuming that M never halted. The particle meets the sparsely dotted line at coordinate m. Each horizontal line represents a configuration. The shaded area represents the letters of the input word $w \in \Sigma^*$ in x that the head of M has not yet read (which the sparsely dotted line goes through).

for all $k, \ell \in \mathbb{Z}$ such that $3|\ell| \geq 2|k|$, we have $\pi_S(h^{k+n}(y)_{\ell-k}) = \pi_S(g^{2k}(x)_\ell) = \pi_S(x_\ell)$. In particular, the word $\pi_S(x_I)$ contains a Turing Machine head in state q_0 followed by the input word w, surrounded by the blank symbols.

Consider now the two remaining tracks of x and y. We know from the above that $g^{2m+2n}(y)_{m+n} = h^{m+n}(y)_0 = (B, \rightarrow, \boxtimes)$ (the intersection of the particle and the densely dotted line in Figure 3). This implies that either the coordinate $g^{2m+2n-i}(y)_{m+n-i}$ contains the final state of M for some $i \in \{0, \ldots, m+n\}$, or each of them contains a right-moving particle. In the latter case, $g^{m+n-1}(y)_0$ contains a left-moving particle, since it is next to a segment border, and so does $g^{m+n-1-j}(y)_j$ for all $j \in \{0, \ldots, m+n\}$ (see the dashed line in the figure). Now, at $j = 0$ we have $m + n - 1 - j > 2j$, while at $j = m + n$, the opposite holds. Thus we have $|(m+n-1-j_0)/2 - j_0| \leq 1$ for some j_0 such that $m + n - 1 - j_0$ is even; denote $m + n - 1 - j_0 = 2\ell$. Then $0 \leq \ell < m + n$, and the cell

$$h^\ell(y)_b = g^{2\ell}(y)_{\ell+b} = g^{m+n-1-j_0}(y)_{j_0}$$

contains a left-moving particle for some $b \in \{-1, 0, 1\}$ (the intersection of the dashed line with the densely dotted line in the figure). But this is impossible since $(h^i(y))_{i \in \mathbb{N}} \in U(w)$, so the choice that none of the cells $g^{2m+2n-i}(y)_{m+n-i} = g^{2m-i}(x)_{m-i}$ contain the final state of M was incorrect. Thus one of them does, implying that M eventually halts, since the initial and final states lie in the same segment (at different times). This finishes the proof of $\tau_{h,1} \cap U(w) \neq \emptyset$ being equivalent to M halting on w.

Finally, we show that h is chaotic, and by Lemma 3, it suffices to prove transitivity. The proof is standard for reversible CA that have 'shifting barriers', in our case borders of segments. Let thus $u, v \in R^n$ be two words of the same length n. Define $w = (B, \leftarrow, \square)(B, \rightarrow, \square)$. Then for all $x, y \in R^\mathbb{Z}$ with $x_{[0,1]} = y_{[0,1]} = x_{[n+2,n+3]} = y_{[n+2,n+3]} = w$ and $x_{[2,n+1]} = y_{[2,n+1]}$, we have $g^i(x)_{[2,n+1]} = g^i(y)_{[2,n+1]}$ for all $i \in \mathbb{Z}$. This is because the evolution of a segment under g is independent of other segments.

Now, let $x \in R^\mathbb{Z}$ be such that $x_{[0,n+3]} = wuw$, and let $y \in R^\mathbb{Z}$ be defined by

$$y_i = \begin{cases} (wvw)_i, & \text{if } i \in [0, n+3], \\ h^{n+4}(x)_i, & \text{otherwise}. \end{cases}$$

By applying the above argument to y, which satisfies $y_{[n+4,n+5]} = y_{[2n+6,2n+7]} = w$, we have that $h^{-n-4}(y)_{[2,n+1]} = u$, and by definition $y_{[2,n+1]} = v$. This shows that h is transitive, and thus chaotic. See Figure 4 for a visualization of this argument. □

The regular expression (1) used in this construction is *local* in the sense that it can be recognized by a DFA whose state only depends on the n symbols it last read. This also applies to the regular language used in the definition of $U(w)$, where the small extra condition of not having left-moving particles in the neighboring coordinates was added.

The reversible cellular automaton we constructed above also has a maximally hard infinite time prediction problem, provided that we choose the machine M correctly.

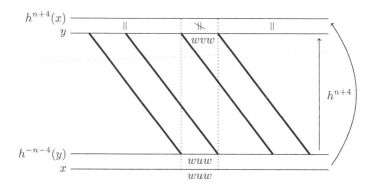

Fig. 4. A schematic spacetime diagram of h. The vertical lines represent configurations, and each thick line is a border of segments. The dotted lines mark the interval $[0, n+3]$.

Theorem 2. *There exists a chaotic reversible cellular automaton whose infinite-time prediction problem is Σ_1^1-complete, even when restricted to the radius-one partition $\mathcal{C}_1$.*

5   Further Discussion

The automaton h constructed in Theorem 1 and Theorem 2 is chaotic, but it is not *expansive*. A reversible cellular automaton $h : S^{\mathbb{Z}} \to S^{\mathbb{Z}}$ is expansive, if there exists $r \in \mathbb{N}$ such that for all distinct pairs $x \neq y \in S^{\mathbb{Z}}$, there exists $k \in \mathbb{Z}$ with $h^k(x)_{[-r,r]} \neq h^k(y)_{[-r,r]}$. Intuitively, this means that all discrepancies between two configurations are propagated to the left and to the right, if we consider both their past and future itineraries. Expansivity can thus be seen as an extreme form of sensitivity to initial conditions, and it makes sense to ask whether an expansive CA can be computationally universal.

Unfortunately, the trace shifts of expansive cellular automata are a deep and mysterious subject, and not much is known about them. In [3], it was shown that if h is an expansive CA, then all of its wide enough traces ($\tau_{h,n}$ for large enough $n \in \mathbb{N}$) have a property called *total chain transitivity*, which makes it difficult to find much structure in them. Also, in [14], it was shown that if h has memory or anticipation 0, then all wide enough traces are actually SFTs. It is currently unknown whether this holds for all expansive CA (as conjectured in [13]), but it would directly imply that their prediction problems are decidable, at least for a fixed clopen partition.

Acknowledgments. The authors are thankful to the anonymous referees for their valuable comments that helped to improve the quality and readability of this article.

References

1. Axelsen, H.B., Glück, R.: What do reversible programs compute? In: Hofmann, M. (ed.) FOSSACS 2011. LNCS, vol. 6604, pp. 42–56. Springer, Heidelberg (2011)
2. Bennett, C.H.: Logical reversibility of computation. IBM J. Res. Develop. 17, 525–532 (1973)
3. Boyle, M.: Some sofic shifts cannot commute with nonwandering shifts of finite type. Illinois J. Math. 48(4), 1267–1277 (2004)
4. Cook, M.: Universality in elementary cellular automata. Complex Systems 15(1), 1–40 (2004)
5. Delvenne, J.-C., Kůrka, P., Blondel, V.: Decidability and universality in symbolic dynamical systems. Fund. Inform. 74(4), 463–490 (2006)
6. Delvenne, J.-C., Kůrka, P., Blondel, V.D.: Computational universality in symbolic dynamical systems. In: Margenstern, M. (ed.) MCU 2004. LNCS, vol. 3354, pp. 104–115. Springer, Heidelberg (2005)
7. Devaney, R.L.: An introduction to chaotic dynamical systems, 2nd edn. Addison-Wesley Studies in Nonlinearity. Addison-Wesley Publishing Company Advanced Book Program, Redwood City (1989)
8. Durand, B., Róka, Z.: The game of life: universality revisited. In: Cellular automata (Saissac 1996). Math. Appl., vol. 460, pp. 51–74. Kluwer Acad. Publ., Dordrecht (1999)
9. Kůrka, P.: On topological dynamics of Turing machines. Theoret. Comput. Sci. 174(1-2), 203–216 (1997)
10. Lukkarila, V.: Sensitivity and topological mixing are undecidable for reversible one-dimensional cellular automata. Technical Report 927, TUCS (2009)
11. Morita, K., Harao, M.: Computation universality of one-dimensional reversible (injective) cellular automata. The Transactions of The IEICE E72-E(6), 758–762 (1989)
12. Morita, K., Shirasaki, A., Gono, Y.: A 1-tape 2-symbol reversible turing machine. The Transactions of the IEICE E72, 223–228 (1989)
13. Nasu, M.: Textile systems for endomorphisms and automorphisms of the shift. Mem. Amer. Math. Soc. 114(546), viii+215 (1995)
14. Nasu, M.: Textile systems and one-sided resolving automorphisms and endomorphisms of the shift. Ergodic Theory and Dynamical Systems 28, 167–209 (2008)
15. Sacks, G.E.: Higher recursion theory. Perspectives in mathematical logic. Springer (1990)
16. Smith III, A.R.: Simple computation-universal cellular spaces. J. Assoc. Comput. Mach. 18, 339–353 (1971)
17. Thomas, W.: Automata on infinite objects. In: Handbook of Theoretical Computer Science, vol. B, pp. 133–191. Elsevier, Amsterdam (1990)
18. Wolfram, S.: Universality and complexity in cellular automata. Phys. D 10(1-2), 1–35 (1983); Cellular automata (Los Alamos, N.M., 1983)

Appendix

Proof of Theorem 2:

Proof. The CA $h : R^{\mathbb{Z}} \to R^{\mathbb{Z}}$ and the proof idea are exactly the same as in Theorem 1, but the machine M now needs to satisfy the claim of Lemma 2.

Now, let $w \in \{0,1\}^*$, and define the Muller-recognizable language $L(w) \subset R^{\mathbb{N}}$ by the infinite regular expression

$$(B, \to, \square)(B, q_0, \square)(w \times (\to, \square)^{|w|})(\#, \to, \square)((0, \to, \square)^*(1, \to, \square))^{\omega} \quad (2)$$

It is similar to (1), except that the head of M is situated right next to the end of the segment, and after the input word w we may have an infinite tail of 0s and 1s, but no particles at all. As before, let $U(w) \subset (R^3)^{\mathbb{N}}$ be the set of configurations whose middle letters form a configuration in $L(w)$, and none of the letters of which contains a left-moving particle.

With a proof mimicking that of Theorem 1, we can now show that $\tau_{f,1} \cap U(w) \neq \emptyset$ if and only if there exists $u \in \{0,1\}^{\mathbb{N}}$ such that M never halts on $w\#u$, and this is Σ_1^1-complete by the choice of M. Namely, if M never halts, then the preimage of a configuration $x \in R^{\mathbb{Z}}$ containing the initial configuration of M with input $w\#u$ for some $u \in (0^*1)^{\omega}$ has its trace in $U(w)$ since no particles are ever introduced. Conversely, if such a configuration exists, then it necessarily simulates a non-halting computation of M, since a particle must be either created or destroyed at the time of halting, both of which are impossible. Furthermore, h is chaotic by the same argument as before.   □

Arbitration and Reversibility of Parallel Delay-Insensitive Modules

Daniel Morrison and Irek Ulidowski

Department of Computer Science, University of Leicester, England

Abstract. We analyse the external behaviour of parallel delay-insensitive modules in order to formalise the notions of arbitration and reversibility, and investigate universality of classes of such modules. A new notation for parallel modules is developed, where inputs can be sets of signals, which is used to define arbitration and module inversion. We show that arbitrating modules are more expressive than non-arbitrating modules, and propose universal sets for two classes of non-arbitrating modules. We demonstrate previously unrealised constructions of $M{\times}N\,Join$ and $M{\times}N\,Fork$ in terms of purely reversible and non-arbitrating modules.

1 Introduction

Delay-insensitive (DI) circuits are a category of asynchronous circuits which make no assumption about delays within modules and lines (wires) connecting the modules, and have no global clock. They were introduced by Keller ([2]) who characterised the conditions required for correct DI operation and gave various universal sets of modules. Much subsequent work by Patra and Fussell ([12,11]) went into finding more efficient universal sets of modules, where efficiency is measured as low *modularity* (the maximum number of input-output lines for modules in a set) and low *cardinality* (the number of modules in a set). Constructions by Keller and by Patra and Fussell of arbitrary *parallel* modules (where multiple signals can be input or output) made no clear distinction between those modules which utilised high-level *arbitrating* behaviour and those which did not. As a result, all current constructions of parallel modules, whether they are arbitrating or not, utilise arbitrating modules.

Reversible modules were originally studied by Fredkin and Toffoli ([1]) who proposed a number of synchronous universal logic gates. More recently, Morita, Lee, Peper and Adachi carried out research into finding efficient universal sets of reversible *serial* modules with memory (where only one signal travels around a circuit), such as *Rotary Element* (*RE*) ([6]), and *Reading Toggle* (*RT*) and *Inverse Reading Toggle* (*IRT*) ([3]). The set of all possible 2-state modules with two, three and four pairs of input/output lines was enumerated in [8]. How these various concepts relate to each other, as well as to cellular automata, was discussed by Morita in [5]. However, a comparatively small amount of research has been carried out into reversible parallel modules.

The behaviour of parallel modules is defined in a *sequential machine* style ([2]) by specifying how sequences of inputs produce sequences of sets of outputs.

S. Yamashita and S. Minato (Eds.): RC 2014, LNCS 8507, pp. 67–81, 2014.

In order to allow concurrent inputs and, at the same time, use the sequential machine style of defining the behaviour of modules, Keller introduced an informal notion of arbitration (see conditions N3 and N6 in Section 2). It says that if two input signals arrive simultaneously or close to each other in time, the behaviour of the module is such as if one signal and then the other arrived (even though the real order of arrival was opposite). We investigate arbitration further and propose several conditions that define its properties precisely.

In order to enable us to define inverses of parallel DI modules we develop a new notation where inputs as well as outputs can be sets of signals. We give an algorithm for converting traditional sequential machine definitions of parallel modules to the new so-called *set notation*, and use this notation to define "high-level" *arbitration* (a form of non-determinism) and inverses of parallel modules. We show how reversibility combined with parallelism presents a new type of *backwards-arbitration*. Our main results are several universal sets for parallel modules which satisfy various properties relating to arbitration, backwards-arbitration and reversibility. In particular, we give for the first time a general construction of $M{\times}N\,Join$ using only reversible and non-arbitrating modules.

2   Asynchronous Delay-Insensitive Modules

We begin by formally defining a DI module.

Definition 1. *A module is defined by the 6-tuple* (Q, I, O, f, g, A) *where 1) Q is a finite set of states, 2) I is a set of input lines, 3) O is a set of output lines, 4) $f : Q \times I \to Q$ is a partial function, the state-transition function, 5) $g : Q \times I \to \mathcal{P}(O)$ is a partial function, the output function, 6) $A : Q \to \mathcal{P}(\mathcal{P}(I))$.*

The initial state of a module is understood implicitly. The set $A(q)$ represents the maximal sets of inputs which may be signalled concurrently in state q. Hence for each $L \in A(q)$, any subset of L may be signalled concurrently.

We note that this differs from Keller's original definitions given in [2], where a distinction is made between a module and an internal *sequential machine* of a module. The definition we give above is a simplification but this does not make a difference in practice.

We introduce some useful notation. Symbols $q, q', q''...$ range over states, and $a, b, c...$ and $B, C, D...$ range over input/output lines and sets of such lines respectively. Given a module M, assume that $f(q, a)$ is defined iff $g(q, a)$ is defined for all q, a. As in [10], we use CCS-like notation ([13], [14]) to succinctly define a module. If $f(q, a)$ and $g(q, a)$ are defined, then $(a, g(q, a)).f(q, a)$ is called an *action* of q, where $(a, g(q, a))$ is an input/output pair and $f(q, a)$ is the resulting state. We specify all actions of q by writing $q = (a_1, B_1).q_1' + \cdots + (a_n, B_n).q_n'$ where $B_x = g(q, a_x)$, $q_x' = f(q, a_x)$ and $f(q, a_x)$ and $g(q, a_x)$ are defined for all $1 \le x \le n$. Then the definition of a module M is given by a set of such equations, one for each state of M, together with a definition of the function A. We say that an action $(a, B).q$ is an *empty output* if $B = \emptyset$. We require that for any q, q': if $f(q, a) = f(q', a)$ and $g(q, a) = g(q', a)$ for all a, then $q = q'$ (no two different states have the same definitions). We also require $a \in L \in A(q)$ iff $(a, B).f(q, a)$ is an action of q for some B. Sometimes we write $(a, B).q' \in q$ to mean $(a, B).q'$ is an action of q.

We outline the operating conditions of modules and networks after Keller [2]:

N1) "I and O are disjoint";

N2) "A module, once having created a signal on a line, cannot "withdraw" the signal before it is assimilated by a module on the opposite of the line";

N3 (arbitration-condition) "If two signals appear on different input lines of a module simultaneously, or very close together in time, the action of the module should be as if one signal, then the other occurred as specified by the sequential machine";

N4) "There may be an arbitrary delay between the assimilation of an input signal by a module and the production of a corresponding output signal. This delay is always finite but is not necessarily bounded";

N5) "At most two modules in a network are ever connected by the same line, and this line must be an input to one module and an output from the other";

N6) "If a signal is produced by one module on an input line to another modules, it must be assimilated before a second signal occurs on the same line."

We modify one of Keller's conditions, and add two further conditions:

N7) A wire has an unbounded but finite delay;

M1) If an input is undefined in a state, then such an input may never occur during operation;

M2) All states are reachable from the initial state.

If a network of modules performs its function correctly regardless of any delays in lines or modules, we say that the network is *delay-insensitive*. We also impose five conditions listed below on the construction of delay-insensitive networks that arise from Keller's arbitration. The conditions are universally quantified over q, a and b (with $a \neq b$):

A1) if $a, b \in L$, where $L \in A(q)$ then $f(f(q, a), b)$ and $f(f(q, b), a)$ are defined;

A2) if $f(q, a)$ and $f(f(q, a), b)$ are defined, and $g(q, a) = \emptyset$ then $f(q, b)$ is defined;

A3) if $f(q, a)$ and $f(f(q, a), a)$ are defined then $g(q, a) \neq \emptyset$;

A4) if $a, b \in L$, where $L \in A(q)$ then $g(q, a) \cap g(q, b) = \emptyset$;

A5) if $a, b \in L$, where $L \in A(q)$ and $g(q, a) \cup g(f(q, a), b) = g(q, b) \cup g(f(q, b), a)$ then q' and q'', where $q' = f(f(q, a), b)$ and $q'' = f(f(q, b), a)$, are *not input discriminating*. States q', q'' are not input discriminating if there exists a binary relation S on states such that $(q', q'') \in S$, where S is defined as follows: if $(q', q'') \in S$ then, $A(q') = A(q'')$ and for all c, whenever $g(q', c)$ and $g(q'', c)$ are defined and equal then $(f(q', c), f(q'', c)) \in S$.

A1 is required as a direct consequence of condition N3, and can be found in [2]. A2 has been identified by us as a condition which must hold as a consequence of M1 and the lack of feedback produced by empty outputs in the DI environment. A3 and A4 correspond directly to Conditions 8 and 9 in [2]. A5 is new and requires that any two identical sequences of inputs and outputs from a given state cannot result in two different states (as a result of arbitration) which have different inputs as specified by function A (but may have different outputs).

This ensures that the environment can determine which sets of inputs are valid based on the preceding input/output sequence. Otherwise, it is possible that the module enters a state where some inputs are not supported, and this cannot be detected by the environment. Similarly to A2, it has been identified by us as a condition which must hold to ensure that the environment behaves correctly in accordance with a module's definition.

Finally, we also require that for any q, a such that $f(q, a)$ is defined, $f(f(q, a), b)$ is defined for some b: this means that modules are not deadlocking, and they always have some input defined in each state.

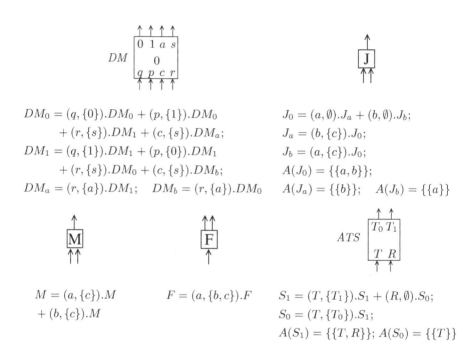

$DM_0 = (q, \{0\}).DM_0 + (p, \{1\}).DM_0$
$\qquad + (r, \{s\}).DM_1 + (c, \{s\}).DM_a;$
$DM_1 = (q, \{1\}).DM_1 + (p, \{0\}).DM_1$
$\qquad + (r, \{s\}).DM_0 + (c, \{s\}).DM_b;$
$DM_a = (r, \{a\}).DM_1; \quad DM_b = (r, \{a\}).DM_0$

$J_0 = (a, \emptyset).J_a + (b, \emptyset).J_b;$
$J_a = (b, \{c\}).J_0;$
$J_b = (a, \{c\}).J_0;$
$A(J_0) = \{\{a, b\}\};$
$A(J_a) = \{\{b\}\}; \quad A(J_b) = \{\{a\}\}$

$M = (a, \{c\}).M$
$\qquad + (b, \{c\}).M$

$F = (a, \{b, c\}).F$

$S_1 = (T, \{T_1\}).S_1 + (R, \emptyset).S_0;$
$S_0 = (T, \{T_0\}).S_1;$
$A(S_1) = \{\{T, R\}\}; A(S_0) = \{\{T\}\}$

Fig. 1. From top-left: *DM* in state DM_0 [10]; *Join, Merge, Fork, ATS* ([2])

To illustrate, in Fig. 1 we define several useful modules. All symbols shown are constants and should not be confused with the variables used in this paper. In the case of *Join*, a and b may arrive concurrently in state J_0 as given by $A(J_0)$. Recall that if a module's correct operation involves each input signal producing exactly one output signal, with no possibility of multiple input signals arriving concurrently, we say that the module is serial. *DM* and *Merge* are examples of serial modules. The function A is not given for modules where no inputs are assumed to be concurrent, as it always consists of the sets $\{a\}$ for each input a.

Consider the behaviour of *ATS*. It is valid in S_1 to send signals on both R and T concurrently, or individually. Depending on the delays in wires, and the order of processing by the module, this can lead to different outcomes. In [2], this is referred to as *non-trivial arbitration*. If the order of processing between two signals does not affect the output or resulting state, it is known as *trivial arbitration*. In the case of non-trivial arbitration, the module can be seen to make a "choice" which affects the overall outcome of the computation. Hence non-trivial arbitration, when combined with the DI environment represents a form of non-determinism.

Trivial and non-trivial arbitration, however, are only defined with respect to pairs of signals. In the general case where several signals may arrive concurrently, leading to different possible states where different sets of inputs may be defined, the situation is much more complex. It is not always clear from the standard notation which modules exhibit non-deterministic (henceforth referred to simply as *arbitrating*) behaviour. High-level arbitration in this sense is briefly mentioned by Keller ([2]), but is not formally defined or further elaborated on.

Furthermore, it is also not clear whether a module exhibits high-level reversibility. For example, simply inverting the definition of *Join* to yield its inverse is not possible using the standard notation, as this would result in empty inputs producing outputs, which is not a valid definition. However *Join*'s high-level behaviour clearly exhibits a form of reversibility.

3   Set Notation for Parallel DI Modules

In this section, we introduce a new notation which describes the high-level behaviour of delay-insensitive modules. We wish to use actions where inputs, as well as outputs, are sets. This will allow us to express that there maybe be several concurrent inputs. Each input set will correspond to a valid combination of individual inputs which may occur in a given state. Since we are also interested in inverses of parallel DI modules, we would like to be able to present the definitions of DI modules in such a way that all actions are not empty output actions. Any module which is not deadlocking will always eventually produce at least one non-empty output in response to a set of inputs.

We present an algorithm (Fig. 2) for converting any definition of M (that satisfies the conditions from Section 2) to a new definition M', which uses our set notation, where each set of inputs causes a non-empty set of outputs, such that M and M' represent the same external behaviour. Informally, the input sets for M' will represent each possible set of inputs which may arrive concurrently to a module in a given state. Hence each $L' \subseteq (L \in A(q))$ (where $|L| \geq 1$) will be the input of an action in state q. Henceforth, we occasionally omit set brackets when representing a singleton set of inputs or outputs.

Example 2. We show the new definition of *Join* after applying this algorithm. It can now be defined as $J_0 = (\{a, b\}, c).J_0$, where this indicates that the combination of inputs $\{a, b\}$ causes an output on c, with no other valid input combinations permitted. It can be verified to possess the same external behaviour of *Join* as defined in Section 2.

The "input sets" in a given state now correspond to the sets of signals that the environment may send before expecting an output. The external operation of a module defined using set notation, and the behaviour of the environment can therefore be understood as follows: 1) The environment chooses one input set to satisfy and signals the corresponding set of lines; 2) When the module receives a complete input set, it selects an action at random which contains the satisfied input set, and executes this action, assimilating the input signals on the lines in the set, and producing signals on the lines in the corresponding output set; 3) When the environment receives the full output set of the action selected by the module, it begins satisfying a new input set.

Input: Module $M = (Q, I, O, f, g, A)$ which satisfies conditions from Section 2.

1) For all q in Q and all $(a, B).q' \in q$, replace $(a, B).q'$ with $(\{a\}, B).q'$

2) **repeat**:$\{\forall q \in Q$ and $\forall L \in A(q)$ with $|L| \geq 2$: if $(B, C).q' \in q$ and $(D, E).q'' \in q$, with $B, D \subset L$ and $B \cap D \neq \emptyset$, then add the following to actions of q if they are not actions already: $(B \cup D, C \cup g(q', D)).f(q', D)$ and $(B \cup D, E \cup g(q'', B)).f(q'', B).\}$
until:$\{\forall q \in Q$ and $\forall L' \subseteq (L \in A(q))$ with $|L| \geq 2$ and $|L'| \geq 1$, $(L', B).f(q, L')$ is an action of q for some $B\}$

3) **repeat**:$\{\forall q \in Q$ and $\forall (B, \emptyset).q' \in q$: replace $(B, \emptyset).q'$ with the sum of all $(B \cup C, D).q''$ where $(C, D).q'' \in q'$ (and $B \neq C)\}$
until:$\{$There are no actions with empty-outputs$\}$

4) Remove states which are unreachable from the initial state.

5) Remove all duplicate actions from each $q \in Q$.

Output: Set notation version of M.

Fig. 2. Algorithm for converting a module to set notation

Clearly, if one input set A is a subset of another A' in the same state, then due to the DI environment, if A' is signalled it is possible that A is "processed" by the module instead of A'. In such a case, signals on the lines $A' \setminus A$ can be seen to remain pending. The next input set signalled by the environment must then contain $A' \setminus A$. The environment cannot send new signals on the lines $A' \setminus A$, it must signal some set B such that $B \cup A' \setminus A$ corresponds to a valid input set. These restrictions are automatically satisfied for an arbitrary module M' defined using set notation, if the original module M satisfies the conditions outlined in Section 2, and the environment interacts with M' as it did with M.

Example 3. The new definition of ATS using set notation is $S_1 = (T, T_1).S_1 + (\{R, T\}, T_0).S_1 + (\{R, T\}, T_1).S_0$; and $S_0 = (T, T_0).S_1$. The definition of S_0 is unchanged by the algorithm, so it suffices to check the behaviour of S_1. If T is signalled alone by the environment, then the behaviour is trivially equivalent to the original definition. If R is signalled, then the signal can be seen to pend at the module as a full input set has not yet been signalled. This is externally equivalent to the original definition, which accepts R but does not produce any outputs. When T is then signalled, one of the two actions containing the input set $\{R, T\}$ may be chosen, with each of the two actions corresponding to processing the inputs in either order. The action $(\{R, T\}, T_0).S_1$ corresponds to processing R

followed by T in the original definition. The action $(\{R,T\}, T_1).S_0$ corresponds to processing T followed by R, which results in the T_1 output and a change to S_0 (where the next T will produce T_0). We also note that if the environment signals $\{R,T\}$ (either concurrently or in any order) in S_1, this may result in the action $(T, T_1).S_1$ being processed by the module instead. In this case, R is seen to pend until another T signal arrives, where the module may then select an action containing $\{R,T\}$, or again force the R signal to pend. This corresponds to the R signal taking an arbitrary length of time to arrive due to the DI environment, or the module repeatedly arbitrating against R in favour of processing T. Hence, the external behaviour of ATS is preserved.

The new definitions of f and g and the new state set Q are outputs of the algorithm in Fig. 2. Maps f and g are now relations (instead of functions) defined over states and sets of inputs, because a set of concurrent inputs may lead to different outputs depending on the actual low-level order of accepting the individual inputs. Hence $f \subseteq (Q \times (\mathcal{P}(I) \setminus \emptyset)) \times Q$, and $g \subseteq (Q \times (\mathcal{P}(I) \setminus \emptyset)) \times (\mathcal{P}(O) \setminus \emptyset)$. The function A is now redundant as each input of an action in the definition of a state is a valid set of concurrent inputs, and vice versa. We note that the CCS-like definitions of serial modules are not modified by the algorithm.

Henceforth, we combine the relations f and g in an obvious way into a single relation T, referred to as transitions, and have $T \subseteq (Q \times (\mathcal{P}(I) \setminus \emptyset)) \times (Q \times (\mathcal{P}(O) \setminus \emptyset))$, where $((q, A), (q', B)) \in T$ represents that the input set A in state q may result in a change to state q' and the output set B. Therefore our modules are now defined using the 4-tuple (Q, I, O, T).

We call a module *reversible* if T is a bijection. We say that a *network is reversible* if all modules within the network are reversible. We define the *inverse* of a reversible module (Q, I, O, T) to be the module (Q, I', O', T') where $I' = O$, $O' = I$, and T' is the inverse of T. The *inverse of a network* is achieved by replacing each module with its inverse and reversing the direction of wires.

We call a module *arbitrating* (*arb* for short) if there are transitions $((q, B), (q', C)), ((q'', D), (q''', E)) \in T$, such that $q = q''$, and either $B \subset D$ or, $B = D$ and either $q' \neq q'''$ or $C \neq E$. We say that a module is *non-arbitrating* (*non-arb*) if it is not arbitrating. Informally, arbitration corresponds to non-determinism. As each possible input set in a given state corresponds to a set of signals arriving, for a module to be deterministic in a delay-insensitive environment, no input set cannot be a subset of another input set in the same state, and no input set can lead to two different output sets or different states. An example of a non-arb module is *Join*. An example of an arb module is ATS, as the set notation definition satisfies the subset condition with $\{T\} \subset \{R,T\}$ in S_1 (Example 3).

Correspondingly, we call a module *backwards-arbitrating* (*b-arb* for short) if there are $((q, B), (q', C)), ((q'', D), (q''', E)) \in T$, such that $q' = q'''$, and either $C \subset E$ or, $C = E$ and either $q \neq q''$ or $B \neq D$. We say that a module is *non-backwards-arbitrating* (*non-b-arb*) if it is not b-arb. For reversible modules, if the inverse of a module is arb then the module is b-arb and vice-versa.

4 Universality of Non-arbitrating Parallel Modules

The main purpose of this section is to realise arbitrary non-arb modules out of simple modules *Merge, Join, Fork* and *DM* in Fig. 1. Firstly, we show that arbitrating modules cannot be realised with non-arbitrating modules. Then, since $M \times N$ *Joins* will be utilised in our construction of arbitrary non-arb modules, we demonstrate how to realise $M \times N$ *Joins* in terms of purely reversible modules *DM* and *Join*. Finally, we present our construction of arbitrary non-arb modules with the help of an example, and prove two universality results.

We begin by showing some limitations of non-arb modules.

Proposition 4. No set of non-arb modules can be universal for arb modules.

Proof. Consider module M: $M_0 = (\{q\}, \{0\}).M_0 + (\{r\}, \{s\}).M_1 + (\{q,r\}, \{1\}).M_0$; $M_1 = (\{q\}, \{2\}).M_1 + (\{r\}, \{s\}).M_0 + (\{q,r\}, \{3\}).M_1$. The module M is arb as $\{q\} \subset \{q,r\}$ in both M_0 and M_1.

Assume for contradiction that a set X which contains only non-arb modules is universal for arb modules. Hence M can be realised as a network N of modules in X. Note that the input sets $\{q\}$ and $\{q,r\}$ result in different outputs depending on the state of M. Similarly, the input $\{r\}$ results in different behaviour (by toggling the state) depending on the state of M.

Consider the set Z of modules in N which process inputs in response to the input $\{q\}$. At least one module in Z must record whether M is in M_0 or M_1. Let any one such module in Z be denoted by z. Let the set of inputs of z which are signalled in response to $\{q\}$ be denoted by the set F. As the input $\{r\}$ changes the state of M, it must change the state of z. Let G be the set of.inputs of z which are signalled in response to $\{r\}$.

Hence if $\{q,r\}$ is signalled in M_0, then by delay-insensitivity, it is possible for signals to arrive on F and G together. Note that $F \cap G = \emptyset$, otherwise this implies that two signals may appear on some $f \in F$, and this would violate condition N6. As a result, z must define actions for the input sets F, G and $F \cup G$. Since $F \subseteq F \cup G$, we obtain that $z \in X$ is arbitrating: contradiction. □

Consider the inverse M^{-1} of the above module M. M^{-1} is reversible and b-arb. Utilising the above argument, it is straightforward to show that M^{-1} cannot be realised with a network of reversible non-arb non-b-arb modules only, giving the following result:

Proposition 5. No reversible non-arb non-b-arb set can be universal for reversible non-arb and b-arb modules.

4.1 Constructing $M \times N$ *Joins* and *Forks* with Reversible Modules

We shall use in our main construction arbitrarily-sized $M \times N$ *Joins* (left of Fig. 3), where at least one of M, N is greater than or equal to 2. We will also utilise $M \times N$ *Forks*, which are inverses of $M \times N$ *Joins*, and are depicted with the same symbol but with the directions of signals reversed. Their definition is not given here. We denote trees of *Join* and *Fork* with symbols J_T and F_T respectively.

We now demonstrate how to construct arbitrary $M \times N$ *Join*s using only the reversible set $\{DM, Join\}$. The right of Fig. 3 shows how to reversibly construct an arbitrary $1 \times N$ *Join* using only $\{DM, Join\}$. Figure 4 shows how to utilise a $1 \times N$ *Join* to reversibly construct an arbitrary $M \times N$ *Join*. We compare our construction with that of Keller in [2], and Patra and Fussell in [12] which both utilise *Merge* and therefore are not reversible. Note also that replacing *Join* with *Fork* in these constructions and relabelling the ports of *DM* (*DM* is shown to be

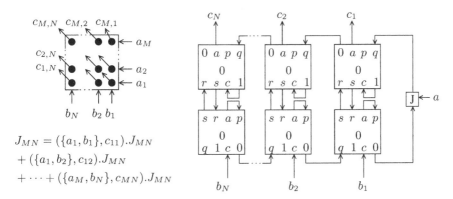

$$J_{MN} = (\{a_1, b_1\}, c_{11}).J_{MN}$$
$$+ (\{a_1, b_2\}, c_{12}).J_{MN}$$
$$+ \cdots + (\{a_M, b_N\}, c_{MN}).J_{MN}$$

Fig. 3. Left: $M{\times}N$ *Join*, Right: Arbitrary $1{\times}N$ *Join* using $\{DM, Join\}$

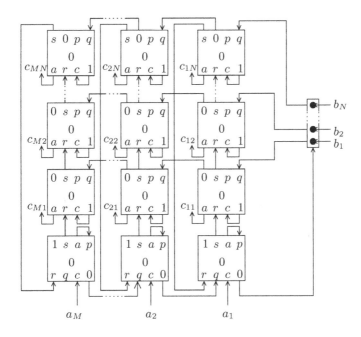

Fig. 4. Arbitrary $M{\times}N$ *Join* using $\{DM, 1{\times}N$ *Join*$\}$

its own inverse in [10]), the inverse of this construction can be achieved, yielding $M \times N$ *Forks*. Hence the reversible set $\{DM, Join, Fork\}$ allows $M \times N$ *Joins* and $M \times N$ *Forks* of arbitrary size to be constructed reversibly. Realisations of 1×3, 1×4, 3×3, 4×3 and 4×4 *Joins* using this construction were verified using Concurrency Workbench ([4]). The details can be found at [9].

4.2   Universal Sets of Non-arbitrating Modules

We note, before we present our main construction and results, that $\{Merge, DM\}$ is universal for serial modules as proven in [10]. Since DM can realise RE ([10]), and since RE is shown in [7] to be able to realise any reversible serial module, we obtain the following result:

Proposition 6. *DM is universal for the class of reversible serial modules.*

In order to realise an arbitrary non-arb module N in terms of our simple modules we shall use three auxiliary modules defined in terms of N. Firstly, we introduce some helpful notation.

Let $RQ(M)$, $RI(M)$, $RO(M)$, $RT(M)$ return the sets of states, inputs, outputs and transitions for any module M respectively. Let $ISets(M) = \{B : ((q, B), (q', C)) \in T(M)\}$. Let $OSets(M) = \{C : ((q, B), (q', C)) \in T(M)\}$. $ISets(M)$, $OSets(M)$ are the sets of input and output sets for M respectively.

Consider any non-arb module $N = (NQ, NI, NO, NT)$ defined as in Section 3. The three auxiliary modules for N are defined as follows:

The module $Seq_N = (SQ, SI, SO, ST)$ is given by $SQ = RQ(N); SI = \{I_i : i \in ISets(N)\}; SO = \{O_i : i \in OSets(N)\}; ST = \{((q, B), (q', C)) : ((q, MapI_N(B)), (q' MapO_N(C))) \in RT(N)\}$, where $MapI_N$ is a bijection that maps SI to $RI(N)$ and $MapO_N$ is a bijection that maps SO to $RO(N)$. Informally, Seq_N is a serial module which represents the behaviour of N but with input sets replaced with single inputs. Seq_N is reversible iff N is reversible.

$SeqQ_N = (SqQ, SqI, SqO, SqT)$ is given by $SqQ = RQ(N); SqI = RI(Seq_N) \cup \{qi\}; SqO = RO(Seq_N) \cup \{q_x : x \in SqQ\}; SqT = RT(Seq_N) \cup \{((x, qi), (x, q_x)) : x \in SqQ\}$. Informally, $SeqQ_N$ extends the functionality of Seq_N with the ability to query the state of the module on a dedicated set of lines, which do not modify the state. $SeqQ_N$ is reversible iff N is reversible.

Finally, $SeqQ'_N = (Sq'Q, Sq'I, Sq'O, Sq'T)$ is $Sq'Q = RQ(N); Sq'I = RI(Seq_N) \cup \{q_x : x \in SqQ\}; Sq'O = RO(Seq_N) \cup \{qi\}; Sq'T = RT(Seq_N) \cup \{((x, q_x), (x, qi)) : x \in SqQ\}$. Informally, $SeqQ'_N$ is equivalent to $SeqQ_N$ but with the query functionality inverted. $SeqQ'_N$ is reversible iff N is reversible.

It is important to note that the auxiliary modules are serial, and Seq_N, $SeqQ_N$ and $SeqQ'_N$ can be realised by DM if they are reversible, and by $\{Merge, DM\}$ otherwise.

Next, we define a non-arb non-b-arb module P, and its auxiliary modules. We will then describe how to construct P using $\{DM, Join, Fork\}$. This allows us to illustrate the method used for the general case.

P is given by:

$S_0 = (\{a,b,c\}, \{x,y\}).S_0 + (\{a,c,d\}, \{y,z\}).S_1;$
$S_1 = (\{a,c,d\}, \{x,y\}).S_1 + (\{a,b,d\}, \{x,z\}).S_0$

The set mappings required for Seq_P, $SeqQ_P$ and $SeqQ'_P$ are:

$MapI_P = \{(I_1, \{a,b,c\}), (I_2, \{a,c,d\}), (I_3, \{a,b,d\})\};$
$MapO_P = \{(O_1, \{x,y\}), (O_2, \{y,z\}), (O_3, \{x,z\})\}$

Finally:

$Seq_P :\quad S_0 = (I_1,O_1).S_0 + (I_2,O_2).S_1;\ S_1 = (I_2,O_1).S_1 + (I_3,O_3).S_0;$
$SeqQ_P :\quad S_0 = (I_1,O_1).S_0 + (I_2,O_2).S_1 + (qi, q_{S_0}).S_0;$
$\qquad\qquad S_1 = (I_2,O_1).S_1 + (I_3,O_3).S_0 + (qi, q_{S_1}).S_1;$
$SeqQ'_P :\ S_0 = (I_1,O_1).S_0 + (I_2,O_2).S_1 + (q_{S_0}, qi).S_0;$
$\qquad\qquad S_1 = (I_2,O_1).S_1 + (I_3,O_3).S_0 + (q_{S_1}, qi).S_1$

The construction is divided into two stages. Stage 1 determines the input set which has been signalled and then updates the state of P accordingly. Stage 2 determines the output set and creates signals on the appropriate output lines.

Stage 1 is shown in Fig. 5. A signal on an input line is forked to several columns of $M \times N$ *Joins*, one for each input set B in the current state of P that contains the signal (determined by querying instances of $SeqQ_P$). These columns contain different numbers and sizes of $M \times N$ *Joins* depending on the module to be constructed. Each $M \times N$ *Join* in a given input set's column synchronises an additional input. Hence synchronising three signals requires two $M \times N$ *Joins*.

Eventually exactly one column produces an output on the bottom $M \times N$ *Join*, corresponding to some input set C of P being satisfied. This signal then removes other instances of the inputs which are part of the completed input set, currently pending on various $M \times N$ *Joins* in other columns. This is achieved by utilising other inputs of the $M \times N$ *Joins*. The order that inputs in a set are synchronised also affects the location of signals which need to be "cancelled". For example, if $\{a,b,c\}$ is satisfied (the leftmost column), the completion signal removes other instances of these inputs from the other input set in this state ($\{a,c,d\}$), which corresponds to removing instances of a and c from the second column of $M \times N$ *Joins* (there are no other instances of b in S_0). However, due to the synchronisation order of the second column, the a and c inputs which have been forked to the second column will have been joined, and hence the single signal corresponding to the completed set $\{a,c\}$ pending on the second $M \times N$ *Join* must be cancelled. Similarly, if $\{a,c,d\}$ in S_0 is satisfied, pending instances of a on the top $M \times N$ *Join* and c on the bottom $M \times N$ *Join* in the leftmost column are cancelled. It is always possible to cancel other forked inputs either individually or as a partially completed set, as they will be pending on some fixed combination of $M \times N$ *Joins*. This is uniquely determined based on the completed input set, the structure of the columns, and the current state of P, as P is non-arb.

After "cancelling" other instances of inputs, the signal is "reversibly merged" using an instance of $SeqQ'_P$, allowing input sets which exist in multiple states to share a single line. This can be seen with the set $\{a,c,d\}$, which exists in both S_0 and S_1, and hence two columns, each representing $\{a,c,d\}$ in a state, are reversibly merged through the middle instance of $SeqQ'_P$. The signal then forks

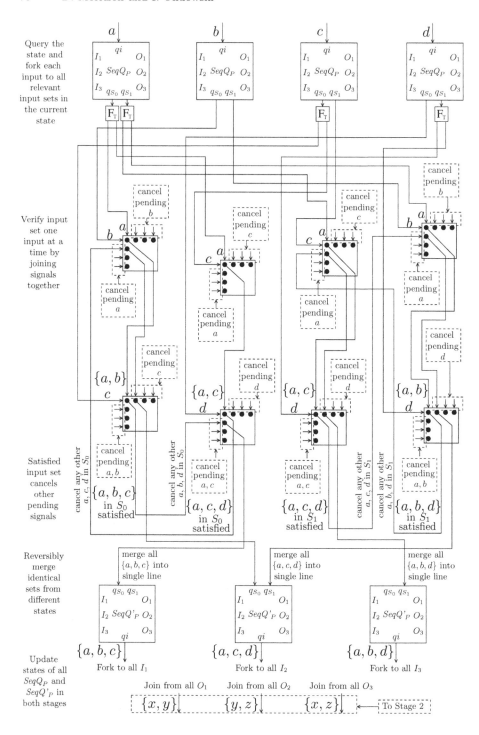

Fig. 5. Stage 1 (input determination and state update) for P

to all thirteen instances of $SeqQ_P$ and $SeqQ'_P$ in both Stages 1 and 2 (Fig. 6), inputting on each module's instance of x such that $MapI_P(x) = C$, where C is the satisfied input set. This updates the state of P depending on the input set. All identical outputs on the various instances of $SeqQ_P$ and $SeqQ'_P$ in both Stages 1 and 2 are joined together using a tree of $Joins$. The output from each tree corresponds to an output set of P. These lines continue to Stage 2.

Stage 2 (Fig. 6) uses a symmetric method to Stage 1. It is achieved by following the construction method of Stage 1 but output sets and resulting states of P are considered (instead of input sets and current states). The entire construction is then inverted, (with $M{\times}N$ $Forks$ replaced with $M{\times}N$ $Joins$, and vice versa) with the exceptions of $SeqQ_P$ and $SeqQ'_P$, which are exchanged. This construction is only possible because P is not b-arb. As P is reversible, Stages 1 and 2 are both reversible. If P were not reversible, then $SeqQ_P$ and $SeqQ'_P$ would not be reversible, and hence Stages 1 and 2 would not be reversible. It is easy to see that any non-arb non-b-arb module can be realised by following a similar construction method to P.

We note that an irreversible version of Stage 2 can be trivially realised with $Merges$ and $Forks$ as shown in [2]. When combined with Stage 1, this is used to realise non-arb b-arb modules.

To compare our construction with that of Keller ([2]), we note that Keller uses arbitrating modules even if the target module is non-arbitrating, and his construction processes one signal at a time. We utilise parallel signals fully, thus realising modules' behaviour, expressed by our new set notation, more directly.

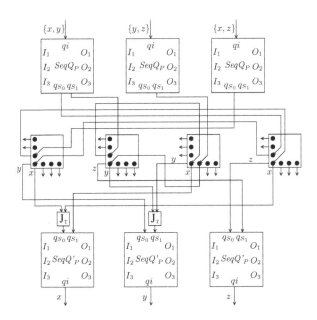

Fig. 6. Stage 2 (output determination) for P

It is easy to see that our construction can be generalised to any non-arb module. This gives us two universal sets for different classes of non-arb modules.

Theorem 7. $\{DM, Fork, Join\}$ is universal for the set of reversible non-arbitrating non-backwards-arbitrating modules, and all constructions of such modules are reversible.

Proof. A reversible non-arb non-b-arb module M has reversible serial instances of $SeqQ_M$ and $SeqQ'_M$ which are realisable by DM (Proposition 6). Hence reversible constructions of Stages 1 and 2 (Figures 5 and 6) can be achieved using $\{DM, Fork, Join\}$ and arbitrarily large $M{\times}N\,Join$s and $M{\times}N\,Fork$s. We showed how to construct any $M{\times}N\,Join$ or $M{\times}N\,Fork$ using $\{DM, Fork, Join\}$.   □

Theorem 8. $\{DM, Fork, Join, Merge\}$ is universal for non-arbitrating modules.

Proof. Theorem 7 proves that $\{DM, Fork, Join\}$ can realise the reversible non-b-arb subclass. Any other module M in this class has instances of $SeqQ_M$ and $SeqQ'_M$ realisable with $\{DM, Merge\}$. Hence, constructions of Stage 1 (Fig. 5) can be achieved using $\{DM, Merge, Fork, Join\}$ and arbitrarily large $M{\times}N\,Join$s and $M{\times}N\,Fork$s (achievable with $\{DM, Fork, Join\}$). Stage 2 can be irreversibly realised for any non-arb module using $\{Merge, Fork\}$.   □

5   Conclusion

In this paper we have introduced a new set notation for describing parallel DI modules. We have defined a clear notion of arbitration, and identified an interesting phenomenon of backwards-arbitration. We have proven limitations when realising reversible modules which utilise backwards-arbitration. Reversible constructions of $M{\times}N\,Join$s and $M{\times}N\,Fork$s in terms of reversible, non-arb modules have been given for the first time. Finally, we have shown how to construct arbitrary non-arbitrating modules within two universal sets of modules.

References

1. Fredkin, E.F., Toffoli, T.: Conservative logic. International Journal of Theoretical Physics 21(3/4), 219–253 (1982)
2. Keller, R.M.: Towards a theory of universal speed-independent modules. IEEE Transactions on Computers 23(1), 21–33 (1974)
3. Lee, J., Peper, F., Adachi, S., Morita, K.: An asynchronous cellular automaton implementing 2-state 2-input 2-output reversed-twin reversible elements. In: Umeo, H., Morishita, S., Nishinari, K., Komatsuzaki, T., Bandini, S. (eds.) ACRI 2008. LNCS, vol. 5191, pp. 67–76. Springer, Heidelberg (2008)
4. Moller, F., Stevens, P.: Edinburgh Concurrency Workbench user manual, version 7.1 (1999), http://homepages.inf.ed.ac.uk/perdita/cwb/
5. Morita, K.: Reversible computing systems, logic circuits, and cellular automata. In: ICNC 2012, pp. 1–8. IEEE Computer Society (2012)

6. Morita, K.: A simple universal logic element and cellular automata for reversible computing. In: Margenstern, M., Rogozhin, Y. (eds.) MCU 2001. LNCS, vol. 2055, pp. 102–113. Springer, Heidelberg (2001)
7. Morita, K.: Reversible computing and cellular automata - a survey. Theor. Comput. Sci. 395(1), 101–131 (2008)
8. Morita, K., Ogiro, T., Tanaka, K., Kato, H.: Classification and universality of reversible logic elements with one-bit memory. In: Margenstern, M. (ed.) MCU 2004. LNCS, vol. 3354, pp. 245–256. Springer, Heidelberg (2005)
9. Morrison, D.: Homepage, Department of Computer Science, University of Leicester (2014), http://www.cs.le.ac.uk/people/dm181
10. Morrison, D., Ulidowski, I.: Reversible delay-insensitive distributed memory modules. In: Dueck, G.W., Miller, D.M. (eds.) RC 2013. LNCS, vol. 7948, pp. 11–24. Springer, Heidelberg (2013)
11. Patra, P., Fussell, D.S.: Building-blocks for designing DI circuits. Technical report, University of Texas at Austin (1993)
12. Patra, P., Fussell, D.S.: Efficient building blocks for delay insensitive circuits. In: Proc. of Async 1994, pp. 196–205. Society Press (1994)
13. Phillips, I.C.C., Ulidowski, I.: Reversing algebraic process calculi. Journal of Algebraic and Logic Programming 73(1-2), 70–96 (2007)
14. Phillips, I.C.C., Ulidowski, I., Yuen, S.: A reversible process calculus and the modelling of the ERK signalling pathway. In: Glück, R., Yokoyama, T. (eds.) RC 2012. LNCS, vol. 7581, pp. 218–232. Springer, Heidelberg (2013)

Reference Counting for Reversible Languages

Torben Ægidius Mogensen

DIKU, University of Copenhagen
Universitetsparken 5,   DK-2100 Copenhagen O,   Denmark
torbenm@diku.dk

Abstract. Modern programming languages and operating systems use heap memory that allows allocation and deallocation of memory to be decoupled, so they don't follow a stack discipline. Axelsen and Glück have presented a reversible heap manager where allocation and deallocation are each other's logical inverses: Freeing a block of memory is done by running the allocation procedure backwards.

Axelsen and Glück use this heap manager to sketch implementation of a simple reversible functional language where pattern matching a constructor is the inverse of construction, so pattern-matching implies deallocation. This requires the language to be linear: A pointer can not be copied and it can only be eliminated by deallocating the node to which it points.

We overcome this limitation by adding reference counts to nodes: Copying a pointer to a node increases the reference count of the node and eliminating a pointer decreases the reference count. We show reversible implementations of operations on nodes with reference counts. We then show these operations can be used when implementing a reversible functional language RCFUN to the reversible imperative language Janus.

1   Introduction

There are basically three ways programs traditionally allocate and free memory: Static allocation, stack allocation and heap allocation. The first two forms are easy to implement reversibly: In static allocation, all memory blocks are available throughout the entire program execution and are neither allocated nor freed during execution, and in stack allocation, allocations and deallocations form a palindromic sequence where each deallocation is a natural inverse of the corresponding allocation. The reversible programming language Janus [5] uses both kinds of allocation: Arrays are statically allocated and a stack is used for storing return addresses of function calls. Janus has also been extended with parameter passing [8], which is also implemented using a stack. Heap allocation, however, does not follow a reversible allocation/deallocation discipline, so it is not obvious how to implement this reversibly without generating garbage data. Axelsen and Glück [2] have described an implementation of heap allocation and deallocation in a reversible setting, though some (relatively harmless) garbage data is generated in the form of a free list, the structure of which depends on the sequence of allocations and deallocations.

We will assume existence of a reversible implementation of explicit allocation and deallocation of nodes (as each other's inverses) in the style of Axelsen and Glück and,

S. Yamashita and S. Minato (Eds.): RC 2014, LNCS 8507, pp. 82–94, 2014.
© Springer International Publishing Switzerland 2014

using these, describe reversible implementations of node construction, pointer copying and pattern-matching, the inverses of which are node destruction, pointer elimination and node sharing. We will show these implementations as procedures in Janus.

Next, we define a language RCFUN similar to the reversible functional language RFUN [9,2] and show how functions in RCFUN can be translated into Janus procedures. We will use the trivial extension of the original Janus to include assertions that is described in [7]. We refer to the latter paper for a description of the syntax and semantics of Janus and for a description of how Janus statements can be reversed.

2   A Heap Manager

The heap manager described by Axelsen and Glück [2] is used for LISP-like data structures built using the nullary constructor Nil and a binary constructor Cons. In order to have all heap cells be the same size, both Nil and Cons cells are represented using three machine words: A tag field and two pointer fields, which in a Nil node are set to 0. Construction and freeing both kinds of cells are done using a reversible procedure get_free that, for allocation, takes no argument and returns a pointer to a three-word cell where all words are 0, and when run in reverse for deallocation takes a pointer to a three-word cell where all words are 0 and returns nothing.

Axelsen and Glück intend their heap manager for implementing a simplified version of the reversible functional language RFUN [9]. The restrictions are that constructors are only Nil and Cons and that values can not be copied. Since pointers to nodes can not be copied, the node can be deallocated at pattern-matching, making construction and pattern-matching basically each other's inverses. This is essentially the same restriction that is used in Bakers reversible Ψ-Lisp [3].

Axelsen and Glück briefly mention the possibility of adding copying to the restricted RFUN language, but not how this would be implemented. Since pattern-matching always deallocates a node, copying values would imply deep copies: Rather than copying a pointer, so the value is shared between two or more variables, the entire tree is copied, so there is only one reference to each node. We want to remove this limitation from the functional language, so heap nodes can be shared by arbitrarily many pointers. We do so by adding reference counts to nodes.

3   Pointer Copying and Reference Counts

We will implement operations on nodes in Janus. In basic Janus, the parameter and return value of get_free are passed through global variables. For example, before a to call to get_free, a global variable p is set to 0 and at return it contains the resulting pointer to the allocated three-word block. Deallocation would set p to point to the block to be freed and uncall (run in reverse) get_free, which would set p to 0 at return.

We want to implement a Janus procedure copy_pointer that takes one argument, which is a pointer, and returns two copies of that pointer. copy_pointer would use two global variables p and q, where p contains a pointer and q is set to zero. A call to copy_pointer will leave p unchanged and set q to be equal to p.

Uncalling `copy_pointer` will require p and q to be identical pointers and set q to zero. Since pointers can be copied, deconstruction of a Cons-node to get its fields does not imply deallocation: It is deallocated only if no other pointers to the node exists. This is where reference counts come in.

We will use a representation of Nil/Cons trees that is somewhat different from what Axelsen and Glück uses: A Nil value is in our representation is pointer with a value of 1 and a Cons value is a pointer (greater than 1) to a three-word block where the first word is a reference count and the two other words are the head and tail fields. The reason we don't use 0 for Nil is that we want to reserve 0 for uninitialised variables and undefined values.

When a Cons-node is allocated, the reference count is set to 1. Each time a (non-null) pointer is copied by calls to `copy_pointer`, the reference count is incremented. Uncalling `copy_pointer` will decrement the reference count (which must be at least two). Deallocating a Cons-node requires that the reference count is 1.

4   Reference-Counting Implementation of Node Operations

We will, assuming an implementation of a reversible allocation/deallocation procedure `get_free` as described above, describe reversible implementations in Janus of node construction, pointer copying and node deconstruction.

We will in our Janus code use e_1 `<>` e_2 as a shorthand for `!(`e_1 `==` e_2`)`, and `else skip` can be omitted, so an if-then-else-fi statement can be written without the else part. We also add `true` and `false` conditions. These can be seen as shorthands for `0 == 0` and `0 == 1`, respectively. We will later introduce a few more shorthand notations.

We treat the heap memory as an array M of words, which can contain either integers or heap pointers represented as integer offsets into M. So if p is a pointer to a Cons-node, `M[p]` is the reference count, `M[p+1]` is the head field and `M[p+2]` is the tail field. So we can write, e.g, `M[p] += 1` to increase the reference-count field of a Cons-node.

4.1   Pointer Copying

The simplest of the procedures is pointer copying. If we did not have to consider reference counts, it could be implemented just by `q += p`, but we additionally have to increment the reference count of the cell that p points to.

```
procedure copy_pointer
  assert q == 0;
  if p > 1 then /* if not Nil */
    M[p] += 1   /* increase reference count */
  fi p > 1;
  q += p;
  assert p == q
```

Note that this implementation allows `copy_pointer` to be used on Nil values. There is no net effect of calling the procedure in this case. The assertions state the preconditions for calling and uncalling this procedure (and, hence, also the postconditions). If these are guaranteed by global invariants (as will be the case in the code-generation scheme shown in Section 6)), there is no need for explicit assertions, but we have included them for clarity. We will, for compactness and ease of reading, use $(x,y) =$ call copy_pointer(z) as a shorthand notation for the sequence

```
p <=> z;
call copy_pointer;
p <=> x;   q <=> y
```

where a<=>b swaps a and b. Similarly, we will use $z =$ uncall copy_pointer(x,y) as shorthand for the reverse call sequence.

4.2   Cons-Node Construction

This procedure will allocate and construct a Cons-node with reference count set to 1. Arguments are in the variables head and tail and the result is returned in c, which before the call must be zero.

```
procedure cons
  assert c == 0 && p == 0;
  call get_free; /* allocate a pointer to 3 zeroed words */
  c <=> p; /* make c point to this */
  M[c] += 1; /* increase reference count to 1 */
  M[c + 1] <=> head; M[c + 2] <=> tail; /* set fields */
  assert c > 1 && M[c] == 1 && head == 0 && tail == 0   && p == 0;
```

Uncalling cons will deallocate a node and return the fields.

We will use $z =$ call cons(x,y) and $(x,y) =$ uncall cons(z) as shorthands similar to the shorthands for copy_pointer.

4.3   Field Access

So far, the only operations we have for shared nodes are copy_pointer and its inverse. This rather limits the usefulness of shared nodes, so we must have a way of accessing the fields of a shared node. The fields procedure below accesses the fields of a Cons-node without deallocating or modifying the node.

In addition to returning the fields, fields returns the node-pointer unchanged, so the reference count of the node is not changed. But, since the fields are copied, the reference counts of these are increased (if they are non-Nil).

```
procedure fields
  assert tail == 0 && head == 0 && c > 1 && M[c] > 0;
  head += M[c + 1]; /* copy fields, increasing reference counts */
  if head > 1 then M[head] += 1 fi head > 1;
  tail += M[c + 2];
  if tail > 1 then M[tail] += 1 fi tail > 1;
  assert c > 1 && M[c] > 0 && head == M[c + 1]&& tail == M[c + 2]
```

Given a (non-Nil) node pointer c, a call to fields returns the fields in the variables head and tail while preserving the value of c.

Uncalling `fields` requires c to contain a pointer to a cons-node and head and tail to contain the values of the fields to this node. At return, head and tail are cleared and c is unchanged.

We will use shorthands $(w,x,y) = $ call `fields`(z) and $z = $ uncall `fields`(w,x,y), where w is the value returned/passed in p.

5   The Reversible Functional Language RCFUN

We will define a modified version of RFUN from [9] that, like the language used in [2], restricts constructors to `Nil` and `Cons`. We will call this language RCFUN, where the C stands for "counting". RCFUN has the following syntax:

$$
\begin{array}{lll}
Program & \rightarrow & Definition^+ \\
Definition & \rightarrow & \textbf{fid } Match \\
Match & \rightarrow & Pattern^+ = Call^* Pattern^+ \\
& | & Match \mid Match \\
Call & \rightarrow & \textbf{vid}^+ = \textbf{fid } \textbf{vid}^+; \\
& | & \textbf{fid } \textbf{vid}^+ = \textbf{vid}^+; \\
Pattern & \rightarrow & \textbf{vid} \\
& | & \texttt{Nil} \\
& | & \texttt{Cons}(Pattern, Pattern) \\
& | & \textbf{vid as } \texttt{Cons}(Pattern, Pattern)
\end{array}
$$

Where **vid** is a variable identifier and **fid** is a function identifier or the special function `copy` that copies a pointer, so it takes one argument and returns two values. This is equivalent to the copy/equality operator $\lfloor \cdot \rfloor$ used [9]. A function is defined by a *Match* with one or more rules using patterns to restrict the arguments.

There are two kinds of calls: One for running a function in the forwards direction and one for running a function backwards: $f\ xs\ =\ ys$; means running the inverse of f on ys to get xs, i.e, the inverse of running f on xs to get ys.

The main differences from RFUN (apart from syntactic details) is that functions in RCFUN are defined by multiple rules, where RFUN uses a single rule and case-expressions, and that functions here can return multiple values.

Additionally, patterns in RCFUN can depend on reference counts as well as the constructor identity: There are two different patterns for Cons-nodes: The pattern $\mathrm{Cons}(x,y)$ matches a Cons-node with reference count 1, i.e., unshared nodes, and z as $\mathrm{Cons}(x,y)$ matches a Cons-node with any reference count, i.e., both shared and unshared nodes. The first form deallocates the node, so the pointer to the node is eliminated. When used as an expression, it allocates a new Cons-node. It is naturally implemented using the cons procedure (in reverse for pattern matching and forwards for building results).

The second form does not eliminate the pointer, so the pointer is explicitly named (as z) and must be used in the body expression. When this form is used as an expression, it takes a pointer z to a Cons-node and two values x and y. It then verifies that x and y are equal to the head and tail fields of the Cons-node. It then returns the Cons-node unchanged. It is naturally implemented using the `fields` procedure (forwards for pattern matching and in reverse for building results). Note that the two kinds of pattern overlap. We will discuss the implications of this in Section 8.

The following restrictions apply to RCFUN programs:

1. Whenever a variable is declared in a pattern or call, it is used *exactly* once within its scope.
2. No two rules in a *Match* can have overlapping argument-pattern lists.
3. The *Pattern* lists that are the results of rules in a *Match* can not overlap. This ensures that the inverse of a function can select rules deterministically. For details of this *symmetric first-match policy*, see [9].

Figure 1 shows and example program in RCFUN that takes two lists and returns the first unchanged and the concatenation of the two lists as the second result.

Running in reverse, this function would deallocate a prefix of the second list that is identical to the first list. Note that calling in reverse requires that the prefix that is deallocated is unshared.

```
append Nil ys = Nil ys
     | xs1 as Cons(x,xs) ys =
          w z = copy x;
          ws zs = append xs ys;
          xs1 as Cons(w, ws) Cons(z,zs)
```

Fig. 1. RCFUN program for appending lists

5.1   Reversibility of Programs

Programs in RCFUN are trivially reversible, as the following inversion scheme shows:

$$\text{Reversing a function definition}$$
$$\mathcal{R}_{\mathcal{F}}[|\mathbf{fid}\ M|] \qquad \doteq \mathbf{fid}^{-1}\ \mathcal{R}_{\mathcal{M}}[|M|]$$

$$\text{Reversing a match}$$
$$\mathcal{R}_{\mathcal{M}}[|Ps = Cs\ Qs||] \doteq Qs = \mathcal{R}_{\mathcal{C}}[|Cs|]\ Ps$$
$$\mathcal{R}_{\mathcal{M}}[|M_1\ |\ M_2|] \doteq \mathcal{R}_{\mathcal{M}}[|M_1|]\ |\ \mathcal{R}_{\mathcal{M}}[|M_2|]$$

$$\text{Reversing a call list}$$
$$\mathcal{R}_{\mathcal{C}}[|Vs = \mathbf{fid}\ Ws;|] \doteq \mathbf{fid}\ Ws = Vs;$$
$$\mathcal{R}_{\mathcal{C}}[|\mathbf{fid}\ Vs = Ws;|] \doteq Ws = \mathbf{fid}\ Vs;$$
$$\mathcal{R}_{\mathcal{C}}[Cs_1\ Cs_2|] \qquad \doteq \mathcal{R}_{\mathcal{C}}[Cs_2|]\ \mathcal{R}_{\mathcal{C}}[Cs_1|]$$

where we use $\doteq$ in the transformation function definitions to distinguish from the syntactic equality sign $=$. The non-overlap restriction on result patterns ensures that an inverted *Match* has non-overlapping rules. Since f^{-1} is the inverse of f, a call $Vs = f\ Ws$ can be translated to $f'\ Vs = Ws$ and $f\ Vs = Ws$ to $Vs = f'\ Ws$.

6   Translation to Janus

We will show how programs in RCFUN can be translated into Janus. Since Janus can be translated to reversible machine code [1] and the get_free (which is used by the Janus code) can be implemented in reversible machine code [2], this shows that RCFUN can be implemented in reversible machine code.

A complication is that RCFUN has local variables, where Janus has only global variables. We handle this by storing the values of variables that are live after a call in a heap-allocated list when the function is called, restoring them after the call. It would suffice to use a stack, but since explicit stacks are not found in Janus, it is easier to use the heap we already have defined.

We use the global Janus variable dump for the variable-save list. We define a procedure store that takes a parameter v and stores v in the dump:

```
procedure store
  head <=> v; tail <=> dump;
  call cons;
  c <=> dump
```

Uncalling store will fetch a variable from the dump. We will use the shorthands call store(x) and $x = $ uncall store.

For simplicity of translation, we will assume that no variables or functions in the RCFUN program clash with variables or procedures used by the Janus procedures cons, copy_pointer and so on that we use in the translated programs. This can be ensured by renaming prior to translation. Hence, we can translate names from RCFUN programs into the same Janus names, so no environments are needed in the translation scheme.

We use global Janus variables A1, A2, ... and R1, R2, ... to, respectively, pass arguments to and results from RCFUN functions. RCFUN variables can, of course, not clash with these either.

We will, below, show a translation scheme for translating RCFUN to Janus. The translation scheme assumes programs are well-formed, in particular that the linearity and unique-matching constraints are obeyed.

The function C_P translates a pattern list to a Janus condition. In addition to a pattern list, C_P also takes a list of Janus expressions that evaluate to the values that the patterns should match.

> *Translating a pattern to a condition*
> $C_P[|P_1 \ \ldots \ P_n|](e_1, \ldots, e_n) \ \doteq C_P[|P_1|](e_1) \ \&\&\ldots\&\& \ C_P[|P_n|](e_n)$
> $C_P[|x|](e) \qquad\qquad\qquad \doteq \texttt{true}$
> $C_P[|\texttt{Nil}|](e) \qquad\qquad\quad\; \doteq e \texttt{ == } 1$
> $C_P[|\texttt{Cons}(P_1, P_2)|](e) \ \doteq e \texttt{ > } 1 \texttt{ \&\& M[}e\texttt{] == } 1 \texttt{ \&\&}$
> $\qquad\qquad\qquad\qquad\qquad\qquad C_P[|P_1|](\texttt{M[}e\texttt{+1]}) \texttt{ \&\& } C_P[|P_2|](\texttt{M[}e\texttt{+2]})$
> $C_P[|x \texttt{ as } \texttt{Cons}(P_1, P_2)|](e) \doteq e \texttt{ > } 1 \texttt{ \&\&}$
> $\qquad\qquad\qquad\qquad\qquad\qquad C_P[|P_1|](\texttt{M[}e\texttt{+1]}) \texttt{ \&\& } C_P[|P_2|](\texttt{M[}e\texttt{+2]})$

The function T_P translates a pattern list into code that defines the variables in the patterns and clears the variables that hold the matched values. It is assumed that the pattern matches and that the variables in the pattern are initially cleared. In addition to a list of patterns, T_P takes a list of variables of the same length. The code, when executed in reverse, will build values from variables. The rules for Cons-nodes have optimised rules for when one or more of the field patterns are variables.

Translating a pattern to deconstructing code

$$T_P[\![P_1 \ \ldots \ P_n]\!](v_1, \ldots, v_n) \doteq T_P[\![P_1]\!](v_1); \ldots; T_P[\![P_n]\!](v_n);$$

$$T_P[\![x]\!](v) \doteq \texttt{x <=> v};$$

$$T_P[\![\texttt{Nil}]\!](v) \doteq \texttt{v -= 1}$$

$$T_P[\![\texttt{Cons}(w_1, w_2)]\!](v) \doteq \texttt{(}w_1, w_2\texttt{) = uncall cons(}v\texttt{)}$$

$$T_P[\![\texttt{Cons}(w_1, P_2)]\!](v) \doteq \texttt{(}w_1, w_2\texttt{) = uncall cons(}v\texttt{)};$$
$$\qquad T_P[\![P_2]\!](w_2);$$
$$\qquad \text{where } w_2 \text{ is a new variable}$$

$$T_P[\![\texttt{Cons}(P_1, w_2)]\!](v) \doteq \texttt{(}w_1, w_2\texttt{) = uncall cons(}v\texttt{)};$$
$$\qquad T_P[\![P_1]\!](w_1);$$
$$\qquad \text{where } w_1 \text{ is a new variable}$$

$$T_P[\![\texttt{Cons}(P_1, P_2)]\!](v) \doteq \texttt{(}w_1, w_2\texttt{) = uncall cons(}v\texttt{)}; \ T_P[\![P_1, P_2]\!](w_1, w_2);$$
$$\qquad \text{where } w_1, w_2 \text{ are new variables}$$

$$T_P[\![x \text{ as } \texttt{Cons}(w_1, w_2)]\!](v) \doteq \texttt{(}x, w_1, w_2\texttt{) = call fields(}v\texttt{)}$$

$$T_P[\![x \text{ as } \texttt{Cons}(w_1, P_2)]\!](v) \doteq \texttt{(}x, w_1, w_2\texttt{) = call fields(}v\texttt{)};$$
$$\qquad \text{where } w_2 \text{ is a new variable}$$

$$T_P[\![x \text{ as } \texttt{Cons}(P_1, w_2)]\!](v) \doteq \texttt{(}x, w_1, w_2\texttt{) = call fields(}v\texttt{)};$$
$$\qquad \text{where } w_1 \text{ is a new variable}$$

$$T_P[\![x \text{ as } \texttt{Cons}(P_1, P_2)]\!](v) \doteq \texttt{(}x, w_1, w_2\texttt{) = call fields(}v\texttt{)};$$
$$\qquad \text{where } w_1, w_2 \text{ are new variables}$$

The function T_C translates calls while keeping track of which variables are used later, i.e, the live variables. T_c handles a function call by saving the live variables (excluding the results of the function), passing the arguments in A1, A2, ..., calling the Janus procedure that implements the function, taking the results from R1, R2, ... and restoring the saved variables. A special case is copy, as it uses different variables for passing arguments and results and because no variables are stored, since copy_pointer doesn't overwrite variables from the RCFUN program.

Translating a call list

$$T_C[\![x\ y\ =\ \texttt{copy } z;]\!]Vs \doteq (\texttt{(}x, y\texttt{) = call copy\_pointer(}z\texttt{)},$$
$$\qquad \{z\} \cup (Vs \setminus \{x, y\}))$$

$$T_C[\![\texttt{copy } z = x\ y;]\!]Vs \doteq (z = \texttt{uncall copy\_pointer(}x, y\texttt{)},$$
$$\qquad \{x, y\} \cup (Vs \setminus \{z\}))$$

$$T_C[\![x_1 \ldots x_m = f\ y_1 \ldots y_n]\!]Vs \doteq (\texttt{call store(}z_1\texttt{)}; \ldots; \texttt{call store(}z_k\texttt{)};$$
$$\qquad \texttt{A1 <=> } y_1; \ldots; \texttt{An <=> } y_n;$$
$$\qquad \texttt{call } f;$$
$$\qquad \texttt{R1 <=> } x_1; \ldots; \texttt{Rm <=> } x_m;$$
$$\qquad z_k = \texttt{uncall store}; \ldots; z_1 = \texttt{uncall store},$$
$$\qquad \{z_1, \ldots, z_k\} \cup \{y_1 \ldots y_n\})$$
$$\qquad \text{where } \{z_1, \ldots, z_k\} = Vs \setminus \{x_1, \ldots, x_m\}$$

$$T_C[\![f\ y_1 \ldots y_n = x_1 \ldots x_m;]\!]Vs \doteq (\texttt{call store}(z_1); \ldots; \texttt{call store}(z_k);$$
$$\texttt{R1 <=> } x_1; \ldots; \texttt{R}m \texttt{ <=> } x_m;$$
$$\texttt{uncall } f;$$
$$\texttt{A1 <=> } y_1; \ldots; \texttt{A}n \texttt{ <=> } y_n;$$
$$z_k = \texttt{uncall store}; \ldots; z_1 = \texttt{uncall store},$$
$$\{z_1, \ldots, z_k\} \cup \{x_1 \ldots x_m\})$$
$$\text{where } \{z_1, \ldots, z_k\} = Vs \setminus \{y_1, \ldots, y_n\}$$
$$T_C[\![Cs_1\ Cs_2]\!]Vs \doteq (J_1; J_2,\ Vs_1)$$
$$\text{where } (J_2, Vs_2) = T_C[\![Cs_2]\!]Vs$$
$$\text{and } (J_1, Vs_1) = T_C[\![Cs_1]\!]Vs_2$$

T_M translates a *Match*. Code is generated that will try the rule patterns in sequence in a nested if-then-else-fi structure. If a rule matches, it will execute the code for the patterns, then code for the calls and finally reversed code for the result pattern. We use the Janus-inversion function $\mathcal{R}$ from [7] for reversing the code. The exit conditions are built from the result patterns. If no rules match, an always-failing assertion is executed.

Translating a match
$$T_M[\![P_1 \ldots P_n = Cs\ Q_1 \ldots Q_m \mid M]\!] \doteq \texttt{if } C_P[\![P_1 \ldots P_n]\!](\texttt{A1}, \ldots, \texttt{A}n) \texttt{ then}$$
$$T_P[\![P_1 \ldots P_n]\!](\texttt{A1}, \ldots, \texttt{A}n);$$
$$\#1(T_C[\![Cs]\!](U[\![Q_1 \ldots Q_m]\!]))$$
$$\mathcal{R}(T_P[\![Q_1 \ldots Q_m]\!](\texttt{R1}, \ldots, \texttt{R}m)$$
$$\texttt{else}$$
$$T_M[\![M]\!]$$
$$\texttt{fi } C_P[\![Q_1 \ldots Q_m]\!](\texttt{R1}, \ldots, \texttt{R}m)$$
$$T_M[\![P_1 \ldots P_n = Cs\ Q_1 \ldots Q_m]\!] \doteq \texttt{if } C_P[\![P_1 \ldots P_n]\!](\texttt{A1}, \ldots, \texttt{A}n) \texttt{ then}$$
$$T_P[\![P_1 \ldots P_n]\!](\texttt{A1}, \ldots, \texttt{A}n);$$
$$\#1(T_C[\![Cs]\!](U[\![Q_1 \ldots Q_m]\!]))$$
$$\mathcal{R}(T_P[\![Q_1 \ldots Q_m]\!](\texttt{R1}, \ldots, \texttt{R}m)$$
$$\texttt{else assert false}$$
$$\texttt{fi } C_P[\![Q_1 \ldots Q_m]\!](\texttt{R1}, \ldots, \texttt{R}m)$$

where #1 is the function that returns the first component of a pair. We used, above, a function U that finds the set of variables used in a pattern list to initialise the variable list when calling T_C:

Finding variables used in pattern
$$U[\![P_1 \ldots P_n]\!] \doteq U[\![P_1]\!] \cup \ldots \cup U[\![P_n]\!]$$
$$U[\![x]\!] \doteq \{x\}$$
$$U[\![x \texttt{ as Cons}(P_1, P_2)]\!] \doteq \{x\} \cup U[\![P_1]\!] \cup U[\![P_2]\!]$$

A function definition is translated by the function T_F simply by defining a Janus procedure where the body is the code for the *Match*.

Translating a function definition
$$T_F[\![f\ Ps = M]\!] \doteq \texttt{procedure } f$$
$$T_M[\![M]\!]$$

As an example, the append function from Figure 1 is translated into the Janus procedure shown in Figure 2. The comments are added for readability.

```
procedure append
  if A1 == 1 && true then /* first rule matches */
    A1 -=1; ys <=> A2;      /* pattern decomposition */
    ys <=> R2; R1 += 1;     /* result building */
  else /* try second rule */
    if A1 > 1 && true then /* 2nd rule matches */
      (xs1, x, xs) = call fields(A1);   /* pattern decomposition */
      ys <=> A2;
      (w, z) = call copy_pointer(x);    /* call to copy */
      call store(xs1); call store(w); call store(z); /* save variables */
      A1 <=> xs; A2 <=> ys;             /* set parameters */
      call append;                      /* recursive call */
      R1 <=> ws; R2 <=> zs;             /* get results */
      z = uncall store; w = uncall store; xs1 = uncall store; /* restore */
      R2 = call cons(z, zs);            /* result building */
      R1 = uncall fields(xs1, w, ws);
    else assert false /* no matching rule, so fail */
    fi R1 > 1 && R2 > 1 && M[R2] == 1   /* 2nd result matches */
  fi R1 == 1 && true       /* first result matches */
```

Fig. 2. The append function from Figure 1 translated to Janus

7 Loops

Since tail-recursive functional programs are hard to make reversible, we introduce an extension to RCFUN that allows tail-recursive definitions to be written as reversible loops. We add the following call construction:

$$Call \rightarrow \mathbf{vid}^+ = \texttt{loop}\ \mathbf{fid}\ \mathbf{vid}^+;$$
$$|\ \texttt{loop}\ \mathbf{fid}\ \mathbf{vid}^+ = \mathbf{vid}^+;$$

Like the normal calls, these are each other's inverses. The loop calls require that the function has the same number of parameters and results and that the pattern matching in both forwards and backward directions is non-exhaustive, so it is possible for matching to fail. The semantics of the call xs = loop f ys is:

1. Call f with the values in ys as arguments and put results (if any) in xs.
2. Swap xs and ys.
3. If ys is defined (i.e, if a matching rule was found), repeat from step 1, otherwise exit loop.

A similar construction has been used for transforming tail-recursive programs to enable syntactic inversion [6]. With this extension, it is fairly easy to write, for example, a list-reversal function for unshared lists:

```
reverse xs =
  xs1 ys0 = makeNil xs;
  xs2 ys1 = loop rev xs1 ys0;
  makeNil ys = ys1 xs2;
  ys

makeNil xs = xs Nil

rev Cons(x, xs) ys = xs Cons(x, ys)
```

The `makeNil` function is just used to introduce and eliminate `Nil` values. The `rev` function matches only if the first argument is a `Cons`-node, so the loop will continue until the `xs1` is `Nil`. At this time, `ys0` holds the reversed list. When the loop stops, the arguments and results are swapped, so `xs2` holds `Nil` and `ys1` holds the reversed list. After removing the `Nil` value by calling `makeNil` in reverse, the reversed list is returned.

To implement the loop construction, we need to change the behaviour of calls that do not match any rules. Currently, this causes an assertion to fail, but instead we want nothing to happen. This causes the argument variables to remain unchanged and the result variables to stay cleared. This way, a non-matching call can be detected at the call site by checking if the result variables are still clear. If we want non-looping calls to report errors when no rules match, we can add an assertion after the call that checks this. With this change, we can implement the loop with the following translation rule:

$$T_C[\![x_1 \ldots x_n = \texttt{loop } f\, y_1 \ldots y_n]\!] Vs \doteq (\texttt{call store}(z_1); \ldots; \texttt{call store}(z_k);$$
$$\texttt{A1 <=> } y_1; \ldots; \texttt{A}n \texttt{ <=> } y_n;$$
$$\texttt{from R1 == 0 do}$$
$$\texttt{call } f; \texttt{ R1 <=> A1; } \ldots; \texttt{ R}n \texttt{ <=> A}n$$
$$\texttt{loop skip until A1 == 0}$$
$$\texttt{R1 <=> } x_1; \ldots; \texttt{R}n \texttt{ <=> } x_n;$$
$$z_k = \texttt{uncall store}; \ldots; z_1 = \texttt{uncall store},$$
$$\{z_1, \ldots, z_k\} \cup \{y_1 \ldots y_n\})$$
$$\text{where } \{z_1, \ldots, z_k\} = Vs \setminus \{x_1, \ldots, x_n\}$$

The translation rule for the reverse case (not shown) is similar.

8 Conclusion and Future Work

We have presented implementation in Janus of reversible reference-counting operations on heap nodes, assuming availability of a heap manager in the style of [2]. We have used these operations to implement a non-trivial reversible functional language RCFUN by translating RCFUN functions into Jason procedures that use the node operations.

The addition of a reversible loop construct to RCFUN makes it easier to write reversible tail-recursive programs, such as list reversal. It is fairly easy to modify the translation scheme to accommodate this addition.

In the current design of RCFUN, Cons and as Cons patterns overlap, which (due to the unique-match restriction) means that you can't use both in different rules of the same function. It is not difficult to change as Cons patterns so they require a reference count greater than 1, so they don't overlap Cons patterns. It would still be possible to make an append function like the one in Figure 1, that works on both a shared and an unshared first argument, but that would require two almost identical versions of the second rule, where the new version differs from the current only in using Cons patterns where the current second rule uses as Cons patterns, so programs would be larger. To avoid this, we could make two distinct versions of as Cons patterns: One that (like in the current design) matches both shared and unshared nodes, and one that matches only shared nodes (so it does not overlap Cons patterns). This would allow the append function in Figure 1 to stay unchanged, but would allow functions that do different things to shared and unshared nodes. The usefulness of this is debatable, so we have chosen the current design where the two patterns overlap.

It is a more serious limitation that the Cons pattern (without as) only works on unshared nodes. In Figure 1, this means that, when calling append in reverse, the prefix of the second argument that is not shared with the first argument must be completely unshared, i.e, have reference count 1. It is not possible to write an append function that allows shared nodes in this prefix without adding an extra parameter that is a copy of the appended list, which makes the function rather useless. The same limitation means that the reverse function in Section 7 only works on unshared lists. It is possible to make an alternative reverse function that works on both shared and unshared lists, but this would need to return a copy of the original list as well as the reversed list, and it would not be tail recursive.

So while being able to share nodes and work on shared nodes at all is a nontrivial extension of previous work [2,3] that allows no sharing, making shared nodes match only as Cons patterns is a serious limitation.

We are currently working on a mechanism for avoiding this limitation and, hence, allow Cons patterns as well as as Cons patterns to match both shared and unshared nodes. Making construction and deconstruction by Cons mutually inverse while working on both shared and unshared nodes, however, requires maximal sharing. Maximal sharing can be implemented using hash-consing [4], which makes construction and deconstruction more costly than in this paper. With maximal sharing, structural equality and pointer equality is the same, so it is natural to add pattern guards that test for equality and non-equality of trees.

It is somewhat annoying to have to use a function (such as makeNil in Section 7) to introduce a constant argument to a function call, so we plan to allow patterns in arguments and results of calls. Additionally, having all data being built from Nil and Cons is somewhat limiting (even though you can encode anything as nil-cons trees), so we plan to add integers and arithmetic to the language. Comparing numbers will also require pattern guards.

References

1. Axelsen, H.B.: Clean translation of an imperative reversible programming language. In: Knoop, J. (ed.) CC 2011. LNCS, vol. 6601, pp. 144–163. Springer, Heidelberg (2011)
2. Axelsen, H.B., Glück, R.: Reversible representation and manipulation of constructor terms in the heap. In: Dueck, G.W., Miller, D.M. (eds.) RC 2013. LNCS, vol. 7948, pp. 96–109. Springer, Heidelberg (2013)
3. Baker, H.G.: Nreversal of fortune–the thermodynamics of garbage collection. In: Bekkers, Y., Cohen, J. (eds.) IWMM-GIAE 1992. LNCS, vol. 637, pp. 507–524. Springer, Heidelberg (1992)
4. Goto, E.: Monocopy and associative algorithms in an extended lisp. Technical Report TR 74-03, University of Tokyo (1974)
5. Lutz, C.: Janus: a time-reversible language. A letter to Landauer (1986), http://www.cise.ufl.edu/~mpf/rc/janus.html
6. Mogensen, T.Æ.: Report on an implementation of a semi-inverter. In: Virbitskaite, I., Voronkov, A. (eds.) PSI 2006. LNCS, vol. 4378, pp. 322–334. Springer, Heidelberg (2007)
7. Mogensen, T.Æ.: Partial evaluation of janus part 2: Assertions and procedures. In: Clarke, E., Virbitskaite, I., Voronkov, A. (eds.) PSI 2011. LNCS, vol. 7162, pp. 289–301. Springer, Heidelberg (2012)
8. Yokoyama, T., Axelsen, H.B., Glück, R.: Principles of a reversible programming language. In: Proceedings of the 5th Conference on Computing Frontiers, CF 2008, pp. 43–54. ACM, New York (2008)
9. Yokoyama, T., Axelsen, H.B., Glück, R.: Towards a reversible functional language. In: De Vos, A., Wille, R. (eds.) RC 2011. LNCS, vol. 7165, pp. 14–29. Springer, Heidelberg (2012)

Constructive Reversible Logic Synthesis for Boolean Functions with Special Properties

Anupam Chattopadhyay[1], Soumajit Majumder[1],
Chander Chandak[2], and Nahian Chowdhury[1]

[1] MPSoC Architectures Research Group, RWTH Aachen University, Germany
anupam.chattopadhyay@umic.rwth-aachen.de
[2] IIT Kharagpur, India

Abstract. Reversible computation is gaining increasing relevance in the context of several post-CMOS technologies, the most prominent of those being quantum computing. The problem of implementing a given Boolean function using a set of elementary reversible logic gates is known as reversible logic synthesis. Though several generic reversible logic synthesis methods have been proposed so far, yet the scalability and implementation efficiency of these methods pose a difficult challenge. Compared to these generic synthesis methods, few reversible logic synthesis approaches for restricted classes of Boolean functions demonstrated better implementation efficiency and scalability. In this paper, we propose a novel constructive reversible logic synthesis technique for Boolean functions with special properties. The proposed techniques are scalable, fast and outperforms state-of-the-art generic reversible synthesis methods in terms of quantum cost, gate count and the number of lines.

1 Introduction

From thermodynamic principles of computing, Landauer [11] pointed out that for every bit of information lost, $kT \cdot \ln 2$ Joules of heat is generated in an irreversible computation, which is recently verified experimentally [3]. Bennett [2] proposed that the computation can be done in reversible manner to achieve theoretically zero power dissipation by building upon Landauer's observations. This concept helped to form the field of reversible computation, which also dictates that the physical reversibility must be accompanied at higher abstraction by logical reversibility. This is a cornerstone for serveral post-CMOS technologies including quantum computing. Reversible logic synthesis accepts an (in)completely specified reversible Boolean function as input and generates a logical representation of the function, where reversible logic gates are used.

Boolean functions serve as prime building block of symmetric-key cryptosystems and error-correcting codes, for which several properties are highly desirable such as nonlinearity, symmetry, correlation immunity and balancedness. The main motivation behind this work is to show that the combinatorial construction of the reversible Boolean functions with specific properties can be done in order to improve the circuit efficiency compared to automated logic synthesis method. In this paper, we focus to two properties namely, *symmetry* and *nonlinearity* of Boolean functions.

S. Yamashita and S. Minato (Eds.): RC 2014, LNCS 8507, pp. 95–110, 2014.

2 Preliminaries

A Boolean function f is of the form $f : \{0,1\}^n \to \{0,1\}$ (or equivalently $f : \mathbb{V}_2^n \to \mathbb{V}_2$). The output of the Boolean function f can be represented as a string s of ones and zeros. It can also be represented as a multivariate polynomial over $GF(2)$. This polynomial can be expressed as a exclusive disjunction (EXOR) of a constant a_0 and one or more conjunctions of the function argument. This is called the Exclusive Sum-Of-Product (ESOP) representation. A less general representation of the ESOP form is known as the Algebraic Normal Form (ANF). The general ANF for a function $f(x_1, .., x_n)$ over n-variables can be written as,

$$f(x_1, .., x_n) = a_0 \oplus a_1 x_1 \oplus \cdots \oplus a_i x_i \oplus \cdots \oplus a_n x_n$$
$$\oplus \cdots \oplus a_{1,2,...,n} x_1 x_2 \cdots x_n \tag{1}$$

Reversible and Irreversible Boolean Functions. An n-variable vectorial Boolean function is *reversible* if all its output patterns map uniquely to an input pattern and vice-versa. It can be expressed as an n-input, n-output bijection or alternatively, as a Boolean permutation function over the truth value set $\{0, 1, \ldots 2^{n-1}\}$. An *irreversible* Boolean function $f_{irr} : \{0,1\}^n \to \{0,1\}^m$ with $n \neq m$ can also be made reversible with the help of extra input lines (ancilla) and/or output lines (garbage lines) such that, $input + ancilla = output + garbage$.

Nonlinearity. The nonlinearity of a Boolean function f on n-variables, denoted by N_f is the minimal Hamming Distance between f and all the affine functions on $\mathbb{V}_2^n$.

The class of Boolean functions having the highest nonlinearity are known as *Bent functions*. They are defined only on $\mathbb{V}_2^{2k}$, i.e. Boolean functions of even number of variables and their nonlinearity is given by $2^{2k-1} - 2^{k-1}$. In contrast, the maximum nonlinearity attainable for a Boolean function $\mathbb{V}_2^{2k+1}$ with odd number of variables still remains an open problem.

Symmetry. A Boolean function $f : \{0,1\}^n \to \{0,1\}$ is called symmetric if its output is invariant under any permutation of its input bits. Equivalently we can say that the value of $f(x)$ is constant for all x's having the same weight.

Direct Sum. The direct sum of two strings x and y, of lengths n and m respectively, denoted by $x \aleph y$ is given by $x \aleph y = (x \otimes y^c) \oplus (x^c \otimes y)$, where $x \otimes y = (x_0 \ AND \ y)...(x_{n-1} \ AND \ y)$ denotes the Kronecker product of two strings producing a string of length nm. y^c denotes complement of y.

Reversible Logic Synthesis. Reversible Boolean logic synthesis is achieved with the help of reversible logic gates. The gates are characterized by their implementation cost in quantum technologies, which is dubbed as Quantum Cost (QC). We use the standard QC values from [13] along with the latest improvements reported in [30] for QC computation. Few prominent reversible logic gates are as following.

- **CNOT gate**: CNOT$(a, b) = (a, a \oplus b)$.
- **CCNOT gate (Toffoli gate)**: CCNOT$(a, b, c)=(a, b, ab \oplus c)$. This gate can be generalized with Tof_n gate, where first $n - 1$ variables are used as control lines. NOT and CNOT gates are denoted as Tof_1 and Tof_2 respectively.
- **Controlled Swap gate (Fredkin gate)**: Fred$(a, b, c) = (a, \bar{a}b \oplus ac, \bar{a}c \oplus ab)$. This is generalized with $Fred_n$ gate $(n > 1)$, where first $n - 2$ variables are used as control lines.
- **Peres gate**: Per$(a, b, c) = (a, a \oplus b, ab \oplus c)$. This gate can be generalized with Per_n gate $(n > 2)$ [30], where first $n - 1$ variables are used as control lines.

2.1 Related Work and Motivation

A Boolean function should possess certain properties for its use in cryptographic applications such as symmetry, balancedness and high nonlinearity. Matsui in [17] showed that Boolean functions of low nonlinearity can be approximated and hence can be consequently attacked using linear cryptanalysis attacks, which makes high nonlinearity a desirable property of cryptographically strong Boolean function. To this effect, researchers came up with multiple construction methods for highly nonlinear Boolean functions with large number of variables. These constructive methods could be adopted for reversible circuit construction, which has not been attempted before this work. This constructive approach not only provides a scalable reversible logic synthesis method for highly nonlinear Boolean functions but also, demonstrates increased efficiency of implementation compared to generic reversible logic synthesis techniques. Symmetry of Boolean functions, while a desirable property for cryptographic applications, has also been shown to be important for general reversible logic synthesis [23].

Existing reversible logic synthesis methods can be broadly classified in two categories - generic [26] and property-specific. In the area of property-specific reversible logic synthesis, Beth and Rötteler [4] suggested synthesis approach for linear reversible circuits using Gaussian Elimination and LU-Decomposition to yield circuits with $O(n^2)$ gates. In [21], an improved algorithm with better speed and asymptotically optimal performance for synthesis of linear reversible circuits is proposed. Younes [34] proposed a factorization algorithm for synthesis of homogeneous Boolean functions. For Symmetric Boolean functions, a synthesis technique is proposed at [15]. This is improved further at [8], where a cascade of Peres gates is utilized to obtain reversible circuits with improved QC.

It has been noted at [15] that the constructive reversible logic synthesis procedures for Boolean functions with special properties are scalable and can outperform, in many cases, the generic synthesis techniques. This forms the key motivation of this work. Besides, it has been shown in a recent work that several Quantum algorithms do require efficient reversible circuits for specific classes of Boolean functions [7]. In this work, we make two contributions. First, we propose a constructive reversible logic synthesis technique for highly nonlinear Boolean functions. Second, we propose a constructive reversible logic synthesis technique for symmetric Boolean functions. For both the cases, we report improved results compared to the current literature.

In contrast to the state-of-the-art synthesis techniques [28,26] for Boolean functions with special propertes, we explore deeper and draw from the classical Boolean function construction techniques from the literature. *The constructive approach presented in this paper have multiple advantages, e.g., scalability, low synthesis runtime and significant implementation efficiency, as we demonstrate via benchmarking with state-of-the-art generic and property-specific reversible synthesis flows.*

3   Synthesis of Highly Nonlinear Functions

In this section, several construction techniques for highly nonlinear Boolean functions and Bent functions are discussed. Those are followed by their reversible circuit synthesis approaches, corresponding theoretical results on the upper bounds of gate count (GC), QC and the total number of lines (L) and comparison with state-of-the-art generic synthesis techniques.

3.1   Construction Method I: [27]

Here, we follow the concatenation-based construction of n-variable, m-resilient Boolean functions. (following Theorem 4,[27]). The idea is to utilize Boolean functions with smaller number of variables to construct a highly nonlinear Boolean function of large variable count. Before the concatenation, *direct sum* function is used. An optimized reversible circuit construction for the direct sum function (denoted as $\aleph$) is developed for the same. We illustrate with the help of a construction of a 14-variable Boolean function with 2nd order resiliency. The values of k and r, which are defined as two parameters for the construction in [27] are chosen as 6. Following the theorem, we concatenate 4 Boolean functions f_i's on $\mathbb{V}_2^{12}$ as $f_i = g_i \aleph \lambda_i$, where g_i is maximum nonlinear function on 6-variables. We choose 4 Bent functions on $\mathbb{V}_2^6$ which are as following.

$$
\begin{aligned}
g_1 &= x_1 x_2 \oplus x_3 x_4 \oplus x_5 x_6, \\
g_2 &= x_1 x_2 \oplus x_3 x_4 \oplus x_5 x_6 \oplus x_2, \\
g_3 &= x_1 x_2 \oplus x_3 x_4 \oplus x_5 x_6 \oplus x_2 \oplus x_3, \\
g_4 &= x_1 x_2 \oplus x_3 x_4 \oplus x_5 x_6 \oplus x_2 \oplus x_3 \oplus x_4
\end{aligned}
\tag{2}
$$

The λ_i's belong to $UL_k(m+1)$ where, $UL_k(m+1) = L_k(m+1) \cup \cdots L_k(k)$ (i.e., $L_k(3) \cup \cdots L_k(6)$) The individual sets $L_k(j)$ denote the set of all k-variable linear Boolean functions which are non-degenerate on exactly j-variables. The choices for the λ_i's are,

$$
\begin{aligned}
\lambda_1 &= L_6(3) = x_7 \oplus x_8 \oplus x_9, \\
\lambda_2 &= L_6(4) = x_7 \oplus x_8 \oplus x_9 \oplus x_{10}, \\
\lambda_3 &= L_6(5) = x_7 \oplus x_8 \oplus x_9 \oplus x_{10} \oplus x_{11}, \\
\lambda_4 &= L_6(6) = x_7 \oplus x_8 \oplus x_9 \oplus x_{10} \oplus x_{11} \oplus x_{12}
\end{aligned}
\tag{3}
$$

For reversible circuit implementation, constructions of g_i and λ_is are straightforward. It is noted that, the reversible logic implementation of *direct sum* is nothing but the $\oplus$ operation of the two functions g_i and λ_i. This allows efficient implementation of this method also via ESOP-based approach. However, the constructive approach considerably reduced the QC of the individual functions, resulting in overall improvement (Table 1). In the table, the shaded cells represent equal or improved performance in comparison with state-of-the-art synthesis methods.

Comparison with the state-of-the-art synthesis methods: We compare the proposed synthesis technique with state-of-the-art reversible logic synthesis methods. The functions are represented by the choice of the parameters - n, k, r and m. The nonlinearity of the functions are denoted by N_f and the maximum achievable nonlinearity (in the case of Bent functions) by $nlmax$. It can be observed that, with the proper choice of r and k, the method can easily scale to large Boolean functions. On the other hand, the choice of a large k and/or r, requires one to first synthesize a large Boolean function.

Table 1. Benchmarking Construction Method I

Function	$N_f/nlmax$	BDD[32]			ESOP[20,10]			MMD[18]			This work		
		Lines	Gates	QC	Lines	Gates	QC	Lines	Gates	QC	Lines	Gates	QC
$(14,6,6,1)$	7836/8028	26	67	179	15	17	157	14	40	886	18	20	88
$(14,6,6,2)$	7836/8028	31	86	238	15	16	148	14	39	660	18	21	91
$(16,6,8,1)$	31856/32368	31	80	208	17	22	262	16	168	5670	20	23	87
$(16,8,6,2)$	31344/32368	36	93	241	17	16	136	16	172	5850	20	27	91

3.2 Construction Method II: Recursive Construction[22]

A construction method presented in [22] generates large Boolean functions of high nonlinearity and resilience recursively like the previous one. A 10-variable, 4-resilient Boolean function of degree 4 and of nonlinearity 480 is constructed using a 7-variable, 2-resilient Boolean function of degree 4 and nonlinearity 56 as described in Theorem 7 [22]. The 7-variable function is first presented below. Note that this function was again found using a constructive method based on 6-variable functions.

$$f(x_1,\ldots,x_7) = (1 \oplus x_7)(1 \oplus x_6)h_1() \oplus (1 \oplus x_7)x_6h_2() \oplus (1 \oplus x_6)x_7h_3() \oplus x_6x_7h_4(), \tag{4}$$

where

$$h_1(x_1,\ldots,x_5) = x_1 \oplus x_2 \oplus x_1x_4 \oplus x_3x_4 \oplus x_2x_5 \oplus x_3x_5 \oplus x_4x_5 \oplus x_1x_4x_5 \oplus x_2x_4x_5 \oplus x_3x_4x_5$$

$$h_2(x_1,\ldots,x_5) = 1 \oplus x_1 \oplus x_2 \oplus x_4 \oplus x_3x_4 \oplus x_2x_5 \oplus x_3x_5 \oplus x_4x_5 \oplus x_1x_4x_5 \oplus x_2x_4x_5 \oplus x_3x_4x_5$$

$$h_3(x_1,\ldots,x_5) = x_3 \oplus x_1x_3 \oplus x_1x_2x_3 \oplus x_1x_4 \oplus x_2x_4 \oplus x_1x_2x_4 \oplus x_3x_4 \oplus x_1x_3x_4 \oplus x_5 \oplus x_1x_5$$
$$\oplus x_1x_2x_5 \oplus x_1x_3x_5$$

$$h_4(x_1,\ldots,x_5) = 1 \oplus x_2 \oplus x_1x_2 \oplus x_1x_2x_3 \oplus x_4 \oplus x_1x_4 \oplus x_1x_2x_4 \oplus x_1x_3x_4 \oplus x_1x_5 \oplus x_2x_5 \oplus x_1x_2x_5$$
$$\oplus x_3x_5 \oplus x_1x_3x_5$$

$$\tag{5}$$

In [22], an n-variable Boolean function F_d is defined to be in *desired form* if it follows the construction

$$F_d = (1 \oplus x_n)f_1 \oplus x_nf_2, \tag{6}$$

where f_1 and f_2 are $(n-1)$-variable functions with their degree being 1 less than F_d. The aforementioned 7-variable function is in *desired form* since, those are constructed recursively using 6-variable functions. Based on the 7-variable function $f(x_1, \ldots, x_7)$, a 10-variable, 4-resilient Boolean function of degree 4 and of nonlinearity 480 is constructed as following. Let $F = x_{n+2} \oplus x_{n+1} \oplus f$ and $G = (1 \oplus x_{n+2} \oplus x_{n+1})f_1 \oplus (x_{n+2} \oplus x_{n+1})f_2 \oplus x_{n+2} \oplus x_n$. Then the target 10-variable function F_1 of specified properties is constructed as $F_1 = (1 \oplus x_{n+3})F \oplus x_{n+3}G$. The construction of the 10-variable function from the 7-variable function can be easily achieved with Toffoli and Fredkin gates, as shown in the Figure 1. The detailed implementation of the constituent functions h_1, h_2, h_3 and h_4 are not shown. These functions were synthesized using an ESOP-based flow including common cube sharing.

The proposed synthesis technique is compared with the existing state-of-the-art synthesis techniques in Table 2. It is interesting to note that, even though the recursive construction allows direct implementation via simple reversible gates, none of the synthesis methods had matching QC or gate count that could be achieved from our constructive technique. The additional 6 lines, compared to the MMD method is contributed due to the fact that the constituent functions were synthesized using ESOP, thereby requiring 4 lines for the constituent functions h_1, h_2, h_3 and h_4. Furthermore, 2 were required for 6-variable functions f_1 and f_2, which were used for constructing $f(x_1, \ldots, x_7)$ as well as for constructing F_1. The improvement in constructive method is due to the following facts

- The *desired form* of a function directly translates to controlled swap gate
- Recursive construction method is based on basic CNOT gates

Evidently, these properties are not utilized by generic synthesis methods.

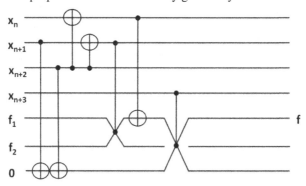

Fig. 1. Construction Method II:10-variable, 4-resilient Boolean function

Table 2. Comparison of Construction Method II with existing synthesis methods

Synthesis Method	Lines	Gates	QC
BDD[32]	42	147	447
ESOP[20,10]	26	89	309
MMD[18]	10	654	55632
This work	16	44	230

3.3   Construction Method III: [9]

An early construction method for Bent functions on $\mathbb{V}_2^{2k}$ was originally proposed in [9]. This construction, known as Maiorana-McFarland construction, has been further generalized in [5]. Numerous developments on Bent function construction followed the basic Maiorana-McFarland technique, such as in [12], authors obtained Bent functions with high resiliency. In this work, we focus on the basic construction as outlined in [9] and [35]. The idea of the construction is to concatenate the linear functions on $\mathbb{V}_2^k$, thereby generating Bent functions on $\mathbb{V}_2^{2k}$.

$$f(y, x) = \pi(y) \cdot x \oplus g(y), x, y \in \mathbb{V}_2^k \qquad (7)$$

where f is the resultant Bent function, π represents a permutation on $\mathbb{V}_2^k$ and g is any Boolean function on $\mathbb{V}_2^k$. There are $2^{2^k}(2^k!)$ such Bent functions, where the possible permutations are covered by the factor $(2^k!)$. For our study, we restricted π to all possible linear functions, and assumed g to be 0, thereby generating $2^k(2^k!)$ Bent functions. The general implementation is as shown in the Fig. 2.

Mapping to Reversible Circuits and Implementation Cost Determination: The aforementioned construction can be realized by applying psuedo-optimal linear reversible circuit synthesis [21] followed by a set of Fredkin gates. This construction has high L, GC and QC due to the multiplexer type functionality where k lines act as control lines and select one from all possible 2^k linear functions on $\mathbb{V}_2^k$. This construction method suffers from scalability issues since, with increasing variable count, the number of linear functions increases exponentially.

Comparison with state-of-the-art synthesis methods: The benchmarking results are presented in Table 3. Note that due to the size constraint, the complete functions are not presented for the studied 8-variable Boolean functions. Instead, only the permutation of the 16 linear functions for the sub-space $\mathbb{V}_2^4$ are given, where $1 \to 0, 2 \to x_1, 3 \to x_2,$ $\cdots, 16 \to x_1 \oplus x_2 \oplus x_3 \oplus x_4$. The total number of lines required remain upper-bounded by 20, which is due to 4 control inputs, 4 inputs for the linear functions, which are reused as part of the total 16 linear functions. Thereby, the upper bound of lines can be generalized as $k + 2^k$ for a bent function construction on $\mathbb{V}_2^k$. In this case, however, the line counts could be further reduced by applying algebraic optimization based on the ESOP formulation (see subsection 3.5). In the same manner, it is possible to determine the generalized costs for the linear function generator part. However, the identification of minimum swap count for a given permutation is non-trivial. Thankfully, the construction method as shown in [35] includes the swaps. Except for the count of lines, the constructive method outperformed ESOP and BDD-based methods both in gate count and QC for most of the permutations. We did not benchmark against MMD as it typically reports even higher gate count and QC compared to ESOP and BDD-based methods.

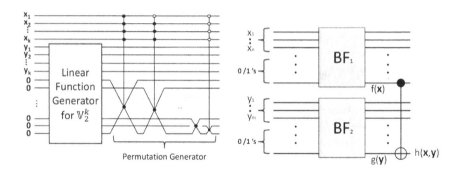

Fig. 2. Construction Method III: Bent Function

Fig. 3. Construction Method IV: Bent Function

Table 3. Benchmarking Construction Method III

Permutation of Linear Functions	Variable	BDD[32]			ESOP[20,10]			This work		
		Lines	Gates	QC	Lines	Gates	QC	Lines	Gates	QC
$\{11, 15, 10, 16, 4, 5, 2, 13, 8, 14, 6, 12, 9, 3, 7, 1\}$	8	22	71	219	9	32	488	18	33	97
$\{7, 14, 5, 13, 1, 16, 6, 3, 10, 12, 9, 2, 4, 11, 8, 15\}$	8	22	68	196	9	35	479	14	30	90
$\{15, 9, 14, 7, 5, 1, 16, 12, 6, 2, 11, 10, 4, 8, 3, 13\}$	8	22	62	174	9	25	353	13	23	71
$\{6, 14, 9, 4, 7, 13, 11, 1, 8, 15, 12, 5, 10, 3, 16, 2\}$	8	22	70	202	9	33	509	19	34	86
$\{11, 13, 16, 15, 8, 7, 2, 14, 10, 5, 4, 9, 3, 12, 1, 6\}$	8	20	62	174	9	36	516	16	35	99
$\{4, 7, 10, 9, 15, 16, 3, 8, 12, 11, 13, 6, 1, 5, 14, 2\}$	8	24	65	169	9	29	461	15	31	87
$\{9, 4, 2, 15, 6, 10, 7, 11, 12, 3, 16, 14, 5, 1, 13, 8\}$	8	22	72	208	9	34	506	15	29	81
$\{16, 9, 10, 7, 15, 4, 5, 12, 2, 1, 6, 13, 11, 8, 14, 3\}$	8	23	68	200	9	33	461	15	30	86
$\{16, 4, 15, 8, 9, 1, 14, 5, 10, 13, 2, 3, 12, 6, 7, 11\}$	8	22	73	201	9	34	490	18	34	98
$\{2, 7, 5, 6, 12, 3, 1, 4, 16, 10, 13, 11, 9, 14, 8, 15\}$	8	22	68	196	9	37	597	16	30	86

3.4 Construction Method IV: [33]

The authors in [33] proposed two theorems for construction of new Bent functions using existing Bent functions. This is particularly interesting for Boolean functions with odd number of variables, where direct constructions methods cannot be used [25].

Theorem 1: Let f and g be Boolean functions on $\mathbb{V}_2^m$ and $\mathbb{V}_2^n$ respectively. Then the Boolean function $h : \mathbb{V}_2^{m+n} \rightarrow \mathbb{V}_2$ defined by $h(\mathbf{x}, \mathbf{y}) = f(\mathbf{x}) \oplus g(\mathbf{y})$ is bent iff f and g are bent.

Theorem 2: If f is a Bent function on $\mathbb{V}_2^n$, then $f \oplus l$ is a Bent function for any affine function l on $\mathbb{V}_2^n$.

Mapping to Reversible Circuits and Implementation Cost Determination: The basic idea of this construction according to theorem 1 is given by Fig. 3. The second construction method can be achieved similarly by performing a CNOT operation between the Bent function and the linear function. The QC of the resulting circuit using this method of construction is simply the sum of QCs of the constituent functions added with 1, which is due to the CNOT gate. The total number of lines for the resulting circuit is $L(f_1) + L(f_2) + m + n$, where f_1 denotes a Bent function on n-variables and f_2 is a Bent function on m-variables for Theorem 1. Here, an ESOP-based implementation of the constituent Bent functions is assumed. f_2 is a linear function on n-variables for Theorem 2 (hence, $m = 0$ for the second construction).

The QC, GC and L for this construction are enlisted in Table 4.

Table 4. Implementation Costs for Construction Method IV

Gate Count	$GC(f_1) + GC(f_2) + 1$
Quantum Cost	$QC(f_1) + QC(f_2) + 1$
Lines	$L(f_1) + L(f_2) + m + n$

Comparison with state-of-the-art synthesis methods: This simple construction of Bent function is compared with BDD-based and ESOP-based methods, when the final Boolean function is subjected to synthesis. We observed an improved performance in most of the cases. The constructive method is scalable to large number of variables, in contrast to the generic methods. An 1-hour timeout set to the benchmarked synthesis methods failed to return a valid circuit in one case (indicated by '-').

3.5 Post-synthesis Optimization

Aforementioned construction techniques show strong algebraic structure and hence there is a wide scope for optimizing the synthesis by using *common cube sharing*. Common cube sharing is a well-studied problem in classical logic synthesis as it helps in minimization of cost and size by identifying the sub-circuits which form the basis for larger functional blocks. This optimization is applied on the Boolean functions obtained following the construction techniques. The implementation costs of these functions, as presented in the following Table 5, is computed after application of the cube sharing algorithm [20]. Note that, such optimizations are present also for the ESOP-based synthesis flows that we compared against and hence, do not provide any undue advantage to the proposed constructive synthesis flow.

Table 5. Benchmarking Construction Method IV

Function		Variable	BDD[32]			ESOP[20,10]			This work		
			Lines	Gates	QC	Lines	Gates	QC	Lines	Gates	QC
f_x	$= x_1 x_2$	2	3	1	5	3	1	5	3	1	5
g_y	$= y_1 y_2 \oplus y_3 y_4 \oplus y_5 y_6$	6	9	11	31	7	3	15	7	3	15
$h_{x,y}$	$= f_x \oplus g_y$	8	12	17	45	9	4	20	10	5	21
f_x	$= x_1 x_2 \oplus x_3 x_4$	4	6	7	19	5	2	10	5	2	10
g_y	$= y_1 y_2 \oplus y_3 y_4 \oplus y_5 y_6 \oplus y_7 y_8 \oplus y_9 y_{10} \oplus y_{11} y_{12}$	12	19	30	78	13	12	88	13	6	30
$h_{x,y}$	$= f_x \oplus g_y$	16	22	40	92	17	24	112	18	9	41
f_x	$= x_1 x_2 \oplus x_3 x_4 \oplus x_5 x_6 \oplus x_7 x_8 \oplus x_9 x_{10} \oplus x_{11} x_{12}$ $\oplus x_{13} x_{14} \oplus x_{15} x_{16}$	16	22	40	92	17	26	214	17	12	44
g_y	$= y_1 y_2 \oplus y_3 y_4 \oplus y_5 y_6 \oplus y_1 \oplus y_2 \oplus y_6$	6	9	12	28	7	6	18	7	6	18
$h_{x,y}$	$= f_x \oplus g_y$	22	-	-	-	-	-	-	24	19	53

4   Synthesis of Symmetric Functions

In contrast to nonlinear Boolean functions, constructive approach for synthesizing symmetric Boolean functions have been studied in the past [15,8], possibly due to their usage in efficient synthesis of general reversible Boolean functions [23]. Before proceeding further, we present some recent results on generalized Peres gates as well as show how cascaded multi-control Peres gates can be realized with lower Quantum costs.

4.1   Quantum Cost of Cascaded, Generalized Peres Gates

Generalization of Peres gates is introduced in [30] with the following definition,

$$Per_n(x_0, x_1, \cdots, x_n) = (x_0, x_0 \oplus x_1, x_0x_1 \oplus x_2, \cdots, x_0x_1 \cdots x_{n-1} \oplus x_n), \ n \geq 2$$
$$\tag{8}$$

Such gates are implemented in an optimized manner with controlled k^{th}-root-of-NOT gates. In the following Fig. 4, Per_3 and its corresponding reversible circuit realization is shown. Here, controlled-V, controlled-V^+ represents controlled k^{th}-root-of-NOT for $k = 2$ and controlled-W, controlled-W^+ represents the same for $k = 4$. In the lower part of the same Fig. 4 an alternative reversible circuit is presented, which locally re-orders the controlled k^{th}-root-of-NOT gates. Since the control lines are exclusive, the resultant Boolean function remains the same.

  In lemma 1 of [30], the number of elementary gates for Per_n is proved to be n^2, which is same as its QC since the elementary gates have a QC of 1. We explore this further considering cascaded, generalized Peres gates. The re-ordering of controlled

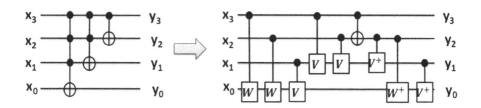

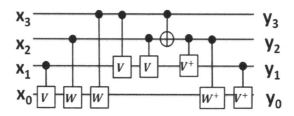

Fig. 4. Generalized Peres Gate Implementation

k^{th}-root-of-NOT gates provides an opportunity to reduce a few adjacent gates. This has been explored in the context of basic Peres gate [19] and for multi-control Toffoli gates [29].

Lemma 1. *Cascading 2 Per_n gates require $n^2 + n$ gates.*

Proof. From lemma 1 of [30], 2 cascaded Per_n gates require $2n^2$ elementary gates. An n-controlled Peres gate, i.e., Per_n consists of three parts. The part in middle implements a Per_{n-1} gate. The first and the last part of the circuit consists of n and $n - 1$ controlled Quantum gates respectively. For two adjacent Per_n gates, by re-ordering, $(n - 1)$ controlled Quantum gates can be cancelled out with their corresponding inverses. This leads to a reduction of $2(n - 1)$ elementary gates. Every Per_n contains a Per_{n-1} inside it, which, in the same manner allows a reduction of $2(n - 2)$ gates. This continues till there is a Per_2 gate, for which a reduction of $2(n - (n - 1))$ gates are possible. Hence, by summing the reductions, we obtain the elementary gate count as following.
$2n^2 - \sum_{i=1}^{n-1} 2(n - i)$
$= 2n^2 - n(n - 1)$
$= n^2 + n$ □

Corollary 1. *Cascading t Per_n gates require $n^2 + (t - 1)n$ gates.*

Proof. For each pair of Per_n gates, a reduction of $n(n-1)$ is obtained. For t number of cascaded Per_n gates, the total reduction from a basic tn^2 gate count is $(t - 1)n(n - 1)$. Hence, the final gate count is,
$tn^2 - (t - 1)n(n - 1)$
$= tn^2 - (t - 1)n^2 + (t - 1)n$
$= n^2 + (t - 1)n$ □

Evidently, the above results also lead to the QC values as we are only considering gates with 1 QC. An application of the above lemma is shown graphically for 2 cascaded Per_3 gates in Fig. 5. It is clear that by cascading as much as possible Peres gates with same control lines, one can obtain a significant reduction in gate count and QC. In the constructive synthesis of symmetric Boolean functions, this property is exploited.

4.2   Constructive Synthesis for Symmetric Functions

Since the symmetric Boolean functions have unique output for a given Hamming weight of the input n-variable Boolean vector $\mathbb{V}_2^n$, we propose an approach based on two phases. First, the Hamming weight computation in $(\lfloor \log_2 n \rfloor + 1)$ lines followed by an evaluation of the function on those lines. Note that, due to the sharing of one target Hamming weight line with one input line, $(\lceil \log_2 n \rceil)$ ancilla lines are needed. The circuit complexity largely depends on the Hamming weight computation, which is done using a ripple-carry adder approach as shown in Fig. 6. This approach is earlier used for Hidden Weighted Bit (HWB) functions in [13]. It can be observed that the Hamming weight computation circuitry is nothing but a series of cascaded, generalized Peres gates. In case of $rd73$, the Hamming weight computation is done with 2 cascaded Per_2

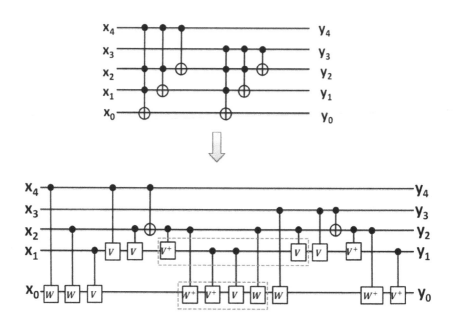

Fig. 5. Cascaded Generalized Peres Gate Implementation

gates and 4 cascaded Per_3 gates, resulting into a total QC of 24. Please note, that to re-duce garbage count, an input line is re-used for storing the LSB of the Hamming weight value. The Hamming weight values directly result into the output. Hence, no further gate is required. In providing the gate count, we report the number of mixed-control Tof_n gates for ease of comparison with previous results.

Table 6. Benchmarking with Property-specific Synthesis Techniques

Function	I/O	[8] (Low Garbage)		[8] (Low QC)		[15]			This work		
		Garbage	QC	Garbage	QC	Garbage	Gates	QC	Garbage	Gates	QC
$2of5$	5/1	-	-	-	-	6	12	32	6	9	15
$rd53$	5/3	5	28	6	20	5	12	36	4*	10	18
$rd73$	7/3	7	46	10	32	7	20	64	6*	16	24
$rd84$	8/4	9	66	13	44	11	28	98	7	20	27
$6sym$	6/1	-	-	-	-	9	20	62	8	16	32
$9sym$	9/1	14	88	19	59	11	28	94	10	22	30

The computation of Hamming weight is further optimized by taking the desired out-put into consideration. For example, the benchmark function $2of5$ produces an output of 1 when the Hamming weight is 2 or 010. However, 110 is not a valid Hamming weight for 5-variable circuit. Therefore, the Hamming weight computation can opti-mize the carry propagation circuitry and an additional line used for the most significant

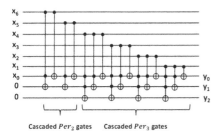

Cascaded Per_2 gates   Cascaded Per_3 gates

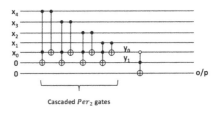

Cascaded Per_2 gates

Fig. 6. Generation of Hamming Weight for $rd73$ **Fig. 7.** Reversible Ciruit: $2of5$

bit. Similarly for $rd84$, the Per_4 gate can be avoided by putting an inverted-control Toffoli gate at the end, which sets the output line indicating Hamming weight of 1000 to true if none of the less Hamming weight values are true. This allows cascading of 5 Per_3 gates. For $9sym$, computing the final two Hamming weights 1000 and 1001 can be avoided, since those do not influence the output. Neither of the Hamming weight values influencing the output, i.e. 3, 4, 5 and 6, has any overlapping bit-pattern in the 3 least significant bits. The complete reversible circuit for $2of5$ is shown in Fig. 7.

Comparison with state-of-the-art synthesis methods: This construction technique easily outperforms both the previous property-specific synthesis flows for symmetric functions in *all the efficiency metrics* as shown in Table 6. In [8], a cascade of 2-control Peres gates are used followed by an extraction-elimination module. In contrast, we do not require any follow-up module and obtain the individual Hamming weight values directly. The values with * in the garbage count are shown to be minimal [13]. Further, it is likely that any approach based on adder circuit and generalized Peres gates may benefit from the results presented in this paper.

4.3 Upper Bounds of Symmetric Functions

In this subsection, we establish novel upper bounds for the gate count and QC for symmetric Boolean functions based on the proposed constructive approach. To the best of our knowledge, no such upper bound for symmetric Boolean functions exist.

Based on a recent result [30], we have an expression of the QC of Tof_n gate as following.

$$2(n-1)^2 - 2(n-1) + 1 \tag{9}$$

While this result is for positive-control Tof_n gates, we use it also for mixed-polarity Tof_n gates. It has been showed in the case of mixed-polarity Tof_n gates, a realization with equivalent QC can be obtained [16]. The only case, where the QC for mixed-polarity is higher, is when all the control inputs are negated. In that case, the QC is

$$2(n-1)^2 - 2(n-1) + 3 \tag{10}$$

Using the proposed constructive approach, we explore the following upper bound calculation based on the circuit for Hamming weight computation using cascaded Per_n gates.

Lemma 2. *The upper bound of QC for an n-variable Hamming weight computation circuit is* $(\lfloor \log_2 n \rfloor)^2 + n(\lfloor \log_2 n \rfloor) + n - 1$.

Proof. For an n-variable Boolean function, the Hamming weight computation requires $(n-1)$ cascaded Per_k gates, where the maximum value of k can be $\lfloor \log_2 n \rfloor + 1$. Considering the worst-case scenario, total $(n-1)$ cascaded $Per_{\lfloor \log_2 n \rfloor + 1}$ gates are needed. By using the result from Corollary 1, the upper bound on QC is $(\lfloor \log_2 n \rfloor + 1)^2 + (n - 2)(\lfloor \log_2 n \rfloor + 1)$. Simplification of this leads to the result.   □

Theorem 1. *The upper bound of QC for an n-variable Symmetric Boolean function is* $(2n + 1)(\lfloor \log_2 n \rfloor)^2 - n(\lfloor \log_2 n \rfloor) + 4n - 1$.

Proof. The computation of Symmetric function is composed of Hamming weight calculation followed by a set of comparators. Each comparator is due to one Hamming weight value. There can be $(n+1)$ different Hamming weights for an n-variable Boolean function. However, at most n Hamming weights can contribute to the generation of the Symmetric function, as otherwise, it will become a constant function. The Hamming weights are stored in $(\lfloor \log_2 n \rfloor + 1)$ lines. Each comparator for a specific Hamming weight value require a mixed-polarity Tof_k gate, where k is at most $(\lfloor \log_2 n \rfloor + 1)$. This leads to the worst-case QC value from the comparator circuit as $n(2(\lfloor \log_2 n \rfloor)^2 - 2(\lfloor \log_2 n \rfloor) + 3)$. By adding the upper bound of QC from the Hamming weight circuit with the comparator circuit, we obtain the result.   □

Clearly, the upper bound derived in Theorem 1 based on the constructive approach is tighter compared to the generic upper bounds presented recently in [1].

It can be also noted that the QC values obtained for benchmark circuits, presented in Table 6 is significantly less than the upper bound presented in Theorem 1. To predict a tighter bound of QC for individual circuits compared to theorem 1, we need to enumerate the number of $Per_1, Per_2 \cdots Per_{\lfloor \log_2 n \rfloor + 1}$ gates, which follows a piecewise function. Let us define the number of Per_k gates for an n-variable Hamming weight computation circuit as $C_n(Per_k)$. It can be easily shown that,

$$
C_n(Per_k) = \begin{cases} 0 & \text{if } n < 2^{k-1} \\ (n+1) - 2^{\lfloor \log_2 n \rfloor} & \text{if } 2^{k-1} \leq n \leq 2^k - 1 \\ 2^{k-1} & \text{if } n \geq 2^k \end{cases}
$$

5   Summary and Future Work

In this paper, a novel, constuctive reversible logic synthesis method is presented for Boolean functions with special properties. It has been shown that this synthesis methods outperforms state-of-the-art, general reversible logic synthesis methods. Detailed experimental studies are presented to support the claim.

Due to the desirability of Boolean functions with specific properties, new constructions are continuously being proposed. The presented techniques can be extended to cover further Boolean function construction methods. The interdependence between the Boolean function properties and the implementation efficiency is an interesting open research problem. Further, we will like to explore the usage of efficient reversible circuits for symmetric Boolean functions in the context of reversible logic synthesis and adder circuit realizations.

Acknowledgement. The authors will like to thank the anonymous reviewers, whose critical feedback helped to improve the paper considerably. The first author will like to acknowledge the help of Prof. Subhamoy Maitra, Indian Statistical Institute, Kolkata, India for understanding several Boolean function construction techniques.

References

1. Abdessaied, N., Soeken, M., Thomsen, M.K., Drechsler, R.: Upper bounds for reversible circuits based on Young subgroups. Information Processing Letters 114(6), 282–286 (2014) ISSN 0020-0190, http://dx.doi.org/10.1016/j.ipl.2014.01.003
2. Bennett, C.H.: Logical Reversibility of Computation. IBM Journal of Research and Development 6, 525–532 (1973)
3. Bérut, A., Arakelyan, A., Petrosyan, A., Ciliberto, S., Dillenschneider, R., Lutz, E.: Experimental verification of Landauer's principle linking information and thermodynamics. Nature, 187–189 (March 2012)
4. Beth, T., Rötteler, M.: Quantum algorithms: Applicable Algebra and Quantum physics. In: Quantum Information, pp. 96–150. Springer (2001)
5. Carlet, C.: Boolean Functions for Cryptography and Error Correcting Codes. In: Crama, Y., Hammer, P. (eds.) Boolean Methods and Models, pp. 257–397. Cambridge University Press (2010), http://www.math.univ-paris13.fr/~carlet/pubs.html
6. Chee, S., Lee, S., Lee, D., Sung, S.H.: On the Correlation Immune Functions and Their Nonlinearity. In: Kim, K.-C., Matsumoto, T. (eds.) ASIACRYPT 1996. LNCS, vol. 1163, pp. 232–243. Springer, Heidelberg (1996)
7. Chakrabory, K., Maitra, S.: Quantum algorithm to check Resiliency of a Boolean function. In: International Workshop on Coding and Cryptography (2013)
8. Deb, A., Das, D.K., Rahaman, H., Bhattacharya, B.B., Wille, R., Drechsler, R.: Reversible Circuit Synthesis of Symmetric Functions Using a Simple Regular Structure. In: Workshop on Reversible Computation, pp. 182–195 (2013)
9. Dillon, J.F.: Elementary Hadamard Difference Set, PhD Dissertation, University of Maryland, College Park, MD (1974)
10. Gupta, P., Agrawal, A., Jha, N.K.: An Algorithm for Synthesis of Reversible Logic Circuits. IEEE TCAD 25(11), 2317–2330 (2006)
11. Landauer, R.: Irreversibility and heat generation in the computing process. IBM Journal of Research and Development 5, 183–191 (1961)
12. Maitra, S., Pasalic, E.: A Maiorana–McFarland type Construction for Resilient Boolean functions on n variables (n even) with nonlinearity. Discrete Applied Mathematics 154(2), 357–369 (2006)
13. Maslov, D.: Reversible Benchmarks (2014), http://webhome.cs.uvic.ca/~dmaslov (last accessed March 2014)
14. Maslov, D., Mathew, J., Cheung, D., Pradhan, D.K.: An $O(m^2)$-depth quantum algorithm for the elliptic curve discrete logarithm problem over $GF(2^m)^a$. In: Quantum Information & Computation, pp. 610–621 (2009)

15. Maslov, D.: Efficient reversible and quantum implementations of symmetric Boolean functions. IEE Proceedings of Circuits, Devices and Systems 153(5), 467–472 (2006)
16. Maslov, D., Dueck, G.W., Miller, D.M., Negrevergne, C.: Quantum Circuit Simplification and Level Compaction. IEEE TCAD 27(3), 436–444 (2008), doi:10.1109/TCAD.2007.911334
17. Matsui, M., Yamagishi, A.: A new method for known plaintext attack of FEAL cipher. In: Rueppel, R.A. (ed.) EUROCRYPT 1992. LNCS, vol. 658, pp. 81–91. Springer, Heidelberg (1993)
18. Miller, D.M., Maslov, D., Dueck, G.W.: A Transformation Based Algorithm for Reversible Logic Synthesis. In: Proceedings of DAC, pp. 318–323 (2003)
19. Moraga, C., Hadjam, F.Z.: On Double gates for Reversible Computing Circuits. In: Proceedings of International Workshop on Boolean Problems (2012)
20. Nayeem, N.M., Rice, J.E.: Improved ESOP-based Synthesis of Reversible Logic. In: Proceedings of the Reed-Muller Workshop (2011)
21. Patel, K.N., Markov, I.L., Hayes, J.P.: Optimal synthesis of linear reversible circuits. Quantum Information & Computation 8(3), 282–294 (2008)
22. Pasalic, E., Maitra, S., Johansson, T., Sarkar, P.: New constructions of resilient and correlation immune Boolean functions achieving upper bound on nonlinearity. Electronic Notes in Discrete Mathematics 6, 158–167 (2001)
23. Perkowski, M., Kerntopf, P., Buller, A., Chrzanowska-Jeske, M., Mischenko, A., Song, X., Al-Rabadi, A., Jozwiak, L., Coppola, A., Massey, B.: Regularity and Symmetry as a Base for Efficient Realization of Reversible Logic Circuits. In: Proceedings of IWLS, pp. 90–95 (2001)
24. Pieprzyk, J., Finkelstein, G.: Towards Effective Nonlinear Cryptosystem Design. In: Proceedings of IEEE Computers and Digital Techniques, vol. 135(6), pp. 143–7062 (November 1988) ISSN:0143-7062
25. Preneel, B., Van Leekwijck, W., Van Linden, L., Govaerts, R., Vandewalle, J.: Propagation characteristics of Boolean functions. In: Damgård, I.B. (ed.) EUROCRYPT 1990. LNCS, vol. 473, pp. 161–173. Springer, Heidelberg (1991)
26. Saeedi, M., Markov, I.L.: Synthesis and Optimization of Reversible Circuits - A Survey. CoRR abs/1110.2574 (2011), http://arxiv.org/abs/1110.2574
27. Sarkar, P., Maitra, S.: Construction of nonlinear Boolean functions with important cryptographic properties. In: Preneel, B. (ed.) EUROCRYPT 2000. LNCS, vol. 1807, pp. 485–506. Springer, Heidelberg (2000)
28. Soeken, M., Frehse, S., Wille, R., Drechsler, R.: RevKit: A toolkit for reversible circuit design. In: Workshop on Reversible Computation, pp. 69–72 (2010)
29. Szyprowski, M., Kerntopf, P.: Reducing Quantum Cost of Pairs of Multi-Control Toffoli Gates. In: International Workshop on Boolean Problems (2012)
30. Szyprowski, M., Kerntopf, P.: Low Quantum Cost Realization of Generalized Peres and Toffoli Gates with Multiple-Control Signals. In: 13th IEEE International Conference on Nanotechnology, pp. 802–807 (2013)
31. Tarannikov, Y.V.: New Constructions of Resilient Boolean Functions with Maximal Nonlinearity. In: Matsui, M. (ed.) FSE 2001. LNCS, vol. 2355, p. 66. Springer, Heidelberg (2002)
32. Wille, R., Drechsler, R.: BDD-based Synthesis of Reversible Logic for Large Functions. In: Proceedings of DAC, pp. 270–275 (2009)
33. Yarlagadda, R., Hershey, J.E.: Analysis and synthesis of bent sequences. IEEE Proceedings on Computers and Digital Techniques 136(2), 112–123 (1989)
34. Younes, A.: Synthesis and Optimization of Reversible Circuits for Homogeneous Boolean Functions. arXiv:0710.0664 [quant-ph] (2007)
35. Zhang, F., Hu, Y., Ma, H., Xie, M.: Constructions of Maiorana-McFarland's Bent Functions of Prescribed Degree. In: International Conference on Computational Intelligence and Security (CIS), pp. 315–319 (2010)

RevVis: Visualization of Structures and Properties in Reversible Circuits

Robert Wille[1,2], Jannis Stoppe[2],
Eleonora Schönborn[1], Kamalika Datta[3], and Rolf Drechsler[1,2]

[1] Institute of Computer Science, University of Bremen, 28359 Bremen, Germany
[2] Cyber-Physical Systems, DFKI GmbH, 28359 Bremen, Germany
[3] Department of Information Technology, Bengal Engineering, Shibpur, India
{rwille,jstoppe,eleonora,drechsle}@informatik.uni-bremen.de,
kdatta.iitkgp@gmail.com
www.informatik.uni-bremen.de/agra/eng/revvis.php

Abstract. The recent interest in reversible computation led to plenty of (automatic) approaches for the design of the corresponding circuits. While this automation is desired in order to provide a proper support for the design of complex functionality, often a manual consideration and human intuition enable improvements or provide new ideas for design solutions. However, this manual interaction requires a good understanding of the structure or the properties of a reversible cascade which, with increasing circuit size, becomes harder to grasp. Visualization techniques that abstract irrelevant details and focus on intuitively displaying important structures or properties provide a solution to this problem and have already successfully been applied in other domains such as design of conventional software, hardware debugging, or Boolean satisfiability. In this work, we introduce *RevVis*, a graphical interface which visualizes structures and properties of reversible circuits. *RevVis* collects relevant data of a given reversible cascade and presents it in a simple but intuitive fashion. By this, *RevVis* unveils information on characteristic structures and properties of reversible circuits that could be utilized for further optimization. A case study demonstrates this by considering circuits obtained from several synthesis approaches.

1 Introduction

Motivated by applications e.g. in quantum computation [1], low-power design [2], or encoder and decoder design [3], research in reversible computation received significant interest in the past. While rather small circuits have (manually) been considered at the beginning, a recent strive for automated and scalable methods supporting the design of several thousand gate circuits can be observed today. This resulted in plenty of (automated) approaches for the synthesis and optimization of reversible circuits in the recent past (see e.g. [4,5] for overviews). Most of them are based on a particular genuine idea, e.g. reversible transformations at a truth-table description, the utilization of proper data structures such as ESOPs, decision diagrams, etc., or the application of templates. But besides

S. Yamashita and S. Minato (Eds.): RC 2014, LNCS 8507, pp. 111–124, 2014.

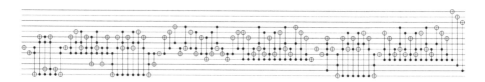

Fig. 1. Existing netlist visualization of reversible circuits

that, also human intuition often led to ideas for new strategies to be exploited or enabled further improvements which could not be detected by a machine.

However, getting a good intuition of a considered circuit requires a deep technical understanding of how design approaches actually realize the respective circuits. Moreover, these approaches may generate circuits with certain structures and properties that are often neither obvious to the developer nor to the user of the design method. Consequently, possible potential in terms of better synthesis or optimization may often not fully be exploited.

In fact, relevant instances of any kind are often equipped with some internal (sometimes hidden) structures or properties that are unknown to the developer and/or designer [6]. One way to unveil these information is to provide a different intuition about a circuit. This can be accomplished by visualization technologies. However, existing visualization schemes for reversible circuits are basically limited to simple netlist representations in which all gates are only arranged in a cascade where black circles and ⊕ respectively represent control and target lines of the gates. In particular for larger circuits, these netlists do not provide a proper intuition of the structure and possible properties of reversible circuits. As an example, consider the netlist visualization of a circuit realizing a division and shown in Fig. 1 (realized by the HDL-based synthesis approach proposed in [7]). Although this circuit is composed of less than 100 gates, it is almost impossible to recognize certain structures and/or properties from this netlist visualization.

As a consequence, advanced visualization techniques are required that go beyond the straight-forward representation of a circuit as a netlist. They should mask irrelevant details as deemed necessary and, in turn, explicitly focus on highlighting the desired structures and properties. In other domains, such visualization techniques have already successfully been applied. For example:

- In the conventional software design, visualizations such as the *CodeCity* [8] are well known. Here, different software classes are placed as "buildings" within an artificial representation of a city. Depending on their properties, e.g. their number of attributes, methods, or lines of code, the ground size or the height of the "buildings" differ. Structural interrelation between classes is e.g. emphasized by placing the corresponding "buildings" in the same "district". Fig. 2a shows such a visualization taken from [8]. Unproportional looking "buildings" immediately pinpoint the designer to problematic classes in the software project. The visualization reveals classes that are too complex in terms of code and may better be split into subclasses or are not well-balanced in terms of their number of attributes to number of methods ratio.

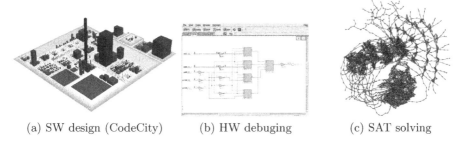

(a) SW design (CodeCity)   (b) HW debuging   (c) SAT solving

Fig. 2. Visualization technologies in other domains

- In the domain of debugging (conventional) hardware, so called *error candidates* are explicitly highlighted in the netlist [9]. They represent logic elements within the circuit that may explain an erroneous behavior. Fig. 2b shows such a visualization (taken from [9]). By this, the designer is explicitly pinpointed to possible reasons for the incorrect behavior and does not have to consider all gates of the circuit at once. Furthermore, by lapping several of such layers, the designer is provided with an intuitive representation of the circuit as well as possible explanations for the error which aids him/her during the debugging process.
- Solvers for Boolean satisfiability (so called SAT solvers [10]) have been shown to be very powerful and, hence, find practical applications e.g. in domains like verification. However, although these approaches are able to efficiently solve instances composed of hundreds of thousands of variables and constraints, much smaller instances remain unsolvable within generous time limits. Understanding what makes a SAT instance hard or not has also been investigated using visualization technologies [11]. For this purpose, instances have been represented by graphs as shown in Fig. 2c (taken from [11]), where nodes represent the variables of the instance and edges the constraints over them. Using a visualization like this intuitively unveils connected sub-functions, important and less important literals, etc. This provides a better understanding about how instances could be solved in a more efficient fashion.

Motivated by these success stories, the application of visualization technologies in the domain of reversible circuit design is investigated in this work. For this purpose, we present the tool *RevVis*, a graphical interface that intuitively visualizes the structure and properties of reversible circuits. For a selected set of metrics and objectives which are relevant in the design of reversible circuits, corresponding data is collected and, afterwards, visualized in a simple fashion. The application of *RevVis* has been evaluated in a thorough case study involving several synthesis approaches that have been proposed in the past. From the different visualizations some already known structures and properties could be confirmed. Beyond that also new characteristics could be unveiled. They may be exploited in the future to further finetune these approaches and to develop corresponding new optimization schemes for the resulting circuits.

The remainder of this paper is structured as follows. The next section briefly reviews reversible circuits and some of the metrics that are considered in the following. Section 3 introduces *RevVis* and, in particular, the visualizations of the selected metrics and objectives. Afterwards, these visualizations are applied for circuits generated by several synthesis approaches. Possible conclusions drawn from that are discussed in Section 4. The paper is eventually concluded in Section 5.

2   Background

This section briefly reviews reversible circuits as well as some of their properties which will be considered later in this paper. In general, reversible logic deals with Boolean functions which are *reversible*. A function $f : \mathbb{B}^n \to \mathbb{B}^m$ over the variables $X := \{x_1, \ldots, x_n\}$ is said to be reversible if (1) its number of inputs and outputs is equal (i.e. $n = m$) and (2) it represents a bijective, i.e. one-to-one, mapping. A reversible circuit G is composed of a cascade of reversible gates $G = g_1 g_2 \ldots g_k$ where g_i represents a reversible gate. In the past, various reversible gates such as the Toffoli gate [12], Fredkin gate [13], or Peres gate [14] have been investigated. In the context of this work, we focus on *Multiple Control Toffoli* gates which are known to be universal.

A Toffoli gate is composed of a (possibly empty) set of *control lines* $C = \{x_{i_1}, \ldots, x_{i_k}\} \subset X$ as well as a single *target line* $x_j \in X \setminus C$ and maps $(x_1, \ldots, x_n)$ to $(x_1, \ldots, x_{j-1}, x_j \oplus x_{i_1} \ldots x_{i_k}, x_{j+1}, \ldots, x_n)$. In other words, the logic value on the target line gets inverted if all the control inputs are at logic 1; otherwise the value on the target is passed as it is. In addition to the (positive) control lines as defined above, Toffoli gates may also be composed of negative control lines. The functionality of such gates is the same as defined above, except that the value on the target line is inverted if all values on positive control lines are assigned 1 and all values on negative control lines are assigned 0. Fig. 3a exemplarily shows a reversible circuit composed of eight Toffoli gates.

In a reversible circuit, sometimes an input line is fed with a constant logic value (0 or 1). Such circuit lines are denoted to have *constant inputs*. Similarly, circuit lines with so called *garbage outputs* may exist, i.e. circuit lines whose output value is a don't care. Garbage outputs may e.g. be needed in order to make an irreversible function reversible (see e.g. [15,16]). The circuit from Fig. 3a has two constant inputs and two garbage outputs.

Finally, the *moving rule* for reversible circuits is partially considered in this work: Two adjacent gates g_1 and g_2 with control lines C_1 and C_2 as well as target lines t_1 and t_2, respectively, can be interchanged if $C_1 \cap \{t_2\} = \emptyset$ and $C_2 \cap \{t_1\} = \emptyset$, i.e. if none of the target lines of one gate is a control line of the other gate. Moving gates through the circuit enables further optimizations, e.g. it allows to remove or merge redundant gates (see e.g. [17,18,19,20]). Hence, the *movability* of a gate is an important metric. Consider a reversible gate sequence $G = g_1 g_2 \ldots g_k$. For every gate $g_i (1 \leq i \leq k)$, the movability of the gate is the number of possible gate positions j $(j \neq i)$ such that g_i can be moved to position j according to the definition from above.

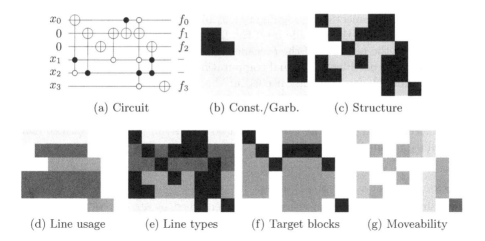

Fig. 3. Different visualizations

3 The RevVis Tool

This section introduces the main features of the proposed visualization schemes which have been implemented in the tool *RevVis*[1]. For a selected set of metrics and objectives, the tool first collects information on the structure and properties of a given reversible circuit, which are then visualized. The visualizations are kept as simple and abstract as possible so that, even for larger designs, an intuitive and easy understanding is possible. In the following, the considered metrics and objectives are introduced. Here, all visualization schemes are illustrated by means of the reversible circuit depicted in Fig. 3a.

Constant Inputs and Garbage Outputs. Constant inputs and garbage outputs are not only essential in order to embed irreversible functions into reversible ones (see e.g. [15,16]), but are also heavily applied in synthesis approaches e.g. based on ESOPs (e.g. [21]) or decision diagrams (e.g. [22]). Optimization approaches such as introduced in [23] rely on the fact how long circuit lines with constants or garbage are unused or not needed anymore, respectively. This is emphasized by the first visualization scheme shown in Fig. 3b. All lines inheriting a constant or garbage line are highlighted by black rows. The width of the rows depends on the number of gates in the cascade in which the respective constant (garbage) is unused (not needed anymore).

Structure of the Circuit. Reversible circuits are composed as a cascade of reversible gates which, in turn, are composed of control lines and target lines. Due to this cascade structure, the structural usage of each line in a circuit may significantly differ. This is visualized in the scheme shown in Fig. 3c. Each control

---

[1] RevVis is available at
http://www.informatik.uni-bremen.de/agra/eng/revvis.php.

and target line connection is highlighted in black. Grey denotes the usage of each circuit line, i.e. the cascade from the first gate in which this circuit line is involved until the last gate of the cascade. White represents parts of the circuit which are not needed for the actual computation. For example, the bottom line of the considered circuit is only needed at the end of the cascade while all remaining lines are needed almost throughout the whole cascade. Although similar to the netlist visualization, this simplified view enables a more intuitive view on the structure of a circuit and can pinpoint to "holes" in the circuit (which can be used e.g. as ancilliae).

Line Usage. The usage of circuit lines is additionally visualized by the scheme shown in Fig. 3d. Here, the visualization is enriched by a color code representing the numerical usage of a circuit line. Lines highlighted red (green) represent the circuit lines with the largest (smallest) number of control and target line connections. Yellow patterns denote the circuit lines which lie between these extremes. White represents parts of the circuit which are not needed for the actual computation. Information like that could e.g. be applied for nearest neighbor optimization (see e.g. [24,25,26,27]). Here, control and target line connections always have to be adjacent, i.e. lines which are heavily used should preferably be put next to each other.

Line Types. The distribution of control and target line connections is an objective of the scheme shown in Fig. 3e. Here, red lines (green lines) denote circuit lines which are entirely composed of target lines (control lines) only; yellow lines denote circuit lines which have both control and target line connections. All actual connections are again highlighted in black. This could provide some inspiration for optimization as e.g. huge parts of the circuit composed entirely of control lines may provide some potential for reduction by factorization (see e.g. [28]).

Target blocks. Fig. 3f shows another scheme which focuses on the target line connections. More precisely, sub-circuits in which all gates have the same target line are highlighted by means of grey blocks (with the target lines additionally highlighted in black). Also this view could provide some inspiration for optimization (in particular, if the possibly different control connections could be merged so that such a cascade can be reduced to some few or even a single gate(s)).

Movability. Finally, the "movability" of gates is visualized in Fig. 3g, i.e. the applicability of the moving rule as reviewed in Section 2 is represented for each gate. Gates highlighted red have a low movability (i.e. can hardly be moved through the cascade), while gates highlighted green can be moved rather flexibly through the cascade. Obviously this view is particularly helpful to investigate optimization approaches relying on the moving rule.

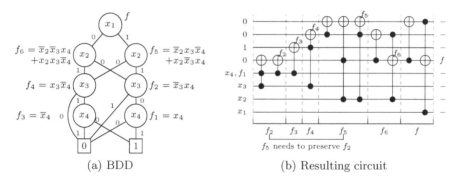

(a) BDD   (b) Resulting circuit

Fig. 4. BDD-based synthesis

4   Applying RevVis

The visualizations proposed in the last section are supposed to provide a representation which allows to grasp a good intuition of the structure and the properties of a given circuit. In order to illustrate that *RevVis* satisfies this purpose, an intense case study has been conducted, in which circuits generated with different synthesis approaches (namely BDD-based synthesis [22], ESOP-based synthesis [21], and HDL-based synthesis [7,29]) have been investigated using *RevVis*. In this section, results of these investigations are exemplarily shown and discussed. For this purpose, first the respective synthesis approach is briefly reviewed. Afterwards, a representative circuit (taken from RevLib [30]) is visualized and corresponding observations are discussed.

4.1   Considering Circuits Obtained by BDD-Based Synthesis

The Synthesis Approach. BDD-based synthesis as introduced in [22] makes use of *Binary Decision Diagrams* (BDDs) [31]. A BDD is a directed graph $G = (V, E)$ where each terminal node represents the constant 0 or 1 and each non-terminal node represents a (sub-)function. Each non-terminal node $v \in V$ has two succeeding nodes $low(v)$ and $high(v)$. If v is representing the function f and labeled with the variable x_i, then the corresponding sub-functions represented by the succeeding nodes are the co-factors $f_{x_i=0}$ ($low(v)$) and $f_{x_i=1}$ ($high(v)$). Thus, a BDD naturally exposes the Shannon decomposition. Having a BDD representing a function f as well as its sub-functions derived by Shannon decomposition, a reversible circuit for f can be obtained as shown by the following example.

Example 1. Fig. 4a shows a BDD representing the function $f = \bar{x}_1\bar{x}_2\bar{x}_3x_4 + \bar{x}_1x_2x_3\bar{x}_4 + x_1\bar{x}_2x_3\bar{x}_4 + x_1x_2\bar{x}_3x_4$ as well as the respective co-factors resulting

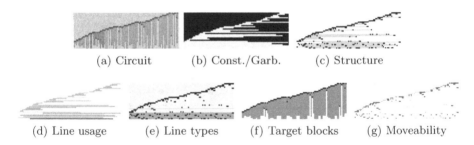

(a) Circuit   (b) Const./Garb.   (c) Structure

(d) Line usage   (e) Line types   (f) Target blocks   (g) Moveability

Fig. 5. Considering a circuit obtained by BDD-based synthesis

from the application of the Shannon decomposition. The co-factor f_1 can easily be represented by the primary input x_4. Having the value of f_1 available, the co-factor f_2 can be realized by the first two gates depicted in Fig. 4b[2]. By this, respective sub-circuits can be added for all remaining co-factors until a circuit representing the overall function f results. The remaining steps are shown in Fig. 4b.

Observations Using RevVis. Fig. 5 shows the visualizations for the circuit *mod5adder_66* which has been obtained using BDD-based synthesis and works as a proper representative for this synthesis scheme. Compared to the simple netlist (see Fig. 5a), these visualizations unveil the clear structure of these circuits. In fact, BDD-based synthesis heavily relies on constant inputs (see Fig. 5b) and subsequently builds up the sub-functions (i.e. the co-factors) of the BDD. This can clearly be seen in Figs. 5c and 5f: New functionality is costantly build up towards the top-right of the circuit. The primary inputs (located at the bottom of the circuit) are frequently used for this purpose. This explains the intense usage of these circuit lines (see Fig. 5d). It also shows very nicely that the usage of the primary inputs depends on the BDD-level, e.g. the primary input represented by the root node of the BDD has a very low usage while primary inputs represented in lower levels of the BDD are accessed more often. As shown in Fig. 5e, all primary input lines are accessed in a read-only fashion (i.e. just control connections are applied in those circuit lines). Finally, Fig. 5g unveils that moveability is usually rather bad in circuits generated by BDD-based synthesis.

By this, several properties of BDD-based circuits which are already known (e.g. the huge number of constant/garbage) are confirmed. Besides that, a clearer intuition of the actual structure and properties is provided. For example, Fig. 5b may offer more precise hints where to merge constants and garbage (similar to the approach presented in [23]). Fig. 5g clearly shows that e.g. optimization approaches like template matching [17] (relying on the moving rule) are not really suitable for BDD-based circuits. Besides that, the clear stepped structure of the overall circuit might be exploitable for further optimizations.

---

[2] Note that an additional circuit line is added to preserve the values of x_4 and x_3 which are still needed by the co-factors f_3 and f_4, respectively.

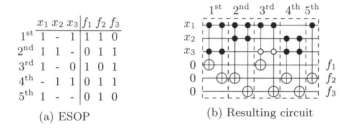

	x_1 x_2 x_3	f_1 f_2 f_3
1st	1 - 1	1 1 0
2nd	1 1 -	0 1 1
3rd	1 - 0	1 0 1
4th	- 1 1	0 1 1
5th	1 - -	0 1 0

(a) ESOP

(b) Resulting circuit

Fig. 6. ESOP-based synthesis

4.2 Considering Circuits Obtained by ESOP-Based Synthesis

The Synthesis Approach. ESOP-based synthesis as introduced in [21] generates a reversible circuit from a Boolean function provided as *Exclusive Sum of Products* (ESOPs). ESOPs are two-level descriptions of Boolean functions that are represented as the exclusive disjunction (EXOR) of conjunctions of literals (called *products*). A *literal* is either a Boolean variable or its negation. That is, an ESOP is the most general form of two-level AND-EXOR expressions.

Having an ESOP representing a function $f : \mathbb{B}^n \to \mathbb{B}^m$, the ESOP-based synthesis approach generates a circuit with $n + m$ lines, where the first n lines work as primary inputs, while the last m circuit lines are initialized to constant 0 and work as primary outputs. Having that, Toffoli gates are selected such that the desired function is realized. This selection exploits the fact that a single product $x_{i_1} \ldots x_{i_k}$ of an ESOP description directly corresponds to a Toffoli gate with control lines $C = \{x_{i_1}, \ldots, x_{i_k}\}$. In case of negative literals, NOT gates or negative control lines are applied accordingly. Based on these ideas, a circuit realizing a function given as ESOP can be derived as illustrated in the following example.

Example 2. Consider the function f to be synthesized as depicted in Fig. 6a[3]. The first product $x_1 x_3$ affects f_1 and f_2. Hence, two Toffoli gates which have target lines f_1 and f_2 and control lines $C = \{x_1, x_3\}$ are added (see Fig. 6b). The third product $x_1 \overline{x}_3$ includes a negative literal. Thus, the Toffoli gates added for this product have a negative control line on x_3. This procedure is continued until all products have been considered. The resulting circuit is shown in Fig. 6b.

Observations Using RevVis. Fig. 7 shows the visualizations for the circuit *rd73_252* which has been obtained using ESOP-based synthesis and works as a proper representative for this synthesis scheme. Compared to the simple

---

[3] The column on the left-hand side gives the products, where a "1" on the ith position denotes a positive literal (i.e. x_i) and a "0" denotes a negative literal (i.e. $\overline{x}_i$), respectively. A "–" denotes that the respective variable is not included in the product. The right-hand side gives the primary output patterns.

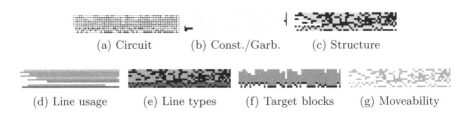

(a) Circuit   (b) Const./Garb.   (c) Structure

(d) Line usage   (e) Line types   (f) Target blocks   (g) Moveability

Fig. 7. Considering a circuit obtained by ESOP-based synthesis

netlist (see Fig. 7a), the characteristic structure is clearly unveiled thanks to the visualizations. In particular, the distinction between input lines (which have control connections only) and output lines (which have target connections only) becomes evident (see Fig. 7e) and also leads to a very regular structure with respect to target blocks (see e.g. Fig. 7f). This provides potential as it may allow to merge gates with equal control lines but different target lines (as discussed e.g. in [19]). Furthermore, approaches relying on the moving rule (e.g. [17]) significantly benefit from this structure as it leads to a very high movability (see Fig. 7g). It may also be observed that, due to the high movability of gates, many target blocks can be merged leading to more potential for optimization. In contrast, constant inputs are used very early in the cascade (see Fig. 7b), i.e. there is no potential to reduce the number of constant/garbage lines using e.g. the method proposed in [23]. Besides that, ESOP-based circuits seem to have a rather irregular structure, i.e. the respective gate connections are distributed rather arbitrarily (see Fig. 7c). However, it can be observed that inputs lines are used more often than output lines (see Fig. 7d). This can be explained by the fact that some factors may have to be applied to several functions and, hence, identical control connections are frequently applied.

4.3   Considering Circuits Obtained by HDL-Based Synthesis

The Synthesis Approach. The strive for more scalable synthesis approaches also led to the definition and consideration of a *Hardware Description Language* (HDL) for reversible circuits in [7]. In order to ensure reversibility in the description, this HDL distinguishes between reversible assignments (denoted by $\oplus=$) and not necessarily reversible *binary operations* (denoted by $\odot$). The former class of operations assigns values to a signal on the left-hand side. Therefore, the left-hand side signal must not appear in the expression on the right-hand side. Furthermore, only a restricted set of assignment operations exists, namely increase (+=), decrease (-=), and bit-wise XOR (^=). These operations preserve the reversibility (i.e. it is possible to compute these operations in both directions). In contrast, binary operations, e.g. arithmetic, bit-wise, logical, or relational operations, may not be reversible and, hence, can only be used in right-hand expressions which preserve the values of the inputs. In doing so, all computations remain reversible since the input values can be applied to reverse any operation. For example, to describe a multiplication (i.e. a*b), a new free

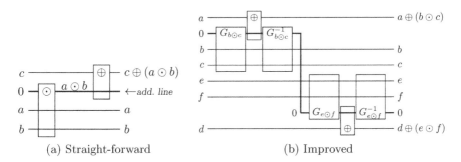

(a) Straight-forward   (b) Improved

Fig. 8. HDL-based synthesis

signal c must be introduced which is used to store the product (i.e. c^=a*b is applied). In comparison to common (non-reversible) languages, this forbids statements like a=a*b.

Having such an HDL description, synthesis approaches like introduced in [7] generate corresponding circuits following a hierarchical scheme. That is, existing realizations of the individual operations (i.e. building blocks) are combined so that the desired circuit is realized. This is illustrated in Fig. 8a for the generic operation $c\oplus = (a\odot b)$. First, the binary operation $\odot$ is realized (using additional circuit lines with constant inputs). Afterwards, the intermediate result is utilized to realize the complete statement including its reversible assignment $\oplus=$.

This scheme has further been improved in [29]. Here, the values of intermediate results are reversed once they are not needed any longer (leading back to the original constant value). Then, no new additional lines might be required to buffer upcoming intermediate results. The general idea is briefly illustrated in Fig. 8b by means of the generic HDL statements $a\oplus = (b\odot c)$ and $d\oplus = (e\odot f)$. First, two sub-circuits $G_{b\odot c}$ and $G_{a\oplus=b\odot c}$ are added ensuring that the first statement is realized. This is equal to the procedure from Fig. 8a and leads to additional lines with constant inputs. But then, a further sub-circuit $G_{b\odot c}^{-1}$ is applied. Since $G_{b\odot c}^{-1}$ is the inverse of $G_{b\odot c}$, this sets the circuit lines buffering the result of $b\odot c$ back to the constant 0. As a result, these circuit lines can be reused in order to realize the following statements as illustrated for $d\oplus=e\odot f$ in Fig. 8b.

Observations Using RevVis. Fig. 9 (Fig. 10) shows the visualizations for the circuit *mult_stmts_3bit* which has been obtained using the straight-forward HDL-based synthesis as illustrated in Fig. 8a (the improved HDL-based synthesis as illustrated in Fig. 8b) and works as a proper representative for this synthesis scheme. More precisely, these circuits realize three HDL-statements over 3-bit variables. The respective cascades for each statement are separated by vertical lines in Fig. 9 and Fig. 10. Compared to the simple netlist (see Fig. 9a and Fig. 10a), these visualizations do not only unveil the structure and characteristics of the respective circuits, but also the differences between the straight-forward and optimized synthesis scheme.

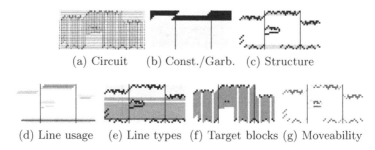

(a) Circuit   (b) Const./Garb.   (c) Structure

(d) Line usage   (e) Line types   (f) Target blocks   (g) Moveability

Fig. 9. Considering a circuit obtained by HDL-based synthesis

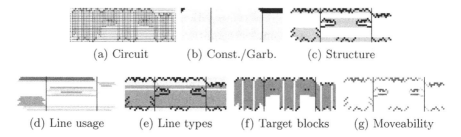

(a) Circuit   (b) Const./Garb.   (c) Structure

(d) Line usage   (e) Line types   (f) Target blocks   (g) Moveability

Fig. 10. Considering a circuit obtained by improved HDL-based synthesis

First of all, the structures sketched in Fig. 8, i.e. the building blocks for binary operations, reversible assignments, and reversing, can also be recognized in the visualizations (see e.g. Fig. 9c and Fig. 10c). In particular for the improved scheme, the symmetry resulting from reversing intermediate results is rather obvious. Here, it can also be observed that just one set of constant circuit lines is needed, while the straight-forward approach uses several constant circuit lines only for a short time (compare Fig. 9b and Fig. 10b). The frequent re-use of these lines in the improved approach is also reflected in the line usage visualization (see Fig. 10d).

Besides that, many circuit lines only have control connections in this example (see Figs. 9e and 10e). This is caused by the fact that the three HDL-statements are of the form $a\oplus = (b\odot c)$, i.e. b and c never occur on the left-hand side of a statement. Finally, the visualization clearly unveils that HDL-based circuits have a rather poor moveability and, hence, do not seem very suitable for optimization schemes such as [17] (see Figs. 9g and 10g).

5   Conclusions

In this work, we considered the visualization of reversible circuits. This is motivated by the fact that certain structures and properties of circuits are often not obvious to the developer or to the user. Furthermore, simple netlist representations do not provide a proper intuition and, hence, are not suitable – particularly for circuits of larger size. In order to address this, we introduced the tool *RevVis* which provides visualization layers for several metrics as well as objectives and, by this, intuitively highlights structures and properties of reversible circuits. The application of *RevVis* has been evaluated in a thorough case study involving several synthesis approaches. This enabled a deeper discussion about both known as well as new characteristics of the obtained circuits and, hence, the considered synthesis schemes. In the future, visualizations as proposed in this work will be beneficial to draw conclusions from newly developed design approaches right from the beginning as well as to gain inspiration for new synthesis and optimization methods.

References

1. Nielsen, M., Chuang, I.: Quantum Computation and Quantum Information. Cambridge Univ. Press (2000)
2. Berut, A., Arakelyan, A., Petrosyan, A., Ciliberto, S., Dillenschneider, R., Lutz, E.: Experimental verification of Landauer's principle linking information and thermodynamics. Nature 483, 187–189 (2012)
3. Wille, R., Drechsler, R., Osewold, C., Garcia-Ortiz, A.: Automatic design of low-power encoders using reversible circuit synthesis. In: Design, Automation and Test in Europe, pp. 1036–1041 (2012)
4. Drechsler, R., Wille, R.: From truth tables to programming languages: progress in the design of reversible circuits. In: Int'l Symp. on Multi-Valued Logic, pp. 78–85 (2011)
5. Saeedi, M., Markov, I.L.: Synthesis and optimization of reversible circuits - a survey. ACM Computing Surveys 45(2) (2011)
6. Walsh, T.: Search in a small world. In: International Conference on AI, pp. 1172–1177 (1999)
7. Wille, R., Offermann, S., Drechsler, R.: SyReC: A programming language for synthesis of reversible circuits. In: Forum on Specification and Design Languages, pp. 184–189 (2010)
8. Wettel, R., Lanza, M., Robbes, R.: Software systems as cities: a controlled experiment. In: International Conference on Software Engineering, pp. 551–560 (2011)
9. Sülflow, A., Wille, R., Genz, C., Fey, G., Drechsler, R.: FormED: A formal environment for debugging. In: University Booth at the Design, Automation and Test in Europe (2009)
10. Eén, N., Sörensson, N.: An Extensible SAT-solver. In: Giunchiglia, E., Tacchella, A. (eds.) SAT 2003. LNCS, vol. 2919, pp. 502–518. Springer, Heidelberg (2004)
11. Sinz, C.: Visualizing SAT instances and runs of the DPLL algorithm. J. Autom. Reasoning 39(2), 219–243 (2007)
12. Toffoli, T.: Reversible computing. In: de Bakker, W., van Leeuwen, J. (eds.) Automata, Languages and Programming. Springer (1980); 632 Technical Memo MIT/LCS/TM-151, MIT Lab. for Comput. Sci.
13. Fredkin, E., Toffoli, T.: Conservative logic. Int'l Journal of Theoretical Physics 21(3-4), 219–253 (1982)
14. Peres, A.: Reversible logic and quantum computers. Phys. Rev. A 32(6), 3266–3276 (1985)

15. Maslov, D., Dueck, G.W.: Reversible cascades with minimal garbage. Trans. on CAD 23(11), 1497–1509 (2004)
16. Wille, R., Keszöcze, O., Drechsler, R.: Determining the minimal number of lines for large reversible circuits. In: Design, Automation and Test in Europe, pp. 1204–1207 (2011)
17. Miller, D.M., Maslov, D., Dueck, G.W.: A transformation based algorithm for reversible logic synthesis. In: Design Automation Conf., pp. 318–323 (2003)
18. Maslov, D., Dueck, G.: Quantum circuit simplification and level compaction. Trans. on CAD 27(3), 436–444 (2008)
19. Wille, R., Soeken, M., Otterstedt, C., Drechsler, R.: Improving the mapping of reversible circuits to quantum circuits using multiple target lines. In: ASP Design Automation Conf. (2013)
20. Datta, K., Rathi, G., Wille, R., Sengupta, I., Rahaman, H., Drechsler, R.: Exploiting negative control lines in the optimization of reversible circuits. In: Dueck, G.W., Miller, D.M. (eds.) RC 2013. LNCS, vol. 7948, pp. 209–220. Springer, Heidelberg (2013)
21. Fazel, K., Thornton, M.A., Rice, J.E.: ESOP-based Toffoli gate cascade generation. In: Pacific Rim Conference on Communications, Computers and Signal Processing, pp. 206–209 (2007)
22. Wille, R., Drechsler, R.: BDD-based synthesis of reversible logic for large functions. In: Design Automation Conf., pp. 270–275 (2009)
23. Wille, R., Soeken, M., Drechsler, R.: Reducing the number of lines in reversible circuits. In: Design Automation Conf., pp. 647–652 (2010)
24. Saeedi, M., Wille, R., Drechsler, R.: Synthesis of quantum circuits for linear nearest neighbor architectures. Quantum Information Processing 10(3), 355–377 (2011)
25. Alfailakawi, M., Alterkawi, L., Ahmad, I., Hamdan, S.: Line ordering of reversible circuits for linear nearest neighbor realization. Quantum Information Processing 12(10), 3319–3339 (2013)
26. Shafaei, A., Saeedi, M., Pedram, M.: Optimization of quantum circuits for interaction distance in linear nearest neighbor architectures. In: Design Automation Conf., p. 41 (2013)
27. Wille, R., Lye, A., Drechsler, R.: Optimal SWAP gate insertion for nearest neighbor quantum circuits. In: ASP Design Automation Conf., pp. 489–494 (2014)
28. Miller, D.M., Wille, R., Drechsler, R.: Reducing reversible circuit cost by adding lines. In: Int'l Symp. on Multi-Valued Logic (2010)
29. Wille, R., Soeken, M., Schönborn, E., Drechsler, R.: Circuit line minimization in the HDL-based synthesis of reversible logic. In: Annual Symposium on VLSI, pp. 213–218 (2012)
30. Wille, R., Große, D., Teuber, L., Dueck, G.W., Drechsler, R.: RevLib: an online resource for reversible functions and reversible circuits. In: Int'l Symp. on Multi-Valued Logic, pp. 220–225 (2008), RevLib is available at http://www.revlib.org
31. Bryant, R.E.: Graph-based algorithms for Boolean function manipulation. Trans. on Comp. 35(8), 677–691 (1986)

Templates for Positive and Negative Control Toffoli Networks

Md Zamilur Rahman and Jacqueline E. Rice

Department of Mathematics and Computer Science,
University of Lethbridge, Lethbridge, AB, Canada
{mdzamilur.rahman,j.rice}@uleth.ca

Abstract. This paper proposes templates for positive and negative control Toffoli gates for post synthesis optimization of reversible circuits. Templates $1-5$ can be applied to two adjacent Toffoli gates $T_1(C_1, t_1)$ and $T_2(C_2, t_2)$ where C_i is the set of controls, $|C_1| = |C_2|$, and $|t_1| = |t_2|$. Templates $6-7$ can be applied to two different size Toffoli gates $T_1(C_1, t_1)$ and $T_2(C_2, t_2)$ where C_i is the set of controls, $|C_1| = |C_2|$ and t_i is the target, $|t_1| = |t_2|$. When applying our templates to circuits generated by the improved shared cube synthesis approach [14] a reduction in quantum cost was achieved for 98 of the 122 circuits. On average a 16.82% reduction in quantum cost was achieved, and in some cases up to 49.60% reduction was obtained.

Keywords: reversible circuit, Toffoli gate, quantum cost, gate count.

1 Introduction

Power dissipation and heat generation are serious problems in today's traditional circuit technologies. According to R. Landauer's observation in 1961, the amount of energy dissipated for each lost bit of information is $KTln2$ where K is the Boltzmann's constant ($1.3807 \times 10^{-23} JK^{-1}$) and T is the Temperature [7]. This is a significant amount of energy for millions of operations. In [1], Bennett said that in order to not dissipate energy the system must be logically reversible. Reversible circuits do not erase any information when operations are performed. In reversible circuits, all operations are performed in a bijective manner. Thus fan-out and feedback operations are not allowed in reversible circuits. Reversible circuits have applications in fields such as quantum computing [15] and optical computing [3]. As a result, reversible logic is being considered as an alternative to conventional logic. Instead of conventional logic gates reversible gates like Toffoli gates, Fredkin gates, and Peres gates are used in reversible circuits.

Several synthesis approaches for reversible logic have been proposed, including transformation based synthesis [11], Exclusive-OR Sum-of-Products (ESOP) based synthesis [5,13] and binary decision diagram (BDD) based synthesis [18]. In this paper we describe a template-based post-processing approach that is based on mixed-polarity Toffoli gates.

S. Yamashita and S. Minato (Eds.): RC 2014, LNCS 8507, pp. 125–136, 2014.

The remainder of this paper is organized as follows. The following section briefly introduces basic concepts in reversible logic. It offers an overview of the Toffoli gate and the cost metrics of a reversible circuit. Section 3 gives the motivations of this work, and the proposed templates are discussed in section 4. Section 6 summarizes the experimental results followed by conclusions in section 7.

2   Background

In this section we provide some brief background and notation to orient the reader.

2.1   Reversible Gates and Reversible Circuits

In this work we focus solely on the Toffoli gate. Other reversible gates are described in *e.g.* [16], which is recommended as a useful introductory article on the topic of reversible logic.

An n-bit Toffoli gate or Multiple Control Toffoli (MCT) gate is a reversible gate that has n inputs and n outputs where $(i_1, i_2, ..., i_n)$ is the input vector, $(o_1, o_2, ..., o_n)$ is the output vector, and $o_j = i_j$ where $j = 1, 2, ..., n - 1$ and $o_n = i_1 i_2 ... i_{n-1} \oplus i_n$. The first $n - 1$ bits are known as controls and the last n^{th} bit is known as the target. This gate passes all the inputs to the outputs and inverts the target bit when all control bits are 1. When $n = 1$, this gate is known as the NOT gate. When $n = 2$, it is referred to as a controlled-NOT (CNOT) gate or Feynman gate. We note that for the sake of simplicity we assume that the nth bit is the target; however the target bit could be any of the n bits with which the gate interacts.

A negative-control Toffoli gate is a gate that may have one or more negative controls. The gate maps the n inputs $(i_1, i_2, ..., i_n)$ to the n outputs $(o_1, o_2, ..., o_n)$ where $o_j = i_j$, $j = 1, 2, ..., n - 1$ and $o_n = \bar{i_1} i_2 ... i_{n-1} \oplus i_n$ and $\bar{i_1}$ is a negative control. This gate passes all the inputs to the outputs and inverts the target bit when all the positive controls have value 1 and negative controls have value 0.

In this paper, $\oplus$ represents the target line, • indicates a positive control, and ○ is used to indicate a negative control line. A Toffoli gate can also be written as $\text{TOF}(C; t)$ where C is the set of controls and t is the target line. The size of a Toffoli gate refers to the number of controls plus target. Figure 1 illustrates several versions of the n-bit Toffoli gate.

A reversible circuit is a cascade of reversible gates without fan-out and feedback. If a reversible circuit is built using only NOT, CNOT, and Toffoli gates (NCT) or Multiple Control Toffoli gates (MCT) it is referred to as a Toffoli circuit.

2.2   Cost Metrics

A reversible function may be realized in different ways, resulting in different circuits. We briefly summarize two common cost metrics used in evaluating reversible circuits.

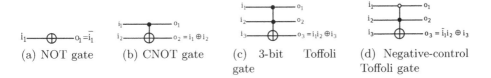

Fig. 1. Toffoli gates

Gate Count. Gate count is the simplest way to evaluate different reversible circuits. This refers to a simple count of the number of gates in a circuit. It does not, however, consider the complexity of the circuit. Consider two circuits where the first circuit consists of three 2-input Toffoli gates and the second circuit consists of two 6-input Toffoli gates. In this case a gate count might indicate that the second circuit is preferable, as it has fewer gates. However, it contains significantly more complex gates.

Quantum Cost. Quantum cost is an important measure for comparison of reversible circuits. The quantum cost of a gate is defined as the number of basic quantum operations needed to realize the gate [8]. Any reversible gate can be decomposed into basic quantum (1×1 and 2×2) gates. The number of basic quantum gates required to implement a circuit is referred to as the quantum cost of the circuit. The quantum cost of the NOT, CNOT, and 3-bit Toffoli gate is 1, 1, and 5, respectively. In general, as the number of controls for a gate increases so does the quantum cost.

The quantum cost of an n-bit negative control Toffoli gate with at least one control is exactly the same as the cost of an n-bit Toffoli gate. When all the controls are negative, an extra cost of 2 is required if zero or $(n-3)$ garbage lines are used. An additional cost of 4 is required when only one garbage line is used [10].

3   Motivation and Related Work

If a circuit is non-optimal then it may be possible to decrease the size and quantum cost of the circuit by replacing sequences of gates with another equivalent sequence of gates; this is known as a template-driven reduction method, or template matching [11]. Template matching is an approach to reduce the number of gates and quantum cost by removing unnecessary gates from the network and has no effect on the functionality of the circuit. Templates for synthesis of positive control Toffoli networks have been classified based on the number of variables and proposed in [9] as well as [6]. For positive and negative control Toffoli gates new merging, moving, and splitting rules are proposed and an algorithm utilizing these rules is proposed in [2]. Templates and rules using both positive and negative control Toffoli gates are also proposed in [4].

4   Proposed Approach

In developing our templates we considered the various ways in which two Toffoli gates with the same target line can appear in a circuit:

1. Two same size gates with controls on the same or different lines, as shown in Figure 2(a), or
2. Two different size gates with controls on the same or different lines, as shown in Figure 2(b).

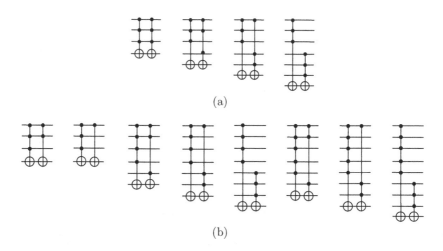

(a)

(b)

Fig. 2. Possible ways for two gates with the same target line to appear in a circuit

We have proposed 7 templates that may be applied in various situations. Templates $1 - 5$ can be applied to two adjacent Toffoli gates $T_1(C_1, t_1)$ and $T_2(C_2, t_2)$ where C_i is the set of controls, $|C_1| = |C_2|$ and t_i is the target, $|t_1| = |t_2|$. In templates $1 - 4$, two gates share the same control line but in template 5 one of the controls of one gate is on a different line. Templates $6 - 7$ can be applied to two different size Toffoli gates $T_1(C_1, t_1)$ and $T_2(C_2, t_2)$ where C_i is the set of controls, $|C_1| > |C_2|$ or $|C_2| > |C_1|$ and t_i is the target, $|t_1| = |t_2|$. In template 6 the two gates may differ, but only by at most 1 line. In template 7, the difference in the size of two Toffoli gates is ≥ 1. In all cases we are interested in Toffoli gates that have the same target line. Details of each type of template are as follows.

Template 1
Template 1 can be applied to two adjacent CNOT gates in the case where one CNOT gate has a positive control and the other has a negative control. In this case the two CNOT gates can be replaced by a single NOT gate [4].

$$T(C; x_t)T(\overline{C}; x_t) \equiv T(; x_t) \tag{1}$$

Template 2
If two Toffoli gates have the same controls, then the two gates negate each other. This property is known as self-reversibility [9].

$$T(C; x_t)T(C; x_t) \equiv I \tag{2}$$

Template 3
If two Toffoli gates have same controls but one of the controls is the inverse, then these two gates can be replaced by one Toffoli gate with all the common controls [2]. An example is shown in Figure 3.

$$T(C \cup x_i; x_t)T(C \cup \overline{x_i}; x_t) \equiv T(C; x_t) \tag{3}$$

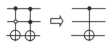

Fig. 3. Template 3

Template 4
If two n-bit ($n \geq 3$) Toffoli gates have controls on the the same lines but two (i.e. x_i, x_j) of the controls have different polarity, then the two n-bit ($n \geq 3$) gates can be replaced by two CNOT gates and one $(n-1)$-bit ($n \geq 2$) Toffoli gate. Equations(4a) and (4b) formalize this, while Figure 4 illustrates two possible ways to apply this template.

$$T(C \cup x_i \cup \overline{x_j}; x_t)T(C \cup \overline{x_i} \cup x_j; x_t) \equiv T(x_i; x_j)T(C \cup x_j; x_t)T(x_i; x_j) \tag{4a}$$
$$T(C \cup \overline{x_i} \cup \overline{x_j}; x_t)T(C \cup x_i \cup x_j; x_t) \equiv T(x_i; x_j)T(C \cup \overline{x_j}; x_t)T(x_i; x_j) \tag{4b}$$

(a)   (b)

Fig. 4. Template 4

Template 5
This template can be applied to two Toffoli gates of the same size where one of the controls is on a different line. In this case the two Toffoli gates can be replaced by two CNOT gates and one Toffoli gate [17]. The three situations in which this may occur are formally described in Equations (5a), (5b), and (5c) and illustrated in Figure 5.

$$T(C \cup x_i; x_t)T(C \cup x_j; x_t) \equiv T(x_i; x_j)T(C \cup x_j; x_t)T(x_i; x_j) \tag{5a}$$

$$T(C \cup \overline{x_i}; x_t)T(C \cup \overline{x_j}; x_t) \equiv T(x_i; x_j)T(C \cup x_j; x_t)T(x_i; x_j) \tag{5b}$$

$$T(C \cup \overline{x_i}; x_t)T(C \cup x_j; x_t) \equiv T(x_i; x_j)T(C \cup \overline{x_j}; x_t)T(x_i; x_j) \tag{5c}$$

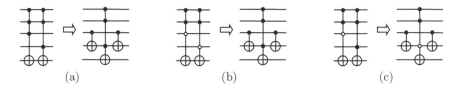

(a)   (b)   (c)

Fig. 5. Template 5

Template 6

If the size of two Toffoli gates differs by 1 and all the controls except the additional control in the larger gate are on the same lines, then this sequence of gates can be replaced by a Toffoli gate of the same size as the larger gate [17]. The two situations are described in Equations (6a) and (6b) and illustrated in Figure 6.

$$T(C; x_t)T(C \cup x_i; x_t) \equiv T(C \cup \overline{x_i}; x_t) \tag{6a}$$

$$T(C; x_t)T(C \cup \overline{x_i}; x_t) \equiv T(C \cup x_i; x_t) \tag{6b}$$

(a)   (b)

Fig. 6. Template 6

Template 7

This template can be applied to two different sized n-bit ($n \geq 3$) Toffoli gates as described in Equations (7aa)-(7db)and illustrated in Figure 7.

$$T(C \cup x_i \cup x_j; x_t)T(C \cup x_k; x_t) \equiv T(x_i \cup x_j; x_k)T(C \cup x_k; x_t)T(x_i \cup x_j; x_k) \tag{7aa}$$

$$T(C \cup x_i \cup x_j; x_t)T(C \cup \overline{x_k}; x_t) \equiv T(x_i \cup x_j; x_k)T(C \cup \overline{x_k}; x_t)T(x_i \cup x_j; x_k) \tag{7ab}$$

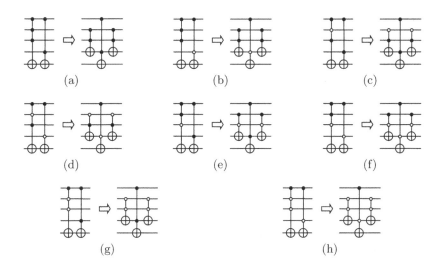

Fig. 7. Template 7

$$T(C \cup \overline{x_i} \cup x_j; x_t)T(C \cup x_k; x_t) \equiv T(\overline{x_i} \cup x_j; x_k)T(C \cup x_k; x_t)T(\overline{x_i} \cup x_j; x_k) \tag{7ba}$$

$$T(C \cup \overline{x_i} \cup x_j; x_t)T(C \cup \overline{x_k}; x_t) \equiv T(\overline{x_i} \cup x_j; x_k)T(C \cup \overline{x_k}; x_t)T(\overline{x_i} \cup x_j; x_k) \tag{7bb}$$

$$T(C \cup x_i \cup \overline{x_j}; x_t)T(C \cup x_k; x_t) \equiv T(x_i \cup \overline{x_j}; x_k)T(C \cup x_k; x_t)T(x_i \cup \overline{x_j}; x_k) \tag{7ca}$$

$$T(C \cup x_i \cup \overline{x_j}; x_t)T(C \cup \overline{x_k}; x_t) \equiv T(x_i \cup \overline{x_j}; x_k)T(C \cup \overline{x_k}; x_t)T(x_i \cup \overline{x_j}; x_k) \tag{7cb}$$

$$T(C \cup \overline{x_i} \cup \overline{x_j}; x_t)T(C \cup x_k; x_t) \equiv T(\overline{x_i} \cup \overline{x_j}; x_k)T(C \cup x_k; x_t)T(\overline{x_i} \cup \overline{x_j}; x_k) \tag{7da}$$

$$T(C \cup \overline{x_i} \cup \overline{x_j}; x_t)T(C \cup \overline{x_k}; x_t) \equiv T(\overline{x_i} \cup \overline{x_j}; x_k)T(C \cup \overline{x_k}; x_t)T(\overline{x_i} \cup \overline{x_j}; x_k) \tag{7db}$$

Moving Rule. Two adjacent gates $g(C_1, t_1)$ and $g(C_2, t_2)$ in a reversible circuit can be interchanged iff $C_1 \cap t_2 = \emptyset$ and $C_2 \cap t_1 = \emptyset$, i.e. the target of each gate is not a control of the other gate [20]. Applying a moving rule increases the possibilities for matching more templates and can lead to further optimization.

5   Steps/Algorithm

The template matching process is performed as follows: Consider two gates $g1$ and $g2$ from the gate list of a circuit.

1. if two gates have the same target line then we begin searching for templates
    (a) if $g1$ and $g2$ match any of the templates then replace $g1$ and $g2$ with the equivalent gates from that template (i.e. $g1'$, $g2'$...) and add the new gates to the new gate list
    (b) move on to consider the next two gates in the circuit (i.e. $g3$ and $g4$); go to step 1
    (c) if no match is found for any template then apply moving rule:
        i. if $g1$ can pass $g2$ then interchange $g1$ and $g2$; add $g2$ into the new gate list, $g1$ and $g3$ become the gates under consideration; go to step 1
        ii. else $g1$ and $g2$ add into the new gate list and consider the next two gates (i.e. $g3$ and $g4$); go to step 1
2. else apply moving rule to $g1$ and $g2$
    (a) if $g1$ can pass $g2$ then interchange $g1$ and $g2$; add $g2$ into the new gate list, $g1$ and $g3$ become the gates under consideration; go to step 1
    (b) else add $g1$ and $g2$ to the new gate list and consider the next two gates in the circuit (i.e. $g3$ and $g4$); go to step 1

The algorithm is iterated until no further reduction is possible.

6   Experimental Results

We have implemented the proposed templates along with the described moving rule in Java. The implemented programs have been run on an Intel Core 2 Duo CPU T6670 @ 2.20GHz×2 systems running Ubuntu 13.04 with 2GiB main memory for 122 benchmark circuits. These benchmarks were obtained from RevLib [19] and preprocessed by applying the improved shared cube synthesis approach from [14]. All the resulting circuits are QMDD (Quantum Multiple-valued Decision Diagrams) verified [12]. Using QMDD, we compare the resulting circuits (after applying templates) with the original circuits, in order to ensure that the behaviour of the circuit has not been modified. The running time is negligible for the program we developed to implement the algorithm discussed in section 5 and the results are listed in Table 1. Table 1 compares the outputs obtained in the current experiment to the results from the improved shared cube synthesis approach in terms of quantum cost and gate count. In this table PrevGC/PrevQC refers to the gate count/quantum cost obtained from the circuit generated by the improved shared cube synthesis approach, while NewGC/NewQC refers to the new gate count/quantum cost as computed from the circuits generated from our template matching post-processing. The proposed templates reduce the quantum cost of circuits 16.82% on average. col4_135 is the best reported circuit in terms of reduction in quantum cost. apex4_103 exhibited the greatest reduction in gate count, at 86%. fredkin_3, x2_223, miller_5, and pcler8_190 showed no changes in gate count but significant reductions in quantum cost.

Table 1. Applying templates with moving rule

Circuit	PrevGC[14]	NewGC	GCImp.(%)	PrevQC[14]	NewQC	QCImp.(%)
co14_135	14	21	-50.00	3472	1750	49.60
cm85a_127	48	54	-12.50	2206	1232	44.15
decod24-enable_32	9	5	44.44	29	17	41.38
bw_116	287	94	67.25	637	387	39.25
4mod5_8	4	4	0.00	21	13	38.10
decod24_10	9	4	55.56	16	10	37.50
C7552_119	89	32	64.04	399	250	37.34
decod_137	89	32	64.04	399	250	37.34
ham15_30	114	46	59.65	263	183	30.42
ham7_29	37	17	54.05	67	47	29.85
rd73_69	43	52	-20.93	856	619	27.69
add6_92	153	159	-3.92	5135	3714	27.67
hwb5_13	49	32	34.69	372	270	27.42
clip_124	78	80	-2.56	3824	2803	26.70
fredkin_3	7	7	0.00	15	11	26.67
mod5d2_17	15	12	20.00	38	28	26.32
mod5d1_16	11	12	-9.09	27	20	25.93
0410184_85	218	256	-17.43	7636	5662	25.85
plus127mod8192_78	36	31	13.89	803	602	25.03
z4_224	34	38	-11.76	489	370	24.34
z4ml_225	34	38	-11.76	489	370	24.34
adr4_93	41	41	0.00	645	489	24.19
apla_107	72	40	44.44	1683	1277	24.12
radd_193	41	43	-4.88	645	490	24.03
dc1_142	31	18	41.94	127	97	23.62
mod5mils_18	11	12	-9.09	30	23	23.33
max46_177	42	52	-23.81	4524	3540	21.75
3_17_6	11	9	18.18	28	22	21.43
cycle10_2_61	42	46	-9.52	1273	1004	21.13
apex4_103	5622	760	86.48	35840	28268	21.13
sym6_63	13	16	-23.08	721	571	20.80
plus63mod8192_80	35	31	11.43	847	672	20.66
majority_176	5	6	-20.00	133	106	20.30
sym10_207	83	105	-26.51	15640	12990	16.94
cm42a_125	42	17	59.52	161	134	16.77
pm1_192	42	17	59.52	161	134	16.77
graycode6_11	12	10	16.67	12	10	16.67
cm151a_129	26	25	3.85	769	642	16.51
4_49_7	20	14	30.00	97	81	16.49
dc2_143	51	39	23.53	1084	906	16.42
sqrt8_205	22	23	-4.55	466	393	15.67
root_197	48	44	8.33	1811	1528	15.63
hwb7_15	233	118	49.36	3015	2551	15.39
hwb6_14	92	52	43.48	839	711	15.26
x2_223	23	23	0.00	433	367	15.24
sao2_199	41	33	19.51	3767	3203	14.97
aj-e11_81	18	11	38.89	74	63	14.86
urf2_73	479	254	46.97	8742	7453	14.74
wim_220	23	14	39.13	139	119	14.39
urf5_76	210	115	45.24	5364	4614	13.98
miller_5	9	9	0.00	29	25	13.79
inc_170	75	32	57.33	892	769	13.79
sqn_203	37	37	0.00	1346	1171	13.00
mlp4_184	80	66	17.50	2496	2174	12.90
hwb8_64	480	261	45.63	8195	7158	12.65
5xp1_90	58	44	24.14	786	687	12.60
cu_141	28	20	28.57	781	687	12.04
rd32_19	6	7	-16.67	25	22	12.00
cm82a_126	17	14	17.65	126	111	11.90
f51m_159	327	359	-9.79	28382	25020	11.85
ex-1_82	6	4	33.33	17	15	11.76
in0_162	245	115	53.06	7949	7014	11.76
f2_158	14	13	7.14	112	99	11.61
9symml_91	52	63	-21.15	10943	9729	11.09

Table 1. (*Continued.*)

Circuit	PrevGC[14]	NewGC	GCImp.(%)	PrevQC[14]	NewQC	QCImp.(%)
sym9_71	52	63	-21.15	10943	9729	11.09
misex1_178	42	22	47.62	332	296	10.84
rd84_70	68	70	-2.94	2329	2079	10.73
table3_209	701	201	71.33	18606	16630	10.62
life_175	50	58	-16.00	6074	5429	10.62
misex3_180	854	576	32.55	49076	43865	10.62
alu3_97	72	56	22.22	1986	1780	10.37
ham3_28	6	5	16.67	10	9	10.00
mod5adder_66	28	26	7.14	353	318	9.92
hwb9_65	1011	554	45.20	23471	21173	9.79
alu2_96	78	82	-5.13	4369	3942	9.77
example2_156	78	82	-5.13	4369	3942	9.77
urf1_72	960	524	45.42	23769	21497	9.56
dist_144	94	82	12.77	3700	3348	9.51
sqr6_204	54	50	7.41	583	528	9.43
sf_232	4	5	-25.00	32	29	9.38
urf3_75	1501	941	37.31	53157	48218	9.29
ex1010_155	1675	775	53.73	52788	48110	8.86
tial_214	459	483	-5.23	43412	39731	8.48
dk17_145	34	27	20.59	1014	930	8.28
urf6_77	1862	287	84.59	39386	36314	7.80
alu_9	4	5	-25.00	40	37	7.50
misex3c_181	822	581	29.32	49720	46069	7.34
rd53_68	17	19	-11.76	220	206	6.36
squar5_206	31	29	6.45	221	207	6.33
plus63mod4096_79	32	28	12.50	676	634	6.21
4mod7_26	12	11	8.33	84	79	5.95
urf4_89	4293	2972	30.77	169830	160548	5.47
pcler8_190	18	18	0.00	323	308	4.64
alu4_98	454	456	-0.44	41127	39331	4.37
ex3_152	4	5	-25.00	76	73	3.95
one-two-three_27	8	5	37.50	38	37	2.63
ex2_151	7	8	-14.29	146	143	2.05
cm163a_133	35	27	22.86	546	536	1.83
Average			**16.68**			**16.82**

7   Conclusion and Future Work

This paper proposes two new templates for positive and negative control Toffoli gates (templates 4 and 7). Template 4 can be applied to two $\geq$ 3-bit Toffoli gates with controls on the same lines while template 7 can be applied to two different size $\geq$ 3-bit Toffoli gates. 98 of the 122 circuits generated by the improved shared cube synthesis approach [14] showed improvement in quantum cost after applying our templates. Results show that the proposed templates can reduce the quantum cost up to 49% (on average, 16.82%) and the gate count up to 86% (on average, 16.68%). Future work may pursue several avenues related to this work, including identifying additional templates, particularly for Toffoli gates with different target lines, and also improving the template matching algorithm. Of course, the issue of template matching with negative controls has not yet been thoroughly studied, and as we pursue this work a broader investigation will also be required.

Acknowledgments. This research was funded by a grant from the Natural Sciences and Engineering Research Council of Canada (NSERC). We also would like to acknowledge the efforts of the reviewers in providing interesting and thoughtful comments to help us improve the work; this was greatly appreciated.

References

1. Bennett, C.H.: Logical reversibility of computation. IBM J. Res. Dev. 17(6), 525–532 (1973)
2. Cheng, X., Guan, Z., Wang, W., Zhu, L.: A simplification algorithm for reversible logic network of positive/negative control gates. In: 2012 9th International Conference on Fuzzy Systems and Knowledge Discovery (FSKD), pp. 2442–2446 (2012)
3. Cuykendall, R., Andersen, D.R.: Reversible optical computing circuits. Optics Letters 12(7), 542–544 (1987)
4. Datta, K., Rathi, G., Wille, R., Sengupta, I., Rahaman, H., Drechsler, R.: Exploiting negative control lines in the optimization of reversible circuits. In: Dueck, G.W., Miller, D.M. (eds.) RC 2013. LNCS, vol. 7948, pp. 209–220. Springer, Heidelberg (2013)
5. Fazel, K., Thornton, M.A., Rice, J.E.: Esop-based Toffoli gate cascade generation. In: IEEE Pacific Rim Conference on Communications, Computers and Signal Processing, PacRim 2007, pp. 206–209 (2007)
6. Iwama, K., Kambayashi, Y., Yamashita, S.: Transformation rules for designing CNOT-based quantum circuits. In: Proceedings of the Design Automation Conference, pp. 419–424 (2002)
7. Landauer, R.: Irreversibility and heat generation in the computing process. IBM Journal of Research and Development 44(1.2), 261–269 (2000)
8. Maslov, D., Dueck, G.W.: Reversible cascades with minimal garbage. IEEE Transactions on Computer-Aided Design of Integrated Circuits and Systems 23(11), 1497–1509 (2004)
9. Maslov, D., Dueck, G.W., Miller, D.M.: Toffoli network synthesis with templates. IEEE Transactions on Computer-Aided Design of Integrated Circuits and Systems 24(6), 807–817 (2005)
10. Maslov, D., Dueck, G.W., Miller, D.M., Negrevergne, C.: Quantum circuit simplification and level compaction. IEEE Transactions on Computer-Aided Design of Integrated Circuits and Systems 27(3), 436–444 (2008)
11. Miller, D.M., Maslov, D., Dueck, G.W.: A transformation based algorithm for reversible logic synthesis. In: Proceedings of the Design Automation Conference, pp. 318–323 (2003)
12. Miller, D.M., Thornton, M.A.: Qmdd: A decision diagram structure for reversible and quantum circuits. In: 36th International Symposium on Multiple-Valued Logic, ISMVL 2006, p. 30 (May 2006)
13. Rice, J.E., Nayeem, N.M.: A shared-cube approach to esop-based synthesis of reversible logic. Facta Univ. Ser.: Elec. Energ. 24(3), 385–402 (2011)
14. Nayeem, N.M.: Synthesis and Testing of Toffoli Circuits. Master's thesis, University of Lethbridge (2011)
15. Nielsen, M., Chuang, I.: Quantum Computation and Quantum Information. Cambridge Univ. Press (2000)
16. Pan, W.D., Nalasani, M.: Reversible logic. IEEE Potentials, 38–41 (February/March 2005)

17. Sasanian, Z.: Technology Mapping and Optimization for Reversible and Quantum Circuits. PhD thesis, University of Victoria (2012)
18. Wille, R., Drechsler, R.: Bdd-based synthesis of reversible logic for large functions. In: 46th ACM/IEEE Design Automation Conference, DAC 2009, pp. 270–275 (2009)
19. Wille, R., Große, D., Teuber, L., Dueck, G.W., Drechsler, R.: RevLib: An online resource for reversible functions and reversible circuits. In: Int'l Symp. on Multi-Valued Logic, pp. 220–225 (2008), RevLib is available at `http://www.revlib.org`
20. Wille, R., Soeken, M., Otterstedt, C., Drechsler, R.: Improving the mapping of reversible circuits to quantum circuits using multiple target lines. In: 2013 18th Asia and South Pacific Design Automation Conference (ASP-DAC), pp. 145–150 (January 2013)

Minimal Designs of Reversible Sequential Elements

Anindita Banerjee[1], Anirban Pathak[2], and Gerhard W. Dueck[3]

[1] Bose Institute
[2] Jaypee Institute of Information Technology
[3] University of New Brunswick

Abstract. In this paper we propose minimal designs of reversible sequential elements. The proposed designs have been synthesized using exact multiple control Toffoli network synthesis algorithm with SAT/SMT techniques. The designs have minimal gate count, minimal garbage bits, optimal quantum cost and optimal delay. The optimized sequential circuits are compared with results from earlier proposals. For a fair comparison, previous circuits designed using non-standard gates are converted into equivalent minimal NCT circuits.

Keywords: Reversible sequential circuits, elementary quantum gates, low power design, quantum cost, circuit complexity, minimization, Boolean satisfiability.

1   Introduction

Reversible computation is at the forefront of ongoing research. This promising technology has extensive applications in low power CMOS [1], nanotechnology [2], optical computing [3], DNA computing [4] and quantum computing [5]. In conventional circuits, logic elements are normally irreversible. According to Landauer's principle [6] erasure of each bit of information dissipates at least $kTln2$ Joules of energy where k is Boltzmann constant and T is the absolute temperature at which the operation is performed. By 2020 this energy loss will become a substantial part of energy dissipation, if Moore's law continues to be in effect. In 1973 Bennet [7] has shown that the energy dissipation problem can be circumvented by using reversible logic. This is so because reversible computation does not require to erase any information. In 1980 Toffoli [8] introduced the notion of universal reversible gates which paved way for reversible computation[1]. Sequential reversible logic was first discussed by Toffoli [8]. Thereafter, Fredkin and Toffoli [10] presented reversible JK flip flop and Picton [11] suggested reversible SR latch. So far most of the work reported in sequential reversible logic are oriented towards synthesis of flip flops or gated latches [12–22].

The quantitative measures or cost metrics have been used to compare a set of designs with another set and gradually optimal designs have been obtained

---

[1] The history of reversible logic is presented in [9].

S. Yamashita and S. Minato (Eds.): RC 2014, LNCS 8507, pp. 137–148, 2014.

in earlier works. The inherent difficulty behind not achieving the minimality condition underlies in the reversible circuit optimization techniques used so far. Moreover optimization techniques can optimize a circuit but can not ensure minimality. In recent past Große *et al.* [23] have shown that Boolean satisfiability (SAT) can be used to exactly optimize reversible circuit. They have presented exact synthesis algorithm that finds minimal Toffoli network realization for a given reversible (Boolean) function using SAT/SMT techniques and problem specific knowledge. This algorithm is incorporated in an excellent toolkit called RevKit [24]. In RevKit one can provide a reversible truth table of a function and obtain a minimal reversible circuit. The SAT technique in [23] has provision for don't care values (the reversibility is still guaranteed since only reversible gates are part of the solution) while the constants have to be assigned a fixed value.

For the first time in literature minimal reversible sequential circuits are proposed. We have checked the minimality using the exact synthesis algorithm. Specifically, using this technique we have ensured that the proposed designs of reversible sequential elements have minimum circuit cost. We have critically compared the proposed designs with the existing designs of [12, 13, 15–17, 25]. The comparison clearly indicates that the proposed circuits are better than the earlier reported circuits. In the next section we have provided the background and in Section 3 we have discussed the earlier approaches and their limitations. In Section 4, we have presented our work and in Section 5, we have given a protocol for comparing our designs with the earlier proposals. Finally we conclude in Section 6.

2   Background

A latch is defined as a bistable memory unit. It is possible to enable and disable the latch by a control input such that the latch responds to input signals only when the control signal is 1 otherwise it maintains the previous state. This is called gated latch and it is level sensitive. In this paper we will use the name Clock pulse (C) for the control signal.

A reversible logic circuit comprises of reversible gates. This gate is reversible if it has equal number of inputs and outputs and the Boolean function is bijective.

Fan out and feedback are not allowed in a reversible circuit but these are required for the design of a sequential circuit. Fortunately, there is a solution for the feedback and this was first addressed by Toffoli [8]. Toffoli has shown that reversible sequential circuits can be constructed provided the transition function of the circuit block, without the feedback loop, is unitary.

Fanout is not allowed in a reversible circuit because there is one input signal and many output signals which makes it irreversible. To circumvent this problem a CNOT gate is used to copy the signal in a circuit which restores bijectivity.

Whichever synthesis algorithm we follow, it is important to choose a gate library [26] which is universal. The physical complexity of gates may not be the same in two different implementations of reversible circuits. For example, it may be easy to build an arbitrary gate 'A' in MOSFET technology but it may not be that easy to implement in optical based technology [27]. Therefore the choice of gate library has a significant role in designing. In this work we have used NCT gate library which comprises of NOT, CNOT (Feynman) and Toffoli gates.

Circuit cost is also denoted by gate count. If one is allowed to introduce a new gate or if a complex gate library is used then the gate count can be considerably reduced. For example, let us consider the Half Adder circuit proposed in [26]. It is implemented using 2 gates therefore its gate count is 2. Now we can put the two gates in a box and consider the box as one gate. The gate count in that case is 1. This gate can now be claimed as a new gate which reduces the gate count. It should be noted that these gates do not contribute to any universal reversible gate library. This may be clearly understood from a quantum gate perspective since reversible gate is only a special case of quantum gate. An n-qubit quantum gate is represented by $2^n \times 2^n$ unitary matrix. Product of any arbitrary number of unitary matrices is always unitary. Moreover serial connection of such gates correspond to multiplication of their matrices and parallel connection corresponds to tensor multiplication of their matrices. Therefore, if we put a set of reversible quantum gates in a black box then it can be visualized as a new gate. Thus the gate count can be reduced to 1. For example in [28] the circuit cost of a Full Adder circuit from NCT gate library is 4, in [29] it is reduced to 2 by using Peres gate which is a relatively complex gate and is not a member of NCT gate library and in [30] it is further reduced to 1. All the differences in circuit cost of Full Adder is because of choice of non-standard gate libraries. Consequently it is important to define an unique gate library for comparison of circuit cost. Moreover it should be noted that the optimal realizations of reversible gates reported in literature are not unique.

A garbage bit is an additional output to make a function reversible. It can be rightly said that garbage bits are don't cares. In [31] it is reported that at least $\lceil log_2(q) \rceil$ number of garbage outputs are required to make a function reversible, where q is the maximum number of times an output pattern is repeated in the truth table. There can be many ways in which garbage value can be assigned which affects the complexity. Recently Miller et al. [32] have shown that addition of new working lines (i.e., essentially additional garbage bits) may be helpful to reduce quantum cost of a circuit. Thus the reduction of a particular cost metric may be obtained at the expense of another one.

Quantum cost is used to measure the implementation cost of a quantum circuit. For a reversible function it is the number of primitive quantum gates needed to implement the function. All (1×1) and (2×2) gates are considered as quantum primitive gates and their quantum cost is one. The Toffoli gate can be constructed using 5 elementary gates and consequently, its quantum cost is five [33].

Delay is considered as an important measure to evaluate a logic design. Toffoli [8] has considered a unit wire for a specific delay that connects the output with input. Therefore, delay in wires and gates play an important role in analyzing a sequential circuit. Kaye [34] has defined that a reversible circuit design can be visualized as a sequence of discrete time slices and the depth is summation of total time slices. In [35] authors have reported that delay is directly proportional to depth and the delay for 1x1 and 2x2 primitive gates is 1. In [17] authors have calculated the delay in their designs of reversible sequential elements by counting total number of primitive gates in the critical path. Interestingly, Maslov *et al.* [36] have prescribed a level compaction algorithm to optimize the depth of a circuit (level compaction). The protocol provides minimal delay.

In CMOS technology the reversible gates can be realized by transistors. The TrC [37] of a circuit is the total number of transistors required to implement the circuit. The transistor cost (TrC) of a TOFn is given by $8n$ where n is the number and that of CNOT gate is 8. TrC for generalized Fredkin gate is $8(n+1)$ where n is the number of control lines of the generalized Fredkin gate. Thus the TrC of usual Fredkin gate is 16. This is a linear cost metric. Transistor cost is applicable to reversible circuits only and it has no role in determination of quality of a quantum circuit since a quantum circuit cannot be realized with transistors.

We have evaluated our designs with respect to the NCT gate library and reported total number of gates/circuit cost (CC), number of garbage bits (G), delay and quantum cost (QC) which are shown in Table 1-Table 12.

3   How to Design Sequential Circuits

3.1   Earlier Approaches

In the previous section we have mentioned that in order to design a reversible sequential circuit we have to design transition function as unitary (U). Now if we know the truth table of U and wish to decompose U in terms of finite number of logic gates, we can use one of the three existing approaches.

1. The first approach is the direct substitution method where an irreversible gate is substituted with an equivalent reversible gate. Picton [11] has used Fredkin gate, Rice [25] has used Toffoli gate and Fredkin gate, Thapliyal et al. [12] have used NEW gate and Fredkin gate and Thapliyal and Vinod [13] have used NEW TOFFOLI gate.
2. The second approach is the augmented truth table approach [15] where one starts with an augmented truth table and apply a suitable synthesis algorithm to obtain the reversible circuit for the function.
3. The design methodology presented in [17] maps the characteristic equation of the latch into a reversible design. This approach is not very different from the second approach as one needs to make a modified truth table in this case too.

Limitations of Earlier Approaches

1. In the first approach the resource cost is higher which means large number of gates and garbage bits. This is so because each irreversible gate is substituted by a reversible gate/circuit.

2. If we operate the traditional flip flop in SET condition (i.e., S=1 and R=0) then the output will be $Q^+ = 1$ and $\overline{Q}^+ = 0$ for following two cases: (i) when the previous state was in SET condition and (ii) when the previous state was in RESET condition. Since we obtain same result for two different cases, it always violates bijectivity. This fact is reflected in the behavior of reversible truth table of Toffoli based reversible SR latch in Table 4, Table 6, Table 7 and Table 11 of [25]. Interestingly in [17] through Verilog HDL using simulation flow it is shown that the SR latch designed using direct substitution method by Peres gates do not satisfy the behavior of SR latch in all possible input cases. Another important observation that points to the fact that these circuits are not gated in nature (i.e., they do not have Enable/Clock signal).

3. All the earlier designs from first approach have inherited the unstable condition of the conventional SR latch which is observed when S=1 and R=1. Thus it can not go beyond the limits of classical computation.

4. The second approach is not a unique approach, as mentioned in [15], the designs of latches depend on the output column, therefore different values assigned to these output columns will affect the design.

5. The third approach will result in reversible circuits belonging to different gate libraries. To be more clear in [17] the designs include gates from two gate libraries NCT gate library and generalized Fredkin gate library. In [13] some new gates have been introduced (MFG and MTG) and are implemented in the design along with NCT and Fredkin gate libraries.

4   New Designs for Reversible Sequential Elements

In this section we present some designs of reversible sequential elements. The design process is that we have obtained the circuit and verified its minimality in terms of circuit cost from the SAT based exact synthesis algorithm presented in [23] using RevKit [24] and obtained the minimal circuit cost. Further we have obtained the optimal quantum cost by substituting the Toffoli gate by its primitive gates in respective circuit and optimizing it by technique prescribed by [38, 39]. The delay is calculated from the elementary circuit by applying the optimization algorithm presented in [36].

The SR latch is the traditional building block of sequential element. We have already discussed in Sec 3.1 that designing SR latch using direct substitution violates bijectively. In [17] they have used a modified truth table and proposed the design of an SR latch with output Q. For our comparison purpose, we have added in their circuit one CNOT gate for the $\overline{Q}$ output (as per their strategy). We can also remove one CNOT gate at the end whose output gives $\overline{Q}$ and compare it with their design, but still our proposed design is better. We have proposed SR latch using augmented truth table approach with minimal circuit cost. In Figure 1a we have shown the reversible SR latch with output Q and $\overline{Q}$. The SR Latch has 1 CCNOT and 4 CNOTs therefore its TrC is 48. Thus the proposed SR latch is designed from augmented truth table approach. Its circuit cost is 5, TrC is 48, quantum cost is 7 and delay is 7.

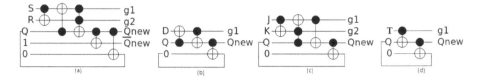

Fig. 1. (a) SR latch (b) D latch (c) JK latch (d) T latch

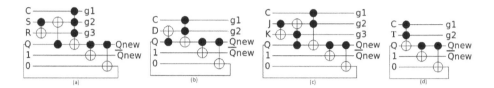

Fig. 2. (a) Gated SR latch (b) gated D latch (c) gated JK latch (d) gated T latch

We have presented reversible D latch in Figure 1b. It comprises of 3 CNOTs thus its TrC is 24. Its quantum cost and delay is 3.

JK latch is similar in function to SR latch with the difference that it toggles the output when both the input signals J and K are 1 and its reversible design is presented in Figure 1c. It comprises of 1 CCNOT and 3 CNOTs thus its TrC is 40.

T latch is a memory device that toggles the output when the input signal T is equal to 1 otherwise it stores the last state and it can be best represented by a CNOT gate with delay, quantum cost and circuit cost equal to 1. Reversible T latch is presented in Figure 1d. It consists of 2 CNOTs thus its TrC is 16.

Gated SR latch is presented in Figure 2a. In the literature gated SR latch with two outputs is presented in [12], it has been implemented by a NEW gate, Fredkin gate and CNOT gate. We have provided the comparison using the comparison protocol. A design of gated SR latch with one output was provided in [17]. We have compared our resources with them. The results are identical.

Gated D latch is presented in Figure 2b with outputs Q and $\overline{Q}$. In literature gated D latch with one output is presented in [15, 16] with Fredkin gate and Feynman gate and its quantum cost is 6. In literature gated D latch with two outputs is proposed in [12] with NEW gate, Fredkin gate and CNOT gate. Its quantum cost is 31. Other works like in references [13] and [16] have implemented it with Fredkin and CNOT gates and its quantum cost is 7. For gated D latch with Q output the circuit cost is just less than 1 from the gated D latch with two outputs because it consumes one more CNOT gate and that is the only difference in these two designs. This is similar for gated JK latch and gated T latch shown in Figure 2c and Figure 2d respectively.

In Figure 2c we have shown the gated JK latch with two outputs Q and $\overline{Q}$. Its circuit cost is 5, quantum cost is 9 and delay is also 9. In [13] a gated JK latch is proposed with two outputs using MFG (modified Fredkin gate) and the quantum cost of MFG is 5. We have presented minimal reversible circuit of MFG

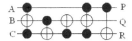

Fig. 3. NEW gate introduced by [40]

Fig. 4. MFG introduced in [13]

in Figure 4. Gated JK latch with two outputs are presented in [16] where they have used two Fredkin gates and MFG. Another design is presented in [12] using NEW gate, Fredkin and CNOT gates. Chuang and Wang [15] have presented gated JK latch with one output using CCCNOT and its optimized quantum cost is 13 [28] therefore the design will have quantum cost of $2*13+1*5+1*1 = 32$.

In Figure 2d gated T latch is presented. It comprises of one CCNOT and two CNOTs for Q and $\overline{Q}$ outputs. The design was first published in [Figure 6 [14]]. Identical design was proposed independently in [15]. In [13] similar design is used but instead of two CNOTs they have used one Fredkin gate for two outputs (i.e., Q and $\overline{Q}$). In [16] Peres gate is used instead of Toffoli as it brings down the quantum cost. In proposed work we have optimized the elementary circuit of gated T Latch by removing the end gate CNOT which has target at the garbage bit. Thus its quantum cost is 4.

We have reported the circuit cost, quantum cost, garbage bits and delay of proposed gated reversible latch with outputs Q and $\overline{Q}$ in Table 5 - Table 8 and the same for gated reversible latch with single output Q in Table 9 - Table 12. In these tables we have compared proposed work with existing works. For the designing of flip flops which are edge triggered sequential elements we follow the traditional way of combining two gated latches with an inverter. The proposed designs can be used to construct respective flip flops in the same manner.

Table 1. Comparison of reversible SR latches with S and R as primary input and Q and $\overline{Q}$ as outputs

SR latch	CC	QC	G	D
[13]	6	10	2	10
[17]	6	8	2	8
[25]	6	10	2	10
[25]	4	10	2	10
Proposed	5	7	2	7

Table 2. Comparison of reversible D latch with Q as output

D latch	CC	QC	G	D
[17]	4	6	2	6
Proposed	3	3	1	3

Table 3. Comparison of reversible JK latch with Q as output

JK latch	CC	QC	G	D
[17]	8	12	3	12
Proposed	4	5	2	5

Table 4. Comparison of reversible T latch with Q as output

T latch	CC	QC	G	D
[17]	3	5	2	5
Proposed	2	2	1	2

Table 5. Comparison of Gated SR latch with output Q and $\bar{Q}$

Gated SR latch	CC	QC	G	D
[12]	7	27	8	52
Proposed	7	17	3	17

Table 6. Comparison of Gated D latch with output Q and $\bar{Q}$

Gated D latch	CC	QC	G	D
[12]	19	23	8	23
[13]	6	10	2	10
[16]	5	7	2	7
Proposed	4	6	2	6

Table 7. Comparison of Gated JK latch with output Q and $\bar{Q}$

Gated JK latch	CC	QC	G	D
[12]	25	35	12	35
[13]	10	15	3	15
[16]	9	12	3	12
Proposed	5	9	3	9

Table 8. Comparison of Gated T latch with output Q and $\bar{Q}$

Gated T latch	CC	QC	G	D
[12]	26	36	12	36
[13]	4	10	2	10
[16]	4	6	2	6
Proposed	3	6	2	6

Table 9. Comparison of Gated SR latch with output Q

Gated SR latch	CC	QC	G	D
[17]	6	16	3	16
Proposed	6	16	3	16

Table 10. Comparison of Gated D latch with output Q

Gated D latch	CC	QC	G	D
[15]	4	6	2	6
[16]	4	6	2	6
Proposed	3	5	2	5

Table 11. Comparison of Gated JK latch with output Q

Gated JK latch	CC	QC	G	D
[15]	4	32	3	32
[16]	8	12	3	12
Proposed	4	8	3	8

Table 12. Comparison of Gated T latch with output Q

Gated T latch	CC	QC	G	D
[15]	2	6	2	6
[16]	3	5	2	5
Proposed	2	5	2	5

5   Comparison Protocol

Since the earlier designs of reversible circuits use different gate libraries. For the purpose of comparison of circuit complexity of our proposals with the existing proposals we have followed the steps given below:

1. Equivalent circuit: An equivalent minimal circuit is obtained for each non-NCT gates using exact algorithm [23], for example a Fredkin gate was used in [11, 41] requires 3 NCT-gates, CCCNOT gate was used in [15] requires 3

Toffoli gates (staircase structure in [42]) and Modified Fredkin gate in [13] requires 4 NCT gates.

2. Substitution: The equivalent circuits are then substituted in the designs and thus the essential logic remains the same.

3. Re-optimization: After obtaining the NCT equivalent and logic conserving circuits of earlier proposals, the optimization techniques (i.e. template matching algorithm, moving rule and deletion rule) are applied. Further quantum cost optimization [38, 39, 43] is applied to the circuit and thereafter quantum cost is calculated.

4. Cost of resources: Number of NCT gates present in these circuits is counted and this count is considered as gate count/circuit cost of the circuit. We have also calculated the garbage bits, quantum cost and delay of the circuit.

5. Comparison: We have compared our resources with the existing resources of [12, 13, 15–17, 25] and have found that the present proposals are better. The results of comparison are presented in Table 1 - Table 12.

6   Conclusions

We have proposed minimal designs for SR Latch, D latch, JK latch and T latch with their corresponding gated latches. With the help of RevKit we have ensured that the designs obtained independently (by using local optimization tools) are minimal as far as NCT gate count is concerned. We have also obtained TrC, quantum cost, delay and number of garbage bits. As it does not make any sense to compare a set of circuits prepared in one gate library with a set of circuits prepared in another gate library, we have devised a protocol for comparison. We have used this systematic protocol to compare the cost metrics of our proposal with that of the existing proposals in [12, 13, 15–17, 25]. The comparison revealed that the proposed designs have minimum gate count or circuit cost, minimum garbage bits, optimal quantum cost and optimal delay.

References

1. De Vos, A., Desoete, B., Adamski, A., Pietrzak, P., Sibinski, M., Widerski, T.: Design of reversible logic circuits by means of control gates. In: Soudris, D.J., Pirsch, P., Barke, E. (eds.) PATMOS 2000. LNCS, vol. 1918, pp. 255–264. Springer, Heidelberg (2000)

2. Merkle, R.C.: Two types of mechanical reversible logic. Nanotechnology 4, 114–131 (1993)

3. Knill, E., Laflamme, R., Milburn, G.J.: A scheme for efficient quantum computation with linear optics. Nature 409, 46–52 (2001)

4. Kari, L., Păun, G., Rozenberg, G., Salomaa, A., Yu, S.: Dna computing, sticker system and universality. Acta Informatica 35, 401–420 (1998)

5. Nielsen, M.A., Chuang, I.L.: Quantum computation and quantum information. Cambridge University Press, New Delhi (2002)

6. Landauer, R.: Irreversibility and heat generation in the computing process. IBM J. Res. Dev. 5, 183–191 (1961)

7. Bennet, C.H.: Logical reversibility of computation. IBM J. Res. Dev. 7, 525–532 (1973)
8. Toffoli, T.: Reversible computing. In: de Bakker, J.W., van Leeuwen, J. (eds.) ICALP 1980. LNCS, vol. 85, pp. 632–644. Springer, Heidelberg (1980)
9. Bennett, C.H.: Notes on the history of reversible computation. IBM J. Research and Development 32, 16–23 (1988)
10. Fredkin, E., Toffoli, T.: Conservative logic. Int. J. Theo. Phys. 21, 219–253 (1982)
11. Picton, P.: Multivalued sequential logic design using fredkin gates. MVL Journal 1, 241–251 (1996)
12. Thapliyal, H., Shrinivas, M.B., Zwolinsky, M.: A beginning in the reversible logic synthesis of sequential circuits. In: Proc. of Military and Aerospace Programmable Logic Devices (MAPLD) International Conference, Washington D.C. (2005)
13. Thapliyal, H., Vinod, A.P.: Design of reversible sequential elements with feasibility of transistor implementation. In: Proc. of the 2007 IEEE International Symposium on Circuits and Systems, ISCAS, p. 625 (2007)
14. Banerjee, A., Pathak, A.: On the synthesis of sequential circuits. arXiv:quant-ph, 0707.4233v1, pp. 1–9 (2007)
15. Chuang, M., Wang, C.: Synthesis of reversible sequential elements. J. Emerg. Technol. Comput. Syst. 3, 19.1–19.19 (2008)
16. Thapliyal, H., Ranganathan, N.: Design of reversible latches optimized for quantum cost, delay and garbage outputs. In: Proc. of 23 Int. Conf. on VLSI Design (2010)
17. Thapliyal, H., Ranganathan, N.: Design of reversible sequential circuits optimizing quantum cost, delay and garbage outputs. ACM J. on Emerging Technologies in Computer Science 6, 1–14 (2010)
18. Sayeem, A.S.M., Ueda, M.: Optimization of reversible sequential circuits. J. of Computing 2, 208–214 (2010)
19. Banerjee, A.: Synthesis, optimization and testing of reversible and quantum circuits. PhD thesis, Jaypee Institute of Information Technology, A-10, Sector-62, Noida, India (March 2011)
20. Bhagyalakshmi, H.R., Ventatesha, M.K.: Design of sequential circuit elements using reversible logic gates. World Applied Programming 2, 263–271 (2012)
21. Mamun, M.S.A., Mandal, I., Hasanuzzaman, M.: Efficient design of reversible sequential circuit. IOSR J. of Comp. Engg. 5, 42–47 (2012)
22. Singla, P., Gupta, A., Bhardwaj, A., Basia, P.: An optimized design of reversible sequential digital circuit. In: Proceedings of NCET (2013)
23. Große, D., Wille, R., Dueck, G.W., Drechsler, R.: Exact multiple control Toffoli network synthesis with SAT techniques. IEEE Trans. on CAD 28, 703–715 (2009)
24. Soeken, M., Frehse, S., Wille, R., Drechsler, R.: Revkit: A toolkit for reversible circuit design. In: Workshop on Reversible Computation (2010), http://www.revkit.org
25. Rice, J.E.: An introduction to reversible latches. The Computer Journal 51, 700–709 (2008)
26. Wille, R., Große, D., Teuber, L., Dueck, G.W., Drechsler, R.: RevLib: An online resource for reversible functions and reversible circuits. In: Int'l Symp. on Multi-Valued Logic, pp. 220–225 (2008), RevLib is available at http://www.revlib.org
27. Brien, J.L.O., Pryde, G.J., White, A.G., Ralph, T.C., Branning, D.: Demonstration of an all-optical quantum controlled-not gate. Nature 426, 264–267 (2003)
28. Maslov, D., Dueck, G.W., Scott, N.: Reversible logic synthesis benchmark page (2007)
29. Haghparast, M., Mohammadi, M., Kavi, K., Eshghi, M.: Optimized reversible multiplier circuit. J. Circuits Syst. Comp. 18, 1–13 (2009)

30. Islam, M.S., Rahman, M.M., Begum, Z., Hafiz, M.Z.: Low cost quantum realization of reversible multiplier circuit. Information Technology J. 8, 208–213 (2009)
31. Dueck, G.W., Maslov, D.: Reversible function synthesis with minimum garbage outputs. In: Proc. International Symposium on Representations and Methodology of Future Computing Technologies, pp. 154–161 (2003)
32. Miller, D.M., Wille, R., Drechsler, R.: Reducing reversible circuit cost by adding lines. In: 40th Proc. of International Symposium on Multi-Valued Logic, pp. 217–222 (2010)
33. Smolin, J.A., DiVincenzo, D.P.: Five two-bit quantum gates are sufficient to implement the quantum Fredkin gate. Phys. Rev. A 53, 2855–2856 (1996)
34. Kaye, P., Laflamme, R., Mosca, M.: An introduction to quantum computing. Oxford University Press, New York (2007)
35. Mohammadi, M., Eshghi, M.: On figures of merit in reversible and quantum logic designs. Quantum information Process 8, 297–318 (2009)
36. Maslov, D., Dueck, G.W., Miller, D.M., Negrevergne, C.: Quantum circuit simplification and level compaction. Proc. Computer-Aided Design of Integrated Circuits and Systems 27, 436–444 (2008)
37. Van Rentergem, Y., De Vos, A.: Optimal design of a reversible full adder. Int. J. Unconventional Computing 1, 339–355 (2005)
38. Banerjee, A., Pathak, A.: An algorithm for minimization of quantum cost. Appl. Math. Inf. Sci. 6, 157–165 (2012)
39. Rahman, M. M., Dueck, G.W., Banerjee, A.: Optimization of reversible circuits using reconfigured templates. In: De Vos, A., Wille, R. (eds.) RC 2011. LNCS, vol. 7165, pp. 43–53. Springer, Heidelberg (2012)
40. Biswas, A.K., Hasan, M.M., Chowdhury, A.R., Babu, H.: Efficient approaches for designing reversible binary coded decimal adders. Microelectron. J. 39, 1693–1703 (2008)
41. Rice, J.E.: A new look at reversible memory elements. In: Proc. of International Symposium on Circuits and Systems ISCAS, p. 1243 (2006)
42. Barenco, A., Bennett, C., Cleve, R., DiVincenzo, D., Margolus, N., Shor, P., Sleator, T., Smolin, J., Weinfurter, H.: Elementary gates for quantum computation. Phys. Rev. A 52, 3457–3467 (1995)
43. Banerjee, A., Pathak, A., Mazder, R.R., Dueck, G.W.: Two qubit quantum gates to reduce the quantum cost of reversible circuit. In: 41st International Symposium on Multivalued Valued Logic (May 2011)

Quantum Circuit Optimization by Hadamard Gate Reduction

Nabila Abdessaied[2], Mathias Soeken[1,2], and Rolf Drechsler[1,2]

[1] Institute of Computer Science, University of Bremen, Germany
[2] Cyber-Physical Systems, DFKI GmbH, Bremen, Germany
{nabila,msoeken,drechsle}@informatik.uni-bremen.de

Abstract. Due to its fault-tolerant gates, the Clifford+T library consisting of Hadamard (denoted by H), T, and CNOT gates has attracted interest in the synthesis of quantum circuits. Since the implementation of T gates is expensive, recent research is aiming at minimizing the use of such gates. It has been shown that T-*depth* optimizations can be implemented efficiently for circuits consisting only of T and CNOT gates and that H gates impede the optimization significantly.

In this paper, we investigate the role of H gates in reducing the T-*count* and T-*depth* for quantum circuits. To reduce the number of H gates, we propose several algorithms targeting different steps in the synthesis of reversible functions as quantum circuits.

Experiments show the effect of H gate reductions on the costs for T-*count* and T-*depth*. Our approach yields a significant improvement of up to 88% in the final T-*depth* compared to the best known T-*depth* optimization technique.

1 Introduction

Quantum computing has shown promising results, e.g., for solving certain problems that require exponential running time in classical computers. Quantum computers exploit quantum mechanical effects and their underlying model makes use of qubits. In contrast to Boolean logic, qubits do not only represent the classical 0 and 1 states but also a superposition of both leading to a theoretically enormous speed-up in computing. The Deutsch-Jozsa algorithm [1] as well as the Shor's factorization algorithm [2] from Shor are the famous examples.

As a result, the synthesis of quantum circuits has become an active research area and many theoretical implementations for this kind of circuits have been presented [3]. To that end, since quantum operations are reversible, as a first step a reversible circuit is synthesized for the desired Boolean function after which, the resulting circuit is mapped to a functionally equivalent quantum circuit. It is also possible to build the quantum circuit for the requested Boolean function directly without going through the reversible circuit synthesis stage [4]. For the synthesis of, or mapping to, quantum circuits, several universal quantum gate libraries were introduced. One of the most used libraries is the Clifford+T library which is particularly interesting due to its fault-tolerant implementation [5].

S. Yamashita and S. Minato (Eds.): RC 2014, LNCS 8507, pp. 149–162, 2014.
© Springer International Publishing Switzerland 2014

After designing the quantum circuit, optimization techniques are often applied in order to produce a cheaper equivalent circuit. These optimization methods for the resulting Clifford+T circuits mainly focus on reducing the number of T gates and hence the T-*depth* on the resulting circuit because fault-tolerant implementations of T gates are considerably more expensive than those of the Clifford gates [6]. Thus, a couple of optimization techniques [7,8] targeting the T-*depth* minimization were introduced. The major obstacle facing the T-*depth* minimization techniques is the H gates since T gates cannot commute across such gates. For that reason, attempts for tackling this problem were either to reduce the T-*depth* for quantum circuits over the gate library {$CNOT$, T} or to extend the same approach for the Clifford+T library circuits by optimizing the T-*depth* of subcircuits between the H gates boundaries [9]. To the best of our knowledge, no one has studied the effect of minimizing H gates for reducing the T-*depth* so far.

In this paper, we study the characteristics of H gates and show how they significantly restrain the movement of T gates and hence limit the ability to better parallelize T gates. We prove that reducing the not needed H gates leads to a more efficient minimization of the T-*depth*. To do so, we introduce a new methodology which aims to eliminate the H gates as a preprocessing step for improving the T-*depth* optimization results of quantum circuits.

The remainder of the paper is structured as follows: first the basics on reversible and quantum circuits are introduced in Sect. 2. The next section outlines the general idea. Section 4 gives a detailed description of the implementation of the presented approach, and experimental results are evaluated and interpreted in Sect. 5. The paper is concluded in Sect. 6.

2   Background

To keep the remainder of this paper self-contained, this section briefly introduces the basics on reversible circuits, quantum circuits, and the corresponding mapping from reversible to quantum circuits.

2.1   Reversible Circuits

A Boolean function $f : \mathbb{B}^n \to \mathbb{B}^n$ is said to be *reversible* if it is bijective, i.e., if each input pattern is uniquely mapped to a corresponding output pattern, and vice versa. Reversible functions can be realized by reversible circuits that consist of at least n lines. Reversible circuits are cascades of reversible gates that belong to a gate library. One gate library that is often used consists of multiple control Toffoli gates [10].

Definition 1. *Given a set of variables* $X = \{x_1, \ldots, x_n\}$, *a* multiple control Toffoli *gate* $T(C, t)$ *has control lines* $C = \{x_{j_1}, x_{j_2}, \ldots, x_{j_l}\} \subset X$ *and a target line* $t \in X \setminus C$. *The gate maps* $t \mapsto t \oplus h(x_{j_1}, x_{j_2}, \ldots, x_{j_l})$ *where* h *is defined as* $h : (x_{j_1}, x_{j_2}, \cdots, x_{j_l}) \mapsto (x_{j_1} \wedge x_{j_2} \wedge \cdots \wedge x_{j_l})$. *All remaining other lines are passed through unaltered.*

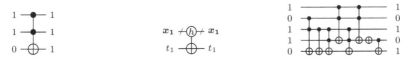

(a) Toffoli gate   (b) Multiple control Toffoli gate   (c) Reversible circuit

Fig. 1. Reversible circuitry

In [11] it has been shown that any reversible function $f : \mathbb{B}^n \to \mathbb{B}^n$ can be realized by a reversible circuit with n lines when using Toffoli gates.

Example 1. Figure 1(a) shows a Toffoli gate with two control lines. The control lines are either denoted by ● as depicted in Fig. 1(a) or represented by a Boolean function $h : \boldsymbol{x_1} = (x_{1_1}, x_{1_2}, \cdots , x_{1_l}) \mapsto (x_{1_1} \wedge x_{1_2} \wedge \cdots \wedge x_{1_l})$ as sketched in Fig. 1(b). The target line is denoted by $\oplus$. Figure 1(c) shows different Toffoli gates in a cascade forming a reversible circuit.

2.2   Quantum Circuits

Instead of bits, quantum circuits manipulate qubits which can represent the classical Boolean values but also a superposition of them. A *qubit* $|\varphi\rangle$ is a vector $\begin{pmatrix} a \\ b \end{pmatrix}$ where $a, b \in \mathbb{C}$ such that $|a|^2 + |b|^2 = 1$. If $a = 1$, then $|\varphi\rangle$ represents the classical 0, denoted $|0\rangle$, and if $b = 1$, then $|\varphi\rangle$ represents the classical 1, denoted $|1\rangle$.

In general, a quantum gate acting on n qubits represents a $2^n \times 2^n$ unitary matrix [12]. A matrix U is unitary if $U^\dagger U = UU^\dagger = I$ where $U^\dagger = (U^*)^T$ is the conjugate transpose of U. Using this gate definition many quantum mechanical effects such as superposition and entanglement can be formulated. Although Toffoli gates represent a unitary matrix, they are too general and thus not suitable for realizing quantum circuits [13]. In this paper, we make use of a gate library that is universal for quantum computation as well as its gates can be implemented in a fault-tolerant way.

Definition 2. *We consider the gate library* $\{H, Z, S, T, CNOT\}$ *with*

$$H = \frac{1}{\sqrt{2}} \begin{pmatrix} 1 & 1 \\ 1 & -1 \end{pmatrix}, Z = \begin{pmatrix} 1 & 0 \\ 0 & -1 \end{pmatrix}, S = \begin{pmatrix} 1 & 0 \\ 0 & i \end{pmatrix}, T = \begin{pmatrix} 1 & 0 \\ 0 & e^{\frac{i\pi}{4}} \end{pmatrix}, \text{CNOT} = \begin{pmatrix} 1 & 0 & 0 & 0 \\ 0 & 1 & 0 & 0 \\ 0 & 0 & 0 & 1 \\ 0 & 0 & 1 & 0 \end{pmatrix} \quad (1)$$

as the universal gate set. Note that the $S^\dagger$, $T^\dagger$, *and* NOT *gates can be implemented with* SSS, $SSST$, *and* HZH, *respectively. The* S *and* $S^\dagger$ *gates are square roots of the* Z *gate (given by the matrix in (1)). Similarly, the* T *and* $T^\dagger$ *gates are given by matrices that are the fourth root of the* Z *gate.*

A single qubit gate $G(t)$ *over the inputs* $X = \{x_1, \ldots, x_n\}$ *consists of a single target line* $t \in X$, *while a* CNOT *gate* $G(c, t)$ *comprises, in addition, a single control line* $c \in X$ *with* $t \neq c$.

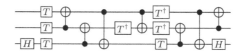

Fig. 2. Quantum circuit realizing a Toffoli gate

The above gate library is often referred to as the Clifford+T library. The so-called T-*depth* refers to the number of T-stages where each stage consists of one or more T or $T^\dagger$ gates that can be performed concurrently on separate qubits. The total number of incorporated T or $T^\dagger$ gates in the whole circuit is denoted by T-*count* while the total number of H gates is denoted by H-*count*. A root of Z gate denotes Z, S, T, $S^\dagger$, or $T^\dagger$.

Example 2. Figure 2 shows a quantum circuit consisting of sixteen Clifford+T gates. This circuit represent one of the optimal realization of a Toffoli gate as depicted in [7, Fig. 13]. The circuit has a T-*count* of 7, a T-*depth* of 3, and an H-*count* of 2.

3   General Idea

In this work, we propose an optimization approach that aims for reducing the T-*depth* in a given quantum circuit as a main goal. In this section we motivate the impact of H gates on minimizing the T-*depth* in quantum circuits, afterwards we outline the proposed approach.

Mapping reversible circuits to quantum circuits can be done with different quantum library gates such as the *NCV* [12] or *NCV*-$|v_1\rangle$ [14] libraries. But recently the Clifford+T gate library has attracted most attention since it is composed of fault-tolerant logical gates [5]. Because it has been demonstrated that the fault-tolerant implementation of the T gates is surpassing the cost of the Clifford gates [6], many works have addressed the optimization of quantum circuits by minimizing the T-*count* [8] and the T-*depth* [9,15].

The algorithm presented in [8] describes a method that performs an exhaustive search for a circuit that implements an n-qubit unitary matrix U using the minimal number of T gates. The work introduced in [7] addressed the optimization of T-*depth* for small circuits composed of four qubits at maximum. This is done by applying an exhaustive search algorithm to find the optimal T-*depth* realization. Another approach proposed a polynomial run-time algorithm for reducing the T-*depth* and the T-*count* of quantum circuits over the gate library $\{CNOT, T\}$ [9]. The algorithm deletes redundant T gates by computing the total phase and parallelizing the T gates through Matroid partitioning. The idea is based on decomposing a given function into minimal number of linear Boolean functions and then resynthesize each one with an optimal T-*depth* realization. This algorithm is extended to circuits built with the Clifford+T library. In this case, the same approach is applied for the subcircuits between the H gates, afterwards an optimization process is applied which detects the identical gates and deletes them.

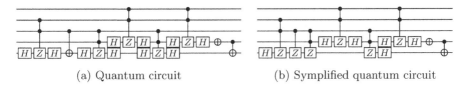

| (a) Quantum circuit | (b) Symplified quantum circuit |

Fig. 3. Equivalent quantum circuit for Fig. 1(c)

So far, as it is explained above, all the optimization techniques proposed algorithms for improving the *T-depth* for quantum circuits in the absence of, or locally between, *H* gates. But no work has introduced an approach for optimizing quantum circuits including *H* gates since they present the bottleneck for finding the optimal *T-depth*, i.e., they cannot interact with neighbouring gates and thus block the movement of any other gates across them. This restricts possible rearrangements of *T* gates and hence reduces the ability to perform *T* gates in parallel or apply possible reduction rules to a target circuit. Also when considering the algorithm [9] explained above and taking into account that the *H* gates are reduced before, this will allow to have larger subcircuits to resynthesize comparing to the first subcircuits: thus we get a bigger chance to get more parallel *T* gates and hence lower *T-depth*. Following the previous observations, therefore we present an approach that minimizes the *H-count* of quantum circuits, enabling better optimization results for the *T-depth* and the *T-count*.

Example 3. Figure 3(a) depicts the equivalent quantum circuit for the reversible circuit drawn in Fig. 1(c) according to [9]. Following their algorithm, the circuit is partitioned into a set of subcircuits located between the *H* gates. As it is shown in Fig. 3(a) we have 7 subcircuits. Next step, each subcircuit is resynthesized with an optimal *T-depth* quantum circuit. The application of the algorithm to the quantum circuit gives a circuit with a *T-depth* equal to 11 and a *T-count* equal to 27. However, one can reduce the *H-count* which yields an equivalent circuit depicted in Fig. 3(b). Applying the same algorithm to this circuit, which has 5 subcircuits, results in a circuit with a *T-depth* of 9 and a *T-count* of 23.

4   Optimization Approaches

Motivated by the idea outlined in the previous section, we propose a design flow (depicted in Fig. 4) for the synthesis of a reversible function realized using gates from the Clifford+*T* library. First, the desired function is realized as a reversible

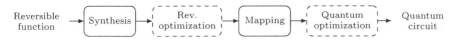

Fig. 4. Design flow for quantum circuits

circuit with Toffoli gates by applying existing synthesis methods such as [16–18]. To achieve better H gate reductions, we have taken the benefits of existing work aiming to optimize reversible circuits; for instance [19,20], and applied the template matching technique introduced in [20] to the reversible circuit. Afterwards, we have incorporated an alternative mapping technique that yields circuits which are particularly suitable for H gate reductions. Finally, the obtained quantum circuit is optimized by applying an algorithm that aims at the T-$depth$ optimization based on H gate minimizations. To resume, although we have employed the existing optimization algorithms at the reversible optimization level, our main contributions are on the mapping and quantum optimization steps.

4.1   Optimizations at the Reversible Level

In order to enhance the obtained circuit from a synthesis approach, a post synthesis process, also called reversible optimization stage, is applied. There are many existing methods targeting the optimization of reversible circuits for either reducing the number of lines [21], number of gates [20], depth [22], or quantum cost [23]. We are interested in techniques that lead to lower quantum cost. Smaller circuits are likely to have less H-$count$ and therefore would have better T-$depth$ but this is not always guaranteed.

Among the interesting work that focus on reducing the quantum cost for a given reversible circuit are template matching algorithms as described in [20], the window optimization introduced in [23], and finally the algorithm outlined in [24], that is similar to the template matching algorithm but includes better gate movement properties in the whole circuit. For this work, one can apply all of these approaches along with any other method leading to optimized quantum cost. For our experiments, we have included only the template matching approach [20].

4.2   Optimizations in the Mapping

After realizing and optimizing the reversible circuit for a given reversible function, each reversible gate is mapped to its equivalent quantum circuit as described in [13]. This mapping strategy is optimized with respect to quantum cost [25]. Afterwards, a second mapping technique that leads to an even lower quantum cost was described in [26]. Another functional mapping algorithm was presented in [27]: the described method searches for gates that have the same controls but different targets and decomposes them with a special decomposition.

According to Lemma 7.3 in [13], a reversible Toffoli gate with c controls (where $c \geq 3$) can be mapped to a network consisting of two identical gates with m controls and two other identical gates with $c - m + 1$ controls, where $m \in \{2, \cdots, c-2\}$ and each of them are placed alternately. One has a lot of freedom on how to choose the controls and the order for each gate. As an example, Fig. 5(b) presents a possible mapping for the circuit depicted in Fig. 5(a) where the partitioning of controls is done with respect to their order in the original gates. However an alternative application of Lemma 7.3 [13] results in a circuit with two identical adjacent gates which can be removed as shown in Fig. 5(c). By removing these gates, at least two H gates are eliminated.

Hence our approach aims to apply a special mapping technique that is particularly suitable for circuits in which H gates cancel. This technique, instead of mapping reversible gates one by one and each on his own side, gathers gates as shown in the schemas in Fig. 6 and finds a suitable partitioning of the controls that leads to reversible gates that cancel and thus reduces the H-count.

This mapping technique can be applied when a pair of reversible gates have one of the structures explained as below:

- Gates having a structure similar to the Peres gates as sketched in Fig. 6(a), i.e., a control line of the first is a target line of the other, besides they share one or more controls and the first gate has its target in a non shared line.
- Gates having their targets in the same line and sharing one or more control lines as depicted in Fig. 6(b).
- Gates having their target in non shared lines as described in Fig. 6(c). Also they have one or more control lines in common.
- Gates having a structure similar to the swap gates but also they share one or more control lines as outlined in Fig. 6(d).

Example 4. Consider the case of the pair of gates depicted in Fig. 5(a). Using the new mapping scheme, we obtain the circuit drawn in Fig. 5(c) that contains 2 identical reversible gates with 3 controls each. The removal of these gates will lead to a reduction of 16 H gates compared to the classical mapping algorithm.

4.3   Optimizations at the Quantum Level

There are many optimization schemes that aim for quantum cost reduction for circuits based on the *NCV* library. In particular, the application of quantum template matching [28] or the merging and deletion rules together with functional moving rules as explained in [24] are beneficial for decreasing the quantum cost. However, post mapping optimization techniques designed for quantum circuits based on Clifford+T gates are limited to the reduction of identical gates as described in [9] and the identities shown in [29].

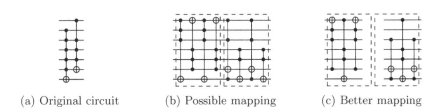

(a) Original circuit   (b) Possible mapping   (c) Better mapping

Fig. 5. Reversible circuit mapping

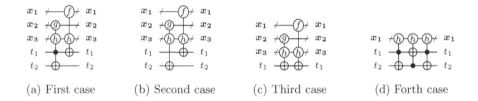

(a) First case   (b) Second case   (c) Third case   (d) Forth case

Fig. 6. Functional mapping

The optimization approach that we introduce is based on a greedy algorithm that traverses repeatedly the circuit and looks for any possible cascade replacement with a cheaper equivalent cascade or any identity deletion. These two operations are known as merging and deleting rules. This scheme can additionally be improved by applying the moving rules for quantum circuits. In fact, in the Clifford+T library, additionally to the moving rules defined in [28], a CNOT gate $G(c, t_1)$ and a root of Z gate $(Z, S, T, S^\dagger, T^\dagger)$ $G(t_2)$ can be interchanged if $t_1 \neq t_2$ as it is sketched with all other possible moving rules in Fig. 7. Furthermore, the following moving and deletion rules can be exploited for the Clifford+T circuits:

Hadamard Gates Reduction. The circuit is mapped in order to locate identical H gates or one of the cascades sketched in Fig. 8. Identical gates that could be moved together are deleted from the circuit and other identified templates are replaced by its equivalent cascade that do not contain any H gate.

Merging and Deleting Gates Reduction. Taking the benefits of the moving properties for Clifford+T gates depicted on Fig. 7, additional reductions are possible for the remaining gates of the library. The algorithm searches for the templates shown in Fig. 10 and replaces these by their cheaper realization.

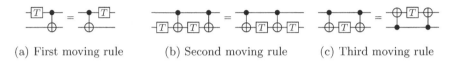

(a) First moving rule   (b) Second moving rule   (c) Third moving rule

Fig. 7. Moving rules for the Clifford+T gates

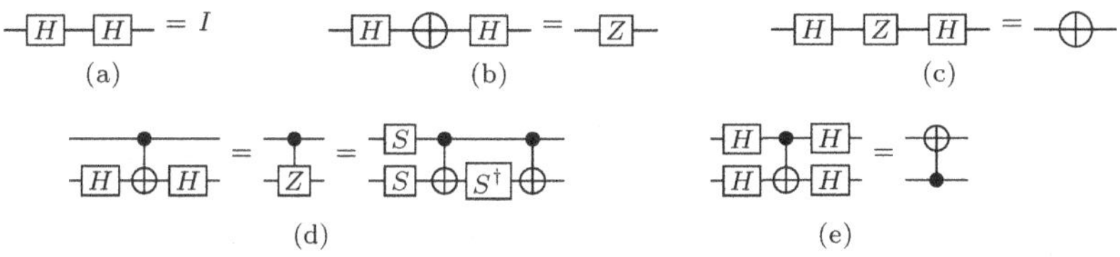

Fig. 8. Reduction rules for the H gates

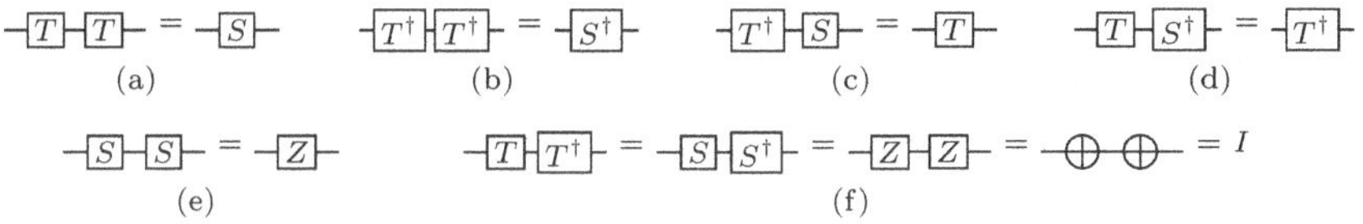

Fig. 9. Reduction rules for the remaining gates

5   Experimental Results

In this work, we proposed considerations of H gate minimizations to optimize quantum circuits build using the Clifford+T library. We have observed that eliminating H gates often leads to quantum circuits with a much smaller T-*depth*. Motivated by this, we introduced an improved design flow that aims at having lower H-*count* when generating the corresponding quantum gate cascades. The proposed idea described above has been implemented in the open source toolkit *RevKit* [30]. The experimental evaluation has been carried out on an Intel Core i5 Processor with 4 GB of main memory using the benchmarks taken from [31,32] database.

To determine the best synthesis approach with respect to T-*depth*, we have generated for each benchmark its corresponding circuits utilizing the following synthesis approaches: the transformation based synthesis approach (TBS [16]), the Reed-Muller synthesis approach (RMS [33]), the Young subgroups based synthesis approach (YSG [34]), and the ESOP based synthesis approach [17]. Due to space constraints, we have not detailed results for the ESOP based synthesis approach.

The experimental results are shown graphically in the plots in Fig. 10. The values of x-axis and the y-axis (logarithmic scale) denote the benchmark and the T-*depth*, respectively. Each plot contains three different scenarios: the T-*depth* of the original quantum circuits, the T-*depth* of the optimized circuits based on [9], and the T-*depth* of the optimized circuits based on our technique. One can clearly see that the T-*depth* and the H-*count* related to each other. Besides, most of the cases, the Reed-Muller synthesis approach [33] outperforms the other synthesis techniques in terms of producing lower T-*depth* circuits. The same observations are found for the H-*count* as it is shown in Fig. 10. In the rest of the paper we consider only the results of the Reed-Muller synthesis approach.

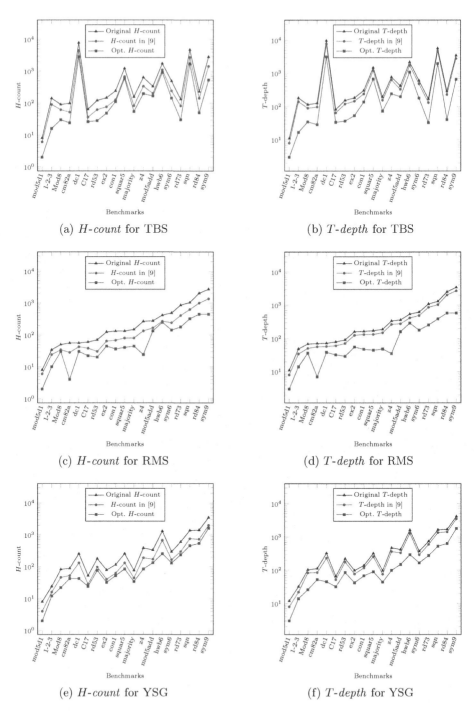

(a) *H-count* for TBS

(b) *T-depth* for TBS

(c) *H-count* for RMS

(d) *T-depth* for RMS

(e) *H-count* for YSG

(f) *T-depth* for YSG

Fig. 10. *H-count* and *T-depth* for original benchmark, optimized *T-depth* benchmarks, optimized *H-count* and *T-depth* benchmarks

Table 1. Experimental evaluation for Reed-Muller synthesized circuits where L, QC, HC, TC, TD, Time, ΔH, and TD Imp. refer to the number of lines, the quantum costs, the H-count, the T-count, the T-depth, the needed run-time, the H gate reductions, and the T-depth improvement with respect to the optimized circuits based on [9], respectively.

| Benchmark | | Original circuit | | | | T-depth opt. in [9] | | | | | H-count+T-depth opt. | | | | | ΔH | TD |
Id	L	QC	HC	TC	TD	QC	HC	TC	TD	Time	QC	HC	TC	TD	Time		Imp.
cm82a	8	456	56	196	71	462	28	142	56	0.004	108	4	23	7	0.000	-24	88%
z4	11	2140	266	931	337	2222	134	639	266	0.056	467	24	93	35	0.031	-110	87%
sym9	10	21510	2688	9408	3419	22423	1346	6364	2688	4.061	7087	446	1470	580	0.044	-900	78%
rd84	15	16188	2020	7070	2520	16803	994	4756	2021	5.537	7062	444	1402	578	0.011	-550	71%
rd73	10	6885	858	3003	1086	7091	406	2031	859	0.637	3027	178	607	254	0.071	-228	70%
majority	6	1188	148	518	189	1220	80	364	149	0.019	644	44	114	48	3.701	-36	68%
squar5	13	1082	132	462	172	1209	80	322	133	0.021	675	40	136	44	0.001	-40	67%
con1	9	1062	132	462	164	1066	68	330	132	0.015	685	36	126	47	0.124	-32	64%
sym6	7	3888	486	1701	619	3924	240	1143	487	0.187	2224	142	422	178	0.125	-98	63%
sqn	10	8411	1034	3619	1301	8734	626	2523	1035	1.067	4519	322	947	388	35.478	-304	63%
mod5d1	5	68	8	28	11	88	6	20	8	0.001	31	2	7	3	0.104	-4	63%
rd53	7	569	70	245	91	606	30	171	71	0.005	427	20	73	29	0.681	-10	59%
1-2-3	5	285	34	119	48	313	24	87	34	0.002	149	10	37	14	2.090	-14	59%
ex2	6	997	124	434	160	1027	64	300	125	0.015	665	44	130	55	0.076	-20	56%
C17	7	486	60	210	79	520	38	152	60	0.004	344	22	77	32	0.205	-16	47%
mod5add	6	2251	276	966	361	2317	166	670	277	0.055	1863	134	390	161	2.108	-32	42%
dc1	11	503	56	196	72	691	42	142	57	0.003	525	30	86	38	11.806	-12	33%
hwb6	6	3489	414	1449	541	3868	268	1035	414	0.135	3630	248	698	291	6.870	-20	30%
Mod8	5	406	50	175	68	413	34	131	50	0.003	408	30	91	36	0.032	-4	28%

Table 1 summarizes the obtained result. All benchmarks are listed in the first column. Then, the number of lines (L), the quantum costs (QC), the H-count (HC), the T-count (TC), and the T-depth (TD) of the respective circuit realizations as well as the needed run-times $(Time)$ are provided.

The H gate reductions and the relative T-depth improvement of the circuits obtained by the proposed technique with respect to the optimized circuits based on the approach presented in [9] are provided in the columns denoted by ΔH and TD $Imp.$, respectively.

In total three different aspects are studied: (1) the results of circuits generated from the Reed-Muller synthesis approach, (2) the results of optimized circuits using the algorithm introduced in [9], and (3) the results of the optimized circuits using the technique reviewed in Sect. 4 in addition to the approach. in [9].

Applying the T-depth optimization approach described in [9] reduces the T-depth significantly. However, it is clearly observed that these results can be improved when applying the approach based on H gate reductions. Our proposed approach leads to additional T-depth reductions of 10% in average. The results confirm the impact of eliminating H gates on the T-depth.

As can be seen, in particular our scheme leads to significant H-count reductions. Over all circuits, reductions up to 900 H gates can be obtained, therefore, this enables further improvements of the overall T-depth as it is shown in Table 1. The T-depth is reduced by 60% on average and in the best case $(cm82)$ by 88%.

H-count and T-depth are related to each other and more the H gates are reduced, more the T-depth is lower. This explains the variation of the T-depth improvement for each benchmark. For example, when a circuit contains many Toffoli gates that have their targets in the same line, then after quantum mapping the majority of H gates will be at the same line and many will cancel. Therefore the T-depth is reduced significantly $(Z4, Sym9)$. Whereas, when Toffoli gates have their targets in different lines then the H-count cannot be much improved, hence the T-depth is not much decreased $(Mod8)$.

6   Conclusion

In this paper we introduced a scheme for optimizing the T-depth of quantum circuits based on H gate reductions. To that end, we incorporated a 3-*level* strategy targeting the optimization of circuits at the reversible, mapping and quantum level to achieve better H-count reductions and hence possible further T-depth improvements. Experimental results have shown significant T-depth reductions which reach over 80% for quantum circuits.

References

1. Deutsch, D., Jozsa, R.: Rapid solution of problems by quantum computation. Proceedings of the Royal Society of London. Series A: Mathematical and Physical Sciences 439(1907), 553–558 (1992)
2. Shor, P.W.: Algorithms for quantum computation: discrete logarithms and factoring. Foundations of Computer Science, 124–134 (1994)
3. Shende, V.V., Bullock, S.S., Markov, I.L.: Synthesis of quantum-logic circuits. IEEE Transactions on Computer-Aided Design of Integrated Circuits and Systems 25, 1000–1010 (2006)
4. Kliuchnikov, V., Maslov, D., Mosca, M.: Fast and efficient exact synthesis of single-qubit unitaries generated by Clifford and T gates. Quantum Information & Computation 13(7-8), 607–630 (2013)
5. Jones, N.C.: Logic synthesis for fault-tolerant quantum computers. arXiv preprint arXiv:1310.7290 (2013)
6. Fowler, A.G., Stephens, A.M., Groszkowski, P.: High-threshold universal quantum computation on the surface code. Physical Review A 80(5), 52312 (2009)
7. Amy, M., Maslov, D., Mosca, M., Roetteler, M.: A meet-in-the-middle algorithm for fast synthesis of depth-optimal quantum circuits. IEEE Trans. on CAD of Integrated Circuits and Systems 32(6), 818–830 (2013)
8. Gosset, D., Kliuchnikov, V., Mosca, M., Russo, V.: An algorithm for the T-count. arXiv preprint arXiv:1308.4134 (2013)
9. Amy, M., Maslov, D., Mosca, M.: Polynomial-time T-depth optimization of Clifford+T circuits via matroid partitioning. arXiv preprint arXiv:1303.2042 (2013)
10. Toffoli, T.: Reversible Computing. In: de Bakker, J., van Leeuwen, J. (eds.) ICALP 1980. LNCS, vol. 85, pp. 632–644. Springer, Heidelberg (1980)
11. Shende, V.V., Prasad, A.K., Markov, I.L., Hayes, J.P.: Synthesis of reversible logic circuits. TCAD 22(6), 710–722 (2003)
12. Nielsen, M., Chuang, I.: Quantum Computation and Quantum Information. Cambridge Univ. Press (2000)
13. Barenco, A., Bennett, C.H., Cleve, R., DiVinchenzo, D., Margolus, N., Shor, P., Sleator, T., Smolin, J., Weinfurter, H.: Elementary gates for quantum computation. Physical Review A 52, 3457–3467 (1995)
14. Sasanian, Z., Wille, R., Miller, D.M., Drechsler, R.: Realizing reversible circuits using a new class of quantum gates. In: Design Automation Conference, pp. 36–41 (2012)
15. Selinger, P.: Quantum circuits of T-depth one. Physical Review A 87(4), 42302 (2013)
16. Miller, D.M., Maslov, D., Dueck, G.W.: A transformation based algorithm for reversible logic synthesis. In: Design Automation Conference, pp. 318–323 (2003)
17. Fazel, K., Thornton, M., Rice, J.: ESOP-based Toffoli gate cascade generation. In: IEEE Pacific Rim Conference on Communications, Computers and Signal Processing. PacRim 2007, pp. 206–209 (2007)
18. Soeken, M., Wille, R., Hilken, C., Przigoda, N., Drechsler, R.: Synthesis of reversible circuits with minimal lines for large functions. In: Asia and South Pacific Design Automation Conference, pp. 59–70 (2012)
19. Wille, R., Große, D., Dueck, G., Drechsler, R.: Reversible logic synthesis with output permutation. In: 2009 22nd International Conference on VLSI Design, pp. 189–194 (2009)

20. Maslov, D., Dueck, G., Miller, D.: Simplification of Toffoli networks via templates. In: Proceedings of the 16th Symposium on Integrated Circuits and Systems Design, pp. 53–58 (2003)
21. Wille, R., Soeken, M., Drechsler, R.: Reducing the number of lines in reversible circuits. In: IEEE Design Automation Conference, pp. 647–652 (2010)
22. Abdessaied, N., Wille, R., Soeken, M., Drechsler, R.: Reducing the depth of quantum circuits using additional circuit lines. In: Dueck, G.W., Miller, D.M. (eds.) RC 2013. LNCS, vol. 7948, pp. 221–233. Springer, Heidelberg (2013)
23. Soeken, M., Wille, R., Dueck, G., Drechsler, R.: Window optimization of reversible and quantum circuits. In: 2010 IEEE 13th International Symposium on Design and Diagnostics of Electronic Circuits and Systems, pp. 341–345 (2010)
24. Sasanian, Z., Miller, D.M.: Reversible and quantum circuit optimization: A functional approach. In: Glück, R., Yokoyama, T. (eds.) RC 2012. LNCS, vol. 7581, pp. 112–124. Springer, Heidelberg (2013)
25. Maslov, D., Dueck, G.: Improved quantum cost for n-bit Toffoli gates. Electronics Letters 39, 1790 (2003)
26. Miller, D.M., Wille, R., Sasanian, Z.: Elementary quantum gate realizations for multiple-control Toffoli gates. In: 41st IEEE International Symposium on Multiple-Valued Logic, pp. 217–222 (2011)
27. Wille, R., Soeken, M., Otterstedt, C., Drechsler, R.: Improving the mapping of reversible circuits to quantum circuits using multiple target lines. In: Asia and South Pacific Design Automation Conference, pp. 145–150 (2013)
28. Maslov, D., Dueck, G., Miller, D., Negrevergne, C.: Quantum circuit simplification and level compaction. IEEE Transactions on Computer-Aided Design of Integrated Circuits and Systems 27(3), 436–444 (2008)
29. Soeken, M., Miller, D.M., Drechsler, R.: Quantum circuits employing roots of the Pauli matrices. Physical Review A 88, 042322 (2013)
30. Soeken, M., Frehse, S., Wille, R., Drechsler, R.: Revkit: A toolkit for reversible circuit design. Journal of Multiple-Valued Logic & Soft Computing 18(1) (2012), RevKit is available at http://www.revkit.org
31. Wille, R., Große, D., Teuber, L., Dueck, G.W., Drechsler, R.: RevLib: an online resource for reversible functions and reversible circuits. In: 38th IEEE International Symposium on Multiple-Valued Logic, pp. 220–225 (2008), RevLib is available at http://www.revlib.org
32. Maslov, D.: Reversible logic synthesis benchmarks page, http://webhome.cs.uvic.ca/~dmaslov/ (last accessed January 2011)
33. Maslov, D., Dueck, G.W., Miller, D.M.: Techniques for the synthesis of reversible Toffoli networks. ACM Transactions on Design Automation of Electronic Systems (TODAES) 12(4), 42 (2007)
34. De Vos, A., Van Rentergem, Y.: Young subgroups for reversible computers. Advances in Mathematics of Communications 2(2), 183–200 (2008)

Mapping NCV Circuits
to Optimized Clifford+T Circuits

D. Michael Miller[1], Mathias Soeken[2,3], and Rolf Drechsler[2,3]

[1] Dept. of Computer Science, University of Victoria, Victoria, BC, Canada V8W 3P6
mmiller@cs.uvic.ca
[2] Institute of Computer Science, University of Bremen, 28359 Bremen, Germany
{msoeken,drechsle}@informatik.uni-bremen.de
[3] Cyber-Physical Systems, DFKI GmbH, 28359 Bremen, Germany

Abstract. The need to consider fault tolerance in quantum circuits has led to recent work on the optimization of circuits composed of Clifford+T gates. The primary optimization objectives are to minimize the T-count (number of T gates) and the T-depth (the number of groupings of parallel T gates). These objectives arise due to the high cost of the fault tolerant implementation of the T gate compared to Clifford gates. In this paper, we consider the mapping of a circuit composed of NOT, Controlled-NOT and square-root of NOT (NCV) gates to an equivalent circuit composed of Clifford+T gates. Our approach is heuristic and proceeds through three phases: (i) mapping a circuit of NCV gates to a Clifford+T circuit; (ii) optimization of the placement of the T gates in the Clifford+T circuit; and (iii) optimization of the subcircuits between T gate groupings. The approach takes advantage of earlier work on the optimization of NCV circuits. Examples are presented to show the approach presented here compares well with other approaches. Our approach does not add ancilla lines.

1   Introduction

Quantum circuits are an important model of quantum computation and there is thus considerable interest in the synthesis and optimization of such circuits [9, 11, 15]. Recently, there has been particular interest in circuits composed of Clifford+T gates [2, 3, 14] where a major objective is to minimize the number of T gates and particularly the T-depth of the circuit. This is motivated by the importance of fault tolerance in quantum computations [5, 18] and by the fact the cost of the fault tolerant implementation of a T gate can exceed the cost of implementing a Clifford gate by a factor of 100 or more [2].

Previously, there has been work on the optimization of NCV circuits [4, 13]. In this paper, we consider the mapping of an NCV circuit to an equivalent circuit composed of Clifford+T gates with particular emphasis on optimizing T-count and T-depth. The approach is heuristic but as examples will show, the approach compares well with other methods. In particular, we compare our method to circuits produced by the matroid partitioning approach described by Amy *et al.* [2] which optimizes T-count and T-depth. Our approach is comparable for those parameters and yields lower circuit depth in certain cases. We do not consider the addition of ancilla lines in this work.

S. Yamashita and S. Minato (Eds.): RC 2014, LNCS 8507, pp. 163–175, 2014.
© Springer International Publishing Switzerland 2014

Table 1. Gate definitions

Type	Symbol	Matrix	Diagram	Type	Symbol	Matrix	Diagram
NOT	N	$\begin{pmatrix} 0 & 1 \\ 1 & 0 \end{pmatrix}$	$\oplus$	CNOT	C	$\begin{pmatrix} 1 & 0 & 0 & 0 \\ 0 & 1 & 0 & 0 \\ 0 & 0 & 0 & 1 \\ 0 & 0 & 1 & 0 \end{pmatrix}$	
controlled V $(V = \sqrt{N})$	V	$\begin{pmatrix} 1 & 0 & 0 & 0 \\ 0 & 1 & 0 & 0 \\ 0 & 0 & \frac{1+i}{2} & \frac{1-i}{2} \\ 0 & 0 & \frac{1-i}{2} & \frac{1+i}{2} \end{pmatrix}$	$\boxed{V}$	controlled $V^\dagger$	$V^\dagger$	$\begin{pmatrix} 1 & 0 & 0 & 0 \\ 0 & 1 & 0 & 0 \\ 0 & 0 & \frac{1-i}{2} & \frac{1+i}{2} \\ 0 & 0 & \frac{1+i}{2} & \frac{1-i}{2} \end{pmatrix}$	$\boxed{V^\dagger}$
Hadamard	H	$\frac{1}{\sqrt{2}}\begin{pmatrix} 1 & 1 \\ 1 & -1 \end{pmatrix}$	$\boxed{H}$				
T gate	T	$\begin{pmatrix} 1 & 0 \\ 0 & e^{\frac{i\pi}{4}} \end{pmatrix}$	$\boxed{T}$	T gate^{-1}	$T^\dagger$	$\begin{pmatrix} 1 & 0 \\ 0 & e^{\frac{-i\pi}{4}} \end{pmatrix}$	$\boxed{T^\dagger}$
Phase	S	$\begin{pmatrix} 1 & 0 \\ 0 & i \end{pmatrix}$	$\boxed{S}$	Phase^{-1}	$S^\dagger$	$\begin{pmatrix} 1 & 0 \\ 0 & -i \end{pmatrix}$	$\boxed{S^\dagger}$

The rest of the paper is organized as follows. Section 2 provides the background for the work. Our NCV to Clifford+T mapping approach is described in Section 3 and examples are given in Section 4. The paper concludes with suggestions for further work in Section 5.

2   Background

We assume the reader is familiar with the basics of quantum circuits and their representations and only provide the notation and specifics required for this work. A full review of the background can be found in the literature, *e.g.* [11].

Definition 1. *A* quantum circuit *is a model of quantum computation representing a sequence of quantum operations. Each operation is represented by a* quantum gate *and the circuit is a cascade of gates where the circuit lines represent the* qubits *(quantum bits) of a quantum system. A quantum circuit has no fanout or feedback.*

The gates used in quantum circuits are commonly defined by unitary matrices and we do so in Table 1 which shows the gates used in this paper. U will denote an arbitrary quantum operation. Note that since the matrices of interest are unitary, the adjoint (denoted by †) is the inverse.

The C, V and $V^\dagger$ gates are controlled gates and the operation is applied to the target line if, and only if, the control line (indicated by a •) is 1.

The Toffoli gate [11] is like the CNOT except it has two controls which must both be 1 for the target to be inverted. This has been generalized to multiple-control Toffoli (MCT) gates [4] which have a number of controls all of which must be 1 for the target to be inverted.

Quantum Gate Properties. The following quantum gate properties are important in this work.

1. (a) $H = H^{-1}$ (b) $S = TT$ (c) $S^\dagger = T^\dagger T^\dagger$
2. (a) $\boxed{U_1}$ ≡ $\boxed{U_1}$ (b) ≡

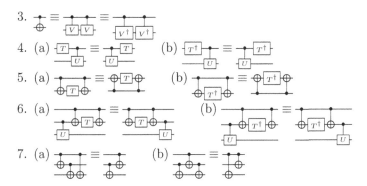

We refer to the structures in Property 5 as CTC structures where the T can be a T or $T^\dagger$ gate. Note the three gates in the structure have a common target and the two CNOTs have a common control. Applying Property 5(a) or (b) will be referred to as *flipping* the CTC structure.

Property 6 is somewhat surprising and provides considerable flexibility in moving gates. It is a direct consequence of Properties 4 and 5.

Property 7 gives two important identities for reducing the number of CNOT gates in a circuit. The applicability of Property 7(a) was illustrated in [17]. Note the equivalence shown is a particular example. The general rule is that interchanging 2 CNOTs which share a qubit as target for one and control for the other introduces a third CNOT with control and target from the unshared lines of the initial pair of gates. Property 7(b) is a direct consequence of 7(a). These properties have not been widely used in the literature but are in fact quite effective as will be shown below.

In this paper, we refer to three types of circuits:

- MCT: which are composed of MCT gates which includes NOT, CNOT and Toffoli gates;
- NCV: which are composed of N, C, V and $V^\dagger$ gates; and
- Clifford+T: which are composed of the Clifford gates N, C, H, S and $S^\dagger$, together with T and $T^\dagger$ gates.

The following define key characteristics used in evaluating circuits.

Definition 2. *A circuit level is defined as a sub-sequence of gates in a circuit that can be applied in parallel. We assume in this work that two or more gates can operate at the same level if they operate on disjoint qubits and can be grouped together in the circuit.*

Definition 3. *Circuit depth is the number of levels in the circuit.*

Definition 4. *The T-count of a Clifford+T circuit is the total number of T and $T^\dagger$ gates in the circuit.*

Definition 5. *The T-depth of a Clifford+T circuit is the number of levels in the circuit that contain one or more T or $T^\dagger$ gates.*

3   Mapping NCV Circuits to Clifford+T Circuits

In this section, we present a heuristic approach to mapping an NCV circuit to a Clifford+T circuit. The approach involves a sequence of steps as outlined in the following where we use the development of a Clifford+T circuit implementing a full adder as a running example.

Initial Expansion. A V gate can be expanded to Clifford+T gates as shown in (1) [16]. Note that the T on the top line can be placed as shown, between the two CNOTs, or above the left H. The T on the bottom line can be moved to be between the left-side H and CNOT gates. Provided the top T is not between the CNOTs, the CNOT-$T^\dagger$-CNOT structure can be flipped. For a $V^\dagger$ gate, interchange T and $T^\dagger$ gates in (1) and the above observations apply.

$$a \; \xrightarrow{\quad} \equiv \xrightarrow{\qquad\qquad} \boxed{T} \qquad\qquad b \; \boxed{V} \qquad \boxed{H}\!\oplus\!\boxed{T^\dagger}\!\oplus\!\boxed{T}\boxed{H} \tag{1}$$

Given the above, an NCV circuit can be expanded to a Clifford+T circuit by expanding each V and $V^\dagger$ gate. Our approach does this by traversing the NCV gates from the inputs (left side) to the outputs (right side). In doing this, recall that H is self-inverse so two adjacent H gates on the same qubit cancel and are not included in the expansion.

T and $T^\dagger$ gates outside CTC structures are specially considered as T and $T^\dagger$ are inverses so cancel if next to each other on the same qubit. Also two successive T gates form an S and two successive $T^\dagger$ gates form an $S^\dagger$. Our approach uses a simple counting procedure to track the T and $T^\dagger$ gates and only places a gate when forced to when an H gate or CNOT target is encountered as the circuit is traversed or the end of the circuit is reached. The details of our method are outlined in the following algorithm description:

Initial Expansion Algorithm. Let n be the number of qubits (lines) in the circuit. $\mathcal{H}$ is the set of lines with pending H gates. For each line i, $\mathcal{T}_i$ is a counter of the T and $T^\dagger$ gates on line i. By incrementing for the former and decrementing for the latter, cancellations are directly accunted for. Let g denote the current gate and let t represent its target. c will represent the control if g is a controlled gate.

1. Set $\mathcal{H} = \emptyset$ and set $\mathcal{T}_i = 0$ for $1 \le i \le n$. Start at the leftmost gate in the circuit.
2. If g is a controlled gate and $c \in \mathcal{H}$,
    (a) If $\mathcal{T}_c > 0$ add $\lfloor \mathcal{T}_c/2 \rfloor$ S gates, and a T gate if $\mathcal{T}_c$ is odd, immediately to the left of gate g on line c.
    (b) Else if $\mathcal{T}_c < 0$ add $\lfloor \mathcal{T}_c/2 \rfloor$ $S^\dagger$ gates, and a $T^\dagger$ gate if $\mathcal{T}_c$ is odd, immediately to the left of gate g on line c.
    (c) Set $\mathcal{T}_c = 0$.
    (d) Add an H gate on line c immediately left of gate g and remove c from $\mathcal{H}$.

3. If g is a V or $V^\dagger$ gate with target t:
   (a) If $t \notin \mathcal{H}$ add H, S, T gates as described in 2(a)-(d) above substituting t for c.
   (b) Put t into set $\mathcal{H}$.
4. If g is a V gate,
   (a) Add 1 to $\mathcal{T}_t$ and add 1 to $\mathcal{T}_c$.
   (b) Replace gate g with three gates CNOT-$T^\dagger$-CNOT using control c and target t.
5. Else if g is a $V^\dagger$ gate,
   (a) Subtract 1 from $\mathcal{T}_t$ and subtract 1 from $\mathcal{T}_c$.
   (b) Replace gate g with three gates CNOT-T-CNOT using control c and target t.
6. Else add H, S, T gates as described in 2(a)-(d) above substituting t for c.
7. Set g to the next gate to the right in the circuit. If there is no such gate the procedure is done.
8. Go to step 2.

To illustrate the application of this algorithm, consider the reversible full adder circuit in Fig. 1(a) [11]. Each Toffoli-CNOT pair is in fact a Peres [11] gate. Figure 1(b) is an optimal NCV realization found by expanding the two Peres gates and then canceling two gates [10]. The Clifford+T circuit shown in Fig. 1(c) illustrates key features of the initial expansion process. The T gates placed on the controls of the three V gates (1,2,3) are positioned as far right as possible. Note that a T and $T^\dagger$ gate cancellation coming from gates 3 and 5 occurs on line d and the T gates from gates 1 and 2 combine to form an S gate which is again placed as far right as possible.

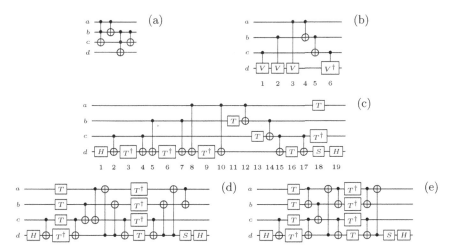

Fig. 1. Full adder

T Gate Parallelization. T gate parallelization means moving T and $T^\dagger$ gates, each on a unique circuit line, to the same circuit level so that they can operate in parallel. The objective is to reduce the T-depth of the circuit. We consider three types of T and $T^\dagger$ gate moves:

I. A T or $T^\dagger$ gate that can be moved to the desired position unimpeded, *i.e.* it can pass over all intervening gates with no additional gate movement or alteration.
II. Moving the T or $T^\dagger$ gate to the desired position requires moving one or more CNOTs and/or requires that a CTC group be flipped.
III. A sequence of Type I and Type II moves is required to reposition a T or $T^\dagger$ gate.

Our approach to T gate parallelization is outlined below. Note that this algorithm addresses only Type I and Type II moves. Type III moves are applied afterwards. Several illustrative examples are given in the next section.

T Gate Parallelization Algorithm. Let n be the number of qubits (lines) in the circuit.

1. Start at the leftmost CTC structure in the circuit.
2. Let p be the position of the T or $T^\dagger$ in the CTC structure.
3. Set $X1_i$ to be the position of the leftmost T gate that can be moved to position p on line i by a Type I move. Set $X1_i = \emptyset$ if no such T gate exists.
4. Set $X2_i$ to be the set of the positions for all T gates that can be moved to be in position p on line i (the set may be empty). Note that in doing this each CTC structure is entered twice as it can be moved flipped or unflipped, *i.e.* the T or $T^\dagger$ can end up on one of two possible lines.
5. Let t be the target line and c be the control line in the CTC being considered. If $X1_t \neq \emptyset$ and $X1_c = \emptyset$, flip the CTC structure; otherwise set $X1_t = \emptyset$.
6. For each line i, if $X1_i \neq \emptyset$ move the T or $T^\dagger$ gate from position $X1_i$ to position p on line i (a Type I move) and set $X2_i = \emptyset$.
7. For each line i, if $X2_i \neq \emptyset$ move the T or $T^\dagger$ gate from position j to position p on line i (a Type II move) where j is the position of the leftmost gate identified in $X2_i$. Remove j from any other $X2_k$, $k > i$.
8. Go right to the next CTC structure and go to step 2. If there is no such structure, the procedure is done.

As an example, applying our T gate parallelization approach to the circuit in Fig. 1(c) yields the circuit in Fig. 1(d). First, the left parallelization is accomplished by moving T gates from positions 18, 11 and 13 left on lines a, b and c respectively using Type I moves. Second, the right parallelization requires the gate groups (5,6,7) and (8,9,10) to be flipped and then gates 8 and 9 have to be shifted left. The group (15,16,17) then has to be shifted into position by a Type II move. To do that requires gate 14 to be moved left which requires gate 14 be moved past gate 12 (recall that gate 13 has already been moved to the left parallelization). Moving gate 14 past gate 12 creates the CNOT(a;c) gate in Fig. 1(d). Lastly, the $T^\dagger$ gate in position 18 is moved left to join the parallelization.

CNOT Reduction. A circuit composed solely of CNOTs is a linear reversible circuit. As can be seen in Fig. 1, a Clifford+T circuit typically has a number of linear subcircuits. It is thus useful to consider optimization of a circuit of CNOT gates.

As shown in Patel *et al.* [12], this problem can be expressed in terms of operations on a matrix over GF(2). In particular, the operation of a CNOT gate can be expressed as a matrix row operation. In particular, the operation of a CNOT with control α and target β corresponds to replacing row β by the mod-2 sum of rows α and β.

For example, consider the 6 CNOT gates between the two T gate paralleliza-tions in Fig. 1(d). Starting from a 4×4 identity matrix and applying (α, β) row additions in the order $(c, d), (b, c), (a, c), (d, a), (d, b), (c, d)$, corresponding to the 6 CNOTs gates from the adder, yields the matrix in (2). This matrix represents the functionality of the 6 CNOTs. The problem here is to determine if there is a more efficient CNOT circuit performing the same functionality.

$$\begin{pmatrix} 1\,0\,1\,1 \\ 0\,1\,1\,1 \\ 1\,1\,1\,0 \\ 1\,1\,0\,1 \end{pmatrix} \tag{2}$$

One approach is to use Gaussian elimination over GF(2). This is typically not optimal. Patel *et al.* [12] have given a method that is typically more effec-tive in terms of CNOT count but is not always optimal. For example, applying their method to the matrix in (2) yields a circuit that can be further reduced using Property 7. Also, the Patel method was not designed to take advantage of levelizing CNOTs, *i.e.* positioning two or more CNOTs into one circuit level.

CNOT Optimization Algorithm. Given a 0-1 matrix M, let M_i denote the ith row of M and let $|M_i|$ denote the number of 1's in that row. Our method proceeds as follows:

1. Set $X = \emptyset$. (Note: The set X is key to making choices that allow levelization.)
2. If M is the identity matrix, go to step 10.
3. For all possible pairs, find the pair (α, β) such that $\alpha \notin X$, $\beta \notin X$ and $|M_\beta| - |M_\beta + M_\alpha|$ is maximal, and there is a 1 in the β position in $|M_\beta + M_\alpha|$ where the addition is modulo 2.
4. If the maximum value found in step 3 is 0, apply the Patel *et al.* method [12] to M to complete the solution.
5. If no (α, β) is found in step 3, set $X = \emptyset$ and go to step 2.
6. If an (α, β) is found in step 3, add a CNOT with control α and target β to the solution. Note that the gates are generated in order from right to left.
7. Replace M_β by $M_\beta + M_\alpha$ where the addition is modulo 2.
8. Add α and β to X.
9. Return to step 2.
10. Property 7 is systematically applied to further reduce the number of CNOTs.

Applying the above method to the matrix in (2) yields the (α, β) sequence: $(a,b), (c,d), (d,a), (b,c), (a,b), (c,d)$ which corresponds to the CNOT sequence shown in Fig. 1(e). Note that while there are 6 CNOTs in both circuits, the sequence in Fig. 1(d) requires 5 levels, while the sequence in Fig. 1(e) requires only 3. Using CNOT reduction, the CNOTs at the right end of Fig. 1(d) can also be reduced as shown in Fig. 1(e) saving one level in the circuit. The circuit in Fig. 1(e) is the same as identified in [3, 16].

4   Examples

In this section we provide a number of examples to illustrate the application of our approach. In particular, these examples illustrate certain aspects of optimizing T gate parallelization not illustrated in the full adder example.

Toffoli Gate with Two Controls. It is well-known [4] that the 2-control Toffoli gate depicted in Fig. 2(a) can be realized by 5 NCV gates as shown in Fig. 2(b). Figure 2(c) is found by expanding the V and $V^\dagger$ gates in Fig. 2(b) to Clifford+T gates. Note that the H gates that would fall between gates 1 and 3 and between 3 and 5 cancel as do a T from the expansion of gate 1 and a $T^\dagger$ from the expansion of gate 3 on line c.

The next step is T gate parallelization. Gates 1e and 5d can be moved to be above gate 1c using Type I moves since there are no intervening CNOT targets or H gates. Similarly, gate 3d can be moved above 3b as a Type I move. Gate 5b is moved above 3b by a Type II move. In particular, the gate group (5a,5b,5c) is flipped and then the gates are moved into the positions shown in Fig. 2(d).

The circuit in Fig. 2(d) has T-count 7, T-depth 3 and 12 levels. The number of levels can be reduced by shifting gate 3d left; flipping the gate group (3a,3b,3c); and then shifting gate 5e left. This yields the circuit in Fig. 2(e) which has 11 levels since gates 5a and 3d can be combined in a single level. Note that no CNOT optimization is possible for this circuit. The T-count of 7 and T-depth of 3 are optimal but a circuit with 10 levels has been found previously [16].

The Function a2x [2]. The function a2x can be realized by 2 Toffoli gates as shown in Fig. 3(a). An NCV realization is shown in Fig. 3(b). Note that the realizations for the Toffoli gates have been arranged so that a V from the left Toffoli combines with a CNOT from the right Toffoli to yield the $V^\dagger$ gates marked by the arrow. This reduction is possible since a CNOT can be replaced by two identical $V^\dagger$ gates which then leads to a V-$V^\dagger$ cancellation. Using the initial expansion and T gate parallelization techniques in the manner described in the above examples yields the circuit in Fig. 3(c).

Figure 3(d) shows two CNOT optimizations. The 3 leftmost CNOTs in Fig. 3(c) are reduced to 2. The 3 CNOTs between the right two T gate parallelizations are also reduced to 2.

Figure 3(d) also shows the insertion of 2 identical CNOTs at positions 3 and 4. This is possible since they functionally cancel. The reason for the insertion is so that the gate group (4,5,6) can be flipped and then moved to the positions shown in Fig. 3(e) with the effect of reducing the T-depth by 1. There is also a resulting CNOT reduction shown in Fig. 3(e). The gates in position 1 and 2 have been interchanged which results in the gate from position 3 being eliminated. Our final circuit has T-count 12, T-depth 4 and circuit depth 20. The circuit in [2] also has T-count 12 and T-depth 4. It has 23 levels.

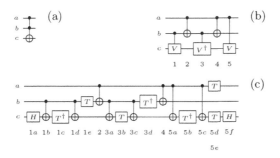

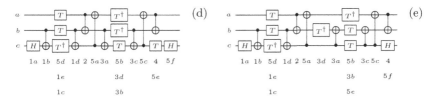

Fig. 2. 2-control Toffoli gate

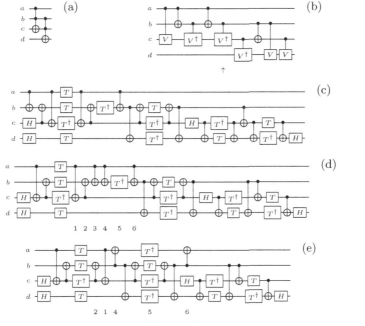

Fig. 3. a2x

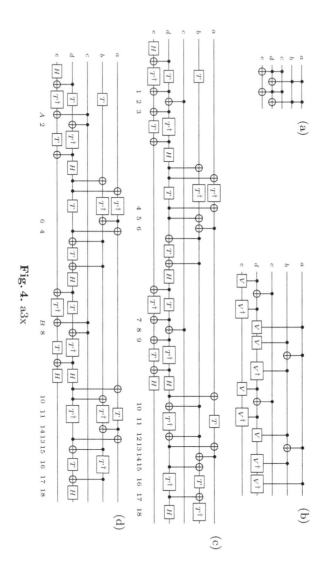

Fig. 4. a3x

The Function a3x [2]. The Toffoli gate circuit for ax3 is shown in Fig. 4(a). Note that this circuit implements the 3-control Toffoli gate $TOF(a, b, c; e)$ using d as an ancillary line. The mapping to NCV gates we use is shown in Fig. 4(b). Note that the mapping for the 2 Toffoli gates with target e are chosen so that a total of 4 NCV gates, 2 from each Toffoli, cancel, so each Toffoli maps to 3 gates. Likewise, the 2 Toffoli gates with target d are mapped so that 2 CNOTs cancel so that each of these Toffoli gates is mapped to 4 gates. The $V/V^\dagger$ assignment for the rightmost Toffoli is chosen so that there are 3 V and 3 $V^\dagger$ on line d which heightens the opportunity for cancellations during the expansion process. This mapping is, up to reordering, the NCV realization given in [13].

Figure 4(c) shows the Clifford+T circuit after T gate parallelization is almost complete. This circuit has T-depth 9. However by doing the following in order: flipping the gate group at (10,11,12); moving the $T^\dagger$ from position 16 to position 11; flipping the gate group at (15,16,17) and then moving the $T^\dagger$ from position 18 to position 16, the T-depth can be reduced to 8. Note that gates (1,2,3) in Fig. 4(c) become gates A,2 in Fig. 4(d). Likewise, gates (4,5,6) become 6,4 and gates (7,8,9) become B,8. These changes are the result of CNOT reductions.

Our final circuit has T-count 18 and T-depth 8 with circuit depth 33. Amy et al. [2] give a circuit for a3x with T-count 16 and T-depth 8. Their circuit has circuit depth 40. Which of the two circuits is truly better will likely be technology dependent. The fact they have the same T-depth makes the reduction from 40 to 33 circuit levels attractive.

The Function 3_17. Our final example is known as 3_17 [19]. The NCV circuit is shown in Fig. 5(a). Fig. 5(b) shows the circuit after the Type I and Type II

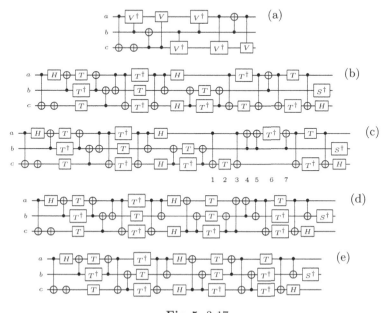

Fig. 5. 3_17

moves in the T gate parallelization phase. The circuit in Fig. 5(c) is derived from the one in Fig. 5(b) by moving the $T^\dagger$ gate into position 6 and adding the two CNOTs in positions 4 and 5. The gate group (1,2,3) can be flipped and moved left and the gate group (5,6,7) can be flipped and moved right. Doing both of those operations yields the circuit in Fig. 5(d) with T-depth 4 rather than 5. CNOT reduction then yields the final circuit, Fig. 5(e).

5 Conclusion and Future Work

In this paper, we have presented a method for mapping an NCV circuit to a Clifford+T circuit. Several examples were presented to illustrate the approach. The results show that the method is promising as it produces results comparable to earlier methods.

More work is required to determine how effective the method will be for larger NCV circuits. The methods presented are heuristic and further study is required to determine if the choices made are in fact the most effective. It would be most interesting to look at the integration of our methods with the matroid partitioning approach due to Amy *et al.* [3], particularly our CNOT optimization approach.

In this paper, we have assumed that gates can be applied in parallel, *i.e.* at the same circuit level, if they involve different qubits. Depending on the technology, a different assumption may apply. For example, the *nearest neighbour* constraint requires that the target and control for a controlled gate must be adjacent circuit lines [7]. In that case, the CNOT optimization phase of our approach must be modified or another appropriate nearest neighbour CNOT optimization technique [1,6,8] can be applied. Other constraints may apply for other technologies and again the CNOT optimization phase must be appropriately adjusted. The initial expansion and T-gate parallization phases are not affected.

H gates are particularly problematic for our approach since they put limits on the movement of other gates in the circuit and can affect the ability of our methods to optimally parallelize T gates. Work to limit or to judiciously place H gates would be valuable. In addition, it is not clear that minimal NCV circuits are the best starting point since non-minimality may in some instances lead to better H gate placement.

Acknowledgment. This work was supported in part by a Discovery Grant from the Natural Sciences and Engineering Research Council of Canada.

References

1. AlFailakawi, M., AlTerkawi, L., Ahmad, I., Hamdan, S.: Line ordering of reversible circuits for linear nearest neighbour realization. Qunatum Inf. Process. 12, 3319–3339 (2013)
2. Amy, M., Maslov, D., Mosca, M.: Polynomial-time T-depth optimization of Clifford+T circuits via matroid partitioning, arXiv:quant-ph/1303.2042v2 (2013)
3. Amy, M., Maslov, D., Mosca, M., Roetteler, M.: A meet-in-the-middle algorithm for fast synthesis of depth-optimal quantum circuits. IEEE Trans. on CAD 32(6), 818–830 (2013)

4. Barenco, A., Bennett, C.H., Cleve, R., DiVincenzo, D.P., Margolus, N., Shor, P., Sleator, T., Smolin, J.A., Weinfurter, H.: Elementary gates for quantum computation. Phys. Rev. A 52(5), 3457–3467 (1995)
5. Buhrman, H., Cleve, R., Laurent, M., Linden, N., Schrijver, A., Unger, F.: New limits on fault-tolerant quantum computation. In: Foundations of Computer Science, vol. 27, pp. 411–419. IEEE Computer Society (2006)
6. Chakrabarti, A., Sur-Kolay, S., Chaudhury, A.: Linear nearest neighbor synthesis of reversible circuits by graph partitioning. CoRR, arXiv:1112.0564v2 (2012)
7. DiVincenzo, D.P., Bacon, D., Kempe, J., Burkard, G., Whaley, K.B.: Universal quantum computation with the exchange interaction. Nature 408, 339–342 (2000)
8. Khan, M.H.A.: Cost reduction in nearest neighbour based synthesis of quantum Boolean circuits. Engineering Letters 16, 1–5 (2008)
9. Lukac, M.: Quantum Inductive Learning and Quantum Logic Synthesis. BiblioLabsII (2011)
10. Maslov, D., Dueck, G.W., Miller, D.M., Negrevergne, C.: Quantum circuit simplification and level compaction. IEEE Trans. CAD 27(3), 436–444 (2008)
11. Nielsen, M.A., Chuang, I.L.: Quantum Computation and Quantum Information. Cambridge University Press (2000)
12. Patel, K., Markov, I.L., Hayes, J.P.: Optimal synthesis of linear reversible circuits. Quantum Information and Computation 8(3&4), 282–294 (2008)
13. Sasanian, Z., Miller, D.M.: Mapping a multiple-control Toffoli gate cascade to an elementary quantum gate circuit. Multiple-Valued Logic and Soft Computing 18(1), 83–98 (2012)
14. Selinger, P.: Quantum circuits of T-depth one. Phys. Rev. A 87, 042302 (2013)
15. Shende, V.V., Bullock, S.S., Markov, I.L.: Synthesis of quantum logic circuits. IEEE Trans. on CAD 25(6), 1000–1010 (2006)
16. Soeken, M., Miller, D.M., Drechsler, R.: Quantum circuits employing roots of the Pauli matrices. Phys. Rev. A 88, 042322 (2013)
17. Soeken, M., Thomsen, M.K.: White dots *do* matter: Rewriting reversible logic circuits. In: Dueck, G.W., Miller, D.M. (eds.) RC 2013. LNCS, vol. 7948, pp. 196–208. Springer, Heidelberg (2013)
18. Weinstein, Y.S.: Non-fault tolerant T-gates for the [7,1,3] quantum error correction code. Phys. Rev. A 87, 032320 (2013)
19. Wille, R., Große, D., Teuber, L., Dueck, G.W., Drechsler, R.: RevLib: An online resource for reversible functions and reversible circuits. In: Int'l Symp. on Multi-Valued Logic, pp. 220–225 (2008), RevLib is available at **www.revlib.org**

2D Qubit Layout Optimization for Topological Quantum Computation

Nurul Ain Binti Adnan, Shigeru Yamashita,
Simon J. Devitt, and Kae Nemoto

College of Information Science and Engineering, Ritsumeikan University,
1-1-1 Noji Higashi, Kusatsu, Shiga 525-8577, Japan

Abstract. Nowadays, *Topological quantum computation* is considered to
be one of the most promising methods in realizing the future of quantum
computation. The circuit model for topological quantum computation
differs from the conventional quantum circuit model even in the logic
level; which is multiple CNOT gates can only be performed at the same
time if the order of qubits satisfies a certain property. Thus, there has
been a wide research to find a good qubit order in one-dimension to
satisfy such a property for topological quantum computation. This paper proposes a new method by using two-dimensional qubit layouts for
topological quantum computation in order to reduce the computational
time steps instead of one-dimensional qubit layouts used by the conventional computer. The general idea is to find a good two-dimensional
qubit layout, so our propose is to find the best set of one-dimensional
qubit layouts exactly by solving a *minimum clique partition problem*, and
by then we will find the best two-dimensional layout that can embed as
many of one-dimensional layouts as possible. The further task may need
a very time-consuming(exponential number of) enumerations because we
try to find the best possible solution by using an efficient graph structure
called πDDs. Indeed, despite this, we still could not find a solution for
larger cases more than 16 qubits (4x4 layout) case in our preliminary
experiment. Thus, we also implement an SA-based method in order to
find a good two-dimensional qubit layout for a reasonable time. Our preliminary experiment shows that the SA-based method works very well
for larger cases.

Keywords: topological quantum computation, qubit layout, circuit
optimization, simulated annealing.

1 Introduction

To realize a quantum computation, we need to have a *fault-tolerant* quantum
gates, i.e., quantum gates with a very low operational error rate. Thus, the
quantum error correction codes were used for that purpose in the conventional
quantum circuit model.

Topological quantum computation [3] is another possible way to have fault-
tolerant quantum gates. Recently, this model of quantum computation has been

S. Yamashita and S. Minato (Eds.): RC 2014, LNCS 8507, pp. 176–188, 2014.

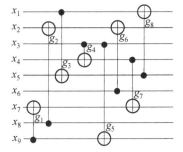

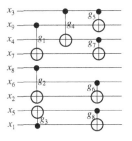

Fig. 1. An initial circuit: 8 Steps

Fig. 2. The optimal one-dimensional qubit layout: 3 Steps

considered to be much more promising than the conventional model of quantum circuits in terms of error corrections. The ways of encoding logical qubits in topological quantum computation differs from the conventional quantum circuit model, and thus the logical primitive operations are also very different. The primitive operation called a *braiding operation* can be seen as a drawing line between logical qubits with some special rules when we designing a quantum circuit. As the property of the topological quantum computation model are different from the conventional quantum circuit model, the design strategy also should be different from the conventional quantum circuit design.

To briefly understand the difference between the conventional quantum circuit model and topological quantum computation; let us see the circuit in Fig. 1. In the conventional quantum circuit model, we often assume that the multiple CNOT gates can be performed at the same time if their interacting qubits are different, and the *depth* of the circuit can also be calculated based on this assumption. For example, in the Fig. 1 we can perform g_1 and g_2 at the same time. First, an important observation here is that such a relation of two gates does not change even if we change the qubit order(qubit layout); while the gate order remain fixed. Thus, it is not important to consider about the qubit order in the conventional quantum circuit design.

In contrast to the above, in topological quantum computation, we can only assume that any two gates can be performed parallelly if only their gate symbols on the circuit diagram are not overlapped in the horizontal direction. (More discussion will be given later.) For example, we cannot perform g_1 and g_2 in the circuit (as shown in Fig. 1) at the same time like in the conventional circuit model.

As described above, it should now clear that the qubit order (i.e., qubit layout) is really important for the computation time for topological quantum computation unlike the conventional quantum circuit model. Thus, there is an existing work [5] to find a good qubit order; the method proposed in this paper can optimize the circuit from Fig. 1 to the Fig. 2. Here, the two circuits are logically equivalent but with different initial qubit orders. The number of the logical time steps in the circuit in Fig. 1 is 8, which is optimized to 3 as shown in Fig. 2.

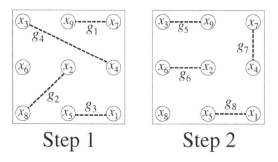

Fig. 3. The optimal two-dimensional qubit layout: 2 Steps

Our Contribution

In this paper, we propose a method by using two-dimensional qubit layout whereas the conventional methods considers only one-dimensional qubit layout. In one-dimensional qubit layout, it is shown that one single qubit order does not allow us to perform the above circuit with two time steps. For example, at the one-dimensional qubit layout of the qubit order as shown in Fig. 2, the three gates, g_4, g_1 and g_5 (and g_7), are overlapped with each other; so we need at least three time steps. In contrast, if we layout the qubits two-dimensionally as shown in Fig. 3, we can perform the circuit with only two logical time steps. This is because the two-dimensional qubit layout allows us to perform g_1, g_2, g_3 and g_4 at the same time as shown at the left-hand side of Fig. 3. Our proposed method is to find the best of two-dimensional qubit layout efficiently; will be mentioned in the followings.

As far as we know, this is the first systematic method to find a good two-dimensional qubit layout suitable for topological quantum circuits.

This paper is organized as follows. The next section explains the logic circuit model for topological quantum circuits, and its design flow. The section also describes terminology used mainly in the one-dimensional case because it is also useful to understand our two-dimensional case. Then, Section 3 proposes our method how to find a good two-dimensional qubit layout. After that, Section 4 shows some experimental results and Section 5 concludes the paper with further future work.

2   A Circuit Optimization Problem for Topological Quantum Computation

In this section, we will first review about the basic circuit model for topological quantum computation mainly from [3]. Then, we will explain a design scheme on how to implement a quantum circuit in logic level for the circuit model. We also explain some terminologies used in the previous optimization method for one-dimensional case [5] because they are also useful for this paper.

Finally, we formulate a logic level circuit optimization problem for the proposed design scheme. Readers who have the background knowledge of the topic may skip this section.

2.1 Logic Circuit Model for Topological Quantum Computation

Here we explain a logical circuit model for topological quantum computation based on the implementation scheme proposed by [3]. In the scheme, first we prepare a group of physical qubits called *surface code data qubits* to express the quantum state of a single logicala qubit. By the way of preparation that there are two types of logical qubit codes: *smooth* and *rough* qubits.

We can apply a specific elementary logical operation to a logical qubit by performing measurements to a specific group of physical qubits that are relevant to the logical qubit code. A group of measurements to a specific group of physical qubit can be illustrated as a drawing in the physical space corresponding to the qubits. Such a group of measurements is called *a brading operation*. An important property of brading operations is that multiple brading operations can be done at the same time if their corresponding drawings are not overlapped with each other in the physical space.

A CNOT operation to logical two qubits that are encoded into different types of qubits (i.e., smooth and rough qubits) can be performed simply by just a single brading operation between the two coded qubits. However, it is not always possible to encode the target and the control qubits of all the CNOT gates into different types of qubits. For example, if we want to apply three CNOT gates between x_1 and x_2, between x_2 and x_3, and between x_3 and x_1, the three pairs of qubits, (x_1, x_2), (x_2, x_3) and (x_3, x_1) should be encoded into different types; this is impossible.

Therefore, we have to encode logical qubits into the same type (say, smooth) code. Then, a CNOT gate between two smooth qubits can be implemented by three brading operations by adding two ancilla qubits. This is shown in Fig. 4 where each horizontal line represents a logical qubit (smooth or rough) code, and times goes from the left to the right in the figure. In the figure, only the second line corresponds to a rough qubit code (the other lines corresponds to smooth qubit codes). The dotted rectangles in the figure represent brading operations. M_X and M_Z in the figure mean measurements in the X and the Z bases, respectively. In the implementation of a CNOT gate, the logical qubit for the target bit is moved to the ancilla (smooth) qubit as the shows in the figure. Thus, for one logical qubit, we need to use a pair of two smooth logical qubit codes. In the following, we consider such a pair of two logical qubit (smooth) codes as one logical qubit in the logic level. Also note that we need an additional rough logical qubit code for each CNOT gate as explained, but such additional qubits are irrelevant to our discussion, and so we will simply ignore them in the following.

The above is a very intuitive perspective of the model discussed in [3], and thus an exact and detail discussions should be found in that paper.

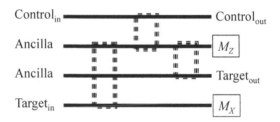

Fig. 4. A CNOT between two logical qubits of the same type

2.2 A Design Procedure for Topological Quantum Computation

To realize topological quantum computation, we consider the following design procedure.

Step 1. Logic level quantum circuit design.
Step 2. Conversion to *braiding operations*.

This design flow is similar to the one for the conventional quantum circuits. For the first step, as usual, we have to decompose a target quantum algorithm into a sequence of CNOT gates and some elementary single qubit gates that can be done in the topological quantum computation.

Then as a second step, the following logic circuit model is our proposal based on the model described in Section 2.1.

– We prepare two smooth qubits for each logical qubit.
– One of the two smooth qubits is used to encode a logical qubit, and the other smooth qubit is used as an ancilla qubit when we want to perform CNOT gates as described in Section 2.1.
– Two smooth qubits for a logical qubit are placed adjacently, and each pair of two qubits are placed in a line. In other words, if we have n logical qubits, $x_1, \cdots, x_n$, we place $2n$ smooth qubits, $x_{1_a}, x_{1_b}, x_{2_a}, x_{2_b}, \cdots, x_{n_a}, x_{n_b}$ in a line where x_{i_a} and x_{i_b} are used for x_i. However, in the logic level it is good enough for us to only consider about one encoded qubit for each logical qubit in our problem. The reason is that we can simply consider x_{1_a}, x_{1_b} as one qubit as they are placed adjacently. Therefore, in the following, we consider that one logical qubit is placed at one place in the logic level circuits for our problem.

2.3 Terminology Used for One-Dimensional Layout

In the followings, we assume logical qubits are placed in a line, named $x_1, x_2, \cdots, x_n$ for a circuit with n logical qubits. We ignore one-qubit gates for simplicity, i.e., our target circuits consist of only CNOT gates. However, the generalization is almost trivial. The target and the control qubits of gate g_i are denoted by $T(g_i)$ and $C(g_i)$, respectively.

First we introduce a terminology "overlapped" for one-dimensional qubit layouts as follows.

Definition 1. *A pair of gates g_i and g_j are said to be* **overlapped** *with a given qubit order if the group of qubits placed between $T(g_i)$ and $C(g_i)$, and the group of qubits placed between $T(g_j)$ and $C(g_j)$ have at least one common qubit with the given qubit order. If g_i and g_j are not overlapped, they are said to be* **non-overlapped** *with each other.*

For example, g_1 and g_2 in Fig. 1 are overlapped with this qubit order. The reason is as follows. Since $T(g_1) = 7, C(g_1) = 9$ and $T(g_2) = 2, C(g_2) = 8$, the group of qubits placed between the control and the target qubits of g_1 are x_7, x_8, x_9, and the group qubits placed between the control and the target qubits of g_2 are $x_2, x_3, x_4, x_5, x_6, x_7, x_8$. Thus, the two groups of qubits have common qubits, and so g_1 and g_2 are overlapped. However, if we just change the qubit order to get the circuit in Fig. 2, g_1 and g_2 become non-overlapped as we can see from the figure.

If the two logical CNOT gates are non-overlapped, the braiding operations for the two CNOT gates can be performed in one logical time step as we discussed in Section 2.2. Thus, our task is to increase the number of CNOT gates that are non-overlapped with each other after Step. 1 of the above-mentioned design procedure.

We can swap two CNOT gates, g_i and g_j, if $C(g_i) \neq T(g_j)$ and $T(g_i) \neq C(g_j)$. We refer this as **the swapping rule** in the following. For example, g_3 and g_4 in Fig. 1 can be swapped. Also g_4 and g_5 in Fig. 1 can be swapped, and thus we can change the order of g_3, g_4, g_5 in any order. However, g_4 and g_7 in Fig. 1 cannot be swapped because the target qubit of g_4 and the control qubit of g_7 are the same qubit (i. e., x_4).

Based on the circuit model discussed in Section 2.1, the cost of a circuit Q, denoted by $Cost(Q)$, is defined as follows: Let the maximum number of gates that are non-overlapped with each other at the first part of Q be k. In other words, by using the swapping rule, we can move k (k is the maximum possible number) gates to the beginning of the circuit so that the k gates are non-overlapped with each other. (Note that non-overlapped two gates can be swapped by the swapping rule.) Then, $Cost(Q) = Cost(Q') + 1$ where Q' is a circuit obtained from Q by removing the first k gates. This cost is due to the fact that the first k non-overlapped gates can be done in one logical time step in our circuit model.

Our essential task is to find a good qubit order among all the permutations, and thus it seems very difficult.

To explain our method, we also need the following terminology.

Definition 2. *If g_i can be moved to next to g_j by only the swapping rule, g_i and g_j are said to be* **"adjacentable"** *with each other.*

For example, g_4 and g_6 in Fig. 1 are adjacentable because g_4 and g_5 (or g_5 and g_6) can be swapped.

For a given qubit order, if two gates are adjacentable and non-overlapped, their corresponding brading operations can be performed parallelly, and thus the computational steps for the circuit is decreased. Therefore, the existing method [5] tries to find a "good" one-dimension qubit order such that as many adjacentable gates as possible become non-overlapped.

3   Two-Dimensional Qubit Layout Optimization

In this section, we propose to use two-dimensional qubit layouts, and also show an efficient method to find a good two-dimensional layout. Let us again see the motivational example as shown in Figs. 2 and 3 where the logical time steps are three and two when the qubits are placed in one-dimension and two-dimension, respectively. From the example, it seems that a two-dimensional qubit layout is always better than any one-dimensional qubit layout. This is indeed true as stated formally in the following; our design approach is based on this fact.

Theorem 1. *If a group of gates can be performed at the same time in a one-dimensional qubit layout, there should be a two-dimensional qubit layout by which we can perform the same group of gates at the same time.*

The proof is obvious by seeing the fact that a one-dimensional qubit order can be always embedded into a two-dimensional qubit layout. For example, the qubit layout as shown in Fig. 3 contains one-dimensional qubit orders, such as $x_3, x_9, x_7, x_4, x_2, x_6, x_8, x_5, x_1$ and $x_7, x_9, x_3, x_4, x_1, x_5, x_8, x_2, x_6$. The qubit order: $x_3, x_9, x_7, x_4, x_2, x_6, x_8, x_5, x_1$ allows us to perform g_5, g_6, g_7 and g_8 in Fig. 1 at the same time. Also, g_1, g_2, g_3 and g_4 in Fig. 1 can be performed at the same time with the qubit order: $x_7, x_9, x_3, x_4, x_1, x_5, x_8, x_2, x_6$. In other words, the qubit layout as shown in Fig. 3 can provide us the above two one-dimensional qubit layouts; two time steps are enough if we use the two-dimensional layout.

In the case of two-dimensional layouts, we need to modify the terminology "overlapped" as follows, which should be obvious.

Definition 3. *A pair of gates g_i and g_j are said to be **overlapped** with a given two-dimensional qubit layout if the line between $T(g_i)$ and $C(g_i)$ and the line between $T(g_j)$ and $C(g_j)$ cross each other in the given two-dimensional qubit layout. If g_i and g_j are not overlapped, they are said to be **non-overlapped** with each other.*

For example, in the qubit layout as shown in Fig. 3, g_i whose target and control bits are x_3 and x_4, respectively, and g_j whose target and control bits are x_2 and x_8, respectively, are non-overlapped whereas g_i and g_k whose target and control bits are x_2 and x_7, respectively, are overlapped. This is because two lines between x_3 and x_4, and between x_2 and x_8, are not crossed, but two lines between x_3 and x_4, and between x_2 and x_7, cross each other in the layout as shown in Fig. 3.

As in the case of one-dimensional layouts, our essential task is to find a "good" two-dimensional qubit layout such that as many adjacentable gates as possible become non-overlapped. The difficulty here is that a two-dimensional qubit layout allows many pairs of two gates to be non-overlapped unlike one-dimensional layouts; there are so many possibilities for a "good" layout.

Therefore, in order to do the search efficiently, we divide the whole problem into the following two sub-problems, each of which can be solved optimally.

- First, we divide all the gates into the smallest number of gate groups such that all the gates in each group are *possibly non-overlapped* whose definition is explained below.

- Second, we enumerate the possible two-dimensional qubit layouts for each gate group so that all the gates in the gate group can be non-overlapped. Let such a set of two-dimensional qubit layouts for the gate group G_i be P_i. After that, we can find a good layout which is included in as many P_i as possible.

The definition of *possibly non-overlapped* is as follows.

Definition 4. *Two gates are said to be* **possibly non-overlapped** *if $T(g_i)$ and $C(g_i)$ are different from neither $T(g_j)$ nor $C(g_j)$, and the two gates are adjacentable.*

Equivalently, if two gates are possibly non-overlapped, there is at least one qubit layout which allows the two gates to be non-overlapped.

Unlike the one-dimensional case, a two-dimensional qubit layout allows many pairs of gates to be non-overlapped. So, it is expected that possibly non-overlapped gates become no-overlapped with one specific qubit layout more often than the one-dimensional case. If that happens, we can perform all the gates in one group of possibly non-overlapped gates at one time step; this means that the number of whole necessary time steps is expected to be equivalent to the number of groups of possibly non-overlapped gates. Thus, in the first sub-problem, we would like to find the smallest number of gate groups.

Finding a group of *possibly non-overlapped* gates can be easily formulated as finding a clique in a graph. Namely, we can find a good solution by casting the problem to a clique cover problem as follows. There are many state-of-the-art methods for the problem, and we just use an exact method to solve minimum clique partition problem [2] in our experiment.

A method to solve the first sub-problem.

Step 1. Construct a graph where each node corresponds to each gate in C, and we have an edge between two nodes iff the corresponding two gates in the given circuit are possibly non-overlapped.

Step 2. Partition the graph obtained at Step 1 into minimal number of cliques, $C_1, C_2, \cdots, C_m$ by using a solver for clique cover problems. From each clique, we get each group, G_i, of possibly non-overlapped gates.

For an initial circuit as shown in Fig. 1, the graph constructed at Step 1 can be shown as in Fig. 5. It is easy to see that the graph can be covered with two cliques: $C_1 = (g_1, g_2, g_3, g_4)$ and $C_2 = (g_5, g_6, g_7, g_8)$. Thus, the group of the possibly non-overlapped gates are selected as: $G_1 = \{g_1, g_2, g_3, g_4\}$ and $G_2 = \{g_5, g_6, g_7, g_8\}$ in this example. This means that in the best case we can perform the circuit in Fig. 1 in two time steps. Thus, we try to find a good two-dimensional qubit layout in the second problem so that the circuit can be performed in two time steps.

In the following, we represent a two-dimensional qubit layout by a qubit order, which is essentially a permutation. More specifically, we order the qubits from the lower left to the upper right to represent a two-dimensional qubit layout. For example, the qubit layout, Layout 1, as shown in Fig. 6 is represented

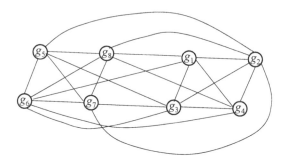

Fig. 5. A Graph at Step 1 for the Circuit in Fig. 1

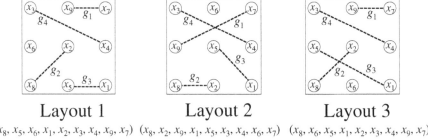

Fig. 6. An example of two-dimensional layouts

by the qubit permutation: $(x_8, x_5, x_6, x_1, x_2, x_3, x_4, x_9, x_7)$ which is essentially a permutation.

To represent and manipulate a set of permutations, there has been proposed an efficient graph structure, πDD [4], which we use in our method. A πDD can represent a set of permutations compactly, and it provides many efficient set operations such as intersection and union for the sets of permutations represented by πDDs. So, instead of enumerating all the possible qubit layouts explicitly, we implicitly represent a set of permutation by using a πDD to enumerate qubit layouts.

For the second problem, our method is as follow.

A method to solve the second sub-problem.

Step 1. We choose G_i from the set of groups obtained at the first problem, one by one, from the beginning of the circuit, and do the following Steps 2. and 3. until such G_i remains.

Step 2. We initialize an πDD P_i as representing all the possible permutations, and go to Step 3.

Step 3. For each pair of two gates in G_i, construct a πDD, p, that represents a set of permutations where two gates are non-overlapped. Then P_i is updated as $P_i \cap p$. This update is repeated for all the pairs of two gates. The final P_i represent a set of permutations corresponding to qubit layouts by which all the gates in G_i can be done at one time step.

Step 4. Our final task is to determine a two-dimensional qubit layouts which is included in as many P_i as possible. We find such a layout by intersecting P_i one by one. If the intersection of all P_i is not empty, we can find the best qubit layout which gives us the smallest computational steps for the given circuit. If the intersection becomes empty at some point, we may choose a layout in the intermediate intersection before it becomes empty.

Note that there is a possibility that P_i becomes empty during the repetition in Step 3. In such a case, there is no qubit layout which allows all the gates in G_i to be non-overlapped. In such a case, we should spend more than one time step to perform the gates in G_i; we just divide G_i into multiple groups so that the final πDD obtained at Step 3 for each group is not empty.

If the intermediate intersection becomes empty during Step 4, we may not get the best layout. However, we expect such a case does not happen so often; indeed in our experiments described in the next section, the intersection does not become empty which means our method can find the best layout.

Let us explain how we construct P_1 for $G_1 = \{g_1, g_2, g_3, g_4\}$ which is the first group of *possibly non-overlapped* gates for the example from Fig. 1. First let us see various two-dimensional qubit layouts in Fig. 6. For example, Layout 1 which is represented as a qubit permutation: $(x_8, x_5, x_6, x_1, x_2, x_3, x_4, x_9, x_7)$, allows g_2 and g_3 to be non-overlapped. Layout 2 also allows g_2 and g_3 to be non-overlapped. Thus, for the pair of gates: g_2 and g_3, the set of permutation, p, created at Step 3 includes Layout 1 and Layout 2, but it does not include Layout 3 where two lines between x_2 and x_8, and between x_1 and x_5 cross each other. For the pair of gates: g_1 and g_4, we also create the set of permutations that includes Layout 1 and Layout 3, but not Layout 2. By using primitive operations on πDDs, we can create a set of permutations to represent the set of layouts where two lines do not cross each other.

If we want to find a layout that allows both pair of gates, (g_2, g_3) and (g_1, g_4) to be non-overlapped, we just perform the intersection operation between the two πDDs representing the two set of permutations obtained as p at Step 3 for (g_2, g_3) and (g_1, g_4). By the intersection, Layout 2 and Layout 3 are automatically excluded from the intermediate candidate set. In this way, we update the intermediate layout candidate set, P_i, by excluding "bad" layouts for the current pair of two gates. We would like to note that the intersection operation can be done very efficiently when we use πDDs.

In conclusion, for each pair of two gates, we make πDDs representing the layouts that allows the two gates to be non-overlapped, and then we update the intermediate P_i as $P_i \cap p$; this means we exclude layouts that does not allow the current pair of two gates to be non-overlapped, from the intermediate layout candidate set. Thus, the final P_1 after Step 3 represents a set of layouts that allows all pairs of gates in $G_1 = \{g_1, g_2, g_3, g_4\}$ to be non-overlapped.

4   Experimental Results

4.1   An SA-Based Heuristic Method

As described in the previous section, our method can find the best layout if the intermediate candidate set does not become empty. There are many efficient solvers for the first sub-problem, i.e., clique cover problems. However, for the second problem, our enumeration-based method obviously cannot deal with many qubits even though we utilize an efficient graph structure, πDD [4], to manipulate sets of permutations.

Therefore, we implemented a simple simulated annealing (SA)-based heuristic to find a good two dimensional layout even for the larger problems. In our implementation, in each iteration, we swap the location of two qubits, and evaluate the depth of the circuit with the new qubit layout. As in the conventional SA-based search, the swap is accepted even though the depth increases when the *temperature* in the SA is high.

The only specific technique used in our implementation is that we do not select a pair of qubits to be swapped by purely randomly, but we select qubits that are used many times for gates with a higher probability. This is because swapping such qubits tends to have more impact on the result.

We would like readers who are not familiar to the simulated annealing to refer such as [1].

4.2   Comparison of the Three Methods

We implemented the two algorithms, our proposed method mentioned in Sec. 3 and the simple SA-based method described in Sec. 4.1 by C++. Then, we compared the two methods with the existing one-dimensional optimization method [5]. Table 1 shows the optimized computational steps of the randomly generated CNOT-based circuits by the three optimization methods. The columns "1D" "2D Optimal" and "2D SA" shows the results for the existing one-dimensional optimization method [5], our proposed method and the simple SA-based method, respectively. The numbers in the parentheses means the ratio of the number of steps to the one by "1D."

The table also reports the computational time (CPU time) for the two methods to run on Linux version 2.6.27 67v15 system on AMD Phenom^{TM} II x6 1055T CPU with 4 GB memory. The numbers in the parentheses means the ratio of the CPU time by "2D SA" to the one by "2D Optimal."

The parameters for the SA are set as follows: The initial temperature is 100°C, and the temperature is multiplied by 0.9 at each iteration until it becomes less than 20°C. At each iteration, we tried 500 different swaps of two qubits.

"2D Optimal" essentially enumerates all the possible qubit layouts, and thus its computational time should increase exponentially even if we use efficient data

Table 1. A comparison of the three methods

Circuit	1D Steps	2D Optimal Time (sec.)	Steps	2D SA Time (sec.)	Steps
9 bits 50 gates	32	34.44	23 (0.72)	0.00005 (1.4×10^{-6})	23 (0.72)
9 bits 100 gates (1)	63	133.44	46 (0.73)	0.00022 (1.6×10^{-6})	46 (0.73)
9 bits 100 gates (2)	63	133.02	43 (0.68)	0.00022 (1.7×10^{-6})	43 (0.68)
16 bits 100 gates (1)	57	2985.48	30 (0.53)	0.00030 (1.0×10^{-7})	30 (0.53)
16 bits 100 gates (2)	58	2644.35	32 (0.55)	0.00029 (1.1×10^{-7})	32 (0.55)
16 bits 200 gates	119	2546.01	65 (0.54)	0.00102 (4.0×10^{-7})	67 (0.56)
25 bits 200 gates	–	–	–	0.00125	48
25 bits 300 gates	–	–	–	0.00244	83

structures for manipulating permutations [4]. Indeed, we cannot complete the computation within 10 minutes for the case of 25 qubits as expected, whose results are shown as "–" in the table. Thus, this exact optimization method may be applicable to small parts of sub-circuits.

On the contrary, the SA-based heuristic is very fast and so it may be applicable to larger circuits. We also found that the optimization ability of the heuristic is very good; it achieves almost the same reduction of the steps as "2D Optimal." Thus, for a larger circuit, such heuristic will be useful.

It should be noted that we noticed the number of the best two-dimensional qubit layouts is very huge by the verification of our exact enumeration. This means that the problems are easy for a heuristic to find the best solution, so there was not a much difference between the two methods. However, we consider that the SA-based heuristic cannot find the best solution like our exact method when the number of best layouts is relatively small which may happen in the practical design.

5 Conclusion

This paper formulates the logic level circuit optimization problem for topological quantum computation. Observing the properties of brading operations in topological quantum computation, we formulate our problem as to find a good gate order and an good initial qubit layout. We also propose an efficient method to try to find the best two-dimensional qubit layout. As far as we know, this is the first systematic synthesis method for topological quantum circuits by considering two-dimensional qubit layout. We should evaluate the proposed approach by using some practical circuits in the future.

Acknowledgments. Some parts of the programs used in this work was implemented by Shinnosuke Hiratsuka and Yohei Ito.

References

1. Aarts, E., Korst, J.: Simulated annealing and boltzmann machines. Wiley, NY (1988)
2. Brélaz, D.: New methods to color the vertices of a graph. Commun. ACM 22(4), 251–256 (1979)
3. Fowler, A.G., Stephens, A.M., Groszkowski, P.: High threshold universal quantum computation on the surface code. Phys. Rev.A 80, 052312 (2009)
4. Minato, S.-I.: πDD: A new decision diagram for efficient problem solving in permutation space. In: Sakallah, K.A., Simon, L. (eds.) SAT 2011. LNCS, vol. 6695, pp. 90–104. Springer, Heidelberg (2011)
5. Yamashita, S.: An optimization problem for topological quantum computation. In: 2012 IEEE 21st Asian Test Symposium (ATS), pp. 61–66 (November 2012)

Cross-Level Validation
of Topological Quantum Circuits

Alexandru Paler[1], Simon Devitt[2], Kae Nemoto[2], and Ilia Polian[1]

[1] University of Passau, Innstr. 43, 94032, Passau, Germany
[2] National Institute of Informatics, 2-1-2 Hitotsubashi, Chiyoda-ku, Tokyo, Japan

Abstract. Quantum computing promises a new approach to solving difficult computational problems, and the quest of building a quantum computer has started. While the first attempts on construction were succesful, scalability has never been achieved, due to the inherent fragile nature of the quantum bits (qubits). From the multitude of approaches to achieve scalability topological quantum computing (TQC) is the most promising one, by being based on an flexible approach to error-correction and making use of the straightforward measurement-based computing technique. TQC circuits are defined within a large, uniform, 3-dimensional lattice of physical qubits produced by the hardware and the physical volume of this lattice directly relates to the resources required for computation. Circuit optimization may result in non-intuitive mismatches between circuit specification and implementation. In this paper we introduce the first method for cross-level validation of TQC circuits. The specification of the circuit is expressed based on the stabilizer formalism, and the stabilizer table is checked by mapping the topology on the physical qubit level, followed by quantum circuit simulation. Simulation results show that cross-level validation of error-corrected circuits is feasible.

Keywords: validation, quantum computing, topological quantum computing.

1 Introduction

Building a large scale quantum computer has been the focus of a large international effort for the past two decades. The fundamental principles of quantum information have been well established [1] and experimental technologies have demonstrated the basic building blocks of a quantum computer [2]. A significant barrier to large scale devices is the inherent fragility of quantum-bits (qubits) and the difficulty to accurately control them. The intrinsic error rates of quantum components necessitates complicated error correction protocols to be integrated into architecture designs from the beginning, and it's these protocols that contribute to the majority of physical resources (both in terms of total number of physical qubits and total computational time) necessary for useful algorithms.

Topological Quantum Computation (TQC) [3,4] has emerged as arguably the most promising error correction model to achieve large scale quantum information processing. This model incorporates a powerful error correction code and

S. Yamashita and S. Minato (Eds.): RC 2014, LNCS 8507, pp. 189–200, 2014.

has been shown to be compatible with a large number of physical systems [5,6]. While experimental technology is not yet of sufficient size to implement the full TQC model, there have been demonstrations of small scale systems and no fundamental issue prevents further expansion to a fully scalable quantum computer.

The TQC hardware is responsible for producing a generic 3-dimensional lattice of qubits, and programming in the TQC model can be separated from the basic functionality of the quantum hardware. Programming a TQC computer requires systematic methods, which are formulated starting from the TQC design stack (Figure 1b) [5]. The stack consists of several abstraction levels that differ from the ones used in classical circuit design. The high level quantum algorithm is first decomposed into a quantum circuit. This circuit does not include any error correction protocols; these can be implemented in multiple ways, leading to circuits requiring a differing number of qubits and/or computational times. We then identify each qubit in the circuit, as logically encoded with the topological code. This transforms each *logical qubit* into a large number of *physical qubits* allowing for the implementation of correction protocols. Such protocols also restrict the types of operations that can be performed on logical data, hence the quantum circuit needs to be further decomposed into gates from an universal set, but which can also be realized within the code. Once these decompositions are complete, the resulting TQC circuit needs to be optimized with respect to the physical resources and then translated to the physical operations sent to the hardware.

The qubit-lattice produced by the hardware embeds the topological quantum circuit and therefore it's physical size (volume) directly relates to the number of physical qubits employed for computation. The computation can be constructed from the circuit in a straightforward, yet suboptimal, way [7] (i.e. it will occupy a 3-dimensional volume much larger than required). The primary goal of TQC circuit synthesis is to construct an automated procedure that not only performs the required translation from circuit to topological circuit, but also to optimize the volume of these structures to ultimately reduce physical resources needed by the hardware. An example of an optimized circuit is presented in Figure 1a.

Validation of topological circuits is therefore a necessity, as optimized circuits often bare little resemblance to their original specification (e.g. Figure 1a). Validation has to be automated, as large topological circuits are complex objects, where the gate list is difficult to be extracted, and unfeasible to verify manually.

In this paper, we introduce the first automated validation method for TQC circuits. The input of the method is a quantum circuit specification, and the procedure verifies that an instance of the quantum circuit exhibits the same functionality as the specification.

For this purpose, we show that the validation problem can be mapped to an equivalent problem that can be efficiently simulated. Direct simulation is necessary to confirm that the topological structure correctly implements the desired circuit. Note that the simulator checks functionality of the topological structure, and it does not simulate error correction within the computation, as this is unnecessary for circuit validation.

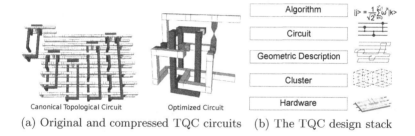

Canonical Topological Circuit   Optimized Circuit

(a) Original and compressed TQC circuits   (b) The TQC design stack

Fig. 1. Topological Quantum Computation (TQC)

2 Background

Quantum circuits are defined as series of quantum gates applied to transform the state of qubits. Classical bits can be either 0 or 1, while a qubit can have an infinity of states that can be visually represented as points on the surface of a unit sphere (the Bloch sphere). Quantum computing is based on the postulates of quantum mechanics: the state space of a quantum system (for our discussion a quantum computer operating on n qubits) is a complex space, where the system's state is represented by unit vectors. For example, the state of a single qubit is represented by a complex vector of length 2, and the 2^n-dimensional state of all n qubits is the tensor product of the component one-qubit states. The difficulty of simulating a general quantum system using a classical computer stems from the exponential increase of the state representation requirements. For example, the possible states of a two-qubit quantum computer where each input qubit is initialized to the $|0\rangle = (1,0)^T$ state is represented using 2^2 complex numbers $(1,0,0,0)^T$. The complex entries of the state vector are called probability amplitudes, and arbitrary tensor products of $|0\rangle$ and $|1\rangle = (0,1)^T$ (e.g. $|000\rangle$, $|100\rangle$, $|1111\rangle$) are called computational-basis-states.

In the quantum circuit formalism, the evolution of the quantum computer's state is dictated by the sequential application of quantum gates. The state, after the application of each quantum gate, is modeled as the outcome of a matrix-vector multiplication, thus the probability amplitudes of each computational basis state are transformed. For this reason, quantum gates can be understood as unitary complex matrices. Single-qubit quantum gates are 2×2 complex matrices, while n-qubit gates are $2^n \times 2^n$ complex matrices. The following gates are particularly relevant for our work.

$$X = \begin{pmatrix} 0 & 1 \\ 1 & 0 \end{pmatrix} \quad H = \frac{1}{\sqrt{2}} \begin{pmatrix} 1 & 1 \\ 1 & -1 \end{pmatrix} \quad CNOT = \begin{pmatrix} 1 & 0 & 0 & 0 \\ 0 & 1 & 0 & 0 \\ 0 & 0 & 0 & 1 \\ 0 & 0 & 1 & 0 \end{pmatrix}$$
$$Z = \begin{pmatrix} 1 & 0 \\ 0 & -1 \end{pmatrix} \quad T = \begin{pmatrix} 1 & 0 \\ 0 & e^{-i\pi/4} \end{pmatrix}$$

A *two-qubit controlled-gate* is applied to two qubits, where one of the qubits is left unchanged, but controls (given its state) the application of a single-qubit gate on to the second qubit. One such gate is the $CNOT$ (Controlled-X) gate, where the first qubit is the control-qubit, and the second-qubit is the target-qubit. Only when the control-qubit is $|1\rangle$ the state of the target qubit is flipped (e.g. $|0\rangle$ becomes $|1\rangle$). Because of its action, the X-gate is called the bit-flip gate.

One of the major differences between classical and quantum computation is the concept of superposition. A qubit is a superposition, if more then one computational basis-state amplitudes is different than zero. The Hadamard gate can be used to construct the $|+\rangle$ and $|-\rangle$ superpositions, because $|+\rangle = H|0\rangle = \frac{1}{\sqrt{2}}(|0\rangle + |1\rangle)$ and $|-\rangle = H|1\rangle = \frac{1}{\sqrt{2}}(|0\rangle + |1\rangle)$. Furthermore, the state of at least two qubits is entangled if their composite state cannot be written as a tensor product. For example, if the CNOT is applied to the $|0\rangle|+\rangle = |0+\rangle$ state, the result $\frac{1}{\sqrt{2}}(|00\rangle + |11\rangle)$ is representing both a superposition and an entangled pair of qubits. Similarly to the X-gate, the Z-gate is called the phase-flip gate, because when applied to a single qubit it flips the sign of the so-called relative phase (e.g. $|+\rangle$ is transformed into $|-\rangle$).

In general, arbitrary quantum computations can be mapped to a discrete set of gates consisting of $\{(H, Z, X, T, CNOT\}$ with any desired accuracy. The H gate is used to construct superpositions, the $CNOT$ to construct entanglement and the T gate is used to achieve arbitrary single-qubit state rotations (visualized as point rotations on the Bloch sphere surface).

2.1 Stabilizer Formalism

The exponential difficulty of describing the evolution of a quantum system originates from the fact that, by incrementing the number of qubits operated on, an exponential increase of the state-space is required. There is a particular type of quantum computations for which this can be overcome by employing the stabilizer formalism. Because $|0\rangle$ is an eigenvector with eigenvalue 1 of Z it is said that $|0\rangle$ is stabilized by Z, and, similarly, $|1\rangle$ is stabilized by $-Z$. Furthermore, using the same idea, $|+\rangle$ is stabilized by X and $|-\rangle$ is stabilized by $-X$. Stabilizer circuits are circuits that can be decomposed into the gates $\{X, Z, P, H, CNOT\}$ where $P = T \times T$. The identity matrix I stabilizes any state, while $-I$ is not a valid stabilizer. The state of such a circuit can be expressed by its stabilizers, and it was shown that for n-qubit circuits n stabilizers are required instead of 2^n-dimensional complex amplitude vectors [1]. A stabilizer table ST is an $n \times n$ table consisting of n independent stabilizers for the n qubits of a computation (e.g. see Figure 3a). The system's evolution of states is based on simple transition rules (e.g. applying a H gate on a qubit stabilized by X, results in the state being stabilized by Z).

$$\text{INITIAL STATE:} |+\rangle|+\rangle|0\rangle \ ; ST = \{XII, IXI, IIZ\}$$
$$\overset{H_1}{\rightarrow} |0\rangle|+\rangle|0\rangle \ ; ST = \{ZII, IXI, IIZ\}$$
$$\overset{CNOT_{2,3}}{\rightarrow} |0\rangle(|00\rangle + |11\rangle) \ ; ST = \{ZII, IXX, IZZ\}$$

The application of some gates, including the T gate, cannot be expressed in a simple manner using the stabilizer formalism. Its application to a state stabilized by X results in a state stabilized by a superposition of stabilizers: $\frac{X+Y}{\sqrt{2}}$, where $Y = iXZ$. Thus, simulating a circuit with T gates using the stabilizer formalism requires doubling the set of stabilizers each time a T is encountered. The application of T gates results in an exponential increase of the state space to be observed. The set of stabilizing gates together with the T gate form an universal gate set, meaning that an arbitrary quantum circuit can be expressed by its stabilizer sub-circuits and a number of applications of T gates (at the expense of an exponential increase in computational resources).

2.2   Measurement-Based Quantum Computing

Arbitrary quantum computations can be mapped to the measurement-based quantum computing paradigm (MBQC). MBQC utilizes an entangled ensemble of qubits (*cluster*) as a computational resource that is measured qubit-wise to perform quantum computations. During the measurement-process it is not necessary to apply any entangling gates, because the cluster is used as the entanglement resource.

In general, measuring a qubit is a probabilistic process dictated by the probability amplitudes of its state. When a qubit is measured in the computational basis (the Z-basis) the qubit's state collapses to either $|0\rangle$ or $|1\rangle$, and when a qubit is measured in the X-basis the possible outcomes are $|+\rangle$ and $|-\rangle$. Furthermore, it is possible to perform *rotated measurements*, meaning that first the qubit's state is rotated and then an X- or Z-basis measurement is performed. In measurement-based computing, the T gate can be applied by using a rotated measurement. Two qubits $|t\rangle = \frac{1}{\sqrt{2}}(|0\rangle + r|1\rangle)$ (where $r = e^{\frac{i\cdot\pi}{4}}$) and $|q\rangle = a|0\rangle + b|1\rangle$ are entangled using $CNOT$ resulting in $|tq\rangle = a|00\rangle + ar|11\rangle + b|01\rangle + br|10\rangle$. The first qubit's Z-measurement will transform the second qubit's state as if it were directly rotated by T: $a|0\rangle + r|1\rangle$ or $a|1\rangle + r|0\rangle$ (this result can be corrected using an X gate) [1].

From the perspective of MBQC, only X- and Z-basis measurements are necessary, iff the cluster to be measured contains already rotated qubits (called injected qubits or *injection points*). This is a technological detail that enables us to both simplify the definition of the computing paradigm, and also to limit the number of qubit states from the initial cluster to only two states: $|+\rangle$ and $|A\rangle = \frac{1}{\sqrt{2}}(|0\rangle + e^{i\frac{\pi}{4}}|1\rangle)$.

In the context of MBQC, the observation, that arbitrary circuits are formed by stabilizer sub-circuits and applications of T gates, can be further refined by noting that arbitrary circuits are formed by only a stabilizer sub-circuit (responsible for entangling the cluster-qubits) and another sub-circuit for measuring the cluster-qubits.

2.3   Topological Quantum Computation

One of the most promising approaches to construct a practical scalable fault-tolerant quantum computer, is based on the topological error-correction code. This code lays at the foundation of topological quantum computing (TQC), which is a measurement-based quantum computing model. In the following a very short introduction to TQC will be offered, while more details are to be found in [4,3].

The TQC cluster has a repeating 3D graph structure, which is obtained by stacking a *unit-cell* along the three axis (width, height and time). The temporal axis is dictated by the order of performing the measurements. The unit-cell is constructed from 18 physical qubits (initialized into $|+\rangle$) and entangled using the Controlled-Z gate according to the pattern indicated in Figure 2a. Morever, for example, by constructing a $2 \times 2 \times 2$ cluster of unit-cells, in the middle of the cluster another unit-cell arises. The initial 8 cells are known as *primal cells*, and the central cell is called a *dual cell*.

Logical qubits are encoded into the cluster by disconnecting individual cluster-qubits (achieved via Z-basis measurement). Logical qubits are defined as pairs of *defects*, where each defect is a *trail of "disconnected" physical cluster-qubits*, and furthermore it can be geometrically abstracted (e.g. Figure 1a). Cluster defects introduce degrees of freedom into the cluster, allowing for the storage of error-protection information. Due to the duality of the graph-structure, two types of logical qubits can be encoded: primal and dual logical qubits, depending on whether qubits are removed from the primal or the dual space.

A logical qubit has a quantum state which is protected against the errors, and the quantum gates can be implemented in a fault-tolerant manner directly on the logical qubits. The logical CNOT gate is always defined on logical qubits of opposite types, but it is still possible to define a logical CNOT between qubits of the same type by using the circuit identities presented in [3]. Initializing and measuring logical qubits is performed by constructing the defect geometries presented in Figure 2b.

A *correlation surface* is a stabilizer defined over the cluster qubits that connect the logical operators of the circuit's inputs to the logical operators of the outputs, such that information is propagated correctly during the circuit operation [3]. The geometrical arrangements of the physical cluster qubits forming a correlation surface are of two possible types: sheets and tubes (see Figure 3b), and the physical cluster-qubits will be always measured in the X-basis. Sheets are spanned between logical qubit defects, while tubes encircle a given defect. The cumulative parity of their measurement indicates how the logical stabilizers of the logical qubits are to be interpreted. The measurement parity of a correlation surface is defined starting from the measurement results of the physical qubits in the surface. The measurement results of an individual qubit are eigenvectors, with associated eigenvalues, of the measurement operator, and 1 and -1 are the two possible eigenvalues for the X-measurement. The *measurement parity* along a correlation surface is the product of the resulting associated eigenvalues.

Finding a correlation surface that connects the logical operators is not to be further detailed into this work, because the methods enabling it are explained in [3].

In TQC the computational universality is achieved by employing injection points in a similar way how the rotational gate T is applied by teleportation as introduced in the context of MBQC. The TQC injection points are cluster qubits initialized into the $|A\rangle$ state (defined in Section 2.2) or $|Y\rangle = \frac{|0\rangle + i|1\rangle}{\sqrt{2}}$ state. Because TQC is an instance of MBQC, logical gate teleportation is achieved by measuring the logical qubits that encode injected states.

3   Validation of TQC Circuits

In order to formulate the cross-level validation of TQC circuits, we start with a consideration of generic (non-TQC) measurement-based fault-tolerant quantum circuits. An arbitrary quantum circuit can be mapped to a construction from a stabilizer sub-circuit followed by a non-stabilizer sub-circuit that contains only rotated measurements. An adequate MBQC-oriented specification of such a "decomposed" quantum circuit is the tuple $QCS = \{ST, J, M\}$, where ST is the stabilizer table of the stabilizer sub-circuit, J is the set of injection points, and M is the ordered set of measurements of these injection points. Given an implementation QC that is also mapped to a tuple $\{ST', J', M'\}$, we are interested in equivalence of both descriptions ($QC \equiv QCS$). If we assume that the number of injection points and their measurement is not changed, as it will directly affect the computation being performed, this question is reduced to the equivalence checking of the stabilizer circuit parts ($ST \equiv ST'$), which has previousuly been investigated in the context of reversible computing [8].

However, checking the equivalence of a TQC description against the specification QCS is more challenging because no complete procedure to translate the geometric description of the topological circuit to the stabilizer table is currently known. In the following, we outline the cross-level approach which checks equivalence without constructing the stabilizer table.

3.1   Problem Statement

In the context of TQC, the stabilizers and the gates are defined at a logical level, which is constructed on top of the cluster-state level (physical qubits). The specification of the circuit (QCS or, more exactly, the stabilizer table of its portion ST) refers to the logical level. In order to check the equivalence of the geometric description against QCS, we map the logical qubits to the cluster state and validate it by simulation. This is done in two steps. First, the geometrical description is mapped to an (unmeasured) cluster. The mapping method can be derived from [9], and the details are omitted here. Then, for every entry of the stabilizer table ST from the specification, the topological computation in the cluster is simulated using a (stabilizer) quantum circuit simulator. Note that the simulated geometry is largely given by the shapes of the logical qubits which are independent from the processed ST entry. Moreover, the ST entry determines the initialization and measurement parts of the logical qubits (see Figure 2b).

In the following paragraphs the validation procedure will be detailed and analyzed.

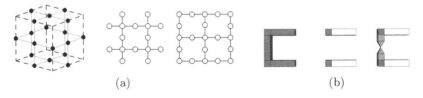

(a)   (b)

Fig. 2. TQC constructs: a) the unit-cell of 18-entangled qubits, and the two repeating layers that are simulate. b) Defect geometries for initialization of primal logical qubits: 1. Z-basis initialisation 2. X-basis initialisation 3. injection point. The defect geometries for measurement are similar.

3.2   Validation Procedure

The cross-validation of circuits is a simulation based procedure of a cluster where the geometric description of the TQC circuit was mapped. Algorithm 1 is synthesizing the details that are presented in the following.

The validation method starts by mapping the geometry to a cluster (Lines 1, 2). The set $TQCC = \{(x, y, z)| \ x, y, z \in \mathbb{N}, measure(x, y, z) \in \{X, Z\}, init(x, y, z) \in \{|+\rangle, |A\rangle, |Y\rangle\}\}$ is specified as a finite set of associated 3D-coordinates of physical qubits, that are marked for measurement in the X- or Z-basis and initialisation into $|+\rangle, |A\rangle$ or $|Y\rangle$. The 3D-coordinates correspond to the geometry presented in Figure 2a. Mapping of defect geometries to the 3D lattice takes an initial cluster $TQCC$, where no measurements were marked, and updates it: Z-basis measurements for defect-internal physical qubits, and X-basis measurements for all others. Injection points (physical qubits initialized into $|A\rangle$ or $|Y\rangle$) are measured in the X-basis.

Logical qubits can contain injection points anywhere along the geometric structure, and the target of validation method is to check that before the injection point will be measured, the logical qubit is correctly stabilized. Otherwise the result of the rotated measurement will be faulty, and the whole quantum computation is compromised. During the validation, as indicated in Section 3, injection points do not need to be explicitly considered. Without affecting the correctness of the method, these are initialized into the $|+\rangle$ state. By *re-interpreting* the injection points, the $TQCC$ set is transformed into $TQCC^+ = \{(x, y, z)|x, y, z \in \mathbb{N}, measure(x, y, z) \in \{X, Z, I\}, init(x, y, z) \in \{|+\rangle\}\}$ (Line 2).

Similar to classical circuits where input and output pins are used for the inputs and the outputs of the circuit, $P_{in} \subset TQCC$ is a set of cluster coordinates of the physical qubits used for initiliazing the logical qubits. The same applies for physical qubits used for logical measurement. These are used to read the information from the TQC circuit; their coordinates are contained in the set

$P_{out} \subset TQCC$ representing the *output pins*. The physical qubits from both sets are marked for either X- or Z-basis measurement, in order to respect the defect geometries from Figure 2b (Line 3). Cluster injection points are elements of P_{out}. Circuit simulation will be performed for each for each logical stabilizer specified in ST, and the P_{in} and P_{out} sets will be constructed accordingly.

A mapped cluster is supporting a logical stabilizer if the correlation surface that connects the corresponding input and output pins has even parity (Lines 19, 23). In the absence of errors (which is assumed during the validation of circuit functionality) the topology of the 3D-cluster guarantees that the measurement parity of all the unit-cell face-qubits is even [4]. The existence of the logical stabilizer support is proven by computing the parity of a correlation surface, as even parity indicates that the stabilizer can be correctly constructed using physical-cluster qubits.

In order to check the existence of all the logical stabilizers specified in ST, the validation method checks each entry in the table sequentially (Lines 4 – 23). Depending on the logical stabilizer to be checked, the injection point coordinate will be marked in $TQCC^+$ (Line 7) with either an X-basis measurement (if the logical qubit should be stabilized by logical-X) or with a Z-measurement (if the logical qubit should be stabilized by logical-Z).

Checking the support of a logical stabilizer is performed by simulations of the cluster, and the simulation involves the following steps. The first step is to compute the presumed correlation surface of the investigated stabilizer (Line 8). A correlation surface connects, only for the logical qubits referenced by the stabilizer, the input to the output pins. In the second step all the physical qubits are measured according to their markings from $TQCC^+$. In a third step, the existence of the stabilizer is determined based on the parity of the correlation surface (Lines 10 – 18). The error-correction is neglected, as it does not manifest itself in the validation of the specification $QC = \{ST, J, M\}$.

During the second step, the measurements are performed. This can be done in an arbitrary order, but we adopt a layered approach. One of the three dimensions of the cluster is defined to be the temporal axis. In a cluster of size $m \times n \times t$, we can reduce memory requirements by instead simulating a physical lattice of $t - 1$ $m \times n \times 2$ *layer pairs* of the cluster dynamically.

Each layer pair (Line 13) consists of two cross-sections of the cluster (e.g. Figure 2a). Layer i contains all physical qubits with t-coordinate equal to i.

In the i-th simulation run ($i = 0, \ldots, t - 1$), layers i and $i + 1$ are considered. The first simulation run considers only qubits from layers 1 and 2 with all connections between these layers. However, X and Z measurements are only performed on qubits with the t-coordinate 1. In the second simulation run, the qubits from the second layer, which retain their states from the first simulation run, are entangled with (hitherto unconsidered) qubits from layer 3 (initialized to $|+\rangle$) according to the unit-cell structure that is used throughout the complete $m \times n \times t$ cluster. Only second-layer qubits are measured, which influences the entangled third-layer qubits. This process is continued until the qubits of the final layer t are measured.

Algorithm 1. Cross-level Validation

Require: Circuit TQC as a geometrical description and the specification QCS
 1: Compute $TQCC$ starting from the geometry of TQC
 2: Compute $TQCC^+$ from $TQCC$ by marking injection points as $|+\rangle$ initialized
 3: Compute $P_{in}^q, P_{out}^q \subset TQCC^+$
 4: **for all** stabilizer s from ST of QCS **do**
 5:     $SIMTQC \leftarrow TQCC^+$
 6:     **for all** Logical qubit q stabilized by s **do**
 7:         Mark in $SIMTQC$ at $coord \in P_{in}^q, P_{out}^q$ the geometric patterns for initialisation and measurement of q according to s
 8:         Compute for $s$the correlation surface $CORS$
 9:     **end for**
10:     $parity \leftarrow 1$
11:     Construct layer l_0 of $SIMTQC$
12:     **for all** Layer l_i of $SIMTQC$, $i > 0$ **do**
13:         Construct l_i and Entangle with l_{i-1}
14:         **for all** Cluster qubits cq in l_{i-1}, $cq \in CORS$ **do**
15:             $ev \leftarrow$ measure cq in X-basis
16:             $parity = parity \cdot ev$
17:         **end for**
18:     **end for**
19:     **if** $parity = -1$ **then**
20:         **return** TQC is NOT valid according to QCS
21:     **end if**
22: **end for**
23: **return** TQC is valid according to QCS

---

4 Results

To evaluate the practicality and the scalability of the validation procedure the quantum circuit simulator CHP [10] was integrated for the cluster simulation step. Checking the complete stabilizer truth table ST requires between 1 and $|ST|$ simulations.

We considered TQC circuits consisting of logical CNOT gates acting on logical qubits. Their sizes are expressed as an *equivalent volume* [7], a quantity that measures the volume of a topological structure compared to a set of independent regularly stacked logical CNOT gates. Our results indicate that reduced TQC circuits of those equivalent volumes are feasible to simulate, and thus to validate. Average simulation times for one pair of layers in such circuits are reported in Figure 4. For example, the number of physical qubits required to be simultaneously simulated for the circuit having the equivalent volume of three CNOT gates was 1462, and this number was $84,052$ for the equivalent volume of 243 CNOT gates. These results suggest that even large and complex topological quantum circuits can be validated in reasonable time.

The selection of one of the three axes in the cluster as the temporal axis is arbitrary, which provides an additional degree of freedom for validation. The complete computation is confined to a 3D volume where the three edges may have different

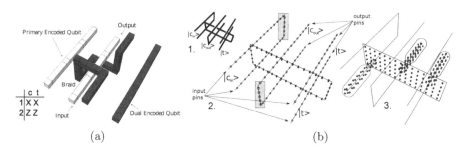

(a)   (b)

Fig. 3. The logical CNOT: a) Two pairs of defects of opposite type are braided. The stabilizer table consists of two stabilizers and indicates, for example, that if the control-qubit is stabilized by X, after applying the CNOT the target-qubit will also be stabilized by X. b) Validation of a circuit consisting of 3 logical CNOTs: 1. the geometric description; 2. the mapped defect geometry, where Z-measured cluster qubits are indicated along with the input and output pins; 3. the correlations surface for the verification of one of the stabilizers from the specification.

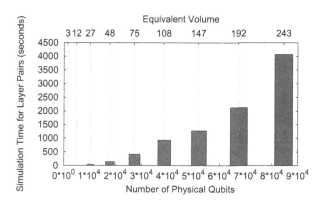

Fig. 4. Average simulation times for pairs of layers

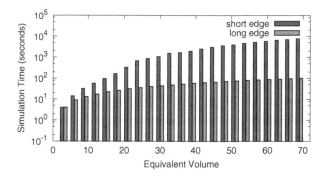

Fig. 5. Simulation times after choosing different temporal axes

lengths. Selecting a short edge as the temporal axis will result in relatively small number of relatively large simulation instances, while selecting a long edge will require more simulations with less qubits per simulation. Note that the simulated functionality is identical for both options. Figure 4 compares the run times for these possibilities. It can be seen that simulation is orders of magnitude faster when the longest edge is selected. This is not surprising as the measurement of stabilizers is of quadratic complexity in the number of qubits, and therefore having to consider less qubits per simulation instance outweighs the higher number of simulation runs.

5   Conclusion

The first validation method for topological quantum circuits was presented. Synthesis of topological quantum circuits often results in non-obvious inaccuracies that currently require a huge manual effort to find and correct, which is clearly impractical even for small circuits. The presented validation procedure maps the geometric description to the actual three-dimensional cluster of physical qubits and simulates these qubits. This abstraction level is much closer to the actual hardware implementation and is well suited to identify any deviations from the specification. Empirical data show the scalability of the procedure to circuits of practical size. As the next step, we plan to develop a validation-guided synthesis procedure for topological quantum circuits, and a more efficient representation of the circuit specification.

References

1. Nielsen, M., Chuang, I.: Quantum Computation and Information, 2nd edn. Cambridge University Press, Cambridge (2000)
2. Ladd, T.D., Jelezko, F., Laflamme, R., Nakamura, Y., Monroe, C., O'Brien, J.: Quantum Computers. Nature 464, 45–53 (2010)
3. Fowler, A., Goyal, K.: Topological cluster state quantum computing. Quant. Inf. Comp. 9, 721 (2009)
4. Raussendorf, R., Harrington, J., Goyal, K.: Topological fault-tolerance in cluster state quantum computation. New J. Phys. 9, 199 (2007)
5. Devitt, S., Fowler, A., Stephens, A., Greentree, A., Hollenberg, L., Munro, W., Nemoto, K.: Architectural design for a topological cluster state quantum computer. New. J. Phys. 11, 83032 (2009)
6. Jones, N.C., Meter, R.V., Fowler, A., McMahon, P., Kim, J., Ladd, T., Yamamoto, Y.: A layered architecture for quantum computing using quantum dots. Phys. Rev. X. 2, 031007 (2012)
7. Fowler, A., Devitt, S.: A bridge to lower overhead quantum computation, arxiv:1209.0510 (2012)
8. Wille, R., Große, D., Miller, D.M., Drechsler, R.: Equivalence checking of reversible circuits. In: 39th International Symposium on Multiple-Valued Logic, ISMVL 2009, pp. 324–330 (2009)
9. Paler, A., Devitt, S.J., Nemoto, K., Polian, I.: Mapping of topological quantum circuits to physical hardware. Scientific reports 4 (2014)
10. Aaronson, S., Gottesman, D.: Improved simulation of stabilizer circuits. Phys. Rev. A. 70, 052328 (2004)

Equivalence Checking
in Multi-level Quantum Systems

Philipp Niemann[1], Robert Wille[1,2], and Rolf Drechsler[1,2]

[1] Institute of Computer Science, University of Bremen, 28359 Bremen, Germany
[2] Cyber-Physical Systems, DFKI GmbH, 28359 Bremen, Germany
{pniemann,rwille,drechsle}@informatik.uni-bremen.de

Abstract. Motivated by its superiority compared to conventional solutions in many applications, quantum computation has intensely been investigated from a theoretical, physical, and design perspective. While these investigations mainly focused on two-level quantum systems, recently also advantages and benefits of higher-level quantum systems became evident. Though this led to several approaches for the representation and realization of quantum functionality in different dimensions, no efficient solution for verifying their equivalence has been proposed yet. In the present paper, we address this problem. We propose a scheme which is capable of verifying the equivalence of two quantum operations regardless of the dimension of their underlying quantum system. The proposed scheme can be incorporated into data-structures such as *Quantum Multiple-Valued Decision Diagrams* (QMDD) particularly suited for the representation of quantum functionality and, by this, enables an efficient verification. Experiments confirm the efficiency of the proposed approach.

1   Introduction

Quantum computation [19] provides a new way of computation based on so called *qubits*. In contrast to conventional bits, qubits do not only allow to represent the (Boolean) basis states 0 and 1, but also superpositions of both. By this, qubits can represent multiple states at the same time which enables massive parallelism. Additionally exploiting further quantum mechanical phenomena such as phase shifts or entanglement enables asymptotic speed-ups for many relevant problems (e.g. database search or integer factorization), offers new methods for secure communication (e.g. quantum key distribution), and has several other appealing applications [19].

Motivated by these prospects, researchers from various domains investigated this emerging technology. While, originally, the exploitation of quantum mechanical phenomena has been discussed in a purely theoretical fashion (see e.g. [10,23] for two well-known quantum algorithms), recently also the consideration of physical realizations (see e.g. [6,8,21]) as well as proper design methods (see e.g. [1]) gained significant interest. However, most of these considerations and implementations focused on two-level quantum systems, i.e. systems based on qubits. But, as a matter of fact, the considered quantum systems offer multiple levels to be exploited. These levels are readily accessible and using them for state

S. Yamashita and S. Minato (Eds.): RC 2014, LNCS 8507, pp. 201–215, 2014.

preparation and read-out has been demonstrated [18]. By this, computations can be performed on so called *qudits* rather than qubits. Researchers investigated possible exploitations of these additional levels e.g. for matters of simplified implementation or improved design of quantum operations. They were able to show that multi-level systems are useful for many promising applications and provide several practical advantages in the design of respective operations (see e.g. [5,12]). This is discussed in detail later in Section 3.

As a consequence, several approaches for representing and realizing quantum functionality in various quantum systems exist. This raises the question of how to verify whether or not two quantum operations given in different quantum systems indeed realize the same function. Although several methods for equivalence checking of quantum functionality have been proposed in the past (e.g. based on simulation [24], decision diagrams [26], or Boolean satisfiability [28]), all of them only supported two-level quantum systems composed of qubits.

In this work, we address the problem of checking functional equivalence between operations that are realized in multi-level quantum systems. This explicitly includes comparisons between realizations in different dimensions, i.e. quantum systems with a different number of levels. For this purpose, we first discuss and define functional equivalence in this context. Afterwards, a verification scheme based on the formal representation of quantum operations by unitary matrices is proposed. Since these matrices grow exponentially with the number of considered qubits, we additionally demonstrate how the proposed scheme can be incorporated into data-structures such as QMDDs [15] which are explicitly suited for the compact representation of quantum operations. By this, an equivalence checker for multi-level quantum systems results. The efficiency of the proposed scheme is confirmed by an experimental evaluation considering a wide range of operations realized in different quantum systems.

The remainder of the paper is structured as follows. In Section 2, preliminaries on quantum computation as well as a proper data-structure for the compact representation of quantum functionality are briefly reviewed. Section 3 discusses recent achievements in the field of multi-level quantum systems and, by this, motivates the present work. A definition of functional equivalence in multi-level quantum systems is then provided in Section 4 before the proposed scheme and an efficient implementation are described in detail. The paper concludes with a summary on the conducted experimental evaluation in Section 5 and our conclusions in Section 6.

2   Preliminaries

This section briefly reviews the basics on quantum computation. Furthermore, we sketch the main ideas of *Quantum Multiple-valued Decision Diagrams (QMDDs)*, a data-structure which is used later for an efficient implementation of the proposed equivalence checking scheme.

2.1   Quantum Computation

Most commonly, the basic building blocks for quantum computation are qubits. A *qubit* is a two-level quantum system, described by a two-dimensional complex Hilbert space. The two orthogonal *basis states* $|0\rangle \equiv \binom{1}{0}$ and $|1\rangle \equiv \binom{0}{1}$ are used to represent the (conventional) values 0 and 1. Any state of a qubit may be written as $|\Psi\rangle = \alpha|0\rangle + \beta|1\rangle$, where α and β are complex numbers with $|\alpha|^2 + |\beta|^2 = 1$. The quantum state of a single qubit is denoted by the vector $\binom{\alpha}{\beta}$. We say that a qubit is in *superposition* if neither of the so called *amplitudes* α or β is zero. A qubit can be *measured*, yielding either the result $|0\rangle$ or $|1\rangle$ with probability $|\alpha|^2$ or $|\beta|^2$, respectively. Such measurement destroys superposition and forces the qubit to the respective basis state. The state of a quantum system with $n > 1$ qubits is given by an element of the tensor product of the single qubit spaces, i.e. a linear combination of the *tensor states* $|0\ldots 0\rangle, |0\ldots 1\rangle, \ldots, |1\ldots 1\rangle$, which are the tensor products of basis states. Consequently, a quantum state is represented as a normalized vector of length 2^n (called the *state vector*), whose components denote the amplitude for each tensor state.

By the postulates of quantum mechanics, the evolution of a quantum system due to a quantum operation can be described by a *unitary transformation matrix* U [19]. Here, the columns correspond to the output state vectors that result when applying the respective operation to the tensor states as inputs. Thus, the entry u_{ij} of the matrix describes the mapping from the input tensor state $|j\rangle$ to the output tensor state $|i\rangle$.

Example 1. Commonly used quantum operations include the *Hadamard* operation H (setting a qubit into a balanced superposition) and the T (or $\frac{\pi}{8}$) operation. The corresponding unitary matrices are defined as

$$H = \tfrac{1}{\sqrt{2}} \begin{pmatrix} 1 & 1 \\ 1 & -1 \end{pmatrix} \quad \text{and} \quad T = \begin{pmatrix} 1 & 0 \\ 0 & e^{\frac{\pi i}{8}} \end{pmatrix}.$$

Applying these operations to a qubit in basis state $|1\rangle$ yields

$$H|1\rangle = \tfrac{1}{\sqrt{2}} \begin{pmatrix} 1 & 1 \\ 1 & -1 \end{pmatrix} \begin{pmatrix} 0 \\ 1 \end{pmatrix} = \tfrac{1}{\sqrt{2}} \begin{pmatrix} 1 \\ -1 \end{pmatrix} = \tfrac{1}{\sqrt{2}}(|0\rangle - |1\rangle) \quad \text{and}$$

$$T|1\rangle = \begin{pmatrix} 1 & 0 \\ 0 & e^{\frac{\pi i}{8}} \end{pmatrix} \begin{pmatrix} 0 \\ 1 \end{pmatrix} = \begin{pmatrix} 0 \\ e^{\frac{\pi i}{8}} \end{pmatrix} = e^{\frac{\pi i}{8}}|1\rangle, \text{ respectively.}$$

While these operations work on a single qubit, there are also operations on multiple qubits. Usually, these are *controlled* operations in the sense that the state of the additional *control qubits* determines which operation is performed on the *target qubit*.

Example 2. An important example of a controlled operation is the *controlled NOT* (CNOT) which flips the two basis states of the target qubit if and only if the control qubit is in the $|1\rangle$-state.

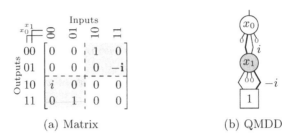

(a) Matrix   (b) QMDD

Fig. 1. Matrix and QMDD representation of a 2-qubit quantum operation

It has been shown that the set of CNOT, H, and T operations (forming the so-called *Clifford+T library*) is *universal* for quantum computation, i.e. operations from this set can approximate every unitary transformation to an arbitrary precision [3]. Moreover, these quantum operations can be implemented in a fault-tolerant fashion [3] – a crucial property since quantum computing is inherently very sensitive to environmental factors such as radiation and, hence, fault-tolerance is even more important than for conventional systems.

2.2   Quantum Multiple-Valued Decision Diagrams

QMDDs [15] have been introduced as a data-structure for the efficient representation and manipulation of quantum operations. The main idea is a recursive partitioning of the respective transformation matrix and the use of edge and vertex weights to represent various complex-valued matrix entries. More precisely, a transformation matrix of dimension $r^n \times r^n$ is successively partitioned into r^2 sub-matrices of dimension $r^{n-1} \times r^{n-1}$. This partitioning is represented by a directed acyclic graph – the QMDD. The following example illustrates main aspects of this data-structure.

Example 3. Figure 1a shows a transformation matrix for which a QMDD as shown in Fig. 1b has been built. Here, the unique *root vertex* (labelled x_0) represents the whole matrix and has four outgoing edges to vertices representing the top-left, top-right, bottom-left, and bottom-right sub-matrix (from left to right). This decomposition is repeated at each partitioning level until the terminal vertex (representing a single matrix entry) is reached. To obtain the value of a particular matrix entry, one has to follow the corresponding path from the root vertex at the top to the terminal vertex and multiply all edge weights on this path. For example, the matrix entry $-i$ from the top right sub-matrix of Fig. 1a (highlighted bold) can be determined as the product of the weights on the highlighted path of the QMDD in Fig. 1b. For simplicity, we omit edge weights equal to 1 and indicate edges with a weight of 0 by stubs.

QMDDs are canonical representations, if normalization of edge weights (as described in [15]) is performed. Thus, they are very convenient for equivalence checking. Indeed, due to standard decision diagram techniques like *unique tables*, this task can be performed in $\mathcal{O}(1)$ by comparing root vertices.

3   Motivation: Multi-level Quantum Systems

Research on quantum computation is considered in numerous facets. Originally, the exploitation of quantum mechanical phenomena e.g. for data-base search [10], factorization [23], and other applications has been discussed in a purely theoretical fashion. But in the past decade also several physical realizations have been proposed – including prototypical implementations based on trapped ions [6], photons [21], and superconducting qubits [8]. However, most of these considerations and implementations focused on two-level quantum systems, i.e. systems based on qubits with the basis states $|0\rangle$ and $|1\rangle$ as reviewed in Section 2.1.

But, as a matter of fact, quantum computation allows for multiple basis states. Instead of qubits, *d-leveled qudits* are then used as basic building blocks. These do not rely on only two orthogonal basis states but a total of d basis states $|0\rangle, |1\rangle, \ldots, |d-1\rangle$. More precisely, a qudit is described by a d-dimensional Hilbert space, where the *state space* is formed by all superpositions $|\Psi\rangle = \sum_{i=0}^{d-1} \alpha_i |i\rangle$ for complex-valued α_i with $\sum_{i=0}^{d-1} |\alpha_i|^2 = 1$. Prominent examples of qudits are *qutrits* $(d = 3)$ and *ququarts* $(d = 4)$ which received most attention so far [5, 9, 11, 13, 16].

Multiple qudits with levels $d_0, \ldots, d_{n-1}$ form a $\hat{d}$-level quantum system where $\hat{d}$ is the maximum of the d_i. The underlying Hilbert space is the tensor product of the respective spaces of the single qudits. Accordingly, the state of such systems can be expressed by a state vector of length $\prod_{i=0}^{n-1} d_i$ and is given by a linear combination of the tensor states $|x_0, \ldots, x_{n-1}\rangle$ where $0 \leq x_i < d_i$ for $0 \leq i < n$.

Operations over qudits are described by extended unitary transformation matrices.

Example 4. The qutrit operation X which exchanges the basis states $|0\rangle$ and $|2\rangle$ can be described by the matrix

$$X_{0,2} = \begin{pmatrix} 0\ 0\ 1 \\ 0\ 1\ 0 \\ 1\ 0\ 0 \end{pmatrix}, \text{ while } H_{0,1} = \frac{1}{\sqrt{2}} \begin{pmatrix} 1 & 1 & 0 & 0 \\ 1 & -1 & 0 & 0 \\ 0 & 0 & \sqrt{2} & 0 \\ 0 & 0 & 0 & \sqrt{2} \end{pmatrix}$$

represents the ququart operation that performs the Hadamard operation on basis states $|0\rangle$ and $|1\rangle$, leaving the remaining basis states untouched.

Multi-level systems are not only of theoretical interest [9], but are also useful for promising applications of quantum computation (see e.g. [5, 12]). Moreover, the use of multi-level quantum systems offers several practical advantages compared to qubit systems. More precisely:

– Multi-level quantum systems allow for much more efficient realizations of multi-qubit operations [12]. For example, Fig. 2a shows a minimal implementation (in terms of T-depth, i.e. the number of sequential T operations)

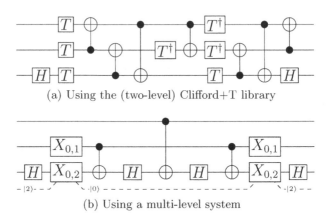

(a) Using the (two-level) Clifford+T library

(b) Using a multi-level system

Fig. 2. Realizations of the Toffoli operation

of a Toffoli operation within the Clifford+T library, i.e. based on a two-level system (taken from [1])[1]. The same functionality can be realized with significantly less operations in a multi-level system using a qutrit as shown in Fig. 2b (taken from [12]).

– A theoretical analysis showed that ququart operations may have a general advantage over qubit operations when it comes to the realization of generalized Toffoli operations. In fact, mapping these Toffoli operations to quantum operations using qubit-based techniques (e.g. [2]) requires an exponential effort. In contrast, a recently proposed four-valued approach can realize each Toffoli operation with linear complexity [22].

These advantages lead to an increased interest in multi-level quantum systems and the implementation of quantum operations in various dimensions. Consequently, as for qubit systems, the synthesis of general quantum functionality has also been studied for multi-level systems [4, 7, 17]. In [7], a generalized CNOT operation is suggested that reacts on an arbitrary control state and swaps an arbitrary pair of states on the target qudit. The advantage of this approach is that it is physically realizable by using standard CNOT operations and certain laser beams (Rabi oscillations) to swap basis states. By this, synthesis of many important multi-level circuits becomes possible with established technology.

Overall, various representations and realizations of quantum functionality for different quantum systems exist. But whether or not two given quantum operations in different dimensions indeed realize the same functionality has hardly been considered yet. This issue is addressed in the following, i.e. we present a scheme which automatically checks for the equivalence of operations in multi-level quantum systems.

---

[1] As established in the literature, horizontal lines represent the qudits and the operations $\boxed{H}$, $\boxed{T}$, •⊕ (CNOT), etc. are applied successively from left to right.

4   Equivalence Checking in Multi-Level Quantum Systems

While, thus far, equivalence checking for quantum functionality has intensely been considered in the past (leading to approaches e.g. based on simulation [24], decision diagrams [26], or Boolean satisfiability [28]), usually only operations in the same dimension have been compared. In this work, we propose a verification scheme which is capable of proving the functional equivalence between quantum operations even if they are realized in different dimensions. For this purpose, this section first discusses fundamental preconditions and provides a precise definition of the functional equivalence that we are going to address. Afterwards, the proposed equivalence checking scheme is introduced. Based on these concepts, we finally illustrate an efficient implementation of the proposed scheme.

4.1   Functional Equivalence for Quantum Operations

The purpose of equivalence checking is to verify whether two quantum operations realize the same functionality. In the following, we denote the two quantum operations to be compared by U_1 and U_2. The underlying quantum systems may have different dimensions d_1 and d_2 (for U_1 and U_2, respectively), where we assume $d_2 \geq d_1$ (without loss of generality). In order to check for equivalence between U_1 and U_2, it is important to have a precise definition of which basis states of the quantum systems actually correspond to each other. Basis states can either be *shared states*, if there is a corresponding basis state in the other system, or *don't care states*, if there is no counterpart.

Example 5. Consider two quantum operations U_1 and U_2, which are realized in a 2-level and 3-level quantum system, respectively. More precisely, the 2-level system consists of three qubits whereas the 3-level system is a hybrid system composed of two qubits and a single qutrit. A possible mapping between basis states is shown in Fig. 3. Here, all basis states are shared states except the $|1\rangle$ state of the qutrit in U_2, which has no counterpart in U_1 and, thus, is a don't care state.

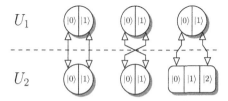

Fig. 3. Possible mapping of basis states between quantum systems

In the following, the correspondence of basis states is represented by a function ψ. It is assumed that ψ is either derived from the specification of the respective technology mapping or directly provided by the designer.

In this work, we require that both quantum systems are composed of the same number of qudits and do not consider corner cases in which e.g. a ququart is realized by two qubits or even more scattered mappings. Although the proposed approach could be extended in order to support also these cases, our simplification is strongly motivated by the following facts:

- It is a natural requirement to enable the same set of measurements for U_1 and U_2. Since only entire qudits can be measured, this is only possible if there is a one-to-one relation between qudits in both systems.
- In order to interpret a measurement result correctly, there may not be cross-mappings between basis states that do not belong to corresponding qudits.

Don't care states may be employed during the operation, like e.g. in the multi-level realization of the Toffoli operation shown in Fig. 2b. But, we assume that neither input nor corresponding output states carry a don't care component.

Having these definitions and assumptions, two quantum operations U_1 and U_2 are *functionally equivalent* ($U_1 \equiv U_2$) if they perform an equivalent transformation on shared states. The behaviour on don't care states, however, may be arbitrary.

Example 6. Consider the matrix $H_{0,1}$ from Example 4 describing a Hadamard operation on a ququart. Assuming the trivial mapping of shared states $\psi(|i\rangle) = |i\rangle$ (for $i = 0, 1$), $H_{0,1}$ is equivalent to the Hadamard operation H on a qubit (from Example 1). However, with the same mapping, this is not the case for

$$H_{0,2} = \frac{1}{\sqrt{2}} \begin{pmatrix} 1 & 0 & 1 & 0 \\ 0 & \sqrt{2} & 0 & 0 \\ 1 & 0 & -1 & 0 \\ 0 & 0 & 0 & \sqrt{2} \end{pmatrix},$$

which also performs a Hadamard operation on a ququart, but on different basis states.

4.2   Proposed Equivalence Checking Scheme

Assume two quantum operations U_1 and U_2 (realized in quantum systems with dimensions $d_2 \geq d_1$) together with a mapping ψ and the corresponding distinction in shared states and don't care states. Then, functional equivalence of these operations can be verified in two steps:

1. Check whether the sub-matrices of U_1 and U_2 representing the mapping of shared input states to shared output states are equivalent.
2. Check whether the sub-matrices of U_1 and U_2 representing the mapping of don't care input states to shared output states (and vice versa) are zero matrices.

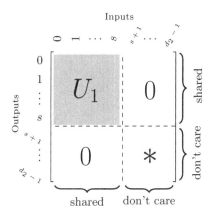

Fig. 4. Matrix of U_2 to be compared against U_1

If both checks evaluate to true, then U_1 and U_2 are equivalent. This scheme is illustrated by means of Fig. 4 on the basis of single qudit systems. More precisely, Fig. 4 shows the matrix representing the quantum operation U_2, i.e. within the higher level system. Without loss of generality, assume that the basis states $|0\rangle, \ldots, |s\rangle$ of the U_1-system are shared states ($s < d_1$) and that ψ maps them to the basis states $|0\rangle, \ldots, |s\rangle$ of the U_2-system. The remaining states are assumed to be don't cares. Then, the top-left $(s+1) \times (s+1)$ sub-matrix of U_2 in Fig. 4 represents the mapping of shared input to shared output states. If $U_1 \equiv U_2$, this mapping obviously has to be equivalent to the corresponding mapping described in U_1. This is checked in Step 1.

Next, we exploit the fact that, as discussed in Section 4.1, only superpositions of shared basis states are applied to U_2, i.e. the basis states $|s+1\rangle, \ldots, |d_i - 1\rangle$ are always prepared (expected) with zero amplitude for input (output) states. Because of that and in order to keep the unitarity of the overall matrix, no further mappings from don't care states to shared states (represented in the top-right sub-matrix) and from shared states to don't care states (represented in the bottom-left sub-matrix) must exist. That is, the corresponding matrices have to be zero matrices. This is checked in Step 2. Note that we do not need to consider the bottom-right sub-matrix representing the mapping from don't care input to don't care output states, since arbitrary behaviour is allowed here.

Example 7. Once again, consider the operations H (from Example 1) and $H_{0,1}$ (from Example 4) together with the trivial mapping of shared states between the underlying 2- and 4-level quantum systems (i.e. $\psi(|i\rangle) = |i\rangle$ for $i = 0, 1$).

The 4-level operation $H_{0,1}$ is equivalent to the 2-level operation H, because (1) the mappings of shared states are equivalent and (2) no mappings from don't care states to shared states and vice versa exist. In contrast, these properties do not hold for the operation $H_{0,2}$ (from Example 6), showing its non-equivalence to the other two operations.

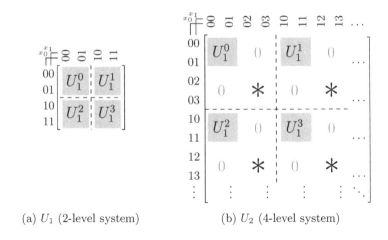

(a) U_1 (2-level system)   (b) U_2 (4-level system)

Fig. 5. Equivalence of operations in multi-qudit systems

This scheme can accordingly be extended to quantum systems composed of an arbitrary number of qudits. Then, however, the checks have to consider the more scattered distribution of the respective sub-matrices. This is sketched in Fig. 5, where U_1 (realized in a 2-level quantum system) is to be compared to U_2 (realized in a 4-level quantum system composed of two ququarts). Here we assume that there are no don't care states in the U_1-system and again, without loss of generality, that ψ maps the basis states $|0\rangle$ and $|1\rangle$ of the U_1-system to the shared basis states $|0\rangle$ and $|1\rangle$ of the U_2-system. As can be seen, all (shared and don't care) basis states are considered separately for each qudit. Accordingly, the sub-matrices to be checked against U_1, the zero matrices, and don't care matrices ($*$) are scattered throughout the whole transformation matrix.

This, however, does not restrict the applicability of the proposed equivalence checking scheme, but of course harms the efficiency of the checks. Note that this is even more the case for more complex mappings of shared states. Then, the matrices under consideration can be in a more dispersed shape and the scheme might result in checking equivalence of many small non-adjacent sub-matrices.

Hence, an efficient implementation of this scheme even in these cases is essential and will be described next.

4.3   Implementation Using QMDDs

While the concepts introduced above are sufficient to check equivalence between arbitrary quantum operations, the matrix representations used thus far constitute a serious hurdle to the applicability of the proposed scheme. In fact, matrix descriptions grow exponentially with the number of qudits in a system. Hence, a naive implementation based on matrices is infeasible for quantum systems of a certain size.

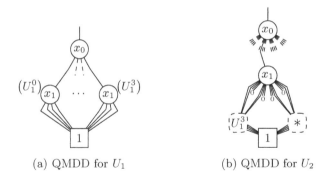

(a) QMDD for U_1 (b) QMDD for U_2

Fig. 6. QMDD representations of the quantum operations sketched in Fig. 5

In order to address this issue, we implemented the proposed scheme by means of the QMDD data-structure introduced in [15]. In this data-structure, each vertex represents a matrix which is partitioned into four sub-matrices (for qubit systems). Each sub-matrix is then represented by a successor of the current vertex. In case of multi-level quantum systems, the number of successors grows accordingly with the number of basis states.

Example 8. Figure 6 sketches the QMDD representations of the quantum operations already discussed in Fig. 5. As U_1 assumes a two-level quantum system, the overall matrix is partitioned into four sub-matrices. In contrast, the four-level system of U_2 is composed of $4 \cdot 4 = 16$ sub-matrices. Hence, the respective nodes have four and 16 successors, respectively. The x_1-vertices in Fig. 6a represent the sub-matrices U_1^0 and U_1^3, respectively (as indicated in brackets). The x_1-vertex in Fig. 6b sketches the second-top-right sub-matrix. Its sub-blocks U_1^3 and $*$ are represented by distinct sets of edges (which are indicated by a correspondingly labelled $\overline{M}$, but are not part of the original QMDD).

Due to efficient techniques like *shared nodes* or *unique tables*, QMDDs are capable of representing quantum functionality for several dozens of qubits and/or qudits. Moreover, computed tables enable a very efficient implementation of the equivalence checking scheme outlined above.

For the purpose of equivalence checking, the QMDD representations of the operations have to be aligned. More precisely, we

- align the number of don't care states for corresponding qudits by "blowing up" vertices with additional successors (e.g. to introduce two additional don't care states for each qubit, all vertices in Fig. 6a are equipped with 12 additional 0-edges),
- align basis states (if the mapping of shared states is non-trivial) by rearranging edges appropriately, and
- align possibly different don't care to don't care mappings ($*$) by setting the corresponding edges to zero.

This transformation can be done in a single traversal of each QMDD and leads to representations of two matrices (of equal size), which are identical if and only if the operations are functionally equivalent. The latter can be verified in constant time by a single unique table look-up, since QMDDs provide canonical representations. By this, equivalence checking can be conducted efficiently even for larger quantum systems. This has been confirmed by an experimental evaluation whose results are summarized and discussed in the next section.

5   Experimental Results

The equivalence checking scheme described above has been implemented in C on top of the original QMDD package presented in [15][2] and evaluated on a wide range of operations realized in different quantum systems. More precisely, we considered

- 2-level and 4-level representations of various quantum operations including Shor's 9-qubit error correcting code (denoted by *9qubitN1* and *9qubitN2*), as well as a 7-qubit encoding (denoted by *7qubitcode*) taken from [14] and instances of Grover's algorithm (denoted by *Grover-k*) and quantum Fourier transforms (denoted by *QFT-k*) taken from [19] (*k* is the number of qubits),
- multi-qubit operations taken from RevLib [27], mainly realizing Boolean functionality for 2-level systems that additionally have been mapped to 4-level representations based on the methods described in [22] (denoted by their respective RevLib identifier), and
- randomly generated quantum operations with up to 25 qubits (denoted *arbitrary*).

In total, 296 benchmarks have been considered. For each of them, the 2-level representation has been compared against the respective 4-level representation. In order to additionally evaluate the performance of the proposed approach for non-equivalent operations, for each pair of representations we introduced an error through random changes (to one of them) and compared this to the original operation. All experiments have been conducted on a 2.8 GHz Intel Core i7 machine with 8 GB of main memory running Linux. The timeout was set to 500 CPU seconds.

The results are summarized in Table 1 for a selection of the conducted experiments[3]. The first two columns provide the identifiers of the respective benchmarks followed by its number of qudits. Afterwards, the run-time (in CPU seconds) for building up the data-structure (QMDD) as well as performing the actual equivalence check (EC) is provided for both cases, i.e. when both operations are equivalent and when they are not equivalent. As can be seen, the

---

[2] We thank the authors of [15] for providing us with their implementation of the QMDD package.

[3] Due to space limitations, we were not able to provide the numbers for all benchmarks.

Table 1. Experimental evaluation

Benchmark	#Qudits	Equivalence QMDD	Equivalence EC	Non-Equivalence QMDD	Non-Equivalence EC
		Runtimes (s)			
7qbitcode	7	< 0.01	< 0.01	< 0.01	< 0.01
9qubitN1	9	< 0.01	< 0.01	< 0.01	< 0.01
9qubitN2	17	0.04	< 0.01	0.04	< 0.01
Grover-5	11	0.41	< 0.01	0.38	< 0.01
Grover-6	13	0.04	< 0.01	0.05	< 0.01
QFT-5	5	< 0.01	< 0.01	0.01	< 0.01
QFT-7	7	0.01	0.01	0.02	< 0.01
add16_174	49	0.03	< 0.01	0.02	< 0.01
add32_183	97	0.08	< 0.01	0.08	< 0.01
alu2_199	16	117.84	0.01	115.94	0.02
alu3_200	18	224.42	0.04	217.3	0.04
apla_203	22	14.77	0.02	15.3	0.02
bw_291	87	> 500	–	> 500	–
cm163a_213	29	1.63	< 0.01	1.74	0.03
cu_219	25	4.36	< 0.01	4.59	0.02
cycle10_293	39	22.91	< 0.01	25.29	< 0.01
ham15_107	15	103.77	0.31	88.6	0.25
hwb7_61	7	3.24	< 0.01	2.94	< 0.01
lu_326	299	> 500	–	> 500	–
mod5add_306	32	326.98	0.4	307.95	0.36
arbitrary10	10	0.7	< 0.01	0.73	< 0.01
arbitrary15	15	15.04	0.2	25.41	0.55
arbitrary20	20	26.76	0.15	41.34	0.35
arbitrary25	25	> 500	–	> 500	–

proposed scheme is able to efficiently check the equivalence of two quantum operations for the majority of all benchmarks. In fact, for 224 out of the 296 benchmarks, we were able to check their equivalence in less than a minute. While the actual equivalence check can always be conducted in almost no time, the limiting factor is the time needed for the construction of the representation of the respective quantum functionality, i.e. the QMDD in this case. Hence, the efficiency of the proposed scheme only relies on the chosen description mean. As improving those is an active research area (see e.g. the work on alternative representations such as *XQDDs* [26], *QuIDDs* [25] or improvements on QMDDs themselves [20]) and the proposed scheme can easily be adapted to other representations, further benefits can be expected here in the future.

6   Conclusions

In this work, we presented a scheme for checking the equivalence between two quantum operations working in different quantum systems. By this, the recent developments showing the advantages and benefits of multi-level quantum systems are taken into account. The proposed scheme can be incorporated into data-structures particularly suited for the representation of quantum functionality. An experimental evaluation confirmed that this enabled an efficient and fast equivalence checking which is mainly limited by the representation of the applied quantum functionality.

References

1. Amy, M., Maslov, D., Mosca, M., Roetteler, M.: A meet-in-the-middle algorithm for fast synthesis of depth-optimal quantum circuits. IEEE Trans. on CAD 32(6), 818–830 (2013)
2. Barenco, A., Bennett, C.H., Cleve, R., DiVincenzo, D.P., Margolus, N., Shor, P., Sleator, T., Smolin, J.A., Weinfurter, H.: Elementary gates for quantum computation. Physical Review A 52(5), 3457–3467 (1995)
3. Boykin, P.O., Mor, T., Pulver, M., Roychowdhury, V., Vatan, F.: A new universal and fault-tolerant quantum basis. Information Processing Letters 75(3), 101–107 (2000)
4. Bullock, S.S., O'Leary, D.P., Brennen, G.K.: Asymptotically optimal quantum circuits for d-level systems. Physical Review Letters 94(23), 230502 (2005)
5. Cabello, A., D'Ambrosio, V., Nagali, E., Sciarrino, F.: Hybrid ququart-encoded quantum cryptography protected by Kochen-Specker contextuality. Physical Review A 84(3), 030302 (2011)
6. Cirac, J.I., Zoller, P.: Quantum computations with cold trapped ions. Physical Review Letters 74(20), 4091–4094 (1995)
7. Di, Y.M., Wei, H.R.: Synthesis of multivalued quantum logic circuits by elementary gates. Physical Review A 87, 012325 (2013)
8. Galiautdinov, A.: Generation of high-fidelity controlled-not logic gates by coupled superconducting qubits. Physical Review A 75(5), 052303 (2007)
9. Greentree, A.D., Schirmer, S., Green, F., Hollenberg, L.C., Hamilton, A., Clark, R.: Maximizing the Hilbert space for a finite number of distinguishable quantum states. Physical Review Letters 92(9), 097901 (2004)
10. Grover, L.K.: A fast quantum mechanical algorithm for database search. In: Theory of Computing, pp. 212–219 (1996)
11. Klimov, A., Guzman, R., Retamal, J., Saavedra, C.: Qutrit quantum computer with trapped ions. Physical Review A 67(6), 062313 (2003)
12. Lanyon, B.P., Barbieri, M., Almeida, M.P., Jennewein, T., Ralph, T.C., Resch, K.J., Pryde, G.J., O'Brien, J.L., Gilchrist, A., White, A.G.: Simplifying quantum logic using higher-dimensional Hilbert spaces. Nature Physics 5(2), 134–140 (2008)
13. Mc Hugh, D., Twamley, J.: Trapped-ion qutrit spin molecule quantum computer. New Journal of Physics 7(1), 174 (2005)
14. Mermin, N.D.: Quantum Computer Science: An Introduction. Cambridge University Press (2007)
15. Miller, D.M., Thornton, M.A.: QMDD: A decision diagram structure for reversible and quantum circuits. In: Int'l Symp. on Multi-Valued Logic, p. 30 (2006)
16. Moreva, E., Maslennikov, G., Straupe, S., Kulik, S.: Realization of four-level qudits using biphotons. Physical Review Letters 97(2), 023602 (2006)
17. Muthukrishnan, A., Stroud Jr, C.: Multivalued logic gates for quantum computation. Physical Review A 62(5), 052309 (2000)
18. Neeley, M., Ansmann, M., Bialczak, R.C., Hofheinz, M., Lucero, E., O'Connell, A.D., Sank, D., Wang, H., Wenner, J., Cleland, A.N., et al.: Emulation of a quantum spin with a superconducting phase qudit. Science 325(5941), 722–725 (2009)
19. Nielsen, M., Chuang, I.: Quantum Computation and Quantum Information. Cambridge Univ. Press (2000)
20. Niemann, P., Wille, R., Drechsler, R.: On the "Q" in QMDDs: Efficient representation of quantum functionality in the QMDD data-structure. In: Dueck, G.W., Miller, D.M. (eds.) RC 2013. LNCS, vol. 7948, pp. 125–140. Springer, Heidelberg (2013)

21. O'Brien, J.L., Akira Furusawa, J.V.: Photonic quantum technologies. Nature Photonics 3(12), 687–695 (2009)
22. Sasanian, Z., Wille, R., Miller, D.M.: Realizing reversible circuits using a new class of quantum gates. In: Design Automation Conf., pp. 36–41 (2012)
23. Shor, P.W.: Algorithms for quantum computation: discrete logarithms and factoring. Foundations of Computer Science, 124–134 (1994)
24. Viamontes, G.F., Markov, I.L., Hayes, J.P.: Checking equivalence of quantum circuits and states. In: Int'l Conf. on CAD, pp. 69–74 (2007)
25. Viamontes, G.F., Markov, I.L., Hayes, J.P.: Quantum Circuit Simulation. Springer, New York (December 2009)
26. Wang, S.A., Lu, C.Y., Tsai, I.M., Kuo, S.Y.: An XQDD-based verification method for quantum circuits. IEICE Transactions 91-A(2), 584–594 (2008)
27. Wille, R., Große, D., Teuber, L., Dueck, G.W., Drechsler, R.: RevLib: an online resource for reversible functions and reversible circuits. In: Int'l Symp. on Multi-Valued Logic, pp. 220–225 (2008), RevLib is available at http://www.revlib.org
28. Yamashita, S., Markov, I.L.: Fast equivalence-checking for quantum circuits. Quantum Information & Computation 10(9&10), 721–734 (2010)

BDD Operations for Quantum Graph States[*]

Hidefumi Hiraishi[1,2] and Hiroshi Imai[1,3]

[1] Department of Computer Science, IST, The University of Tokyo
[2] ERATO Kawarabayashi Large Graph Project, National Institute of Informatics
[3] NanoQuine, The University of Tokyo

Abstract. A quantum graph state determined by an underlying graph is very fundamental in quantum computation and information, such as measurement-based quantum computing, stabilizer states and codes. For a graph state, a reversible operation, called the local complementation, transforms it to another graph state, and local Clifford operations map it to a stabilizer state. Besides these operations, taking the inner product of a graph/stabilizer state with an arbitrary complete product state leads to analyzing measurements for an arbitrary basis and solving a #P-complete problem of computing the partition function of a graph in Ising model. We recently observe that a graph state naturally corresponds to a Boolean function associated with a graph, and apply our top-down construction algorithm for the function. In this paper, we further discuss BDD operations for the above-mentioned operations on them. Specific bounds on the sizes and computational times of these BDDs are given in terms of the linear rank-width of a graph, and an efficient exact exponential algorithm for the Ising partition function is derived.

1 Introduction

Quantum computing opens us a new vista for a new model of computing based on new principles of quantum mechanics. In order to reveal intrinsic power of quantum computing, typical and useful quantum states have been investigated, such as a maximally entangled state like EPR state, GHZ states. As more general classes of quantum states, graph states and stabilizer states have been investigated in these years. Quantum graph states, determined by underlying graphs, are fundamental in measurement-based quantum computing (MBQC) where a graph state is prepared as an initial quantum resource to be consumed by a series of measurement for computation. Quantum stabilizer states are defined under the stabilizer formalism in quantum information which have applications for quantum error correcting codes, classical simulation and others. A class of stabilizer states form a proper superclass of graph states.

[*] This work was supported by Project for Developing Innovation Systems of the Ministry of Education, Culture, Sports, Science and Technology (MEXT), Japan. Also, the work by the second author is supported in part by the Grant-in-Aid for Scientific Research of MEXT, Japan.

S. Yamashita and S. Minato (Eds.): RC 2014, LNCS 8507, pp. 216–229, 2014.

BDD is a data structure representing Boolean functions, proposed more than a half century ago, and a paper [3] is a seminal work identifying the uniqueness with respect to variable ordering and introducing operations among BDDs. BDD has diverse applications in many branches of computer science [12,13,14]. Furthermore, quantum BDDs are proposed. Since finite-dimensional quantum states are represented as a vector and a matrix, through this connection the MTBDD in [8] directly represents quantum state. There are specific operations on quantum states, which are exploited in quantum BDDs such as [30,29,21,31].

In [11], for an underlying graph G of n vertices and m edges, a simple Boolean function of n variables can represent a graph state, and its BDD can be constructed by a top-down construction algorithm from the root, as in [23]. The BDD width is shown to be bounded by $2^{lrw(G)+1}$ for the linear rank-width $lrw(G)$ (see [18]) of a graph G. This BDD itself can be constructed in $O(n^2 2^{lrw(G)})$ time.

In this paper we first discuss applying a unitary transformation, called local complementation at a vertex v, from a graph state to another graph state over BDDs. Within the stabilizer formalism in quantum information, a specific unitary transformation is given [22,25,10] as the tensor product of n 1-qubit unitary matrices, specifically $deg(v) + 1$ non-identity unitary matrix and $n - deg(v) - 1$ identiry matrices, where $deg(v)$ is the degree of vertex v. In general frameworks of quantum BDDs, these unitary operations can be performed over them by extending Bryant's operations over Boolean BDDs. However, this approach may face a well-known barrier of Bryant's approach, i.e., blow-up in size in intermediate BDDs treated in the process of apply operations and its time may dependent on $deg(v)$ which may be proportional to n in dense graphs. We show that a local complementation can be performed in time linear to the BDD size of an original graph in the worst case, by taking the exclusive-or, XOR, of the BDD of a graph and a BDD representing the local complementation. This width and computational time of this BDD is $O(n2^{lwd(G)})$, whose time is smaller by a factor of n to the time bound to construct this transformed BDD from scratch.

Next we consider a representation of a stabilizer state when it is given as the product of a graph state and a local Clifford unitary matrix, which is a tensor product of n 1-qubit unitary matrices of a certain finite set of 1-qubit unitary matrices. We are interested in computing the inner product of this stabilizer state with an arbitrary complete product state. This can be done by first computing the multiplication of the product state with the above-mentioned local Clifford matrix, which is again another complete product state, and then by taking the inner product of this computed product state with the BDD representing the underlying graph state. With this, the BDD of a graph state can be further utilized. Applying this to a specific stabilizer state in [27], we can efficiently compute the partition function of a graph in Ising model. For a $n = k \times k$ square lattice graph with non-zero external magnetic field, this yields We may interpret in this framework an $O(k^3 2^k)$-time algorithm [11] for the Ising partition function, which is better than an $O(k^3 4^k)$-time algorithm using a BDD representing all the spanning trees of the underlying graph in [23]. We further refer to a Boolean function corresponding to the stabilizer state in [27], and discuss its BDD from the viewopoint of graph width parameters.

Since this paper bridges many research fields, such as quantum computing, graph minor theory and BDD, we try to use many examples to give idea on their connection smoothly. In the remaining part of this introduction, we summarize strongly relevant research results in such fields. From the standpoint of quantum computing, the power of MBQC starting with a graph state is related to the rank-width of its underlying graph [28]. Efficient classical simulation of MBQC for graphs with bounded rank-width [26] can be extended to computing the partition function of Ising model efficiently [27]. From the graph-theoretic viewpoint, the rank-width of a graph is introduced in [19] (see also [18]) in terms of vertex-minors as an extension of graph minor theory (e.g., see [20] introducing the tree-width). The rank-width is investigated in terms of vertex-minors and local complement operations in [16], and is used for MBQC in [28]. Both aspects are combined via Boolean BDDs here. Concerning the Ising partition function, Sekine, Imai and Tani [23] treated the BDD representing all spanning tree of a graph, propose the above-mentioned top-down algorithm, and analyzed the BDD width in terms of path-width (different terminology there, but using modern one here) of the graph. It has strong connection with 'Exact Exponential Algorithms' (e.g., see a book [6]) as well as complexity-theoretic issues about the Tutte polynomial of a graph [2,5,32]. It would be interesting to note, at the end of this introduction, that an approximation algorithm for the Ising partition function has been analyzed intensively in these year (e.g., see [24]), and also an approximation quantum algorithm for computing the Tutte polynomial on some curves and points in the Tutte plane, while this paper is concerned with exact algorithms [1].

2   Basic Definitions

A one-bit quantum state, called a 1-qubit state, is a complex vector in $\mathbf{C}^2$ with norm 1. By adopting a bracket notation, the normal orthogonal basis is represented, by ket vectors, which are column vectors, as

$$|0\rangle = \begin{pmatrix} 1 \\ 0 \end{pmatrix}, \quad |1\rangle = \begin{pmatrix} 0 \\ 1 \end{pmatrix}$$

A n-qubit state is a complex vector $|\phi\rangle$ in $\mathbf{C}^{2^n}$ with norm 1, and its orthonormal basis is given by

$$|x_1 x_2 \ldots x_n\rangle := |x_1\rangle \otimes |x_2\rangle \otimes \cdots \otimes |x_n\rangle \in \mathbf{C}^{2^n} \qquad (x_i \in \{0, 1\})$$

where $\otimes$ is the tensor product, or Kronecker prodct. We also use an orthogonal basis $|+\rangle$. $|-\rangle$ defined by

$$|+\rangle = \frac{1}{\sqrt{2}}(|0\rangle + |1\rangle), \qquad |-\rangle = \frac{1}{\sqrt{2}}(|0\rangle - |1\rangle).$$

In the sequel we will ignore the so-called global phase (e.g., see [15] of a quantum state when required.

Consider an undirected graph $G = (V, E)$ with vertex set V and edge set E. We assume it is simple and connected. For $S \subseteq V$, define $E(S)$ to be a set of edges whose two vertices are both in S (i.e., the edge set of a subgraph induced by S). For the vertex set $V = \{v_1, v_2, \ldots .v_n\}$ ($|V| = n$), consider a n-qubit quantum state $|x_1 x_2 \ldots x_n\rangle \in \mathbf{C}^{2^n}$ ($x_i \in \{0, 1\}$). For $S \subseteq V$, its characteristic vector is defined as $\chi_S^V = (x_1, x_2, \ldots, x_n)$ with $S = \{i \mid x_i = 1\}$. Then, a graph state $|G\rangle$ for graph G is defined by

$$|G\rangle = \frac{1}{2^{|V|/2}} \sum_{S \subseteq V} (-1)^{|E(S)|} |\chi_S^V\rangle \qquad (1)$$

Graph states can be defined under the so-called stabilizer formalism where more definitions about fundamentals of quantum computing are necessary. Pauli spin matrices are

$$\sigma_x = \begin{pmatrix} 0 & 1 \\ 1 & 0 \end{pmatrix}, \quad \sigma_y = \begin{pmatrix} 0 & -i \\ i & 0 \end{pmatrix}, \quad \sigma_z = \begin{pmatrix} 1 & 0 \\ 0 & -1 \end{pmatrix}$$

For n unitary matrices $A_1, \ldots, A_n$ in $\mathbf{C}^{2\times2}$, $U = A_1 \otimes A_2 \otimes \cdots \otimes A_n$ operates on $|\phi\rangle$, mapping it to another quantum state. When $A_i = A$ for $i \in S_A$ and $A_i = B$ for $i \in S_B$ and other A_i's are all an identity matrix with $S_A, S_B \subseteq S, S_A \cap S_B = \emptyset$, the corresponding unitary matrix U in $\mathbf{C}^{2^n \times 2^n}$ is denoted by $A^{S_A} B^{S_B}$. For a graph $G = (V, E)$, define a unitary matrix K_v for $v \in V$, operating on n-qubit states, by

$$K_v = (\sigma_x)^{\{v\}} (\sigma_z)^{\delta(v)}$$

where $\delta(v)$ is defined to be a set of vertices adjacent to v in the graph G. A graph state $|G\rangle$ satisfies $K_v |G\rangle = |G\rangle$ for each $v \in V$, which is another characterization of graph states. Stabilizer states can be defined by more general stabilizers. We here simply give its characterization theorem:

Theorem 1 ([9,22,25], see also [10]). *A quantum state $|\phi\rangle$ is a stabilizer state iff $|\phi\rangle = U|G\rangle$ for a graph state $|G\rangle$ and a unitary matrix U obtained by the tensor product of each 1-qubit unitary matrix which are products*

$$H = \frac{1}{\sqrt{2}} \begin{pmatrix} 1 & 1 \\ 1 & -1 \end{pmatrix}, \quad S = \begin{pmatrix} 1 & 0 \\ 0 & i \end{pmatrix}$$

The unitary transform in the theorem is called local Clifford unitary.

A binary decision diagram (BDD) represents a Boolean function in a compact and operational manner. See [3]. Here we explain it through an example. In Fig.1(a), for an ordering of x_1, x_2, x_3, this labeled complete binary tree represents the sign $+$ and $-$ of $|K_3\rangle$ by 0 (false) and 1 (true), respectively. By unifying two nodes in the tree such that trees rooted at each of them are isomorphic, including labels, we derive a BDD. A BDD obtained by performing this unifying operation as much as possible is called a quasi-reduced ordered binary decision diagram

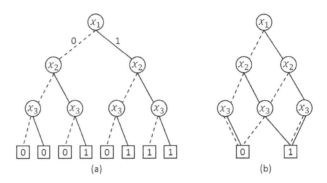

Fig. 1. For a graph state $|K_3\rangle = (|000\rangle + |001\rangle + |010\rangle - |011\rangle + |100\rangle - |101\rangle - |110\rangle - |111\rangle)$ of a complete graph K_3, (a) a complete binary tree represents it as a Boolean function, and (b) its QOBDD

(QOBDD). A QOBDD is a layered diagram such that i-th level corresponds to x_i for the variable ordering. The width of a level is the number of nodes in the level, and the width of QOBDD (we below write it simply as BDD) is the maximum among widths of levels. In Fig.1, the BDD width is 3.

3   BDD of a Graph State

The paper [11] introduces a Boolean function $f_G(x_1, \ldots, x_n)$ for $G = (V, E)$ with vertex set V and edge set E by

$$f_G(\chi_T^V) = \bigoplus_{e=(v_i,v_j)\in E} (x_i \wedge x_j). \quad \text{for } T \subseteq V, \tag{2}$$

where $\oplus$ is the exclusive-or, XOR, operation. Identifying the value of this Boolean function with integers 0 (False) and 1 (True), we see that this function represents the graph state. In fact, it gives an explicit representation by a straight-line program produced from the BDD of this function as in the following example of $|K_3\rangle$. Denoting an intermediate variable in the program corresponding to a node for x_i with j-th left among the nodes in the same level by $[x_i]_j$, the program becomes as follows:

$$[x_2]_1 := |0\rangle;$$
$$[x_2]_2 := |1\rangle;$$
$$[x_3]_1 := [x_2]_1 \otimes |0\rangle;$$
$$[x_3]_2 := [x_2]_1 \otimes |1\rangle + [x_2]_2 \otimes |0\rangle;$$
$$[x_3]_3 := [x_2]_2 \otimes |1\rangle;$$
$$[0] := [x_3]_1 \otimes (|0\rangle + |1\rangle) + [x_3]_2 \otimes |0\rangle;$$
$$[1] := [x_3]_2 \otimes |1\rangle + [x_3]_3(|0\rangle + |1\rangle);$$
$$\text{output } \tfrac{1}{2\sqrt{2}}((-1)^0[0] + (-1)^1[1]);$$

The BDD of this function is first investigated in Hiraishi, Imai, Iwata and Lin [11], and here we summarize its results to investigate BDD operations for graph states followingfurther. This BDD representation can be directly applied to computing useful functions of graph states.

Lemma 1. *For a graph state* $|G\rangle$ *with its BDD, given a complete product quantum state* $|\alpha\rangle = \otimes_{i=1}^{n}(a_i|0\rangle + b_i|1\rangle) \in (\mathbf{C}^2)^{\otimes n}$ *the inner product* $\langle\alpha|G\rangle$ *can be computed in size proportional to the size of the BDD.*

This inner product computation is a main problem here, and will be discussed in a more general setting for stabilizer states in section 6.1. In fact, this is exactly a necessary operation of computing the partition function of Ising model via a type of graph state [27], and is covered in section 6.2.

We are interested in investigating BDDs of f_G. Let us first consider a variable order $x_1,\ldots,x_n$ in BDDs. For $S \subseteq V$, we denote $V - S$ by $\overline{S}$. For $i = 1,\ldots,n-1$, define a subset S_i of V to be $\{v_1, v_2, \ldots, v_i\}$. For $T \subseteq S_i$, define a Boolean function $f_T^i = f_T^i(x_{i+1},\ldots,x_n)$ of variables $x_{i+1},\ldots,x_n$ by

$$f_T^i(x_{i+1},\ldots,x_n) = f_G(\chi_T^{S_i}, x_{i+1},\ldots,x_n)$$

This corresponds to a subfunction in the BDD of f_G. For a vertex $v \in \overline{S_i}$, define $\delta^i(v)$ to be $\{u \mid u \in S_i, (u,v) \in E\}$. For $T \subseteq S$, define $\Gamma_2(T)$ by

$$\Gamma_2(T) = \{v \mid v \in \overline{S_i}, |T \cap \delta^i(v)|\colon \text{odd}\}$$

Then, the following lemma is given in [11].

Lemma 2. *For* $i \in \{1,\ldots,n-1\}$ *and* $T,T' \subseteq S_i$, *we have* $f_T^i(x_i,\ldots,x_n) = f_{T'}^i(x_i,\ldots,x_n)$ *iff* $f_T^i(0,\ldots,0) = f_{T'}^i(0,\ldots,0)$ *and* $\Gamma_2(T) = \Gamma_2(T')$.

This lemma can be used in equivalence test of subfunctions in the top-down BDD construction algorithm from the root.

The width of this BDD can be analyzed as follows. Consider the adjacency matrix $A(S,\overline{S})$ of a bipartite subgraph of G such that its rows and columns correspond to S and $\overline{S}$, respectively, and its uv-element ($u \in S$, $v \in \overline{S}$) is 1 if there is an edge connecting u and v, and 0 otherwise. Following the notation in Oum [16], denote the rank of this matrix $A(S,\overline{S})$ over $GF(2)$ by $\text{cutrk}_G(S)$, we have.

Lemma 3. $|\{\Gamma_2(T) \mid T \subseteq S\}| \le 2^{\text{cutrk}_G(S)}$.

This has connection with discussions about defining and analyzing the rank-width of a graph G. In an analogous manner of defining the path-width from the tree-width, we may define the linear rank-width as follows (see [18]). For any permutation τ on V, consider a vertex oder $v_{\tau(1)}, v_{\tau(2)}, \ldots, v_{\tau(n)}$ and $S_i' = \{v_{\tau(1)}, v_{\tau(2)} \cdots, v_{\tau(i)}\}$, the linear rank-width of graph G with respect to the permutation τ is defined to be

$$lrw(G,\tau) = \max\{\text{cutrk}_G(S_i') \mid i = 1,\ldots,n-1\}$$

and the linear rank-width G is defined to be

$$lrw(G) = \min\{lrw(G, \sigma) \mid \forall \text{permutation } \tau\}$$

Note that $rwd(G) \leq lrw(G) \leq pw(G)$.

Theorem 2 ([11]). *For a graph G, there is a QOBDD representing $|G\rangle$ with width at most $2^{lrw(G)+1}$, and can can be constructed in $O(n^2 2^{lrwd(G)})$ time.*

Similar arguments hold for a generalized graph state $|\varphi_{\tilde{G}}\rangle$ in [27] for the Ising partition function.

4   Local Complementation in BDD

Local complementation at vertex v is an elementary operation in chordal graph recognition and vertex-minor theory. Recall that $\delta(v)$ is a set of vertices adjacent to v in the graph. The local complementation at v deletes edges connecting vertices in $\delta(v)$ and adds new edges between two vertices in $\delta(v)$ which are not connected by an edge in the original graph. That is, it takes the complement on a subgraph induced by $\delta(v)$ with respect to a complete subgraph on $\delta(v)$. See Fig.2.

Fig. 2. Local complementation at v

The local complementation corresponds to a fundamental unitary transformation among graph states:

Theorem 3 ([25], see also [10]). *(1) A stabilizer state $U|G\rangle$ for a local Clifford unitary U and a graph G is a graph state of a graph G' iff G' can be obtained by a series of local complementations from G.*

(2) Local complementation at vertex v maps a graph state $|G\rangle$ by a local Clifford unitary, with imaginary unit i,

$$\sqrt{(-1)^{|\delta(v)|}i} \cdot \sqrt{-i\sigma_x}^{\{v\}} \sqrt{i\sigma_z}^{\delta(v)}$$

$$\text{with} \quad \sqrt{-i\sigma_x} = \frac{1}{\sqrt{2}} \begin{pmatrix} 1 & -i \\ -i & 1 \end{pmatrix}, \quad \sqrt{i\sigma_z} = \frac{1}{\sqrt{2}} \begin{pmatrix} 1+i & 0 \\ 0 & 1-i \end{pmatrix}$$

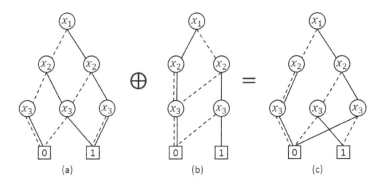

Fig. 3. How to obtain the QOBDD of a graph state $|P_3\rangle = (|000\rangle + |001\rangle + |010\rangle + |011\rangle + |100\rangle - |101\rangle - |110\rangle + |111\rangle)$ of a path graph P_3 connecting vertices v_2, v_1, v_3 in this order

This gives a complete characterization of a local Clifford unitary transformation corresponding to a local complementation from the viewpoint of stabilizers. This local Clifford unitary matrix is a tensor product of $deg(v)+1$ non-identity matrix, where $deg(v) = |\delta(v)|$, and applying a quantum BDD algorithm for such non-identity matrix may take time dependent on $deg(v)$ with a possible blow-up in size for intermediate BDDs.

BDD as well as Boolean functions provides an efficient way of transformation of local complementation at v as follows. Denote a complete graph of vertices in $\delta(v)$ by $K_{\delta(v)}$, and then a Boolean function $f_{K_{\delta(v)}}$ is given by

$$\bigoplus_{i,j\in\delta(v),\ i\neq j} (x_i \wedge x_j)$$

For this function we have the following.

Theorem 4. *(1) For a graph G' obtained by the local complementation at v from G,*

$$f_{G'} = f_G \oplus f_{K_{\delta(v)}}.$$

and $|G'\rangle = D|G\rangle$ where D is a diagonal matrix whose diagonal element corresponding to $S \subset V$ is given by 1 if $|S \cap \delta(v)| \equiv 0, 1 \mod 4$ and -1 if $|S \cap \delta(v)| \equiv 2, 3 \mod 4$.

(2) The width of a graph state of a complete graph is bounded by 4.

(3) The width of BDD representing G' is bounded by $2lrw(G)$.

(4) From the BDD for a graph state of G, that for a graph state of G' can be obtained in time linear to the original BDD size, and in time $O(n2^{lwd(G)})$.

Proof. (1) It is known that the local complementation is performed with taking the exclusive-or with a edge set of the complete graph, and this simply states it in a level of Boolean functions.

(2) The rank-width of a complete graph is 1, and using Theorem 2, the width is bounded by $2 \cdot 2^1 = 4$.

(3) It is shown, in Proposition 2.6 of [16], that $\mathrm{cutrk}_G(S)$ for every $S \subset V$ is invariant under local complementation at a vertex, and hence $cutrk_G$ for the width of each level in the BDD does not change.

(4) This can be achieved by using Bryant's algorithm [3]. $\square$

Viewing graph states in a discrete setting, the diagonal unitary transform in (2) above may give different implications compared with the local Clifford unitary transform.

5   Measurements in BDD

In the measurement-based quantum computing, stating with an initial graph state $|G\rangle$, a sequence of measurements by Pauli spin matrices σ_x, σ_y and σ_z are performed. Applying σ_x on vertex v_i corresponds to pivot for an edge $(v_i, v_j) \in E$ with deletion of v_i. σ_y on v_i corresponds to local complementation at v_i followed by deletion of v_i. σ_z on v_i corresponds to deletion of v_i. See [10,16].

These can be handled within the framework of BDDs. Deletion of v_i in BDD can be done by setting $x_i = 0$ (and some post processing). Local complementation at v_i can be done by considering a complete graph G' of vertices adjacent to v_i, taking XOR between the original BDD and BDD representing $f_{G'}$. The resulting BDD has width at most the width of the original BDD. Pivot is a series of 3 local complementations, and can be done similarly with no increase in BDD width. A step of the measurement-based quantum computing can be simulated on the BDD in time bounded by the original BDD size.

Furthermore, concerning measurements with respect to an arbitrary basis, we can compute the inner product of each of graph states with a basis. We have the following.

Theorem 5. *A step of the measurement-based quantum computing can be simulated on the BDD in time bounded by the original BDD size. In a series of $O(n)$ local complementation operations of a graph state starting from graph G, all the inner products of each intermediate graph states with a basis can be computed in $O(n^2 2^{lwg(G)})$ time.*

Note that the time bound stated at the end of this theorem is also the time bound in Theorem th:lrw. It should be noted that, the technique in the next section can lead to the same bound, and merits of directly maintaining BDDs should be investigated further.

6   Weighted BDD for a Stabilizer State

In the BDD for a graph state $|G\rangle$, 0-edge and 1-edge are made to correspond to $|0\rangle$ and $|1\rangle$, respectively. We can extend this to a weighted case. For each qubit

$|x_i\rangle$, consider a 1-qubit unitary matrix U_i, and, in the BDD, associate 0-edge and 1-edge with 1-qubit weights $w(x_i.0)$ and $w(x_i, 1)$, respectively, defined by $w(x_i, 0) = U|0\rangle$ and $w(x_i, 1) = U|1\rangle$. Then, this weighted BDD represents a quantum state $U_1 \otimes \cdots \otimes U_n |G\rangle$, which is shown in the following subsections on typical quantum states.

It should be noted that this type of operation is discussed in section 6.1 of doctoral dissertation of Viamontes [29] and implemented in his QuIDDPro [30]. The algorithm utilizes Bryant's apply operation in a clever manner. Our case treats the problem of computing the inner product of a stablizer state represented as above with an arbitrary complete product state, and, as described in the introduction ours is not intended to be a quantum BDD.

For local complementation at vertex v, we show how to obtain the BDD of a transformed graph state, together with a general theory of local Clifford unitary transformation in Theorem 3. A weighted BDD on the original BDD can be considered similarly to the other examples, and we can discuss more about relation between these BDDs. Details will be given in a full paper.

6.1 Representing a Stabilizer State by a Weighted BDD

There exists a stabilizer state which is not any graph state, and therefore BDD representations of graph states cannot be applied indirectly. For a stabilizer state $U|G\rangle$ for a local Clifford unitary U and graph G as above, by introducing edge weights, complex numbers in general, the stabilizer state can be represented indirectly on the BDD of a graph state. This broadens applicabilities of BDD in representing these quantum states.

We discuss this approach with using the so-called GHZ-state as a running example. A 3-qubit GHZ state $|\phi_{GHZ}\rangle$ is given as

$$\frac{1}{\sqrt{2}}(|000\rangle + |111\rangle).$$

Applying a local Clifford unitary $I \otimes H \otimes H$ to this state, it is transformed to

$$\frac{1}{\sqrt{2}}(|0\rangle \otimes |+\rangle \otimes |+\rangle + |1\rangle \otimes |-\rangle \otimes |-\rangle) = |P_3\rangle$$

where $|P_3\rangle$ is a graph state of P_3 as in Fig.3. Since $HH = I$, we have

$$|\phi_{GHZ}\rangle = I \otimes H \otimes H|P_3\rangle$$

Then, it is natural to associate weights to two edges of node x_i representing assignments weights corresponding to $I \otimes H \otimes H$ as in Fig.4.

A computational process is also shown to compute the stabilizer state along the BDD in a top-down fashion, which is more or less common in BDD applications. The program size is proportional to the BDD size. However, if we expand the output thoroughly, the number of terms would blow up to 2^n, which is meaningless to compute. However, a complete expansion is not necessary in

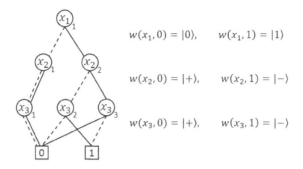

$$w(x_1, 0) = |0\rangle, \qquad w(x_1, 1) = |1\rangle$$

$$w(x_2, 0) = |+\rangle, \qquad w(x_2, 1) = |-\rangle$$

$$w(x_3, 0) = |+\rangle, \qquad w(x_3, 1) = |-\rangle$$

$[x_2]_1 := w(x_1, 0);$
$[x_2]_2 := w(x_1, 1);$
$[x_3]_1 := [x_2]_1 \otimes (w(x_2, 0) + w(x_2, 1));$
$[x_3]_2 := [x_2]_2 \otimes w(x_2, 0);$
$[x_3]_3 := [x_2]_2 \otimes w(x_2, 1);$
$[0] := [x_3]_1 \otimes (w(x_3, 0) + w(x_3.1)) + [x_3]_2 \otimes w(x_3, 0) + [x_3]_\otimes w(x_3, 1);$
$[1] := [x_3]_2 \otimes w(x_3, 1) + [x_3]_3 \otimes w(x_3, 0);$
output $\frac{1}{2\sqrt{2}}((-1)^0[0] - (-1)^1[1]);$

Fig. 4. Representing GHZ state by QOBDD

many cases, and the BDD representations can be used in various ways. For example, it would be rather straightforward to compute the inner product of a state with a complete product state based on this program. This example is a very small-scale, yet gives an idea about handling generalized n-qubit GHZ states fast. The following is a stronger statement of Lemma 1.

Lemma 4. *The results of Lemma 1 hold for a stabilizer state $U|G\rangle$ when a local Clifford unitary U and a graph state $|G\rangle$ are given.*

6.2   Partition Function of the Ising Model and a Stabilizer State

In section 2, we described an operator K_v, stabilizer for graph states. In computing the partition function of the Ising model, a stabilizer state for a graph is used.

Given a graph $G = (V, E)$, we first introduce a new vertex in the middle of each edge to derive a expanded graph $\tilde{G}$ with vertex set V and $v_E = \{v_e \mid e \in E\}$. $\tilde{G}$ is called a decorated graph, and in it v_e is adjacent to two vertices which are connected by e in G. Define an operator $\tilde{K}_v$ for each vertex $v \in V$ and an operator $\tilde{K}_e$ for each $v_e \in V_E$ by

$$\tilde{K}_v = (\sigma_x)^{\{v\}} \cdot (\sigma_x)^{\{\, v_e \mid v_e \text{ is adjacent to } v \text{ in } \tilde{g} \,\}}$$
$$\tilde{K}_e = (\sigma_z)^{\{v_e\}} \cdot (\sigma_z)^{\{\, v \mid v \text{ is adjacent to } v_e \text{ in } \tilde{g} \,\}}$$

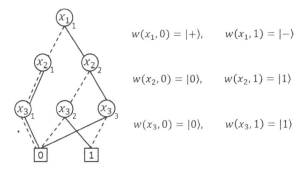

$$w(x_1, 0) = |+\rangle, \qquad w(x_1, 1) = |-\rangle$$

$$w(x_2, 0) = |0\rangle, \qquad w(x_2, 1) = |1\rangle$$

$$w(x_3, 0) = |0\rangle, \qquad w(x_3, 1) = |1\rangle$$

Fig. 5. A weighted BDD for a stabilizer state related to the Ising model

With these operators $\tilde{K}_v$ ($v \in V$) and $\tilde{K}_e$ ($v_e \in V_E$), a stabilizer state $\phi_{\tilde{G}}$ is defined, which is invariant under these operators. This stabilizer state $\phi_{\tilde{G}}$ is obtained from a graph state $|\tilde{G}\rangle$ by applying the Hadamard transform H to each vertex $v_e \in V_E$ (e.g., see p.5 of [4]). Hence this state can be represented by a weighted BDD.

As an example, suppose the original graph consists of a single edge, and its decorated graph. This is nothing but a path graph P_3 connecting v_2, v_1, v_3 in this order with $V = \{v_2, v_3\}$ and $V_E = \{v_1\}$. Then, the weighted BDD becomes as in Fig.5. Through calculation,

$$|\phi_G\rangle = \frac{1}{2}(|000\rangle + |011\rangle + |101\rangle + |110\rangle)$$

This argument can be generalized to any graph G, and, combining Lemma 4, this gives another interpretation of computing the partition function of the Ising model from the graph state $|\tilde{G}\rangle$, especially that for a $k \times k$ grid graph in $O(k^3 2^k)$ time [11].

For a decorated graph of $\tilde{G}$, consider a Boolean function

$$\bigvee_{e=(u,v) \in E} (x_u \oplus y_e \oplus x_v)$$

with Boolean variables x_v with $v \in V$ and y_e with $e \in E$. The support for this function with 0 corresponds to the stabilizer state. The width of BDD of this function can be characterized in terms of the path-width $pw(G)$. In general, the path-width of a graph can be much larger than its linear rank-width, for example, they are n and 1, respectively, for a complete graph of n vertices. In the problem of Ising partition function, a class of decorated graphs is considered. It is left open to investigate the path-width and linear rank-width of a graph this class.

7   Concluding Remarks

We have discussed applications of Boolean BDDs for quantum graph states and stabilizer states. Also, connection of these BDDs with graph width parameters such as linear rank-width and path-width has been discussed. Research in these directions seem to have interesting open problems, including one mentioned at the end of the last section, would deserve further investigation.

Acknowledgment. The authors would like to thank anonymous reviewers for their valuable comments which help improve the manuscript.

References

1. Aharonov, D., Arad, I., Eban, E., Landau, Z.: Polynomial Quantum Algorithms for Additive approximations of the Potts model and other Points of the Tutte Plane, arXiv:quant-ph/0702008 (2007)
2. Björklund, A., Husfeldt, T., Kaski, P., Koivisto, M.: Computing the Tutte Polynomial in Vertex-Exponential Time. In: Proceedings of the 49th Annual IEEE Symposium on Foundations of Computer Science, pp. 677–686 (2008)
3. Bryant, R.E.: Graph-Based Algorithms for Boolean Function Manipulation. IEEE Transactions on Computers 35(8), 677–691 (1986)
4. De Las Cuevas, G., Dür, W., Van den Nest, M., Briegel, H.J.: Completeness of Classical Spin Models and Universal Quantum Computation. Journal of Statistical Mechanics: Theory and Experiment P07001 (2009)
5. Dell, H., Husfeldt, T., Wahlén, M.: Exponential Time Complexity of the Permanent and the Tutte Polynomial. In: Abramsky, S., Gavoille, C., Kirchner, C., Meyer auf der Heide, F., Spirakis, P.G. (eds.) ICALP 2010. LNCS, vol. 6198, pp. 426–437. Springer, Heidelberg (2010)
6. Fomin, F.V., Golovach, P.A., Lokshtanov, D., Saurabh, S.: Intractability of Clique-Width Parameterizations. SIAM Journal on Computing 39(5), 1941–1956 (2010)
7. Fomin, F., Kratsch, D.: Exact Exponential Algorithms. Texts in Theoretical Computer Science, An EATCS Series. Springer (2010)
8. Fujita, M., McGeer, P.C., Yang, J.C.-Y.: Multi-Terminal Binary Decisoin Diagrams: An Efficient Data structure for Matrix Representation. Formal Methods in System Design 10, 149–169 (1997)
9. Grassl, M., Klappennecker, A., Rotteler, M.: Graphs, Quadratic Forms, and Quantum Codes. In: Proceedings of the 2002 IEEE International Symposium on Information Theory, p. 45 (2002) (see also arXiv:quant-ph/0703112)
10. Hein, M., Dür, W., Eisert, J., Raussendorf, R., Van den Nest, M., Briegel, H.-J.: Entanglement in Graph States and Its Applications. In: Quantum Computers, Algorithms and Chaos. Proceedings of the International School of Physics "Enrico Fermi", vol. 162, pp. 115–218 (2006)
11. Hiraishi, H., Imai, H., Iwata, Y., Lin, B.: Representing Quantum Graph States by Binary Decision Diagrams (submitted 2014)
12. Knuth, D.E.: The Art of Computer Programming. Fascicle 1: Bitwise Tricks & Techniques; Binary Decision Diagrams, vol. 4. Addison-Wesley Professional (2009)
13. Meinel, C., Theobald, T.: Algorithms and Data Structures in VLSI-Design: OBDD—Foundations and Applications. Springer (1998)

14. Minato, S.: Binary Decision Diagrams and Applications for VLSI CAD. Kluwer Academic Publishers (November 1996)
15. Nielsen, M.A., Chuang, I.C.: Quantum Computation and Quantum Information. Cambridge University Press (2000)
16. Oum, S.: Rank-Width and Vertex-Minors. Journal of Combinatorial Theory, Series B 95(1), 79–100 (2005)
17. Oum, S.: Approximating Rank-Width and Clique-Width Quickly. ACM Transactions on Algorithms 5(1), Article 10, 20 (2008)
18. Oum, S.: Dynamic Survey on Rank-Width and Related Width Parameters of Graphs,
    http://mathsci.kaist.ac.kr/~sangil/2013/dynamic-survey-on-rank-width/
19. Oum, S., Seymour, P.: Approximating Clique-Width and Branch-Width. Journal of Combinatorial Theory, Series B 96(4), 514–528 (2006)
20. Robertson, N., Seymour, P.D.: Graph minors. IV. Tree-Width and Well-Quasi-Ordering. Journal of Combinatorial Theory, Series B 48, 227–254 (1990)
21. Samoladas, V.: Improved BDD Algorithms for the Simulation of Quantum Circuits. In: Halperin, D., Mehlhorn, K. (eds.) ESA 2008. LNCS, vol. 5193, pp. 720–731. Springer, Heidelberg (2008)
22. Schlingemann, D.: Stabilizer Codes can be Realized as Graph Codes. Quantum Information & Computation 2(4), 307–323 (2002)
23. Sekine, K., Imai, H., Tani, S.: Computing the Tutte Polynomial of a Graph of Moderate Size. In: Staples, J., Katoh, N., Eades, P., Moffat, A. (eds.) ISAAC 1995. LNCS, vol. 1004, pp. 224–233. Springer, Heidelberg (1995)
24. Sinclair, A., Srivastava, P., Yin, Y.: Spatial Mixing and Approximation Algorithms for Graphs with Bounded Connective Constant. In: Proceedings of the IEEE 54th Annual Symposium on Foundations of Computer Science, pp. 300–309 (2013)
25. Van den Nest, M., Dehaene, J., De Moor, B.: The Invariants of the Local Clifford Group. Physical Review A 71, 022310 (2005)
26. Van den Nest, M., Dür, W., Vidal, G., Briegel, H.J.: Classical Simulation versus Universality in Measurement-Based Quantum Computation. Physical Review A 75, 012337, 15 (2007)
27. Van den Nest, M., Dür, W., Briegel, H.J.: Completeness of the Classical 2D Ising Model and Universal Quantum Computation. Physical Review Letters 100, 110501, 4 (2008)
28. Van den Nest, M., Miyake, A., Dür, W., Briegel, H.J.: Universal Resources for Measurement-Based Quantum Computation. Physical Review Letters 97, 150504, 4 (2006)
29. Viamontes, G.F.: Efficient Quantum Circuit Simulation. Doctoral Dissertation. Department of Computer Science and Engineering, The University of Michigan (2007)
30. Viamontes, G.F., Markov, I.L., Hayes, J.P.: Improving Gate-Level Simulation of Quantum Circuits. Quantum Information Processing 2(5), 347–380 (2003)
31. Wang, S.A., Lu, C.Y., Tsai, I.M., Kuo, S.Y.: An XQDD-Based Verification Method for Quantum Circuits. IEICE Trans. Fundamentals E91-A(2), 584–594 (2008)
32. Welsh, D.J.A.: Complexity: Knots, Colourings and Counting. London Mathematical Society Lecture Note Series, vol. 186. Cambridge University Press (1993)

Author Index